New Developments in the Theory of the Historical Process

Poznań Studies in the Philosophy of the Sciences and the Humanities

Founding Editor
Leszek Nowak (1943–2009)

Editor-in-Chief
Katarzyna Paprzycka-Hausman (*University of Warsaw*)

Editors
Tomasz Bigaj (*University of Warsaw*) – Krzysztof Brzechczyn (*Adam Mickiewicz University*) – Jerzy Brzeziński (*Adam Mickiewicz University*) – Krzysztof Łastowski (*Adam Mickiewicz University*) – Joanna Odrowąż-Sypniewska (*University of Warsaw*) – Piotr Przybysz (*Adam Mickiewicz University*) – Mieszko Tałasiewicz (*University of Warsaw*) – Krzysztof Wójtowicz (*University of Warsaw*)

Advisory Committee

Joseph Agassi (*Tel-Aviv*) – Wolfgang Balzer (*Munchen*) – Mario Bunge (*Montreal*) – Robert S. Cohen†(*Boston*) – Francesco Coniglione (*Catania*) – Dagfinn Follesdal (*Oslo, Stanford*) – Jacek J. Jadacki (*Warszawa*) – Andrzej Klawiter (*Poznań*) – Theo A.F. Kuipers (*Groningen*) – Witold Marciszewski (*Warszawa*) – Thomas Müller (*Konstanz*) – Ilkka Niiniluoto (*Helsinki*) – Jacek Paśniczek (*Lublin*) – David Pearce (*Madrid*) – Jan Such (*Poznań*) – Max Urchs (*Wiesbaden*) – Jan Woleński (*Krakow*) – Ryszard Wójcicki (*Warszawa*)

VOLUME 119

The titles published in this series are listed at *brill.com/ps*

New Developments in the Theory of the Historical Process

Polish Contributions to Non-Marxian Historical Materialism

Edited by

Krzysztof Brzechczyn

BRILL

LEIDEN | BOSTON

Cover illustration: Photograph by Luemen Rutkowski, published in 2018 via unsplash.com

This publication was financially supported by the previous Institute of Philosophy and Faculty of Social Sciences and the present Faculty of Philosophy, Adam Mickiewicz University in Poznań, Poland.

The Library of Congress Cataloging-in-Publication Data is available online at https://catalog.loc.gov
LC record available at https://lccn.loc.gov/2022004882

Typeface for the Latin, Greek, and Cyrillic scripts: "Brill". See and download: brill.com/brill-typeface.

ISSN 0303-8157
ISBN 978-90-04-50727-2 (hardback)
ISBN 978-90-04-50728-9 (e-book)

Copyright 2022 by Krzysztof Brzechczyn. Published by Koninklijke Brill NV, Leiden, The Netherlands.
Koninklijke Brill NV incorporates the imprints Brill, Brill Nijhoff, Brill Hotei, Brill Schöningh, Brill Fink, Brill mentis, Vandenhoeck & Ruprecht, Böhlau and V&R unipress.
Koninklijke Brill NV reserves the right to protect this publication against unauthorized use. Requests for re-use and/or translations must be addressed to Koninklijke Brill NV via brill.com or copyright.com.

This book is printed on acid-free paper and produced in a sustainable manner.

Contents

Preface   VII
  Krzysztof Brzechczyn
List of Tables and Figures   XXVIII
Notes on Contributors   XXXI

PART 1
Leszek Nowak on Non-Marxian Historical Materialism

1. Religion as a Class Structure: A Contribution to Non-Marxian Historical Materialism   3
   Leszek Nowak

2. The Truth Unbearable for All   52
   Leszek Nowak

3. Hegel and Liberalism: On the Issue of the Nature of Historiosophy   57
   Leszek Nowak

4. The Problem of the So-Called Social Transformation   77
   Leszek Nowak

5. The End of History or Its Repetition?   96
   Leszek Nowak

6. Marxism versus Liberalism: A Certain Paradox   106
   Leszek Nowak

7. On-the-Verge Effect in a Historical Process: An Attempt at an Interpretation in the Light of Non-Marxian Historical Materialism   119
   Leszek Nowak

8. Hegel's Chuckle, That is, Marxism and Liberalism in Polish Politics   134
   Leszek Nowak

9. On the Prediction of the Totalitarization of Capitalism: An Attempt at an Evaluation after Twenty Years Later   150
   Leszek Nowak

PART 2
On Totalitarization of Capitalism, Democratization of Real Socialism and Development of Non-European Societies

10 The Problem of Totalitarization of the Capitalist Society   189
    Tomasz Zarębski

11 The Problem of the Accumulation of Class Divisions in Contemporary Capitalism: An Attempt at a Theoretical Analysis   217
    Mieszko Ciesielski

12 How Does Democracy Evolve in Autocracy?   239
    Tomasz Banaszak

13 On Coalitions and Party Splintering: A Contribution to the Theory of Power in Non-Marxian Historical Materialism   256
    Marcin Połatyński

14 On Two Types of Democratization. Poland and Czechoslovakia. An Attempt at Theoretical Analysis   265
    Lidia Godek

15 The Social Structure of the Ottoman Society: An Attempt at a Theoretical Analysis   294
    Eliza Karczyńska

16 The Dynamics of Power in Postwar China: An Attempt at a Theoretical Analysis   314
    Dawid Rogacz

Name Index   335
Subject Index   340

Preface

Krzysztof Brzechczyn

Professor Leszek Nowak (1943–2009) was a co-founder of the Poznań School of Methodology and an author of seven original scientific theories with a wide reach: the concept of an excellent lawmaker in the methodology of law, the idealizational theory of science in the philosophy of science, the adaptive reconstruction of Marxian historical materialism, a categorial interpretation of Marx and Engels's dialectics, non-Marxian historical materialism in the philosophy of history, non-Christian model of man in philosophical anthropology, and negativistic unitarian metaphysics. During his scientific career, Nowak wrote 28 books[1], edited 21 joint publications, and authored about 600 published scientific works (Brzechczyn 2007; 2011; on Nowak's scientific output see also: Klawiter, Łastowski 2007). In 1974–1999 Nowak was the head of the Department of Dialectics of Cognition. In 1975, he founded the "Poznań Studies in the Philosophy of the Sciences and the Humanities" series, continued to this day, and "Poznańskie Studia z Filozofii Nauki" (Poznań Studies in the Philosophy of Science).

During the 1st National Convention of Delegates of the Independent Self-Governing Trade Union "Solidarity" in September–October 1981 in Gdańsk, Nowak was an expert in the 11th Program Group named "The Union and the State Authorities and the Polish United Workers' Party." After the imposition of martial law on December 13, 1981, he was detained (interned). After his release from prison on December 9, 1982, Nowak resumed work at the university and the underground publicistic work. In October 1984, the Minister of Science and Higher Education decided to suspend Nowak's academic teaching rights. In 1985, Nowak was expelled from the university. He returned to the university after 1989.

This introduction has three parts. In the first one, I will present professor Nowak's biography, in the second one – a short characteristic of his theory of the historical process, and in the third one – the concept of this volume.

---

1 Works published post mortem: Nowak (2011; 2018; 2019).

1 An Outline of Leszek Nowak's Biography

Leszek Nowak was born on January 7, 1943 in Więckowice near Brzesko and he grew up in Międzychód, where he graduated from high school. It was then that he became fascinated with leftist thinking. He read Marx's *Capital* while still in high school. In 1960, he began studying law at Adam Mickiewicz University in Poznań. During his studies, he was an active member of the Students' Philosophical Group at the university, and he organized regular student sessions. During the second year of study, he joined the Polish United Workers' Party. Nowak graduated from the university in 1965. His Master's thesis "Powinność i obowiązywanie. Problem statusu terminów teoretycznych w naukach prawnych" (Duty and Validity. The Problem of the Status of Theoretical Terms in Legal Science) was written under the supervision of professor Zygmunt Ziembiński. Simultaneously, Nowak was a distance student of philosophy at the University of Warsaw. His Master's thesis "Model, prawda względna, postęp nauki" (Model, Relative Truth, Scientific Progress) written under the supervision of Janina Kotarbińska was defended in 1966.

Since September 1965, he was employed in the Department of Legal Applications of Logic of the Chair of the Theory of the State and Law. On May 30, 1967, he defended his doctoral dissertation titled *Problemy znaczenia i obowiązywania normy prawnej a funkcje semiotyczne języka* (The Problems of the Meaning and Validity of a Legal Norm and the Semiotic Functions of Language), written under the supervision of professor Zygmunt Ziembiński.

Nowak began to study Marx's philosophy in a more systematic manner. This study was accompanied by a political idea layed out by Nowak as follows:

> socialism needs its good, nonconformist – critical – theory which would reveal its hidden mechanisms and, in that way, provide an intellectual basis for the party for more effective politics which would, as was my belief at the time, lead to the implementation of Marxian ideals. One paradigmatic example was Keynes's theory which, I thought, allowed the transformation of the likewise not so pretty pre-war capitalism into something at least bearable for the people. The idea was to build a Keynes-type theory of socialism. Being very critical of the political practice of the system, and especially of its ideology – I was already sure that it was gibberish – that theory was to be faithful to the Marxian message and addressed to the people who I believed implemented it – the party.
>
> NOWAK 1988b, p. 37

The basis for that reform was to be the construction of a non-standard theory of socialism which would still remain within the framework of Marxian historiosophical assumptions. On the basis of that idea, Nowak decided on the order of the reconstruction of Marx's thought: from methodology (the idealizational conception of science), through the reconstruction of ontological assumptions (the categorial interpretation of dialectics), to Marxian social philosophy (the adaptive interpretation of historical materialism).

In October 1970, Nowak moved to the Department of Logic and Methodology of Science in the newly formed Institute of Philosophy. In the first half of the 1970s, he was very active in the realms of scientific research, organization, and didactics. Almost every year, he published one or two books. In 1974, he became the head of the Poznań Dialectics Department, where his doctoral students could find employment. In October 1976, the Polish Council of State conferred the title of professor (*profesor nadzwyczajny*) of humanities on him. Aged 33, Nowak became the youngest professor in the Polish People's Republic.

He gradually ceased to identify himself with the socialist reality of the Polish People's Republic, and he became one of the most radical critics of the system. It seems that factors from three spheres: political and social, empirical, and theoretical contributed to the change of Nowak's perception of real existing socialism. According to professor Władysław Balicki, Nowak:

> was strongly influenced by Polish 1970 protests and the subsequent events. When Edward Gierek came to power, he propagated the idea of petty-bourgeois money making. Nowak would prefer him to propose a program of fundamental social changes. Gierek's program disappointed him. The crisis of worldview was instantaneous. A month earlier, Nowak defended the socialist form of government, and now he declared he had had enough of it.
> BALICKI 2003, p. 72

The empirical sources included the underground ('secondary') circulation of literature which reached the university circles. They revealed the history and the social mechanism of real socialism. Nowak himself points to the pivotal role of Solzhenitsyn's *The Gulag Archipelago*:

> The avalanche of facts related in the book killed the natural propensity of my dogma-enslaved mind to ascribe secondary importance to facts which put the system in a bad light (and dismiss them as an 'exception', 'error,' or a 'deviation'). I still remember the thought which struck me after another hundred of pages: 'God, if that was the case there, it means that

> every party member had to be immersed in that quagmire, which means that the system is a quagmire.' Solzhenitsyn turned my value structure upside down – the great size of the Gulag and all it entailed could not be incorporated into the vision of the party which – with deviations and inevitable costs – implements Marx's ideals.
>
> NOWAK 1981, p. 4

According to Nowak, some of the most important sources of the ideological transformation were theoretical factors indicating the limited nature of Marx's theory (Nowak 1987). A systematic reconstruction of Marx's philosophy was to inspire Nowak to try and create a version of historical materialism which would explain the functioning of real socialism with all its deficiencies (pathologies) and failures. Nowak made those attempts since at least 1976, and as a result, he could point to the theoretical limitations of Marx himself and of Marxism. One of them was the paradox of historicism. In Nowak's words:

> In the first half of the 1970s, we worked, in a rather big team, on the categorial interpretation of dialectics and the adaptive interpretation of historical materialism. When both conceptions were quite well developed, I noticed a contradiction between them. Roughly speaking, it consisted in the fact that according to categorial dialectics, the nature of all phenomena is variable, while Marxian historical materialism presupposes that they are everlasting and eternal because of the perpetual mutual relationship of productive forces and relations of production. Marxian historical materialism, then, presupposes a metaphysical concept of history. Given my orientation toward reconstruction, I was then quite shocked: Marxism must be wrong somewhere, and that 'somewhere' was in the foundations of the system – the dialectics or historical materialism.
>
> NOWAK 1981, 5

Nowak tried to create a version of historical materialism which would explain the development of socialist societies. Andrzej Klawiter gave the following account of those attempts:

> Nowak informed two people from his team about the project: Piotr Buczkowski and me. It was in the spring of 1977. He proposed that the three of us should start working on such a theory. Since May 1977, we met regularly, once a week, in his home at private seminars to discuss what form the theory of the socialist society should assume ... Buczkowski and I realized quite early that we were not starting from scratch and that

> Nowak invited us to take part in a project he had been developing for some time.
>
> KLAWITER 2013, p. 83

An outline of such a theory, in the form of a long typescript entitled *U podstaw teorii procesu historycznego* (On the foundations of the theory of the historical process; Nowak 1979), was completed in September 1979. It was distributed as a samizdat in the main higher education institutions. However, it was not easy to publish it as a book. Because of censorship, the official publishing houses would not publish even the most theoretical fragments of the work. Nowak's attempts at convincing Western publishing houses to publish the text failed because the conception was contrary to the main ideological trends. He described those efforts as follows:

> that materialist but non-Marxian historiosophy was unacceptable within the framework of the main contemporary ideological trends ... For Marxists (who still held a strong position among intellectuals), I was a renegade, and for conservatists, nationalists, church people, or neoliberals who were just entering the scientific market, I was a Marxist.
>
> NOWAK 2006, p. 170

Nowak also tried to make Polish publishing houses abroad interested in the book, but they unanimously refused to publish it. "Instytut Literacki did that in a record time – it sent the typescript back to me, to Frankfurt, in ten or eleven days. You can browse through a book in such a time in a publishing house but not read it" (Nowak 1985, 53). In September 1979, Nowak submitted the typescript to the Towarzystwo Kursów Naukowych (Scientific Course Association) with the same result. Polish independent publishing houses championed the same ideological movements as the Western ones (Nowak 2006, 170).

In the summer of 1980, Nowak signed the letter of 60 intellectuals from Poznań who supported the demands of people on a strike in Gdańsk, and on August 28, 1980, he left the Polish United Workers' Party. He became a member of the Independent Self-Governing Trade Union "Solidarity" formed in autumn 1980 at Adam Mickiewicz University in Poznań, and as the political situation changed, he took up the position of the associate dean for students' affairs. He also became an ideological mentor for the new student movement. According to Jacek Bartkowiak:

> the beginnings of self-government at the Poznań university were revolutionary. The atmosphere was pervaded by the spirit of radical syndicalism.

> The movement grew under the ideological patronage of professor Leszek Nowak ... The initial project of self-government provided for two structures: the Academic Self-Government of Adam Mickiewicz University in Poznań, which was to include all the students, academic staff, and administrative staff of the university, and students' self-government.
>
> BARTKOWIAK 2014, pp. 23–24

Piotr Lissewski, a student of political science and journalism at the time, remembers professor Nowak's lectures as follows:

> Professor Nowak's voice differed from other voices. It introduced order into the intellectual chaos. It was formally precise and clear, with a transparent, distinctive axiological substrate. It was not a conviction, view, or vision. It was a transmission of the cognitive proof, from the problem, through the method and source, to the statement of reasons, all presented in a very accurate and structured way. That evoked respect, even among later critics, and we had the impression of being our professor's intellectual companions, following the leader on the road toward the 'truth, good, and beauty.'
>
> LISSEWSKI 2013, p. 95

The second area of Nowak's social activity were numerous lectures and publications, intended to popularize the theory and lead to the publication of a book: "The only solution for me were the spontaneously created local publishing houses of Solidarity, independent from the Warsaw and Cracow opposition. Still, in order to publish the book, I had to be known at the grassroots level of Solidarity, hence my lecturing and publishing activity in 1980–1981." (Nowak 2006, p. 170) Nowak's opinion pieces and articles were published in bulletins of Solidarity in Gdańsk, Kalisz, Katowice, Koszalin, Cracow, Łódź, Poznań, Słupsk, and Szczecin.

Gradually, his concept of a strategy for union work in the conditions of increasing social polarity in 1981, which was based on non-Marxian historical materialism, became noticed by the managers of Solidarity. During the 1st National Convention of Delegates of the Independent Self-Governing Trade Union "Solidarity," Nowak was an expert in the 11th program group: "The union and the state authorities and the Polish United Workers' Party" led by Lech Kaczyński and Andrzej Małachowski. This program group prepared two alternative proposals: fundamentalists' and pragmatists'. Nowak was the main co-creator of the fundamentalists' project. Lech Kaczyński, who reported during the congress on October 8, 1981 results of program group's work noted that the alternative pragmatists' proposal was directed toward both the union and the authorities of the Polish People's Republic and their allies. According to Kaczyński, fundamentalists believed that "words – even if they are from the program of Solidarity – mean nothing at all to our authorities and to the authorities of the Union of Soviet Socialist Republics" (Kaczyński 2013, p. 87; on Nowak's political ideas at that time, see: Brzechczyn 2012). For that reason, as related by Kaczyński:

> the program should only be directed to the member masses. It should reflect their feelings and, in a way, put them in order. And what are those feelings? First of all, there is a deep resentment of our political system which incapacitates the society and which is seen by Poles as oppressive and causing all kinds of social evil. Such a system can be described in different ways. Among fundamentalists, professor Nowak's theory of so-called triple rule has become very popular, and they used that theory in their document.
> LECH KACZYŃSKI (1981) 2013, p. 87

An indirect result of Nowak's publicistic and social activity was his detainment during the night between December 12 and 13, 1981. During his stays in internment centers in Gębarzewo (December 13, 1981–February 1982), Ostrów Wielkopolski (February–July 1982), Gębarzewo again (July–August 1982), and Kwidzyn (September–December 9, 1982), Nowak gave lectures to co-prisoners and did scientific work. At first, he was troubled the most by the lack of books. Wojciech Wołyński remembers that: "Just after the transportation from Gębarzewo to Ostrów, he moved his table to the tiny window of the cell and turned it into a creative workshop. He did the same in the two subsequent prisons" (Wołyński 2002, p. 405). Nowak took part in the detainees' protest actions. Despite certain doubts, he also participated in the March hunger strike in Ostrów Wielkopolski. During his stay in Kwidzyn, he finished writing a brochure entitled "O konieczności socjalizmu i konieczności jego zaniku" (On the Necessity of Socialism and of its Disappearance; Nowak 1982), which was published in 100 copies by other co-internees by means of the ink and pin method. Nowak was released from prison on December 9, 1982. He was released only after other internees who were to be released on that day declared that they will not go unless Nowak is released as well.

He returned to the university where he continued his work as the head of the Poznań Department of Dialectics of Cognition and the vice dean of the Faculty of Social Sciences. He returned to lecturing and publicistic activity (under his own name). In 1983, the Reidel publishing house published Nowak's book, *Property and Power. Towards a non-Marxian Historical Materialism*

(Nowak 1983b). In 1983–1988, there were 14 underground editions of Nowak's August 1983 brochure *Anty-Rakowski, czyli co wygwizdali wicepremierowi robotnicy* (Anti-Rakowski, or, what workers booed at the deputy prime minister; Nowak 1983a). Nowak's publicistic activity drew the attention of the apparatus of repression. On February 10, 1984 the voivodeship Office of the Public Prosecutor in Poznań initiated an investigation in the case of the "distribution of works and publications signed with the name of Leszek Nowak, the content of which contains texts and false information which denigrate the form of government of the Polish People's Republic, the main governing bodies of the Polish People's Republic, and the Polish United Workers' Party, and which instigate social unrest."[2] In March 1984, while Nowak and his family were in Frankfurt where he was a visiting professor, his house was searched and 43 texts (manuscripts of articles, typescripts, and single copies of illegal publications) were confiscated. Nowak was not arrested because an amnesty law was passed on July 21, 1984. As a result, the investigation was discontinued on September 17, 1984.

A month later, on October 19, 1984, the Minister of Science and Higher Education, Benon Miśkiewicz, suspended Nowak's right to perform the duties of an academic teacher. That decision spurred protests of the academic circles in Poznań and the whole country. Nevertheless, Nowak was dismissed from the university on February 14, 1985. For the next three years, he was refused a passport 12 times. In 1988, he went to the l'Universita degli Studi in Catania at the invitation of professor Francesco Coniglione. Subsequently, he was a fellow at the Netherlands Institute for Advanced Study (Wassenaar), the Berlin Institute for Advanced Study (1989–1990 academic year), and the Australian National University in Canberra.

The reinstatement of Leszek Nowak became a postulate of the student strikes in May 1988 at Adam Mickiewicz University in Poznań and one of the issues raised by the academic circles in the 1988–1989 academic year. On April 10, 1989, the Senate of Adam Mickiewicz University in Poznań passed a resolution concerning the reinstatement of Nowak. In May 1989, the Minister of Science reinstated Nowak to his former position, as of April 1, 1989.

After his return to Poznań, Nowak received the position of a full professor (*profesor zwyczajny*). In 1991, he was a candidate to the Sejm from the list of the Labor Union (he was not elected). He wrote about social issues to "Głos Wielkopolski," "Gazeta Poznańska," "Bez Dogmatu," and "Przegląd Tygodniowy."

---

2   The Archive of the Institute of National Remembrance, Po 04/3531, The decision on the initiation of an investigation, February 10, 1984.

In his columns, he discussed critically the role of the Catholic church in Poland after 1989 and the quality of Polish political elites. Disappointed with the course of the transformation, he left Solidarity in 1994. In the second half of the 1990s, as his health deteriorated, he gradually limited his university duties. In 1999, he resigned from the position of the head of the Epistemology Department, and he focused on the creation of a system of unitarian metaphysics, which he presented in his three-volume work *Byt i myśl* (Being and thought, Nowak 1998, 2004, 2007). The fourth volume remained unfinished as Nowak died on October 20, 2009 (it was edited by his wife and published posthumously in 2019).

2   On Leszek Nowak's Theory of the Historical Process

It is possible to distinguish three overlapping phases of Nowak's intellectual development: reconstructive, generalizing, and unifying (for a detailed reconstruction Nowak's theory of historical process, see Brzechczyn 2017; 2020b). The first reconstructive period lasted from 1973 to 1979 (if we base it on the publication dates and not the moment when Nowak began writing the text). At that time, Nowak created the adaptive interpretation of historical materialism. During the second period, from 1979 to about 1988, Nowak tried to generalize the Marxian concept of class division and to derive certain theoretical and historiosophical consequences from it. The result was non-Marxian historical materialism (Nowak 1979; 1983b; 1988a; 1991abc; 1991d)[3]. The unifying stage (which began about the middle of the 1980s) started with laying down the anthropological foundations for non-Marxian historical materialism, which enabled Nowak to incorporate certain theses from liberalism and Christian social science into the new theory.[4]

Non-Marxian historical materialism assumed some earlier concepts: the idealizational theory of science, the adaptive interpretation of historical materialism, and the categorial reconstruction of dialectics. The main idea of the reconstruction of Marx's methodology was the conviction that a scientific theory is neither a generalization of facts nor a hypothetical-deductive system (Nowak 1980; Nowak, Nowakowa 2000). The construction of a scientific theory begins

---

[3] *Property and Power* (Nowak 1983b) was reviewed by Sołtan (1984), Schneck (1984) and Berthold (1986), *Power and Civil Society* (Nowak 1991d) – Kubik (1994).

[4] Nowak also reflected on the conditions for the construction of a unified social theory and tried to construct such a theory at a later time, in the 1990s, and in the first decade of the 21st century (see Nowak 1997; 1999; 2003; 2010; 2022a; 2022b).

from a decisive deformation of reality, in the first, most idealized model. An idealizational law has the form of a conditional. The antecedent contains counterfactual assumptions on the basis of which the influence of factors considered to be secondary for the studied phenomenon are omitted. The consequent of an idealizational law shows how the studied phenomenon depends on its primary factors or factor. An idealizational statement obtained in that way is valid on condition that certain idealizational assumptions are made. Next, that simple image of a phenomenon only dependent on the main factor is gradually corrected. Idealizational assumptions which, in the first model, exclude the influence of particular secondary factors are waved aside, while the corrective impact of those initially omitted factors is explained. In that way, a scientific theory is formed which consists of a hierarchy of models that reflect the complexity of the studied phenomena in more and more detail (on Poznań School of Methodology and Nowak's methodological approach, see: Swiderski 1984; Coniglione 2010; Borbone 2011a; 2011b; 2016; 2021 and Kowalewski Jahromi 2021).[5]

Nowak used the idealizing methodology in his reconstruction of Marx's dialectics and social theory. Within the framework of categorial ontology, the contradiction between Marxian dialectics and historical materialism was constructed. It was called the paradox of historicism and consisted in the observation that Marxian dialectics (at least its categorial reconstruction) propounded the variability of the main factors of studied phenomena, while Marxian historical materialism maintained that productive forces and relations of production were always significant determinants of social life, in all societies and historical periods. That paradox gives rise to the question if the repertoire of main factors is or is not subject to change in historical development. If we admit that the main factors change in the course of historical development, the question arises about the nature of those non-economic but still material factors. That question led to the generalized version of Marxian historical materialism in which the functioning of real socialist societies would also be explained.

Non-Marxian historical materialism was an attempt at resolving the contradictory nature of historical materialism. According to that theory, there are three independent class divisions in a society, in the realms of economy, culture, and politics. Those social divisions arise as a social minority appropriates: the means of production in the economy (which creates the division into

---

5 It seems that following opinion of Professor Gereon Wolters: "I would like to mention the Polish philosopher Leszek Nowak (1943–2009), who has launched the contemporary debate on idealization and has greatly contributed to it. He is nonetheless, rarely quoted, although a substantial part of his world is published in English: He just seems to have had the wrong address: University of Poznań (Wolters 2013, p. 10) is too pessimistic.

the owners and the direct producers), the means of coercion in politics (leading to the division into the rulers and the citizens), and the means of spiritual production in culture (which results in the division into the priests and the followers). Social divisions can cumulate, so apart from class societies (with three separate classes), there are supraclass societies, in which the same social class controls politics, the economy, and culture.

Real socialism turned out to be such a supraclass system, as the apparatus of the communist party controlled political, economic, and cultural life. According to that approach, the socialist system was the most oppressive social system in history because it involved a triple monopoly. The basic interest of the class of triple-lords was to maximize its political range of regulation. Therefore, the control over economy and culture was instrumentally subordinated to the maximization of power. For that reason, phenomena considered to be the 'absurdities' of planned economy were not caused by the 'unreasonableness' of the rulers, weakness of political culture, political errors, or distortions of the idea of socialism – they were structurally determined by the realization of the political interest of the triple rule.

The advantage of Nowak's theory was its dynamic approach to the development of socialism based on a conflict of interest between the triple lords and the people. The theses of the basic model of that theory could be presented in the following way.

(i) The principal social division of socialism is the contradiction between the class of triple lords and the people's class; the mechanism of political competition enforces a typical ruler to enlarge his/her sphere of influence. As a result, the scope of political regulation enlarges and the scope of civil autonomy is gradually diminished.

(ii) In the phase of political enslavement (called Stalinism), when all spheres of social life are controlled by the authorities, a new phenomenon appears. Because the sphere of social autonomy becomes much smaller (or disappears altogether), political competition has to lead to the overtaking of social areas controlled by other rulers. In those conditions, blind mechanism of political competition leads to the self-enslavement of rulers who eliminate the surplus of candidates for power and, in that way, stabilize the political system. In theory of power in non-Marxian historical materialism, the social function of the purges it is clearly distinguished from their ideological justification (e.g. that they are carried out to defeat agents or the enemies of the people, to forestall conspiracies, etc.; more on mechanism of political purges, see Siegel 1992; 1993; 1998).

(iii) During the enslavement phase, there appears a trend toward a re-valorization of grassroots social relations. This leads to the outbreak of a revolution, which fails but gives rise to the phase of cyclical development of the system.

(iv) The rulers repress the revolting citizens and, in order to prevent a new revolutionary wave, make concessions to the class of citizens – they withdraw from the regulation of selected spheres of social life. However, after a time, the mechanisms of competition for power once more cause an increase of the citizens' alienation. The greater power regulation triggers another citizens' revolution with a wider social base, which compels the rulers to make even greater allowances. A political society evolves according to the following pattern: citizens' revolution – declassation – concessions – increasing power regulation – another citizens' revolution with a broader social base – etc.

(v) The increasing number of citizens participating in the cyclical political revolutions results in a revolution so massive that the rulers, instead of turning to oppression, must initially make concessions big enough to bring about social compromise.

(vi) The mechanism of social development changes as well and assumes the following form: concessions – greater power regulation – revolution with a broader social base – greater concessions.

When we compare the critique of real socialism based on the assumptions of non-Marxian historical materialism with the critiques made on other ideological-theoretical grounds (of orthodox Marxism, revisionism, or liberalism), we can see that Nowak's critique was more radical and comprehensive from the start.[6]

In the orthodox Marxist critique represented by Karl August Wittfogel (1957) or Milovan Đjilas (1957), the state apparatus is a collective owner (or capitalist, in Đjilas terms) who uses state violence to maximize the surplus product and stimulate economic development. In Wittfogel's approach, the state participated in the production process in order irrigate the farmed land.

According to Đjilas, the state control of the economy and the participation of the state in robust industrialization was caused by the necessity to modernize Eastern European states and to catch up with more civilized Western states. In the approaches mentioned above, the state apparatus is not constituted by a separate type of social interest (power regulation). In Nowak's approach, the

---

6 For a more systematic comparison with other conceptualizations of real socialism, see: Brzechczyn, 2008, 2019.

maximization of power regulation generates greater contradictions than the maximization of the surplus product or of spiritual authority. From his point of view, socialism was a system with the greatest social divisions in history because one triple class (the party apparatus) took over the disposal of three type of material means.

The revisionist critique of socialism was based on the category of alienation, present in young Marx's writings – the idea of people losing control over their products and becoming alienated. In socialism, state bureaucracy was the source of the alienation of individuals. The critique of socialism based on the idea of alienation was ahistorical, and it ignored the actual social divisions because both a party member and an average citizen could become alienated.

The liberal critique of socialism focused on its institutional aspects: the rule of one party and the lack of free elections, a multi-party system, and institutional control of the state. In the social structure of Western European countries, the institutions mentioned above truly controlled political rulers whose social power was counterbalanced by private property and independent social opinion. Nowak argued that, in socialist societies, the state is the ruler, collective owner, and priest. That is why the institutional channels of control over the triple rule are insufficient.

In the second half of the 1980s, Nowak constructed the anthropological foundations for non-Marxian historical materialism, which led to a revision of the theory of power and the whole of his historiosophy. The non-Christian model of man built by Nowak revealed the limitations of the rationalistic concept of human individuals, in which the philosophical justification was drawn from the Judeo-Christian religion. According to the non-Christian model of man, there are three areas of social interactions. In the normal area of social interaction the rule of mutuality prevails. Individual A responds with hostility to hostility from individual B, and responds with kindness to his/her kindness. In this area, the Christian ethical principle of love of one's neighbor is applied. However, in the presented model of social interactions there are thresholds of hostility and kindness.

When individual A faces growing hostility from B, his/her tendency to answer with reflexive hostility decreases. In conditions of extreme hostility from B, individual A becomes 'pathologically' kind towards his/her partner of social interaction, or, in other words, accepts his/her preferences. In these social conditions, individual A is enslaved by individual B and this state of social interactions is called 'the area of enslavement'. In these social conditions, the ethics of the love of one's neighbor should be substituted with the ethics of revolution.

A parallel situation takes place at the opposite end of the area of social interactions. Individual A also responds with kindness to kindness received from B. However, when individual A faces growing kindness, his/her tendency to respond with similar kindness decreases. In the conditions of extreme kindness received from B, individual A does not behave in accordance with his/her own preferences, but according to the counter-preferences of individual B. We describe this as individual A being satanized by individual B and this state of social interaction is named an area of satanization, where the ethical principle of love of one's neighbor should be substituted with the conservative ethics of social strictness.[7]

The anthropological assumptions incorporated into the theory of power make it possible to paraphrase certain right-wing and left-wing intuitions about, among other things, the nature of revolution and power itself. On the one hand, a revolution is a mass protest against political enslavement, leading to renewed interpersonal solidarity (as noticed in left-wing philosophy and ignored in right-wing thinking). On the other hand, it releases mechanisms that satanize the citizens. Since the grassroots committees and revolutionary boards are too weak to prevent the increasing anarchization of public life, post-revolutionary dictatorship is implemented to maintain social order. That dictatorship is formed as ex-revolutionists reach for more and more power, in stark contrast to the ideals they used to profess (which was noticed by right-wing thinkers and ignored by the left-wing ones). According to Nowak:

> the point is that both are true. But traditional paradigms of conservative and radical thinking are so limited that they are unable to notice this two-fold empirical truth.
>
> Yet, both certain "conservative truth" and certain "radical truths" occur. However, they are empirical records, which are neither theoretically explained nor pronounced together. The outlined concept, on the other hand, does allow for both. Both turn out to be a consequence of more primary mechanism, resulting in the last resort from the non-Christian model of man.
>
> NOWAK 1991d, pp. 58–59

---

[7] For some discussions on Nowak's anthropological model and its some application and extensions, see: Garcia de la Sienra 1989; Egiert 1993; Paprzycki 1993; Paprzycka, Paprzycki 1993; Ciesielski 2012; 2013; Brzechczyn 2020a, pp. 219–231.

3   The Concept of This Volume

The idea for this volume was born during my meetings and talks with Professor Leszek Nowak which took place in the first decade of the XXI century. During one of these conversations, prof. Nowak encouraged me to collect hitherto prepared papers from non-Marxian historical materialism and edit them in a special volume of 'Poznań Studies in the Philosophy of the Sciences and the Humanities.' As I recall, Prof. Nowak loosely suggested a title or subtitle for this volume: 'Polish Contributions to the Theory of the Historical Process.' In this way, the content of the present volume and its title reflect Prof. Nowak's inspiration.

The first part of the volume contains a selection of Nowak's works on non-Marxian historical materialism, which are published here in English for the first time. This part begins with a text written together with Piotr Buczkowski and Andrzej Klawiter, *Religion as a Class Structure: A Contribution to Non-Marxian Historical Materialism*. It is an attempt at conceptualizing social divisions in the cultural sphere of social life. In this chapter, the structure of worldview is conceptualized and basic notions (i.e. spiritual domination vs. spiritual autonomy, spiritual alienation and the mechanisms of spiritual class struggle) of the static assumptions of confessional society are introduced into the conceptual apparatus of non-Marxian historical materialism. In the last part of this paper, the development of the idealizational confessional society is presented.

In the two subsequent texts, *Marxism versus Liberalism: A Certain Paradox* and *Hegel and Liberalism: On the Issue of the Nature of Historiosophy*, Nowak analyzes the structure of the substantial philosophy of history. In the first text, he compares liberalism and Marxism from theoretical and ideological perspectives. In the second one, he presents the interrelationships of the normative and descriptive motifs in the philosophy of history inspired by Hegelianism.

The article titled *The Truth Unbearable for All* is an attempt at capturing the historiosophical specificity of Stalinism in the history of the Union of Soviet Socialist Republics. The mechanisms of the development of the Soviet society in the 1930s – which liberated political power from the influence of property and religion – were completely different from the ones in Western Europe. In two articles, *The Problem of the So-Called Social Transformation* and *Hegel's Chuckle, That Is, Marxism and Liberalism in Polish Politics* Nowak interprets – in the light of his theory – the historiosophical assumptions of the socio-political thought of main political parties responsible for the course of the political transformation initiated in Poland after 1989.

In the article titled *On-The-Verge Effect in a Historical Process: An Attempt at an Interpretation with the Assumption of non-Marxian Historical Materialism*

Nowak presents a concretization of the model of the capitalist society trying to accommodate civilizational mechanisms of historical developments. In the two subsequent texts (*The End of History or its Repetitions?* and *On the Prediction of the Totalitarization of Capitalism: An Attempt at an Evaluation after Twenty Years*), he wonders about the status of the still unfulfilled prediction about the totalitarization of the capitalist society.

In the second part of the volume titled *On Totalitarization of Capitalism, Democratization of Real Socialism and Development of non-European Societies*, the developments of non-Marxian historical materialism are presented. Tomasz Zarębski (*The Problem of Totalitarization of the Capitalist Society*) and Mieszko Ciesielski (*The Problem of the Accumulation of Class Divisions in Contemporary Capitalism: An Attempt at a Theoretical Analysis*) analyze theoretical assumptions of the model of the capitalist society which make it possible to explain why the progressive accumulation of political and economic power, predicted by Nowak, might not materialize.

Three subsequent texts: Tomasz Banaszak's *How Democracy Evolves into Autocracy,* Marcin Połatyński's *On Coalition and Party Splintering: A Contribution to Theory of Power in non-Marxian Historical Materialism*, and Lidia Godek's, *On Two Types of Democratization: Poland and Czechoslovakia. An Attempt at an Interpretation* broaden the theory of political society in non-Marxian historical materialism. Those developments enrich the analyses of institutional dimensions of political power.

The two last texts are examples of the application of non-Marxian historical materialism to the history of non-European societies. Eliza Karczyńska interprets the social structures of the Ottoman society (*The Social Structure of the Ottoman Society: An Attempt at a Theoretical Analysis*), and Dawid Rogacz, in his article titled *The Dynamics of Power in Postwar China: An Attempt at a Theoretical Analysis* – the Chinese society.

References

Balicki, W. (2003). Wypowiedź [A Statement]. In: K. Brzechczyn (ed.) *Odwaga filozofowania – rozmowa o obecności Leszka Nowaka w filozofii polskiej. Przegląd Bydgoski. Humanistyczne Czasopismo Naukowe*, 14, 65–81.

Bartkowiak, J. (2014). *Element Antysocjalistyczny. Samorząd Studentów na Uniwersytecie im. Adama Mickiewicza w Poznaniu w latach 1980–1989* [The Anti-Socialist Element. The Students' Self-Government at Adam Mickiewicz University]. Poznań: Fundacja Św. Benedykta.

Berthold, L. (1986) Review of 'Property and Power.' *Zeitschrift Für Politik*, 33 (2), 218–219.

Borbone, G. (2011a). The Legacy of Leszek Nowak. *Epistemologia*, 34, 227–252.

Borbone, G. (2011b). Leszek Nowak and the Idealizational Approach to Science. *Linguistic and Philosophical Investigations*, 10, 125–149.

Borbone, G. (2016). *Questioni di Metodo. Leszek Nowak e la scienza come idealizzazione.* Roma: Acireale.

Borbone, G. (2021). *The Relevance of Models. Idealization and Concretization in Leszek Nowak.* Műnchen: Grin Verlag.

Brzechczyn, K. (2007). Selected Bibliography of Leszek Nowak's Writings. In: J. Brzeziński, A. Klawiter, Th.A.F. Kuipers, K. Łastowski, K. Paprzycka, and P. Przybysz (eds.) *The Courage of Doing Philosophy: Essays Dedicated to Leszek Nowak*, pp. 235–254. Amsterdam/New York, NY: Rodopi.

Brzechczyn, K. (2008). Polish Discussions on the Nature of Communism and Mechanisms of its Collapse. A Review Article. *East European Politics and Societies*, 22 (4), 828–855.

Brzechczyn, K. (2011). Bibliografia publikacji Leszka Nowaka w obiegu niezależnym [A Bibliography of Leszek Nowak's Publications in the Clandestine ('Secondary') Circulation]. In: L. Nowak, *Polska droga od socjalizmu. Pisma polityczne 1980–1989*, edited by K. Brzechczyn, pp. 723–734. Poznań: IPN.

Brzechczyn, K. (2012). On Courage of Actions and Cowardice of Thinking. Leszek Nowak on the Provincionalism of the Political Thought of Solidarność. In: K. Brzechczyn. K. Paprzycka (eds.), *Thinking about Provincialism in Thinking. Poznań Studies in the Philosophy of the Sciences and the Humanities*, vol. 100, pp. 217–234. Amsterdam/New York, NY: Rodopi.

Brzechczyn, K. (2017). From Interpretation to Refutation of Marxism. On Leszek Nowak's non-Marxian Historical Materialism. *Hybris. Internetowy Magazyn Filozoficzny*, 37, 141–178.

Brzechczyn, K. (2019). Between Modernization and Enslavement: The Historiosophical Implications of Two Approaches to the Social Divisions in Real Socialism. In: K. Brzechczyn (ed.) *New Perspectives in Transnational History of Communism in East Central Europe*, pp. 25–42. Berlin: Peter Lang.

Brzechczyn, K. (2020a). *The Historical Distinctiveness of Central Europe: A Study in the Philosophy of History*. Berlin: Peter Lang.

Brzechczyn, K. (2020b). Periodization as a Disguised Conceptualization of Historical Development: a Case Study of a Theory of the Historical Process Developed in the Poznań School of Methodology. In: M. Będkowski, A. Brożek, A. Chybińska, S. Ivanyk and D. Traczykowski (eds.), *Formal and Informal Methods in Philosophy. Poznań Studies in the Philosophy of the Sciences and the Humanities*, vol. 113, pp. 101–125. Leiden/Boston: Brill / Rodopi.

Ciesielski, M. (2012). *Zagadnienie ograniczeń racjonalnego modelu działań ludzkich, Próba ujęcia działania nawykowo-racjonalnego* [The Issue of Limitations of the Rational Model of Human Action. An Attempt at Recognition of Habitual-Rational Action]. Poznań: Wydawnictwo Poznańskie.

Ciesielski, M. (2013). Leszek Nowak's non-Christian Model of Man and Inderdisciplinarity of Humanities. *Studia Europea Gnesnensia*, 7, 87–111.

Coniglione, F. (2010). *Realtà e astrazione. Scuola polacca ed epistemologia post-positivista*. Roma: Bonanno Editore.

Djilas, M. (1957). *The New Class. An Analysis of Communist System*. London: Thames and Hudson.

Egiert, R. (1993). Toward the Sophisticated Rationalistic Model of Man. In: L. Nowak, M. Paprzycki (eds.) *Social System, Rationality and Revolution. Poznań Studies in the Philosophy of the Sciences and the Humanities*, vol. 33, pp. 215–233. Amsterdam-Atlanta: Rodopi.

Garcia de la Sienra, A. (1989). The Christian Model of Man: Reply to Nowak. *Social Theory and Practice. An International and Interdisciplinary Journal of Social Philosophy*, 15 (1), 89–107.

Kaczyński, L. ([1981] 2013). Wypowiedź (Statement). In: G. Majchrzak, J.M. Owsiński (eds.) *Krajowy Zjazd Delegatów NSZZ „Solidarność." Stenogramy*, vol. 2, pp. 85–87. Warsaw: IPN.

Klawiter, A., K. Łastowski (2007). Introduction: Originality, Courage, and Responsibility. In: J. Brzeziński, A. Klawiter, T.A.F. Kuipers, K. Łastowski, K. Paprzycka, P. Przybysz (eds.) *The Courage of Doing Philosophy. Essays Presented to Leszek Nowak*, pp. 7–22. Amsterdam-New York: Rodopi.

Klawiter, A. (2013). Wspomnienie o działalności naukowej Leszka Nowaka [Remembering Leszek Nowak's Scientific Work]. In: K. Brzechczyn (ed.) *Realny socjalizm – „Solidarność" – kapitalizm. Wokół myśli politycznej Leszka Nowaka*, pp. 80–84. Poznań: IPN.

Kowalewski Jahromi, P. (2021). Analytical Philosophy of History in Poland. Inspirations and Interpretations. *Historyka. Studia Metodologiczne*, 51 (special issue), 39–63.

Kubik, J. (1994). Review of 'Power and Civil Society.' *Ethics*, 104 (3), 652–655.

Lissewski, P. (2013). Leszek Nowak – wspomnienie z przełomu epok [Leszek Nowak – a Memory from the Turn of Epochs]. In: K. Brzechczyn (ed.) *Realny socjalizm – „Solidarność" – kapitalizm. Wokół myśli politycznej Leszka Nowaka*, pp. 95–96. Poznań: IPN.

Nowak. L. (1979). *U podstaw teorii procesu historycznego* [On the Foundations of the Theory of the Historical Process]. Poznań: Manuscript.

Nowak, L. (1980). *The Structure of Idealization. Towards a Systematic Interpretation of the Marxian Idea of Science*. Dordrecht: Reidel.

Nowak, L. (1981). Jeśli mamy szansę, to dzięki kryzysowi gospodarczemu i radzieckiemu zagrożeniu [If We Have a Chance, it is Thanks to the Economic Crisis and Threat from the USSR]. *Wakat. Niezależne Pismo Członków NZS*, 4, 5–14.

Nowak, L. (1982). *O konieczności socjalizmu i konieczności jego zaniku* [On the Necessity of Socialism and the Necessity of its Disappearance]. Kwidzyn: Internowa.

Nowak, L. (1983a). Anty-Rakowski, czyli co wygwizdali wicepremierowi robotnicy [Anti-Rakowski, that is What Workers Whistled to the Deputy of the Prime Minister]. *Veto*, 10–11, 126–162.

Nowak, L. (1983b). *Property and Power. Towards a non-Marxian Historical Materialism*. Dordrecht: Reidel.

Nowak, L. (1985). Conversation. *Obecność. Niezależne Pismo Literackie*, 11, 45–56.

Nowak, L. (1987) Science, Marxism and Real Socialism. In: L. Nowak, *Oltre Marx. Per un materialismo storico non-Marxiano*, edited by F. Coniglione, pp. 271–315. Rome: Armando.

Nowak, L. (1988a.) *Władza. Próba teorii idealizacyjnej* [Power. An Attempt at an Idealizational Theory]. Warszawa: In Plus.

Nowak, L. (1988b). Wypowiedź [Statement] in: Marzec '68 w relacjach uczestników i refleksji socjologicznej [March 1968 in the Participants' Relations and in Sociological Reflection]. *Czas. Pismo Społeczno-Polityczne*, 1, 37–38.

Nowak, L. (1991abc.). *U podstaw teorii socjalizmu* [The Foundations of the Theory of Socialism]; vol. 1: *Własność i władza. O konieczności socjalizmu* [Property and Power. On the Necessity of Socialism]; vol. 2: *Droga do socjalizmu. O konieczności socjalizmu w Rosji* [The Road to Socialism. On the Necessity of Socialism in Russia]; vol. 3: *Dynamika władzy. O strukturze i konieczności zaniku socjalizmu* [The Dynamics of Power. On the Structure and Necessity of the Disappearance of Socialism]. Poznań: Nakom.

Nowak L. (1991d). *Power and Civil Society. Toward a Dynamic Theory of Real Socialism*. New York: Greenwood Press.

Nowak, L. (1997). Marksizm versus liberalizm: Pewien paradoks [Marxism versus Liberalism: a Certain Paradox]. In: L. Nowak, P. Przybysz (eds.) *Marksizm, liberalizm, próby wyjścia*, pp. 7–19. Poznań: Zysk i S-ka.

Nowak, L. (1998). *Byt i myśl. U podstaw negatywistycznej metafizyki unitarnej*, t. I: *Nicość i istnienie* [Being and Thought: Foundations of Negativistic Unitarian Metaphysics, vol. I: Nothingness and Existence]. Poznań: Zysk i S-ka.

Nowak, L. (1999). Unifikacja liberalnego i Marksowskiego modelu człowieka [The Unification of the Liberal and Marxian Models of Man]. In: J. Kozielecki (ed.) *Humanistyka przełomu wieków*, pp. 162–178. Warszawa: Wydawnictwo Akademickie Żak.

Nowak, L. (2003). O prognozie totalitaryzacji kapitalizmu. Próba oceny po dwudziestu latach [On the Prediction of the Totalitarization of Capitalism. An Attempt at an

Evaluation after Twenty Years]. In: K. Brzechczyn (ed.). *Ścieżki transformacji. Ujęcia teoretyczne i opisy empiryczne*, pp. 361–400. Poznań: Zysk i S-ka.

Nowak, L. (2004) *Byt i myśl. U podstaw negatywistycznej metafizyki unitarnej* t. II: *Wieczność i zmiana* [Being and Thought: Foundations of Negativistic Unitarian Metaphysics, vol. II: Eternity and Change]. Poznań: Zysk i S-ka.

Nowak, L. (2006). Autoprezentacja [Self-presentation]. In: M. Dźwiniel (ed.), *Ludzie 13 Grudnia. Kim byli, co myślą niektórzy internowani w stanie wojennym Poznaniacy?* pp. 167–181. Poznań: Studio Poligrafia.

Nowak, L. (2007) *Byt i myśl. U podstaw negatywistycznej metafizyki unitarnej* t. III: vol. III: *Enigma i rzeczywistości* [Being and Thought: Foundations of Negativistic Unitarian Metaphysics, vol. III: Enigma and Realities]. Poznań: Zysk i S-ka.

Nowak, L. (2010). O złotym podziale prawdy w teorii rewolucji. Przyczynek do analizy opozycji myślenia lewicowego i prawicowego [On the Golden Rule of Truth in the Theory of Revolution. A Contribution to an Analysis of Leftist and Rightist Thinking]. In: J. Grad, J. Sójka, A. Zaporowski (eds.) *Nauka, kultura, społeczeństwo*, pp. 123–130. Poznań: Wydawnictwo Naukowe UAM.

Nowak, L. (2011). *Polska droga od socjalizmu. Pisma polityczne 1980–1989* [The Polish Road from Socialism. Political Papers 1980–1989], edited by K. Brzechczyn. Poznań: IPN.

Nowak, L. (2018). *Człowiek, ludzie, międzyludzkie. Eseje z nie-Ewangelicznego modelu człowieka* [Man, People and the Inter-Human. Essays from the non-Christian Model of Man] edited by I. Nowakowa. Warszawa: Semper.

Nowak, L. (2019). *Podmiot i system kulturowy* [Subject and Cultural System], edited by I. Nowakowa. Poznań: Wydawnictwo Naukowe UAM.

Nowak, L. (2022a). Marxism versus Liberalism: A Certain Paradox. In: K. Brzechczyn (ed.) *New Developments in Theory of Historical Process. Polish Contributions to Non-Marxian Historical Materialism. Poznań Studies in the Philosophy of the Sciences and the Humanities*, vol. 119, pp.106–118. Leiden/Boston: Brill.

Nowak, L. (2022b). On the Prediction of the Totalitarization of Capitalism: An Attempt at Evaluation after Twenty Years. In: K. Brzechczyn (ed.) *New Developments in Theory of Historical Process. Polish Contributions to Non-Marxian Historical Materialism. Poznań Studies in the Philosophy of the Sciences and the Humanities*, vol. 119, pp. 150–185. Leiden/Boston: Brill.

Nowak, L., I. Nowakowa (2000). *Idealization X: The Richness of Idealization. Poznań Studies in the Philosophy of the Sciences and the Humanities*, vol. 69. Amsterdam/Atlanta: Rodopi.

Paprzycka, K. and M. Paprzycki (1993). How Do Enslaved People Make Revolutions? In: L. Nowak, M. Paprzycki (eds.) *Social System, Rationality and Revolution. Poznań Studies in the Philosophy of the Sciences and the Humanities*, vol. 33, pp. 251–265. Amsterdam-Atlanta: Rodopi.

Paprzycki, M. (1993). The Non-Christian Model of Man. An Attempt at a Psychoanalitic Explanation. In: L. Nowak, M. Paprzycki (eds.) *Social System, Rationality and Revolution. Poznań Studies in the Philosophy of the Sciences and the Humanities*, vol. 33, pp. 205–215. Amsterdam-Atlanta: Rodopi.

Schneck, St. F. (1984). Review of 'Property and Power.' *The American Political Science Review*, 78(4), 1193–1194.

Siegel, A. (1992). *Der Dynamik des Terrors im Stalinismum: Ein strukturtheoretischer Erklärungsversuch*. Pfaffenweiler: Centaurus.

Siegel, A. (1993). The Overrepression Cycle in the Soviet Union. An Operationalization of a Theoretical Model. In: L. Nowak, M. Paprzycki (eds.) *Social System, Rationality and Revolution. Poznań Studies in the Philosophy of the Sciences and the Humanities*, vol. 33, pp. 371–396. Amsterdam-Atlanta: Rodopi.

Siegel, A. (1998). Ideological Learning Under Conditions of Social Enslavement: The Case of the Soviet Union in the 1930s and 1940s. *Studies in East European Thought*, 50(1), 19–58.

Sołtan, K. (1984). Review of 'Property and Power.' *Ethics*, 95(1), 160–162.

Swiderski, E. M. (1984) Humanistic Interpretation and Historical Materialism: The Methodology of the Poznań School, pp. 97–107. In: J.J. O'Rourke, T.J. Blakeley, F.J. Rapp (eds.) *Contemporary Marxism*, Dordrecht: Springer.

Wittfogel, K. (1957). *Oriental Despotism*. New Haven: Yale University Press.

Wolters, G. (2013). European Humanities in Times of Globalized Parochialism. *Bollettino della Società Filosofica Italiana*, 208, 3–18.

Wołyński, W. (2002). Wspomnienie rysownika [A Sketch Artist's Memory]. In: J. Brzeziński, A. Klawiter, Th.A.F. Kuipers, K. Łastowski, K. Paprzycka, and P. Przybysz (eds.) *Odwaga filozofowania. Leszkowi Nowakowi w darze*, pp. 403–408. Poznań: Humaniora.

Tables and Figures

Tables

10.1 Types of State Systems (Nowak 1991a, p. 75)   198
13.1 The typology of forms of party organization   261
14.1 Types of State Systems (Nowak 1991a, p. 75)   271
14.2 Multilinear Development and Progress in Model II   271
16.1 Power hierarchy in China   321

Figures

1.1 The elements of the spiritual structure of a society. Area 1 is the internal (formal) structure of culture. Area 2 represents the integrative function of culture and its practitioners. Area 3 shows the inflammatory function of culture. A spiritual teacher is a creator of culture, his role is to satisfy recipients' spiritual needs. A doctrinaire is a holder of the means of creating cultural messages. The creator of culture can be a doctrinaire if that person imposes his or her views on the recipients (the indoctrinated). The opposition between a doctrinaire and a teacher exists at the level of social roles and not necessarily of people. Sometimes creators of culture play both roles.   10

1.2 The contradiction of interests between spiritual classes. A single field means a set of convictions within the range of which a single priest has spiritual influence over a certain number of bellowers. The sum of those fields is the global range of regulation of the whole class of priests. The illustration shows that the subject matter of these reflections requires a number of simplifications. We will mention two such necessary assumptions here: that particular convictions are logically independent and that they have the same 'weight' for priests. None of them is true, but if we took into account the circumstances omitted in those assumptions, our construction would become too complicated right from the start.   31

1.3 The dependence of class struggle in the momentum of spiritual production on spiritual oppression of the faithful. Abbreviations used: R_1, R_2 – the first (respectively, the second) revolutionary area, p – the area of class peace.   33

1.4 The idealized course of the formation of faith in time. R_I (resp. R_{II}) – the first (resp. the second) revolutionary area, p – the area of class peace. It is assumed that at the starting point of the process, the first confessional society in the discussed society is formed. The continuous curve means the level of spiritual oppression within the framework of that society, created by the priests of faith F (marked F_{ort} since the first schism). The thin curves indicate the level of spiritual oppression in the newly created confessional societies which correspond to the reformed faiths from the F faith family. The thicken continuous curve indicates the level of spiritual oppression in the possibly emerging new faith (based on a new mythical set), U. Broken thick curves indicate the level of spiritual oppression in the confessional societies which correspond to the reformed faiths of the U type. One of them absorbs faith F_{ort} 43

10.1 The development of a model capitalist society in the n-Mhm. Explanations: The areas marked with Roman letters correspond to three historical stages of the development of capitalism: I – from the beginning of the industrial revolution to the end of the 19th century, II – contemporary times, III – the foreseeable future. The remaining designations: K – the great crisis of the 1930s, T – totalitarianism.   194

10.2 An illustration of the decision-making possibilities of the working class if conditions (W_1), (W_2) are fulfilled.   208

10.3 An illustration of the decision-making possibilities of the working class when conditions (W_1) and (W'_2) are fulfilled.   210

11.1 The transition from the class society to the p-totalitarian society. Abbreviations used: rulers – the class of rulers, owners – the class of owners, priests – the class of priests, people – the people class; the people means the three classes which do not have the material social means at their disposal, that is: the citizens, the direct producers, and the followers.   221

11.2 The expanded typology of societies of non-Marxian historical materialism. On the figure, I assume that the societies are in the political version. Abbreviations used: r – the class of rulers, o – the class of owners, pr – the class of priests, p – the people's class; the people means the three classes which do not have the material social means at their disposal, that is: the citizens, the direct producers, and the followers.   223

11.3 A pure three-momentum society   224

11.4 A mixed three-momentum society, the variant with two double derivative classes   224

11.5 A mixed three-momentum society, the variant with two triple derivative classes   224

11.6 A pure two-momentum society, the variant with one derivative class   225

11.7 A pure two-momentum society, the variant with two derivative classes   225

11.8 A mixed two-momentum society, the variant with two single derivative classes   225

11.9 A mixed two-momentum society, the variant with two triple derivative classes   226

11.10 A pure one-momentum society, the variant without derivative classes   226
11.11 A pure one-momentum society, the variant with one derivative class   226
11.12 A pure one-momentum society, the variant with two derivative classes   227
11.13 A mixed one-momentum society, the variant with two single derivative classes   227
11.14 A mixed one-momentum society, the variant with two double derivative classes   227
11.15 A transition from a class society to a society with a tendency toward the accumulation of class divisions (economic with spiritual one and political with spiritual)   235
14.1 Typology of state systemic changes   273
14.2 Extension of typology of state systemic changes   274
15.1 The structure of feudal society (A), society of state feudalism (B) and totalitarian society (C). In order to simplify, the division of the class of owners into the owners of urban and rural economic subsystems is omitted.   297
16.1 The dynamics of relation between the class of rulers and the class of citizens in the People's Republic of China. Explanations: P – the threshold of class peace, R – the area of revolutions, D – the threshold of declassation, T – the threshold of totalitarianism; development phases: 1– the phase of the growth of civil alienation, 2 – the phase of the civil revolution, 3 – the phase of enslavement, 4 – the phase of cyclical declassations, 5 – the phase of cyclical revolutions; 6 – the phase of class peace.   328

Notes on Contributors

Tomasz Banaszak
is a lecturer of political sciences in University of Zielona Góra, Poland. Main areas of interests concern political philosophy and history of political thought.

Krzysztof Brzechczyn
is Professor at the Faculty of Philosophy, Adam Mickiewicz University, Poznań, Poland and the head of Epistemology and Cognitive Science Research Unit. He has recently authored *The Historical Distinctiveness of Central Europe: A Study in the Philosophy of History* (2020). brzech@amu.edu.pl.

Mieszko Ciesielski
is an assistant professor at the Institute of European Culture in Gniezno, Adam Mickiewicz University, Poznań, Poland. mieszko@amu.edu.pl.

Lidia Godek
is an assistant professor at Adam Mickiewicz University, Poznań, Poland. Her research focuses on philosophy of the social sciences and an aesthetic philosophy of politics.

Eliza Karczyńska
graduated philosophy from the Institute of Philosophy, Adam Mickiewicz University, Poznań, Poland.

Leszek Nowak (1943–2009)
was a philosopher, the founder and editor-in-chief Poznań Studies in the Philosophy of the Sciences and the Humanities and co-founder of Poznań School of Methodology. He created three theories of the great scope: idealizational theory of science, non-Marxian historical materialism and unitary metaphysics. In English he published among other: *The Structure of Idealization: Towards a Systematic Interpretation of the Marxian Idea of Science* (1980), *Property and Power: Towards a non-Marxian Historical Materialism* (1983), *Power and Civil Society: Power and Civil Society. Toward a Dynamic Theory of Real Socialism* (1991), *The Richness of Idealization* (with I. Nowakowa 2000).

Marcin Połatyński (1975–2007)
graduated political science from the Institute of Political Science and Journalism, Adam Mickiewicz University, Poznań, Poland.

Dawid Rogacz
is an assistant professor at the Faculty of Philosophy, Adam Mickiewicz University in Poznań, Poland; dawid.rogacz@vp.pl.

Tomasz Zarębski
graduated philosophy from the Institute of Philosophy, Adam Mickiewicz University, Poznań, Poland. He lectures at Gniezno College Milenium.

PART 1

*Leszek Nowak on Non-Marxian
Historical Materialism*

CHAPTER 1

Religion as a Class Structure: A Contribution to Non-Marxian Historical Materialism

Leszek Nowak

Abstract

The aim of this paper is to present a model of spiritual society with separate classes of priests and the indoctrinated (interchangeably the term 'the faithful' is used). In the first part of the paper the three approaches to the phenomenon of religion are presented: formal-axiological, functionalist-sociological and antagonicist-sociological and the introductory notions of mythologization, sublimation and worldview are introduced. In the second part, the confessional society is characterized. The criterion for being a member of the class of priests is to dispose of the material means of spiritual production. The members of the class of the indoctrinated are devoid of such possibility. This social advantage of the class of priests allows them to dogmatize the consciousness of the rest of society. Dogmatization occurs if, for every proposition from class Z, the proposition p that person A has accepted p is a necessary condition for B to accept p. The interest of the class of priest is to dogmatize the collective consciousness of the faithful but the maintenance of spiritual autonomy is in the interest of the class of faithful. The spiritual alienation defined as the ratio between dogmatized beliefs and social consciousness accepted by the faithful determines the dynamic social relations between these two spiritual classes. In the last part of the paper, the sixth-phased evolution of confessional society is presented.

Keywords

confessional society – dogmatization – faith – non-Marxian historical materialism – religion – spiritual dependence

1 Introduction[1]

In Marxian historical materialism, the class nature of religion is viewed as its external characteristic – religion is to be the opium for the masses, a tool for preventing them from taking off the shackles of economic exploitation. That thesis is false, not because of the reason usually given, namely, that it is too radical, but because it is not radical enough – because it is too weak. From the point of view of non-Marxian historical materialism, class division is present in the internal structure of religion. It is inscribed in the unequal access to the means of indoctrination: only priests, and not the faithful, have the means to enforce their convictions. This material – although non-economic – inequality leads to a particular spiritual oppression, the domination of the priest over the faithful, which, in turn, gives rise to the resistance of the class of faithful. The struggle of the spiritual classes is subject to certain regularities which, consequence determine the regularity of the course of the ideal formation of faith. It is the principal aim of this text to reveal those idealizational dependencies.

2 Assumptions

2.1 *It is Not True That Social Being (Socio-Economic Conditions) Determines Consciousness*

It is a classic thesis of Marxism that social being (the socio-economic conditions determined in the last resort by the state of productive forces and of relations of production) determines consciousness. As regards the societies called class societies in Marxism, the meaning of that thesis is that "The ideas of the ruling class are in every epoch the ruling ideas."[2] That sentence expresses both the depth and the weakness of the Marxian approach to social consciousness. It is deep, in the sense that consciousness is here understood not as a factor which integrates 'humanity' or a 'nation' but as an area in which social conflict takes place. For the first time – or, at least, for the first time in a clear and decisive way – social consciousness is discussed within the framework of an

---

1 The paper appears in English translation for the first time. The Polish original „Religia jako struktura klasowa. Przyczynek do nie-Marksowskiego materializmu historycznego" was written in cooperation with Piotr Buczkowski and Andrzej Klawiter. It has appeared in *Studia Religiogica* 20, (1987), 79–128. The abstract and key words have been added by the editor.
2 We should note that this transition from the civilizational to class level is not, by any means, clear in Marxian historical materialism. On the contrary, it leads to an ambiguity and makes the concept fall apart into two essentially separate historiosophies. See: Nowak 1983, pp. 18–31.

antagonicist paradigm and not a solidaristic one. Marx's approach is weak, in that it reduces the issue to economics (at best, with mediations – that is, 'as a last resort'): the discussed ruling class is the class of the owners of the means of production. The "ruling thoughts" are to sanction the owners' interests – in particular, to maximize the surplus product, that is, the exploitation of the direct producers.

However, the thesis that the ideas of the ruling class are ruling ideas is inconsistent with the Marxist understanding of religion. That can be verified simply by referring to what Marx says about religion as a special form of social consciousness:

> Man makes religion, religion does not make man. Religion is, indeed, the self-consciousness and self-esteem of man who has either not yet won through to himself, or has already lost himself again ... [Religion] is the fantastic realization of the human essence since the human essence has not acquired any true reality ... The criticism of religion disillusions man, so that he will think, act, and fashion his reality like a man who has discarded his illusions and regained his senses, so that he will move around himself as his own true Sun. Religion is only the illusory Sun which revolves around man as long as he does not revolve around himself.
> MARX [1843] 1970, pp. 457–458

Religion, then, is an expression of an individual's alienation, of the inability of a person to understand the nature of the forces he is subject to and of the consequent tendency to personify them as an extraterrestrial being. Both classic Marxist thinkers (Marx and Engels, editorial note) maintained the young Marx's view, as presented below:

> All religion, however, is nothing but the fantastic reflection in men's minds of those external forces which control their daily life, a reflection in which the terrestrial forces assume the form of supernatural forces.
> ENGELS [1878] 1987, p. 300

This statement, however, is clearly inconsistent with the thesis that "the ideas of the ruling class are in every epoch the ruling ideas." Alienation is a category independent from class divisions which applies equally to, let us say, a capitalist who is subject to the laws of the market, over which he has no power, and a proletarian who is subject to the law of exploitation, which he cannot oppose. The division into alienated and non-alienated people cuts across the class division (in the Marxist sense of that term) and is not dependent on it.

Religious alienation encompasses what is common for the social condition of the two antagonistic classes, namely, that their members do not have power over the social conditions of their activity and, for that reason, have the same predispositions to project the unexplainable terrestrial forces onto "fantastic supernatural forces." The class point of view (in Marxism) turns out to be too weak to explain the specificity of the religious attitude and of the social sources of religion. That is why classic Marxist thinkers add, *ad hoc*, the perspective of abstract humanism to that point of view. That is also why contemporary Marxists put forth the idea that worldviews are independent from class divisions:

> that a worldview is not unambiguously determined by class – so we can talk about world views of particular epochs, civilizations, social formations and their types, etc. That is how world views differ from ideologies (which could be defined as class-determined specifications of world views). A world view is a correlate of epochs and societies, while an ideology is a correlate of the consciousness of social groups, in particular, of social classes.
>
> RAINKO 1978, p. 78

Those thinkers do not see that this idea falsifies the thesis that "The ideas of the ruling class are in every epoch the ruling ideas," (Marx [1846] 1998, p. 67). It is not accidental, then, that Marxists today only conceptualize a world view in solidaristic terms – the Marxist class paradigm is too weak to allow them to define it in antagonicist terms.

2.2   *Non-Marxian Historical Materialism*

In Marxism, the class approach to social phenomena is encumbered by the error of economism: the only criterion of global divisions of a society into groups with contradictory interests is the criterion of the ownership of the means of production. The use of the means of coercion also entails a division into such two groups, the rulers' class and the citizens' class. The struggle of political classes is subject to particular laws which modify the struggle of economic classes to a great degree – that is how deviations from Marxian historical materialism in pre-capitalist formations (Nowak 1983, pp. 18–101) are explained. From a certain point on in historical development (i.e. late capitalism), the relationships between rulers and citizens become decisive. They lead from class to supra-class societies: rulers overtake the means of production as well as of indoctrination transforming into a triple-class of rulers-owners-priests (Nowak 1983, pp. 211–235). That is why a theory of the movement of the triple-rule system must refer to the theory of political and not economic classes (Nowak 1979, p. 73; 1983, pp. 211–235).

2.3 The Momentum of Spiritual Production in Non-Marxian Historical Materialism

We will now discuss the third class division considered in non-Marxian historical materialism, that is, the division into spiritual classes, together with the mechanism of the development of the momentum of spiritual production, resulting from the struggle of those classes. Let us, however, consider this at matter not at the general level but in a particular area, namely, the issue of faith. If our intention is to be understood correctly – the risk of misunderstandings is high in this case because of the nature of the problem which provokes various emotions – we owe readers some introductory explanations.

Research on the momentum of spiritual production is dominated by a paradigm which could be called, for lack of a better term, formal–axiological: a given domain of spiritual life (science, art, religion, etc.) is assigned a certain value (values), and the researchers proceed to check which formal conditions must be satisfied in that domain if the value(s) is (are) to be realized. For example, the value science is expected to approach is truth. Then, in methodology, researchers ponder what formal properties this domain must have (e.g. how its theories should be built, what structure the theses of those theories should have, etc.) if the truth is to be reached. Within the framework of that paradigm, any questions about what justifies the decision to discuss a given spiritual domain from the point of view of the optimization of a specific value are either not considered at all or are relegated to the functionalist–sociological paradigm of reflections on culture. The latter paradigm points to the functionalist argument for the realized value(s) in a cultural system, and distinguishes it (them) in the social environment of that system. For example, according to one approach, it is claimed that science approaches more comprehensive truths about the world – by method of trial and error – because that is required for social practice to be effective.

It is obvious that both paradigms, the formal–axiological one and the functionalist–sociological one, are not only admissible but virtually indispensable approaches to spiritual production. Nevertheless, using only those paradigms entails the risk of omitting the comprehensive and important question of the spiritual enslavement of one person by another by means of cultural production. Characteristically, the common approaches within the functionalist–sociological paradigm, as they consider the relationship of the sender, cultural message, and recipient from the point of view of its social functions, omit the material element: the means of creating cultural transmission. Taking that element – publishing houses, TV, etc. – into account forces us to ask the elementary question who makes the decisions about which cultural transmission are to reach the recipient, that is, which cultural content is to become a cultural transmission.

The person who makes such decisions, that is, the person who has at his or her disposal the means of cultural transmission, has power over people who do not – the power to shape their minds. That power is, first of all, negative – it is the power to eliminate that cultural content which is rejected by the owner of the means of cultural transmission. It is also positive in that the owner imposes upon the audience that content with which he or she identifies. Making use of the means of transmitting cultural content presupposes an actual inequality between "the sender" and "the recipient." Thus, a sender with the means of transmission can be called a doctrinaire, and a recipient without them – an indoctrinated person. Needless to say, that qualification has nothing to do with the evaluative qualification of cultural content itself: doctrinaires can impose both valuable and worthless – from the perspective of the internal cultural criterion – things on the indoctrinated. The division of a society into doctrinaires and the indoctrinated is only related to the issue of using the means of cultural transmission (which, in this situation, are termed the means of indoctrination). That division, then, should not be considered from the point of view of general social functions (arguments, needs) but from the point of view of a social conflict. The introduction of spiritual classes necessitates a discussion of spiritual production in antagonist terms.

Those ideas will be elaborated upon further in the text.[3] At this point, we would just like to emphasize that the antagonist approach does not, in any measure, eliminate the functionalist–social paradigm, not to mention the formal–axiological one. After all, cultural products are somehow related to particular values. They do have certain functions in society as a whole, but they are also used by some people to gain spiritual power over other people. The only demand of non-Marxian historical materialism is that the latter fact should be theoretically conceptualized, in all areas of spiritual production. Non-Marxian historical materialism is not opposed to studying cultural products from the point of view of the assumed values or to studying the integrative (solidaristic) functions of culture in a society as a whole; but it disagrees with suggestions that the formal–axiological paradigm or the functionalist–sociological paradigm constitute the general, complete and sufficient, theory of culture because

---

[3] The initial intuitions were presented in: Buczkowski, Klawiter, Nowak (1982, pp. 247ff.), also see; Nowak (1991b, pp. 167–182), in English: Nowak 1983, pp. 126–186 [editorial note].

that is not the case – there remains the issue of the spiritual authority of a professor over a student, a journalist over a reader, viewer, or listener, a priest over a believer, etc. Those suggestions can have an ideological function: they can mask a problem which is inconvenient for people who are stronger in that particular field of social struggle (fighting with the use of thoughts). Those people's advantage is not even gained by way of 'healthy competition' but because they have at their disposal the matter of the spiritual life of the society, that is, a monopoly for the means of enforcing their convictions.

A complete structure of spiritual production, then, can be illustrated as in Figure 1.1. (on page 10). Despite its inevitable simplification, this figure has the advantage of presenting clearly the explanations given above. The formal–axiological paradigm in theory of culture analyzes Area 1, while the functionalist–sociological paradigm analyzes Area 2. Non-Marxian historical materialism strives to conceptualize Area 3, based on the conviction that the main factors of development during the momentum of spiritual production – very similarly to the economic and political momentums – are determined in that area, so the main factors for the movement of that area are those which give rise to conflict, whereas those which give rise to consensus (that is, are characteristic of area 2) are important but secondary, and, therefore, negligible in the first approximation. Consequently, one can abstract from Area 2 – but only in the most idealized model of the theory of the movement of spiritual production.[4] That area has to be taken into account, however, in further models of that theory. Obviously, such an approach necessitates a particular understanding of human beings.

The human spiritual needs as well as other solidaristic factors cannot be simply 'added' to improve standard functionalist–sociological concepts. However, those issues are not the subject matter of this text.

Therefore, within the framework of non-Marxian historical materialism, the concept of spiritual domination and spiritual classes has methodological priority over the concept of spiritual needs and the social function of culture: the first models of the idealization theory of the development of spiritual production must refer to antagonist factors, and only their further concretizations should introduce solidaristic factors. As regards formal culture theory and the theory of the development of spiritual production, they are essentially independent from each other. The former even has a logical priority with respect to the latter: one has to assume certain concept of the internal structure of a given kind of cultural products (e. g. scientific theories, literary works) before

---

[4] The methodological assumptions here are those of the idealizational theory of science. See, for example, Nowak 1977d; and also: Nowak 1980; Nowak, Nowakowa 2000 (editorial note).

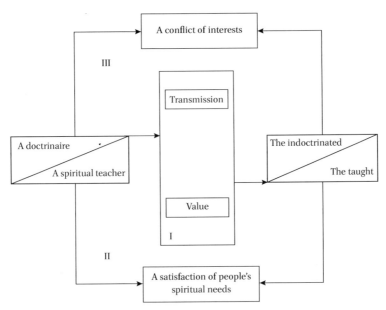

FIGURE 1.1 The elements of the spiritual structure of a society. Area 1 is the internal (formal) structure of culture. Area 2 represents the integrative function of culture and its practitioners. Area 3 shows the inflammatory function of culture. A spiritual teacher is a creator of culture, his role is to satisfy recipients' spiritual needs. A doctrinaire is a holder of the means of creating cultural messages. The creator of culture can be a doctrinaire if that person imposes his or her views on the recipients (the indoctrinated). The opposition between a doctrinaire and a teacher exists at the level of social roles and not necessarily of people. Sometimes creators of culture play both roles.

discussing the issue of spiritual incapacitation[5] of people by some others, by means of spiritual production.[6]

---

5 At this point, we should strongly emphasize that only the relationship between people, and not any content of spiritual transmission from one person to another, has an influence on the relationship of spiritual incapacitation. We may, then, just as well speak about incapacitation by means of noble and ignoble norms, as well as incapacitation without a reference to any norms, effected by means of, for example, scientific theories. An authoritarian professor's assistant who is not allowed either to question any of his master's views or to dare to offer an independent opinion at all, if it is not authorized by references to the master's works as the primary sources of that opinion, is spiritually incapacitated within the area of the relevant field of study, by means of a certain theoretical concept which, authored by the master, is a set of dogmas for the assistant. See: Nowak 1986.

6 Marx's judgment that the "The class which has the means of material production at its disposal, has control at the same time over the means of mental production, so that thereby, generally speaking, the ideas of those who lack the means of mental production are subject

3 The Structure of the Theory of Religion

If the assumptions sketched very briefly above can be regarded as accurate, then certain conclusions can be drawn about the problems discussed in this text. A religious structure, it turns out, can also be presented according to the scheme shown in Figure 1.1. It is true that a religious transmission is characterized by a special internal structure. Therefore, a formal theory of religion as a special kind of cultural structure is necessary. One of the basic human needs – apart from economic needs and the need for social order – is the need for sense. Religious world views – in addition to lay world views – satisfy that need. Priests, then, act as spiritual teachers, while the faithful are taught and supported in their search for meaning. However, priests also play the role of doctrinaires, and conflicts between believers and churches are a well-known social phenomenon, especially in the history of our civilization.

A complete theory of religion, then, should include a formal part (a theory of the structure and evaluation of religious transmission) and a sociological part. If the assumptions of non-Marxian historical materialism are correct, the sociological part should be an idealization theory, its basic model should concern antagonistic relations between priests and the faithful, and solidaristic elements ought to be introduced in subsequent models. There is only one way to learn if those referring to religion assumptions are correct: to put a theory of on them to test. If, having made those assumptions, we obtain an image of the development of a religious formation which corresponds, at least very roughly, to the history of a certain religion, and if, by introducing the factors which have initially been omitted for idealizational reasons, the original model will be developed and in consequence the correspondence between the theoretical concepts and the historical events will increase, then it will provide some arguments for the hypothetical assumption that the sphere of religious phenomena falls within the scope of non-Marxian historical materialism.

In this text, we cannot do more than take the first step in the abovementioned direction. Thus, we will first introduce certain elements of a formal

---

to it" (Marx [1998] 1846, p. 67) is false. The nobility had at its disposal the means of production but not ambos, the bourgeoisie – economy but not universities, the press, or television. The phrase 'have at one's disposal' is here consistently used in one meaning, for example, of having means (of production, coercion, indoctrination) at one's disposal and using means s for the intended purpose, with such decisions being respected. It is only in supra-class systems that one and the same minority takes control over more than one type of material means. For example, in a system of the rule of triple lords, the same people decide about the distribution of: the national income, school curricula, and television programs. However, Marx could not have known such systems.

approach to the structure of religious transmission, in order to sketch, on that basis, an initial model – a purely antagonicist one – of the movement of a religious formation. We must leave the discussion of its concretizations, including those which take into account the integrational functions of religion, for another occasion.

3.1 An Initial Typology of Religion

In order to define the subject matter of this article more precisely, it is worth taking a closer look at certain types of theories of religion. Let us take into account two criteria: (a) whether the variables in the basic model of the theory are specific to the sphere of the phenomena of spiritual production (idiogenic theories) or not (allogenic theories), and (b) whether the relations among those variables found in that model express contradictions among people (antagonicist theories) or the position of a social consensus (solidaristic theories). When we cross those criteria, we get four types of theories:

I. idiogenic–antagonicist, that is, theories which reveal the source of social contradictions specific to the sphere of spiritual production,
II. idiogenic–solidaristic, that is, theories which extract the basis of a social consensus among people from that sphere,
III. allogenic–antagonicist, that is, theories which declare the priority of social contradictions – the external ones, outside of the sphere of spiritual production, from which the regularities of that sphere are derived,
IV. allogenic–solidaristic, that is, theories which derive the basic regularities of the sphere of the spirit from an external basis of social consensus.

Here is how the idiogenic–solidaristic paradigm defines religion:

> [it] is a set of coherent answers to the core of existential questions that confront every human group, the codification of these answers into a creedal form that has significance for its adherents, the celebration of rites which provide an emotional bond for those who participate, and the establishment of an institutional body to bring into congregation those who share the creed and celebration, and provide for the continuity of these rites, from generation to generation.
>
> BELL 1980, p. 333–334

Mircea Eliade's theory follows the same pattern. He claims that

> For religion is the paradigmatic solution for every existential crisis. It is the paradigmatic solution not only because it can be indefinitely repeated but also because it is believed to have a transcendental origin and hence

> is valorized as a revelation received from an other, [emphasis in the original] transhuman world.
>
> ELIADE 1959, p. 210

and that religion gives human life a meaning by determining "the original patterns for all rituals and human activities which have a meaning" (Eliade 1966, p. 404).

The Marxist theory of religion as the opium of the people – that is, for direct producers, opium produced in the interest of the owners' class – was to have been a theory of the allogenic–antagonicist type. However, as we have seen, that intention was not consistently realized: rather, the idea that the source of a religion is the alienation of 'man' resulting from the projection of one's best characteristics on transcendence has idiogenic–solidaristic origins. The Marxist theory of religion is, then, a somewhat eclectic combination of Type 2 and Type 3 motifs.

Given that background, the idea of this article can be defined more clearly. The aim here is to sketch the starting point for a theory of the type 1 religion, that is, the idiogenic–antagonicist religion – just the starting point because the project sketched below will refer, as we will see, to a class of phenomena which is more extensive than that of phenomena usually called religious, and it would probably only be possible to gain models concerning those phenomena through further concretization.

4   The Structure of the Transmission of Faith: Mythologization

4.1   *Idealization vs. Mythologization*

Religious discourse is characterized by referring to such creatures as God, about whom we only know that they have properties not possessed by empirical objects. That gives rise to the idea of comparing those mythical entities with the ideal types discussed in scientific discourse, such as the mass-point. The similarity between them is obvious and manifests itself in the difference from empirical objects, that is, in those beings' 'counterfactuality' (from the extra-confessional points of view). The differences are more interesting. A mass-point is devoid of certain characteristics of physical objects (for example, dimensions), whereas God is to be equipped with some additional characteristics (such as perfection). The ideal type, then, is poorer in comparison to the relevant empirical objects, in that it does not have certain characteristics possessed by them, whereas the type which we might call mythical is enriched with certain characteristic in comparison to those objects. Thus, the procedure of idealization consists in depriving empirical objects, in one's thoughts, of certain properties, and the mythologization procedure – in adding properties to them, in the same fashion. Object a can be turned into an ideal type by subtracting some of its properties or into a mythical type by enriching it with properties it has not had so far. In other words, idealization causes the 'thinning' of the space of the properties registered in the surrounding world, while mythologization 'thickens' them.

That intuition can be explained a little more clearly as follows. A property (characteristic, feature) is but an instance of a magnitude. Let us, then, consider a magnitude which, at some intensities, is attributed to empirical objects. We create an ideal type of those objects by postulating (counterfactually) the existence of an object which has the variable in question to a minimal (e.g. zero) degree, whereas the mythical type of those objects is created by postulating (which, from an extra-confessional point of view, is also a counterfactual operation) the existence of an object which has that magnitude to a maximal degree. The similarity between idealization and mythologization manifests itself in that the procedures consist in a counterfactual (from the non-confessional points of view) extremization of the magnitudes we have at our disposal. The difference lies in the opposite direction of that extremization.

4.2   *The Mythologizing Assumptions*

The explanation above is not entirely accurate because a more exact definition of the idealizational assumptions does not refer just to the syntactic form but to a certain substantive interpretation (Zielińska 1981, p. 30ff). An idealizing assumption of type F is a certain condition stipulating that the considered object should have some such value of the given magnitude p at which its influence upon *F reduces to zero*; those assumptions often have the following form: $p(x) = 0$. That is why we define a mythologizing assumption in this way: mythologizing assumption of type-F is a condition stipulating that the considered object is to have some such value of the given magnitude p at which the influence of p upon *F is maximal*.[7] That is recorded as: $p!_F(x)$, and if the context points to a relativization to magnitude F, we reduce the record of the mythologizing condition to $p!(x)$; we will call magnitude $p!$ an augmented magnitude. Thus, it is a function of mythologizing assumptions to augment appropriate magnitudes.

---

7   It is assumed that appropriate magnitude p belongs to multiple categories, see Nowak 1977c, p. 81ff [editor's note: a magnitude that belongs to multiple categories is affected by different main factors].

4.3 The Mythical Thesis

Ascribing augmented magnitudes to certain mythical objects may serve the purpose of determining some other properties of those objects, that is, to formulate certain theses about them. The theses have a special syntactic structure, namely, the structure of a mythical identity. A mythical identity is the name given to expressions of the following formulas:

(1) B is identical with one and only one x, such that (briefly $B = (^1x)$): since $P(x)$, then $Q(x)$.

The colloquial meaning of "since p, then q" seems to be synonymous with: "since p, then q, and p." In such a case, mythical identity (1) leads to the following existential sentence: "There is an object with properties P and Q," which is compatible with the manner in which the adherents use those identities. Not every mythical identity, though, is based on mythologizing assumptions. The statement that Jesus Christ died on the cross does not require mythologization, while the thesis that he rose from the dead does. Consequently, we will distinguish those mythical identities which are based on certain mythologizing assumptions and call them mythical theses. Strictly speaking, a mythical thesis is an identity which looks as follows:

(2) $B = (^1x)$ (since $p_1!(x)\ \&\ \ldots\ \&\ p_1!(x)\ \&\ p_{k+1}(x)\ \&\ \ldots\ \&\ p_n(x)$, then (if $H!(x)$, then $F(x)$))),

where the first k conditions are mythologizing assumptions, and further conditions, from $k+1$ to n, are realistic assumptions.[8] Augmented magnitudes are called epithets for property F. Epithets and properties are ascribed to a mythical type with proper name B, defined by the sets of mythologizing and realistic conditions enumerated in thesis (2).

4.4 Sublimations

A mythologization can be weaker or stronger, so a mythical type can be characterized with the use of weaker or stronger mythologizing assumptions. From that point of view, it is important how, let us say, heroes and gods differ, and what the difference is between Greek gods, who are not deprived of human characteristics, and the Christian God. We could say that those mythical types are more and more sublimated.

Therefore, we could justify an operation which would lead from 'less' to 'more' mythical theses. Realistic assumptions would, in such an operation, be replaced with proper mythologizing conditions, and the property attributed to the mythical type would be appropriately strengthened (made more subtle or

---

[8] That is, conditions which are neither idealizing nor mythologizing.

precise). Mythical thesis (2) would, then, be directly sublimated as the following identity:

(3) $B = (^1x)$ (since $p_1!(x)$ & ... & $p_k!(x)$ & $p_{k+1}!(x)$ & $p_{k+2}(x)$ & ... & $p_n(x)$, then (if $H!(x)$, then $F^*(x)$)),

where predicative F^* is logically stronger than predicative F, which means it is its special case, and the particular case of F, which is F^*, depends on predicative p_{k+1}.

The direction of concretization is opposite to that of sublimation, just as the direction of the introduction of idealizing assumptions is, in a way, opposite to that of the introduction of mythologizing assumptions. If t' is a concretization of t, then t' is a "less abstract" idealizational statement (in a limiting case – a factual one) than t. If t' is a sublimation of t, then t' is, in a way, a "more mythical" statement than mythical thesis (in a limiting case – a factual one) t, because it is based on a greater number of mythologizing assumptions.

4.5   *Mythologization and Myth*

When we have at our disposal certain partial characteristics, we can try to present a more complete structure of mythologization. It is easily noticeable that the very construction of mythical thesis (2) presupposes a distinction between epithet "$H!$" and epithets "p_1", ..., "p_k." The latter ones only establish the conditions in which the possession of augmented magnitude H is to entail the possession of property F. For example, the thesis that "God out of His goodness and by means of his omnipotent power ... created this world in order to manifest His perfection through the goods he is the disponer of" (*Wprowadzenie*, 1969, p. 42) can be, with some simplifications, reconstructed in the following form:

(4)   God is identical to that one and only one being such that [since the being is infinitely good ($p_1!$) and omnipotent ($p_2!$), then (in order to manifest His highest perfection ($H!$), He created the world (F))].

That thesis presupposes a certain substantive view on what the creation of the world depends on. Obviously, it depends on the creator's "omnipotence" but also on His goodness:

> The good and more than good God did not content Himself with contemplating His Own Self, but out of the overabundance of His goodness, He wanted that there should exist creatures capable of accepting benefits of and participating in His goodness.
>
> JOHN OF DAMASCUS, quoted from: *Wprowadzenie*, 1969, p. 42.

Moreover:

God's goodness does by no means come from a frailty of His which would be a sign of imperfection, but from His absolute perfection. God is good (at the same time) being perfect (...) God is that perfect beauty which never loses itself. When He gives out to us of Himself, he never loses himself. (...) God gives Himself and yet always remains the same Self. To give Himself means for God to be.

JOHN OF DAMASCUS, quoted from: Wprowadzenie, 1969, p. 42.

Hence, the almighty God "does not create out of necessity or because he needs creatures but only out of goodness and in order to show his perfection" (John of Damascus, quoted from: *Wprowadzenie*, 1969, p. 44). We could say that mythical thesis (4) presupposes a certain substantive view which determines what creation depends on: namely on the 'power' of the creator, His goodness, and His perfection manifested in the creation. In order to create the world – everything that exists – one has to be omnipotent, infinitely good, and absolutely excellent; such are the attributes ascribed to the creator of the world, to God.

Let us express that in general terms. Let us consider an image of the essential structure of magnitude F, expressing a given substantive outlook on what magnitude F depends on:

$I(S_F): H$
$\quad H, p_n$
$\quad H, p_n, \ldots, p_1$

H is considered here, to be the main factor for F, and the remaining ones are secondary factors. We will call the following table of augmented magnitudes the image of the mythical structure of magnitude F:

$I(M_F) \, H!, p_n!, \ldots, p_1!$
$\quad \ldots \ldots \ldots$
$\quad H!, p_n!$
$\quad H!$

A mythical structure determines the form of the starting mythical thesis (let us call it the core of the myth):

$(m°) \; B = (^1x) \, [since \, p_1(x) \, \& \, p_2(x) \, \& \ldots \& \, p_n(x), \, then \, (if \, H!(x), \, then \, F(x))]$,

And its further sublimations:

$(m^1) \; B = (^1x) \, [since \, p_1!(x) \, \& \, p_2(x) \, \& \ldots \& \, p_n(x), \, then \, (if \, H!(x), \, then \, F^{(1)}(x))]$

....

$(m^n) \; B = (^1x) \, [since \, p_1!(x) \, i \, p_2!(x) \, \& \ldots \& \, p_n!(x), \, then \, (if \, H!(x), \, then \, F^{(n)}(x))]$,

where, by definition, predicative $F^{(n)}$ is logically stronger than $F^{(n-1)}$, $F^{(n-1)}$ is stronger than $F^{(n-2)}$, etc., until $F^{(1)}$, which is logically stronger than F. We will call thesis (m^n) the final sublimation because it presupposes the augmenting of all magnitudes which are significant for attribute F, or, in short, the myth of attribute F.

We could say that, starting from the same image of an essential structure, it is possible to go in two opposite directions. One can omit the influence of the secondary magnitudes upon the main magnitude in an idealizational law which is subsequently concretized for an ever stricter explanation of an ever greater class of phenomena (through approximations of subsequent, more and more concretized idealizational theses) – that is, use the procedure of idealization and concretization. Alternatively, one can add secondary magnitudes, and, starting from the core of the mythologization, gradually sublimate them and obtain an ever narrower scope of the determination of the property of the subsequent mythical theses, in order to obtain the final sublimation, that is, a myth.

4.6 *Worldview*

We should note that not only religious myths are myths within the meaning given above. A scientific view of science, which makes it a tool for solving all problems (or reduces those which cannot be solved by science to the category of 'pseudo-problems'), is nothing more than an augmenting of the real capabilities of science, and it constitutes the basis for the technocratic myth. The so-called 'good opinion' we have about ourselves, based on the mythologization of our actual predispositions and skills, is also an exemplification of a certain myth – the egotistic one. Lukács's concept of the proletariat which, in its essence, should evince class consciousness based on the understanding of its position in the society and of its role as an actual subject of history – even though the real empirical proletarian class has other convictions (it only has the 'consciousness of class') – is a typical example of a social myth which exponentiates, in thought, some real tendencies exhibited by members of that class. Those short examples are sufficient to demonstrate that the concept of a myth defined above transcends beyond the religious realm. They also appear to show, at least at first sight, that all worldviews, not only religious ones, must be based on mythologizations of what they make their warp – the appropriate mythical types: of man, science, matter, etc. Since it would be difficult to give an explanation of that fact without a reference to serious issues of philosophical anthropology, let us just simply state it here. Still, that statement entitles us to sketch a definition of a worldview. A worldview is a collection of myths of such a kind as makes it possible to rationalize and project life decisions, that is, solve of the adherents' life problems.[9]

---

9 At this point, one should distinguish between a particular worldview and a family of worldviews based on the accepted stratification principles which define the type of magnitudes

4.7 The Internal Development of a Worldview

A worldview, then, is a collection of myths obtained from certain initial theses, that is, mythical cores, by using the procedures of mythologization. A worldview understood in that way retains its identity for as long as it retains the initial set of those cores because they determine which augmented magnitudes are the main ones and which ones are secondary for the given property of a mythical type – in other words, they determine the hierarchization of the epithets of that mythical type. Therefore, a given worldview can develop in accordance with two principles: by extension, that is, by adding a new myth to that body of myths, a myth which derives from a new mythical core and is later developed by means of appropriate sublimations, and by deepening, that is, by revising the secondary parameters of an assumed mythical structure and by adding sublimations. Obviously, it is also possible to combine the two methods, that is, to both broaden and deepen the initial body of myths.

The method of extension does not require more elaborate explanations. Simply speaking, a new myth, (m^t_{p+1}) is added to myth set $(m^n{}_1), (m^F{}_2), ..., (m^s{}_p)$. This new myth is obtained by appropriate sublimations from a new mythical core which pertains to either a new property of the mythical type derived earlier or a property of a new mythical type constituted by that new mythical core. The growth of god pantheons in polytheistic religions is an example of the extension of the worldview.

And here is an example of a development of a worldview by deepening. (For the sake of the simplicity, we will not present a general definition of the concept of deepening; instead, we will limit ourselves to a simple scheme). Let us have a worldview which contains the following myth:

(5) $B = (^1x)$ [since $p!(x)$ & $q!(x)$, then (if $H!(x)$, then $F^{pq}(x)$)].

It is, then, the final sublimation of a mythical core

(6) $B = (^1x)$ [since $p(x)$ & $q(x)$, then (if $H!(x)$, then $F(x)$)]

which presupposes the following mythical structure of magnitude F:

$H!, p!, q!$
$H!, p!$
$H!$

The deepening of that worldview may consist in, for example, an extension its mythical structure:

$H!, p!, q!, r!$
$H!, p!, q!$
$H!, p!$
$H!$

---

which are to be subjected to mythologization.

and the core will assume the following form:

(7) $B = (^1x)$ [since $p(x)$ & $q(x)$ & $r(x)$, then (if $H!(x)$, then $F(x)$)]

and, next, it will be subjected to sublimations, including a new one, on account of newly added parameter r. Consequently, the new – or, rather, old but deepened – myth will assume the following form:

(8) $B = (^1x)$ [since $p!(x)$ and $q!(x)$ and $r!(x)$, then (if $H!(x)$, then $F^{pqr}(x)$)]

Obviously, when a new epithet is added, the old one can be removed. We can assume that the change made in the Christian tradition during the Council of Nicaea – when the Son of God/Messiah was transformed into the Son of God consubstantial with the Father – represented that kind of myth deepening.

4.8 Relationships between Worldviews

A worldview can be extended or deepened, with the use of those methods, because of its believers (internal inspiration) or as a result of the impact of another worldview (external inspiration). Let us take a closer look at the latter case, especially that it will point to other methods of expanding a worldview system.

Let there be worldview S and another worldview, S'. For the sake of simplicity, let us assume that each of those two worldviews consists of one myth: worldview S of myth (5) and worldview S' of the following myth:

(9) $B = (^1x)$ [since $u!(x)$, then (if $G!(x)$, then $F^u(x)$)]

We will say that worldview S has absorbed worldview S' if it has been expanded with myth (9), but worldview S has also been deepened, in the following manner: myth (5) has been transformed, for example, into myth

(10) $B = (^1x)$ [since $p!(x)$ and $G!(x)$ and $q!(x)$ and $u!(x)$, then (if $H!(x)$, then $F^{pGqu}(x)$)].

In such a case, the absorption of worldview S' by S consists in the fact that the main epithet of mythical type b is turned into a secondary epithet of the mythical type B, so the latter type is enriched, as it were, at the cost of the former one. The absorbing worldview is deepened because its myth becomes even more sublimated through the incorporation of, in an inferior position, elements which constitute the absorbed myth. That operation, then, ensures the addition of a new myth to the absorbing worldview (and a new mythical type to the pantheon of that worldview), with a lower position than the already existing myths and mythical types. The absorption also presupposes inequality of partners.

For example, when certain elements of the ancient Slavic religion were absorbed into Christianity, the church practiced the "politics of tolerance and absorption of whatever could be absorbed from the attacked faith without damaging the main corpus of the Christian faith" (Margul 1983, p. 281). For centuries, then, our forefathers' worldview contained pagan myths, in subordinate positions. As lately as 1579, priest Paweł Gilowski's "A Lecture on the Catechism" was published which contained a sizable list of pagan demons identified as types of Christian devils: little devils, because we know about earthly gnomes, domovoys, forest satyrs, topielce, mountain witches, air spirits" (Quoted according to Margul 1983, p. 291).

The Christian myth of the devil as the embodiment of evil has, then, absorbed the demonological myths of the ancient Slavic religion; those myths have been subordinated to the Christian image of Satan, but they were initially preserved.

A more radical change of a worldview consists in a rejection of the sublimations layered over the mythical cores; only the main parameters remain from the relevant mythical structures, and those parameters are later subjected to further sublimations which are entirely different than the previous ones; the mythical cores are preserved but the direction of the sublimation changes. We will call it a reformation of the given worldview. It may happen as a result of an interference of another worldview, but that does not have to be the case. Let us illustrate such a case with the use of our simplified worldview W which only consists of myth (5). A reformation of worldview W consists in the rejection of both myth (5) and the preceding sublimations, whereas mythical core (6) retains its formula (consequent), and the list of secondary parameters is changed. The mythical structure presumed by myth (5) is replaced with another one, with the same main parameter but different secondary parameters, for example:

$H!, v!, w!$
$H!, v!$
$H!$

so the mythical core assumes the following form:
(11) $B = (^1x)$ [since $v(x)$ and $w(x)$, then (if $H!(x)$, then $F(x)$)]
and then is subjected to new sublimations, which results in myth:
(12) $B = (^1x)$ [since $v!(x)$ and $w(x)$, then (if $H!(x)$, then $F^{vw}(x)$)].

Therefore, reformed worldview W^* retains the formula of the initial core of worldview W, and returns, so to speak, to the same sources, but it develops that core in an entirely different way than system W.

A worldview can be changed in an even more radical manner when it merges with another worldview, which means that a third worldview is created which retains the equality of both initial systems: their main parameters remain the main parameter in the third system. Let us once more refer to our simplified schemes: worldview W (myth (5)) and W' (myth (9)). The fusion consists in the overtaking of the following mythical structure:

H!, G!, p!, u!, q!
H!, G!, p!, u!
H!, G!

expressed in core[10]:

(13) $B/b = (^1x)$ [since $p(x)$ and $u(x)$ and $q(x)$, then (if $H!(x)$ and (x), then $F(x)$)]

subsequently sublimated until a new myth is obtained:

(14) $B/b = (^1x)$ [since $p!(x)$ and $u!(x)$ and $q!(x)$, then (if $H!(x)$ and $G!(x)$, then $F^{puq}(x)$)]

One example of a fusion is the fate of the Ancient Egyptian religion in the Hellenistic period. At that time, it was assumed that "Egyptian and Hellenic gods are, in principle, the same characters; they are only called differently in the two countries and each god of one side has a counterpart in a god of the other side" (Margul 1983, p. 62). That is how the "identification of the pantheon" came about. Amun was identified with Zeus, Anubis with Hermes, Isis with Demeter, etc. That identification was but a sign of the creation of a syncretic religion in which Ancient Egyptian beliefs were on a par with Hellenic ones.

5   Spiritual Domination

So far, we have discussed the solidaristic aspect of a religious formation – the fact that since it is always a set of myths, those myths are used for rationalizing and projecting individuals' actions in life.[11] It is time to discuss the antagonicist aspect – the one we find more important, which will manifest itself in the concept of the development of a religious formation, sketched in the next chapter.

5.1   *Authority and Spiritual Dependency*

People's convictions do not only depend on the arguments they are supported but also on whose those convictions are: sometimes we only accept certain propositions because we are aware someone else has accepted them. If for every proposition p from class Z it is a sufficient condition for person B to accept p that person B knows that p has been accepted by person A, then person A can be called an authority for person B with regard to Z. If, however, for every proposition from class Z the knowledge that person A has accepted p

---

10   Symbol B/b means that a given mythical type has two names.

11   The approach presented here emphasizes the 'superior type' – that a worldview is always a set of myths. The *differentia specifica* could be determined in the context of the culture-creating functions of a religion which are not discussed in this article.

is a necessary condition for B to accept p, then we can say that B is spiritually dependent on A with respect to Z.

There is a significant difference between those two situations. If a person finds another person to be an authority in a given field, it does not, by any means, preclude finding another person to be an authority as well, nor does it preclude the first person from attempting to verify the authority, as that person may refer to the authority in a given field not because of a feeling of inferiority but simply because of a lack of time, means, or even interest in gaining greater competence in that field. The situation is very different in the case of spiritual dependency: another person's acceptance of a proposition is a necessary condition for accepting it. Being spiritually depended on another person in relation to a certain field means believing oneself to be incapable of solving issues in that field. A student who does not dare to have an opinion on any matter respecting the learned material without knowing or 'feeling' the teacher's view on it is dependent on that teacher, and both are bad in their roles.

5.2   *Spiritual Domination*

It may happen that one and the same person is both spiritually dependent on and an authority for another person in one and the same range. This means that a necessary and a sufficient condition for the person to accept propositions (from a given class) is her/his belief that they have been accepted by the other. In such a case, we will say that the person is spiritually dominated by the other. In other words: A spiritually dominates B with respect to the range of beliefs Z just in case B accepts every proposition p from Z if and only if B believes that the proposition has been accepted by A; we will call propositions regarding that domain dogmas (of person B on account of person A). It follows that if A has spiritual domination over B with respect to Z, then A is the only authority for B in that respect. Consequently, B will not refer to any other authorities. It also follows that a person who is spiritually dominated by another person in a given domain is not an authority in that domain, even for himself or herself. That means that if that person accepts arguments (for example, logical ones) for a certain proposition, it does not, in itself, constitute a condition for that person to accept that proposition as long as it concerns the field dominated by the other person. Therefore, even if, say, q is a logical consequence of p, and our dominated person B accepts p, it does not follow that B will accept q on that basis – if q belongs to the dominated domain; dogmas are accepted on a different basis than conclusions of deductive reasoning. Also, a person spiritually dominated in a given domain will not make any efforts to determine "If p?", as long as p belongs to that domain– instead, he will try his best to find out how the 'spiritual master' determines that issue.

Here is a description of a person about whom it can be reasonably surmised that he was spiritually dominated – at least with regard to moral and political convictions – by Nazism:

> Hess was the type of ... man with whom it is possible to do anything, because he loves to feel he is wax in the hands of another, and his ambition is to intensify his impersonality, voluntarily to renounce criticism, judgment and self-determination.
> FEST, 1995, p. 223

5.3 Faith

A worldview with the use of which some people wield spiritual power over others – become authorities on worldview matters and make others spiritually dependent in that respect – is called a faith. A faith, then, is a system of myths distinguished by two properties: they allow the adherents to explain and project their life actions, and they are dogmas, that is, they express the adherents' spiritual incapacitation. A person who believes in a certain worldview: religious, lay, or any other – is a person who has given up independent solving of worldview problems and relies, in that respect, totally and unreservedly on the content of dogmas. It is a person who cannot evaluate his or her own action or another person's action on the basis of moral intuition but can only repeat a dogmatic proposition, a person who cannot reject any dogma in any situation and will unconditionally trust the authority regardless of how much life experience and knowledge about the world that the faithful has gained. According to that definition, a the faithful is a 'passive dogmatist', in contrast to an 'active dogmatist' who establishes or announces myths to be believed.

Let us consider the following example:

> Communism [is] the positive transcendence of private property, or human self-estrangement, and therefore as *the real* appropriation of the human essence by and for man; communism therefore as the complete return of man to himself as a social (i.e., human) being-a return become conscious, and accomplished within the entire wealth of previous development. This communism, as *fully developed* naturalism, equals humanism, and as fully-developed humanism equals naturalism; it is the genuine resolution of the conflict between man and nature and between man and man – the true resolution of the strife between existence and essence, between objectification and self-confirmation, between freedom and

necessity, between the individual and the species. Communism is the riddle of history *solved*, and it knows itself to be this solution.

MARX [1844] 1978, p, 84 [*emphasis mine* – L.N.]

Communism understood in that way is but a mythical type which is ascribed, in the quoted passage, with certain magnified parameters [see the phrases spaced out for emphasis the quoted passage]. The quoted fragment is, then, simply a presentation of a social myth. We should not be misled by the fact that it refers to a social form of government and not, for example, to a personal God: the methodological status of that statement is the same as, let us say, that of *Book of Genesis*. In both cases, questions like "will that really be (has that been) the case" can only be answered in one way: through an act of faith, that is, of acceptance of those statements regardless of their origin. Thus, for a believing Marxist, the mere fact that Marx has said a thing will be a sufficient reason for accepting that statement. A Catholic will accept the canonical texts of Catholicism simply because they have been approved within the authority of the Church. Admittedly, in both cases, it is possible to question the relevant myths, but a person who does that ceases to be a Marxist or a Catholic and is no longer considered to be one by members of the respective groups.

5.4   *Religion*

If the communist or liberal (in which free market and democracy are mythologized) doctrines are faiths, then the question arises how to distinguish a religious faith from other faiths. Let us take a look at the following confession of a believer, drawn from a religious publication: "Make me, [God,] your tool. Make use of me when You want to and make me fall into pieces when You want it. Allow me to be Yours." From an extra-confessional perspective, which we allow ourselves to take here, the matters look as follows. The author of those words, as a person who believes in his religion – who is spiritually dominated by his church. After all, representatives of that church tell him what to believe as regards worldview matters, and he is obedient. The church is an authority for him. What is more, the author here does not dare to take a stand on those matters without having determined that it is consistent with the dogmas presented to him by the church. It follows that he is spiritually dependent on the church hierarchy with respect to worldview matters. Indeed, in such a case, according to our definitions, we should state that the author is spiritually incapacitated by his church as regards matters related to a vision of the world, man, human life, etc. At the same time – according to the quoted text, the honesty of which we have, after all, no reasons to doubt – he does not realize that. To be more precise, he is aware of the dependence but associates it with God and not the church, he accepts and even glories in his incapacitation but does it in the face of God and not the priests of the church, and he ideologically transforms the spiritual but earthly dependence into a mystical one.

That seems to be the essence of the religious attitude: the ideological transformation of a spiritual dependence on the church which promulgates certain myths into a dependence on the characters postulated in those myths. Any faith makes the faithful dependent on their priests, with the use of myths. However, only religious faiths are constructed in such a way that the faithful are expected to become dependent on the characters brought to life in the myths which are the actual means of dominating people. Religion, then, is a faith, a worldview with the help of which some people (priests) dominate others (the faithful), with an meta-ideology which presents the faithful as dependent on the characters brought to life by the very myths used to make them dependent. Those auto-ideologies can be more or less sophisticated. Here is an example of the latter kind:

> A human being can come before the presence of God and the mystery of being, of existence. Then, that person has a clear consciousness and a clear heart, has a revelation, an intuition. Truth and the original spirit of the creator reveal themselves to such a person who then reaches the very source. ... Only subjugating oneself to God and the mystery of being gives real freedom.
> BERDYAEV 1937, p. 125, p. 127

At this point, it is difficult for us not to note that the same religious faith which tells the excellent philosopher to oppose lay faith leads him from the critique of the "freedom is the understanding of necessity" formula to the idea that the real freedom lies in the "understanding of subjugation" and that, consequently, freedom is but spiritual incapacitation.

6   The Structure of a Confessional Society

The concept presented here will, however, be an attempt at creating a theoretical conceptualization of the development of faith and not of religion in the meaning defined above. If that definition is justified, then we can immediately see that a materialistic theory of religion must begin with a model applicable to any faith. Religion does not differ from other faiths with respect to the material level (the means of indoctrination are used in any faith) or even to the institutional level (doctrinaires are organized not only in church institutions but also in state or party institutions) but only at the level of self-awareness, that is, the type of the ideology it produces about itself. For a materialist, that type of factors will be the third to be considered in an idealizational theory of faith. In terms of the idealizational theory of science: the class of faiths is an essential type, whereas the class of religion is one of the species of that essential type.[12]

6.1 The Materialist Hypothesis in the Theory of the Momentum of Spiritual Production

The approach we are striving for is based on two initial ideas. The first one has already been mentioned: it is the assumption that – just as is the case with the economic or political momentum – the social conflict proper to spiritual production plays a basic role in its momentum[13] (the antagonicist hypothesis). According to the second one, those who have proper material means at their disposal, that is, the means for shaping convictions (the means of indoctrination), have an advantage in that momentum of spiritual production. That materialist hypothesis can be formulated a little more precisely because the appropriate terms have already been introduced – for any two social groups A and B, if members of group A have at their disposal the means of indoctrination, and members of group B do not, then group A has greater chances to spiritually dominate group B than group B to spiritually dominate group A.

It is difficult to say if both those hypotheses are true. There is no need to decide about that in advance. Just as in the case of all essential hypotheses, there is only one way to ascertain that: trying them out. For that purpose, one has to construct a basic model of the materialist-antagonicist theory of faith and subject it to further concretizations (obtaining, as a derivative model, a concept of religion for further concretization), until one achieves models which are complex enough to be compared with the known empirical and historical regularities. If that purely theoretical work helps understand the factual material, it will mean that the starting point for the whole construction has probably been selected correctly – both initial ideas will gain factual confirmation.

---

[12] Those notions are explicated in Nowak 1977c, pp. 81ff; in English: Nowak 1977b [editorial note].

[13] We use that term here instead of 'cultural momentum' because we would like to understand culture as a general civilizational (independent from class divisions) component of the momentum of spiritual production.

6.2 Classes in the Momentum of Spiritual Production

Both hypotheses lead to a third class division of society (apart from the divisions into owners versus direct producers and rulers versus citizens) – into spiritual classes. In a society, we can distinguish between those who have all means of indoctrination at their disposal – let us call them the class of doctrinaires– and those who do not possess such means – let us call them the class of the indoctrinated.

There will be a subset of the class of doctrinaires consisting of people identifying with the given faith – let us call it a caste of priests– as well as a subset of the class of the indoctrinated consisting of people identifying with that faith – let us call it a caste of the faithful. The sum of those two subsets, that is, the set of the believers of the given faith, is a confessional society. For the sake of simplicity, we will assume that at the starting point of the analyzed process, there is only one faith. Thus, we will consider the structure and development of a single confessional society.

6.3 The Contradiction of the Interests of Priests and the Faithful: The Initial Idea

The antagonicist paradigm in the approach to the momentum of spiritual production encourages one to look for contradiction of interests in a confessional community. According to the program sketched at the beginning of this text, we will look for those contradictions within that community and we will not transfer external conflicts (for example, between work and capital) into the sphere of faith – as we have written above, that was Marx's main mistake with regard to the theory of religion.

Predictably, the assumptions presented above give grounds for the application of such a radically materialist approach. After all, what type of a relationship other than an antagonicist one could there be between a person who spiritually overpowers a fellow man – even if it is done with the use of the most beautiful myths – and that fellow man? Who, then, transforms another person into a being who is dependent on an external instrumentarium, or, rather, who presents himself as the only authorized interpreter of that instrumentarium? It is a person who cannot view even the most incisive and wise recommendations as just a tool which can be used in particular life circumstances – perhaps a better one than the available alternative options – but, instead, sees them as fossilized and canonized dogmas which are not to be questioned by common people, even if an individual's life or the fate of a society were to depend on it. To accept a point of view from which people are a flock which needs a shepherd, or else they will stray, one has to have a great contempt for individual moral sense. Despite the great many shepherds supposedly operating in accordance with the only possible and lifesaving truths – from the *Bible* to *Communist Manifesto* – people still lose their way. It looks like shepherds' role is not as significant as they would have people believe. Also, they probably do not hold themselves in such a high esteem by accident. Materialism enforces the ruthless decision to ignore saints' as well as revolutionists' most noble intentions. Some people are assigned the role of a shepherd and the rest are reduced to the role of sheep, which is in the interest of the former and should be understood, primarily, as motivated by interest. The undeniable best intentions of many priests of all faiths do not have much weight when it comes to understanding confessional processes, just like politicians' intentions – which are not always bad, either – are not very important for understanding power mechanisms.

It should be added that the nature of that contradiction between a priest and the faithful is often obscured, for example, in reflections on human nature which, supposedly, inherently requires a spiritual whip – incidentally, that concept is contradicted by its very proponents as, since times immemorial, individuals have been trained from birth to be adherents of various churches – or when it is reduced to other social conflicts. I have already written about Marx's economic reductionism. Here is another example of reductionism which reduces the priests' interest to the interest of government authorities:

> To them [supporters of – editorial note] the State, as providence, as director of the social life, dispenser of justice, and regulator of public order, is a necessity. [...] They always must have available a more or less ignorant, immature, incompetent people, [...] a kind of *canaille* to govern. This would make them [...] keep the highest places for themselves, [...]. As the privileged guardians of the human flock, strong in their virtuous devotion and their superior intelligence, while prodding the people along and urging it on for its own good and well-being, they would be in a position to do a little discreet fleecing of that flock for their own benefit.
> BAKUNIN [1867] 1971, p. 142

All that is true – about priests. It is only true about the government in so much as the authorities also overtakes priests' basic attribute: the means of indoctrination – that is, in so much as they transform into a double class of rulers–priests.

Actually, the antagonism which divides a confessional community is entirely internal – other divisions may overlap with it, bolster or weaken it, but its principal source is within the adherents' community. Sometimes the antagonism appears to manifest itself on the ideological surface. Here is a fragment of Gratian's decree – a set of church laws from the 12th century:

> There are two types of Christians. The first one is those who have devoted themselves to serving God, to contemplation and prayer, who have separated themselves from the multitude of worldly matters – they are the clergy, consecrated to God and turned toward him. ... God has chosen them all as his own. They are veritable kings because they rule over themselves and others by their virtuous life, in this way building the kingdom of God. The second type of Christians are the lay people ... They can have material goods but only for temporary use. They can also marry, plough fields, file suits, judge one another, bring gifts to altars, pay tithe to the king, and save their souls in that way if their good deeds compensate their faults.
>
> Quoted from: WIERUSZ-KOWALSKI 1970, p. 146; [spacing out mine – L. N.]

If we take the ideology out of this text, we will obtain the very idea we are looking for: that a confessional community is not divided primarily into capital and labor, or authorities and citizens, but into those who have at their disposal effective teams of propagators, a great ceremonial[14], and, today, mass media and those who are subjected to the influence of the former group – that is, into priests and the faithful.

6.4 The Contradiction of the Interests of Priests and the Faithful: Conceptualization

Let us now try to conceptualize those intuitions. Let priest A spiritually dominates over worshipper B_1 with regard to Z_1, worshipper B_2 with regard to Z_2, etc. The sum of the sets of convictions Z_1 Z_2, etc. is the range of priest A's spiritual influence. The range of the spiritual regulation of the class of the faithful by the class of priests is the sum of the ranges of influence of particular priests of that class. In accordance with the definitions accepted earlier in the text, the range of spiritual regulation also includes those convictions which are dogmas because of at least one member of the class of priests. Therefore, the relation between the range of spiritual regulation and the faithfuls' convictions expresses the degree of the dogmatization of those convictions or, in other

---

14 The concept of a ceremonial is developed by Falkiewicz (1980) who assigns it, in that work, a role transcending that of a means of communication, to which it is reduced in this text.

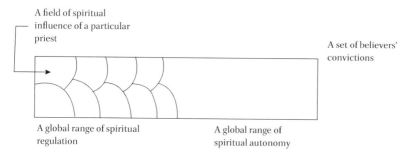

FIGURE 1.2   The contradiction of interests between spiritual classes. A single field means a set of convictions within the range of which a single priest has spiritual influence over a certain number of bellowers. The sum of those fields is the global range of regulation of the whole class of priests. The illustration shows that the subject matter of these reflections requires a number of simplifications. We will mention two such necessary assumptions here: that particular convictions are logically independent and that they have the same 'weight' for priests. None of them is true, but if we took into account the circumstances omitted in those assumptions, our construction would become too complicated right from the start.

words, the degree to which the faithful are spiritually oppressed. Let us illustrate that above (see figure 1.2).

The interest of the class of priests as a whole is to expand the range of spiritual regulation. Just like in the case of the class of rulers, that interest is usually realized not by way of conscious intentions but through mechanisms of competition which require that particular priests expand their areas of influence; those priests who do not participate in the game of soul harvesting and want to help people rather than subdue them are pushed to the margin by those mechanisms.[15] The interest of the class of the faithful consists in the expansion of the range of their spiritual autonomy and, consequently, a reduction of the degree of the dogmatization of collective consciousness. Despite appearances, such a conceptualization is quite obvious – if only we agree that it is normal for normal people to solve their life problems on their own, referring to their own experience and moral sense, and not to surrender, once and for all, their own proposition and blindly accept other people's solutions.

---

15   Similar mechanisms in political sphere are presented in: Nowak 1991a, pp. 25–31.

6.5   The Struggle of Spiritual Classes

Nevertheless, just like in the economic or political momentum (Nowak 1983; 1991a, pp. 31–38 [editorial note]), that contradiction of interests is not directly transformed into a spiritual revolt. Let us begin by defining the issue. An individual who is in revolt against the priests of a given faith goes beyond the framework imposed by them for solving life problems, leaves behind the addiction to those priests, and even stops seeing them as spiritual authorities. That revolt can take many forms: of believing that priests are not the right interpreters of that faith, of converting to another religious or lay faith, etc.[16] The level of the class conflict between the faithful and priests can be determined as a percentage of those who are in revolt against a given class of priests.

The common intuition that 'the greater the oppression, the stronger the protest' fails completely with regard to revolt, including a spiritual one – mainly because a faith is always a worldview, so it can satisfy some spiritual needs, especially people's need to find the meaning of life. The starting point here is the assumption (for which there are, apparently, strong empirical grounds) that to be able to find order in his or her actions in life, every individual must refer to a systematized set of myths – that is, to a worldview. Still, it does not immediately follow that the worldview must be a faith, a means of spiritual enslavement of an individual. On the contrary: the resistance is born if the external intervention in the established worldview structures is weak. That is why people are in revolt against a faith when the level of spiritual oppression – of the dogmatization of collective consciousness – is low. The people in revolt are not the few early the faithful but the surrounding people who, having established their worldviews, defend themselves against the new, different worldview enforced by the priests of the new faith. The low-level spiritual oppression by the priests of the new faith results in the formation of the first revolutionary area or the area of external revolution (external with respect to the confessional society).

The second revolutionary area (the area of internal revolution) encompasses very high levels of spiritual oppression. That is a situation in which the whole or almost the whole collective consciousness is dogmatized and in which a typical member of the faithful community must abide by priests' opinions about almost every matter of life. That situation is also revolutionizing, at least, in the pure momentum of spiritual production when priests do not have at their disposal the means of coercion and cannot apply rulers'

---

[16] Therefore, it is understandable that a spiritual revolt does not have to be connected with any 'active forms of protest' – it can be played out solely in the sphere of thoughts.

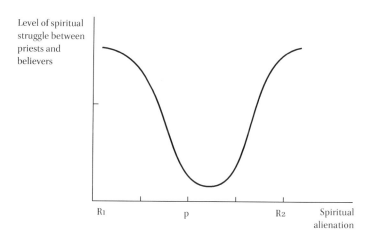

FIGURE 1.3 The dependence of class struggle in the momentum of spiritual production on spiritual oppression of the faithful. Abbreviations used: R_1, R_2 – the first (respectively, the second) revolutionary area, p – the area of class peace.

declassing strategy. People who occasionally submissively follow instructions and recommendations will not necessarily agree to priests' ceaseless and meticulous interventions which do not leave any room for the faithful own opinions about how to evaluate and plan their lives. To sum up, both low and very high values of spiritual oppression and dogmatization of collective consciousness give rise to a revolution, that is, a situation in which a high percentage of people become spiritual rebels as they break free from their role of priests' believers.

When the values of spiritual oppression are average, rebelliousness subsides because in that state, although faith has already encompassed a typical individual's main worldview assumptions – and, consequently, began to play the role of that worldview by providing spiritual order and an idea of the meaning of that person's life – priests still have not gained control over all thoughts of their faithful who are still allowed a certain degree of autonomy in relation to self-evaluation and the planning of one's actions. In the case of average values of spiritual oppression, there is class peace. That can be graphically represented in the form of a reversed bell curve (see Figure 1.3).[17]

---

17 Let us note that the figures presented in this book are purely illustrative. They could only be treated as literal if the appropriate variables were operationalized. However, as regards methodology, that is an entirely different task, see: Brzeziński 1976, p. 14ff.

7 Development of Faith (Model 1)

The notes above concerned the 'statics of faith'. Now, we will try to present a proposal of an approach to the development of faith. It is not a 'generalization' of any empirical or historical studies of religion because theories are not created in that way. They are formed as a result of capturing, in an idealizational manner, some sides of actual courses of events, and approximating them by way of concretizations of the initial, simplified model. The only role of the studies is to provide material for explanations. Needless to say, no theoretical proposal has a monopoly on a good explanation. The only possible criterion is comprehensiveness: that theory turns out to be the closest to truth which explains the most and with the greatest accuracy. The problem in the discussed field of study, however, still appears to be the theoretical explanation of the most elementary things: the main developmental stages of standard religions. Only after a little more light has been shed on those simple things will it be the proper time to explain more complex issues such as non-standard religion histories or details of the development of basic religions.

7.1 *Idealizing Assumptions*

First, we will determine the idealizing assumptions of the initial model. We will begin by accepting a condition which postulates that the discussed society is only divided into spiritual classes (assumption A). This assumption eliminates all processes related to the two remaining social class divisions (economic and political classes) from our model. In other words, in our model, we assume that the momentum of spiritual production is entirely isolated from the economic and political momentums. We also assume that at the starting point of the process, there is only one faith in our idealized society – one confessional community in a non-confessional environment (condition B). In other words, the worldviews of the individuals in that community are all uniform and conform to the priests' faith, whereas the individual, private worldviews from outside of that community are dispersed and cannot be subsumed under any uniform pattern.

We make the simplifying assumption that the class of priests is not organized in any institutional structures (condition C) and that its faith does not encompass any meta-ideology (condition D); the latter requirement makes it impossible to distinguish a religious faith on the basis of Model 1 (see chapter 4). The meaning of those conditions for model 1 is that one cannot, within the framework of that model, refer to the fact that priests are usually organized in a church hierarchy and that their declarations about their calling, in and of themselves, have a certain persuasive power which influences relations with the faithful.

We also omit all inter-social relations, that is, we assume that the discussed society is entirely isolated from other societies (simplification E). Moreover, we make a number of simplifications of lesser importance, such as the condition of simple reproduction of humanity or other conditions which have been mentioned above.

To sum up, we consider the development of priests–the faithful relations in a single confessional community formed within the framework of a society isolated from all other societies. We also assume that the state of the relations between the spiritual classes is not disturbed by any economic or political factors, that it is not influenced by the way in which the church is organized or by the church ideology, and that all factors other than the main one (the level of the class conflict between the faithful and priests) are omitted.

7.2   The Phase of Initial Rejection

Let us consider the development of faith – marked F – beginning from a small confessional community. Regardless of the degree to which the faithful have been spiritually overmastered by priests, the degree of spiritual oppression of the whole community will be small. According to the reverse bell-curve dependence (see Figure 1.3), faith F will encounter strong rejection on the part of all those who feel threatened by priests' aspirations. We could say that a faith emerges in conditions of people's rejection.

Therefore, it is not possible to determine if it will thrive (that is, gain more the faithful) with the use of Model 1 – which, after all, precludes support from the state machinery. Both options are possible: that faith F will survive the stage of early rejection and that it will lose the faithful and disappear.

7.3   The Phase of Absorption of Alternatives

By means of model 1, we cannot determine a condition the fulfillment of which would be sufficient for faith F to survive the phase of early rejection, but we can determine the necessary condition: it is subdued expansion of that faith, that is, expansion which does not eliminate alternative worldviews but absorbs them, that ensures some – even if subordinate – room for the defeated myths in the new mythical set.

As it absorbs the existing alternative worldviews, faith F – we still assume it has survived the dangerous birth stage – constantly grows in numbers. The mechanisms of competition among priests bring about a further increase of spiritual oppression, which – in accordance with the dependence presented in figure 1.3 – ensures class peace: the new faith has the same social function as the old alternative worldviews, but it still leaves much room for spiritual autonomy of the faithful.

7.4   The Schism Phase

Still, the mechanisms of competition never cease to operate, and the priests' class, after it has subdued the whole society, must increase not only the scope but also the intensity of its spiritual authority over individual believers. Consequently, a typical believer's convictions are progressively transformed into dogmas, and the freedom of alternative thinking is limited. The first outcome of that process is the annihilation of the alternative worldviews which have been absorbed by faith F. Priests' competition leads to progressive purification of faith – a proponent, and, in time, even a believer who is overly 'tolerant' of old 'superstitions' can easily be accused of recreance. In time, collective consciousness is dogmatized. Spiritual oppression spreads.

The end result, as pictured in Figure 1.3, is a spiritual revolution (from the faithful's point of view), or a spiritual crisis (from the perspective of faith F priests): a great number of the faithful rebel against the class of priests. The revolt, however, leads them to a worldview vacuum: the existing alternatives have been eliminated in the course of the expansion of faith F, and even if new alternatives appeared, they would not be able to pass through the phase of initial rejection, for the same reason. Therefore, the only solution is to reform faith F. That is done by dividing the class of the faithful into two sub-classes: an orthodox one, which continues to follow the original faith, and a group of schismatics. The schismatics, in turn, divide themselves into priests and the faithful as well and form another confessional society, bound by the principles of the new faith. That new faith is based on the idea of a return to the sources of the original faith. The progress of the spiritual overmastering of the faithful of faith F is presented as a result of 'improper reading' of canonical books; the cores of the myths comprising faith F are maintained but their sublimations are rejected and replaced with new ones. The orthodox faith (F_{ort}) and the reformed faith (F^1_{ref}) have a common starting point but their further development differs.

The reformed faith continues to develop according to the principles we already know: the individual worldviews which have appeared in the course of the spiritual revolution are absorbed and annihilated, in proportion to the expansion, which is extensive at first and later intensive and which culminates in a spiritual revolution within the framework of a reformed confessional society. Generally speaking, the faiths which are coming into existence are subject to the same principles as faith F (or rather F_{ort}, as we have marked it for the sake of differentiation from the reformed faith).

Let us, then, discuss the further development of faith F_{ort}. After the schism, the level of spiritual oppression in the orthodox community drops – as the most rebellious people have transformed into schismatics – and class peace is achieved. However, the same process is recreated: the mechanisms of competition among priests lead to a gradual increase of the dogmatization of the consciousness of the orthodox members of the church and, after some time, there is another spiritual revolution and another schism within the framework of the orthodox confessional community. The orthodox confessional community loses many members (a simple reproduction of people is assumed) as they begin to support reformed faith F^2_{ref}; the reformed faith removes the orthodox sublimations from the common mythical cores in a different way and begins to develop according to the same principles as F and, later, F^1_{ref} did. A new reformation of faith F comes into existence, primarily because individuals with aspirations to become priests are not likely to compete successfully within the already established structures of the first schismatic society, so they have to separate as a new faith (or, rather, a new direction of sublimation from the common core), and create a new caste in which they immediately obtain appropriate positions of priests. That would only be excluded if the second wave of schismatics leaving the orthodox community in question transitioned as a whole to the position of faith F^1_{ref}, that is, joined the first schismatic community. However, that does not happen. The processes we are talking about here – unlike those related to ruling – take a very long time. Therefore, before the second spiritual revolution, the antagonicist nature of the relations within the framework of F^1_{ref} is revealed, and the projects of the reformers of the new reading of mythical cores are supported by the rebels. Thus, the faith considered here, F_{ort}, is subjected to subsequent schisms which lead to the appearance of new faiths, $F^1_{ref}, F^2_{ref}, F^3_{ref}$, etc., which reform the original faith. A uniform confessional community falls apart into a number of sub-communities, each of which is appropriately divided into priests and the faithful.

7.5   The Possibility of a Conversion

That confessional pluralism within the framework of one society weakens the effect of the 'early rejection' mentioned above. Previously, the uniformity of the worldview of the society based on faith F excluded the possibility that a new prophet, if there appeared one, could create a new confessional community on the basis of a completely new faith derived from new mythical cores. However, the more divisions are caused by subsequent schisms (schisms generated by orthodox faith F_{ort} are, in time, followed by schisms of the second order, generated by reformed faiths F^1_{ref}, F^2_{ref}, etc.), the greater the odds that a faith with a different core than the core of faiths from the F family survives the phase of initial rejection – if only there appears a new prophet. The mechanism of the appearance of new mythical cores cannot be grasped by means of a historical materialism, so we have to assume that it is a random mechanism which is external to our model. The only thing we can say about it within the framework of our model is that if a new prophet appears in the phase of the expansion of faith F, then that prophet can, at best, be absorbed by that faith – there is no possibility of his new faith becoming popular. Such an opportunity only materializes during the phase of schisms, most likely in its last stages.

If there exists a project of new mythical cores at that time, it can become the focus of a new confessional community. The effect of the 'initial rejection', although it has been weakened by the pluralism of faiths, is still strong, and the new faith – let us mark it U – vegetates in the form of one of numerous confessional groups, until another spiritual revolution within the framework of faith F_{ort}. At that point, instead of another reformation, there appears an opportunity for the rebels to take a step more radical than a schism: they can completely abandon the mythical cores which constitute faith F_{ort} and are maintained in all its reformations. They can convert to faith U. The degree to which they avail themselves of that opportunity depends primarily on the time factor, that is, on when faith U appeared and when that spiritual revolution takes place. The later the appearance of faith U, the greater the odds of conversion and, consequently, of sudden growth of that faith. First of all, the development of reformed varieties F^1_{ref}, F^2_{ref}, etc. of faith F, which always occurs in accordance with the same pattern (absorption – spiritual revolution – schism) as the faith itself, proves to another wave of the rebellious faithful of faith F that the problem is not that sublimations go in the wrong direction but that the cores of their fathers' faith are faulty and that they should look for the 'truths of faith' in an entirely different tradition, such as U. Second, the later faith U appears, the greater the odds of a conversion not only within the orthodox community but also in the schismatic confessional communities, on an increasingly large scale.

All in all, if there exists a project of a new confessional tradition based on mythical cores different than those of faith F, then in another spiritual revolution, there appears the phenomenon of conversion to new faith U. The scale of that phenomenon depends on the degree of the development of faiths from family F. There is, however, no guarantee that such a project will appear at an appropriate time or even that it will appear at all. At this point as well, then, we can only say, in general, that model 1 allows for two paths of development. If there does not appear a faith with alternative cores, then the schism continues, and the society divides more and more into various confessional communities; however, all those communities are based on a common body of mythical cores of type F. If there appears faith U with a different body of mythical cores (even if it partially overlaps with the old one), then the schism phase is followed by a conversion phase. The rebellious faithful of faith F_{ort} and, possibly, some followers of reformed faiths convert to an entirely different faith.

7.6 The Ecumenism Phase

Regardless of whether there is a purely schismatic or a schismatic-convertive variant of the development of faith F_{ort}, that faith is weakened very much: it transitions from the position of a monopoly to the position of one of many confessions of either the same family or even two different families. Therefore, it is in orthodox priests' interest to merge with other faiths from the same family in order to stop the process of losing the faithful. As long as reformed faiths F^1_{ref}, F^2_{ref}, etc. are in the phase of absorption, that is, as long as they are gaining the faithful, the interest of the priests of faith F_{ort} cannot be realized. However, when those faiths also undergo schisms (of the second order), which means that reformed confessional communities also begin to divide, the interest of orthodox priests meets that of reformed priests – beginning with the oldest variant – faith F_{ort} merges with the older variants of reformed faiths, which is made easier by the fact that the mythical cores of all those faiths refer to the same main parameters, so the fusion only pertains to derivative parameters used in various sublimation procedures within particular faiths.

The fusion entails an increase of the global number of the faithful, so it stops the process of the loss of the faithful of ecumenic faith F^{ek}_{ort}. Equally important is the fact that the new ecumenic community will include communities with various degrees of spiritual oppression. As a rule, the level of oppression is the highest in the orthodox community and lower in the reformed ones – in proportion to the times at which they have joined the new ecumenic faith. As a result, the global spiritual oppression in the ecumenic community lessens, and the spiritual autonomy if the number of the faithful grows. The fusion, then, extends the period of class peace. In a way, we could say that the new, ecumenic priests' class gains a new spiritual territory which can be conquered, and the specter of another revolution is pushed away – however, only for a certain time because, sooner or later, the mechanisms of competition will once more lead to such dogmatization of the collective consciousness that a spiritual revolt will take place. There will be another schism or – if that process is simultaneous with the birth of a new prophet – conversion. It is not possible for the fusions to lead to a solution of the conflict and to a stable augmentation of the influence of the expanded faith – first of all, because the effects which are beneficial for the combined classes of priests (extended class peace) come to an end and there is a new wave of spiritual revolt. It is not even possible for a single faith – faith *W*, possibly modified in some way as regards its mythology – to be re-created as a result of a combination of the previously separated original variants of that faith. After all, various reformed faiths – not to mention different faiths with new mythical cores, which may come into existence – derive from subsequent schisms, of the first or later orders, so there are 'older' and 'younger' faiths in the set. The historical age of a faith, that is, the number of phases from our model it has gone through, is the basic determinant of the interest of its priests' class. A new faith is still expanding – extensively at first, by winning minds, and intensively later, by augmenting its power over their minds – so its priests do not have an interest in a fusion. A mature faith, which undergoes periodical schisms, begins to lose their faithful, but the priests of such a faith may not have an interest in a fusion because it would mean losing a certain number of the faithful – this time, the more orthodox ones. Only the priests of a senile faith begin to have a real interest in a fusion, when that faith is systematically losing the faithful, especially those who belong to the 'silent majority' – more the faithful than it would lose as a result of a fusion with its traditional opponents, which would be 'unacceptable' for the 'loud minority', in particular, for orthodox the faithful. Therefore, we can draw the conclusion that the demand for a fusion on the part of faith F_{ort} meets halfway – at best – with the interest of the priests' castes of the oldest reformed faiths. Other faiths will not be interested in ecumenization because it is not their goal. Not yet. When the idea of ecumenization begins to correspond with their interest, other, younger faiths will react to that idea in the same way the older ones used to respond to faith F_{ort}: they will ignore the appeals for a reconciliation. The behavior of priests' castes, just like the behavior of any human communities, is motivated by interests and not ideals; however, this particular interest – in spiritual authority over fellow men – is often hidden behind exceptionally alluring ideals.

7.7 *The Possibility of Syncretic Religion*

A fusion based on mythical cores of type *F*, that is, those which are preserved in the whole family of reformed faiths of the first order, $F^1_{ref}, F^2_{ref}, ...$, of the second order, etc., can be repeated with various faiths of the same family as they transition into senile age. Even a fusion with faiths of family *U* is not excluded. It is all a matter of the interest of priests' castes which can be determined on the basis of the balance of spiritual profits and losses, measured by the growth or decrease of the spheres of regulation. Obviously, the losses are especially big in the case of a fusion of faiths from different families, so that kind of a fusion can only take place when the possibilities of a fusion based on common mythical cores are exhausted. Actually, according to model 1, a faith of type *F* will merge, sooner or later, with a faith of type U, and create a new, syncretic faith, that is, a faith in which the fusion involves the mythical cores and not the series of sublimation. There are, however, no guarantees that the faith the history of which is described by model 1, that is, faith F_{ort}, will manage to do that in time. It simply depends on the pace of the faithful attrition due to schisms and/or conversions, which cannot be predicted by our purely qualitative models.

Let us consider both cases. Let the pace of the faithful attrition of faith F_{ort} be so slow that faith U_{ort} – which also underwent the described phases of development, especially schisms and/or conversions – reaches 'senile age' as well. In other words, that case boils down to the pace of the faithfuls' attrition of faith F_{ort} being so much slower than the pace of the the faithful attrition of faith U_{ort} that the confessional age of both faiths becomes the same. At that point, those faiths – or rather their priests – will, indeed, be interested in a fusion. Because of the differences between their mythical cores, that fusion will be much more difficult to organize than a fusion within the same family of faiths: both priest castes can expect particularly big losses of the faithful. That is why, at least within the framework of our model, where neither party can count on, for example, support from the state, such a fusion must be preceded by a fusion of the derivative attributes, by a mutual 'exchange' of sublimations. A fusion of cores can only be the final step in the process of syncretization of those faiths. That process results in the coming into existence of syncretic faith F_{ort}/U_{ort}. Contrary to appearances, that does not mean a breakthrough in the process of ecumenization. In particular, it does not automatically mean that the later, reformed faiths of both parties will join the syncretic faith to co-create a great new family of faiths consisting of all branches of all orders of both families. It bears repeating that the problem of a fusion is not a doctrinal but a material issue related to the internal balance of class forces in confessional communities. Thus, as regards doctrinal argumentation, if the two orthodox faiths merge, it will only be of help to the priests of those reformed faiths – on both sides – which need a fusion in order to stop the faithful's attrition. (That circumstance, by the way, cannot be discussed within the framework of Model 1, which omits the meta-ideology of the discussed faiths. We only mention it for the sake of a polemic, in order to deflect objections based on idealistic assumptions).

The coming into existence of syncretic faith F_{ort}/U_{ort} does not, in itself, entail a fusion of the reformed faiths of both families, so the effects of a syncretization do not differ much from the effects of a fusion on the level of sublimation, that is, within the framework of a given family of faiths: the period of class peace of the syncretic faith is somewhat prolonged. That lengthening can, actually, be smaller than the analogous effect of a fusion within the framework of one family because the deeper the level of the mythical structures encompassed by a fusion, the greater the number of the orthodox faithful on both sides who do not join the new faith. A syncretic religion continues to be subject to the same mechanism: competing priests gain more and more power over their faithfuls' spiritual life, which leads to another revolt and another schism and/or conversion. As we can see, in terms of social ramifications, the creation of a syncretic faith does not differ from a fusion: it only postpones the end of the two faiths comprising the syncretic one. Since a syncretic faith can only be formed after the possibilities of a fusion within the separate families have been exhausted, the syncretization of a faith is a harbinger of its demise.

7.8 *The Assimilation Phase*

However, faith F_{ort} does not have to undergo syncretization. If the pace at which its faithful are lost is not smaller than the corresponding pace in faith U_{ort}, a syncretic faith will not be formed: the interest of the priests of faith F_{ort} will not meet the interest of the priests of faith U_{ort}. Regardless of which of the two possibilities is realized, the end result will be the same, except that it will come a little later in the case of syncretization. As the number of the faithful of faith F_{ort} decreases progressively, the position of its priests with respect to priests from other castes weakens: a fusion with faith F_{ort} will yield fewer the faithful than a fusion with one of the other, younger faiths. In other words, faith F_{ort} ceases to be competitive on the 'confession market' – we may be putting it bluntly here, but that term aptly reflects the nature of the mechanisms operating between various priests' castes. The essence of the materialist understanding of faiths – and, consequently, the content of model 1 – are class relations in a confessional community and 'free-market' relations between confessions, with the latter depending on the development of the former.

Such understanding of the nature of faith leads to the conclusion that any faith will, after a time (prolonged in the case of syncretization), lose its ability to combine with another faith. It can vegetate for a while, but the nearest spiritual revolt will lead to the last division of the orthodox confessional community. The priests' class only has one chance at that point: to let itself be absorbed, that is, assimilated with a still powerful confession. The mythical cores which used to constitute a whole family of faiths are relegated to the order of distant sublimations in a new faith, or – in the case of an assimilation to a faith from their own family – the peculiar sublimations of orthodox faith F_{ort} are pushed to further positions in the sublimation chain of the absorbing faith. That is, naturally, but a doctrinal expression of the fate of the class of orthodox priests who are downgraded to lower positions – measured by the power of spiritual

RELIGION AS A CLASS STRUCTURE

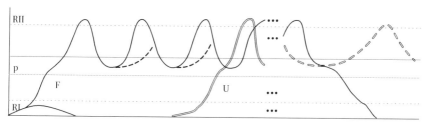

FIGURE 1.4   The idealized course of the formation of faith in time. RI (resp. RII) – the first (resp. the second) revolutionary area, p – the area of class peace. It is assumed that at the starting point of the process, the first confessional society in the discussed society is formed. The continuous curve means the level of spiritual oppression within the framework of that society, created by the priests of faith F (marked F_{ort} since the first schism). The thin curves indicate the level of spiritual oppression in the newly created confessional societies which correspond to the reformed faiths from the F faith family. The thicken continuous curve indicates the level of spiritual oppression in the possibly emerging new faith (based on a new mythical set), U. Broken thick curves indicate the level of spiritual oppression in the confessional societies which correspond to the reformed faiths of the U type. One of them absorbs faith F_{ort}.

influence – in the new confessional community. On the occasion of the first purification of that new faith, they disappear without a trace.

7.9   *The Paganization Phase*

The remaining faction of the confessional community retains the old faith but without priests because even if some priests put being faithful to dogmas before their own spiritual interest (which is possible just like it is possible that some rulers will act for the benefit of the public instead of furthering their own interest), the priest caste of faith F_{ort} will still disappear in a short time. After all, young people aspiring to the rank of a priest – once more, we are talking about a trend and not about all of them – will join strong priest castes and not the one that is dying out. Soon, the faith, deprived of priests, will be paganized, reduced to a superstition practiced by a decreasing number of people who can even hardly be called the faithful.

7.10   *Summary*

Model I presented above paves the way for the development of any faith in the conditions of an isolated confessional community divided into only two spiritual classes and devoid of a church organization, etc. (see Figure 1.4).

It is worth noting that the presented model is a purely formal scheme in that the very concept of a faith is characterized in a formal manner, by means of the concept of mythologization and operation on myths, without any assumptions as to the contents of the faith. Surely, for that reason, many phenomena cannot be captured within our model, but some can still be elucidated with its help.

8   A Discussion of the Application of the Model

8.1   *A Certain Classical Case: The Development of Christianity*

Model 1 is extremely idealized. Nevertheless, if we are not mistaken, we can find its principal characteristics in the historical development of, for example, Christianity.[18] Christianity survived the phase of initial rejection. It happened because factors which cannot be expressed within the framework of model 1 came into play. We will elaborate on that further in the text. Wherever Christianity was developing, it absorbed certain elements of local myths, and, in that way, became more palatable for the adherents to the native tradition. However, when Christianity became a dominant confession, it was purified – the 'pagan' elements were removed. Dogmatization of social consciousness leads to spiritual crises and, consequently, to schisms. In Christianity, the first such division was the so-called East–West Schism which resulted in the separation of the Eastern Orthodoxy. Later, a number of religious movements – Albigensians, Waldensians, Hussites – protested against the spiritual power of the centralized church. The subsequent schisms – Lutheranism, Calvinism, Anglicanism – which led to the creation of new, stable confessional communities, turned out to be more lasting. The new confessions, in turn, were subject to the normal principles of development and divided themselves, as a result of their own schisms. After all, those schisms consisted in returns to the basic mythical cores of Christianity. They removed the layers of sublimations accumulated by churches, in order to go back to the living truths of the gospel.

Since the Enlightenment, a new process has been taking place: the scientistic conversion. A new confessional community has been forming, based entirely on a new set of mythical cores, that is, the myths of: human beings' unlimited cognitive powers, progress through the mastery over nature, and a rational organization of social life. Scientists, sometimes unwittingly, become idols of the scientistic faith, the priests of which are the 'priests of mass culture'. The socialist faith – especially its Marxist version – is the outcome of a

---

18   Needless to say, considering faith in antagonist categories does not, by any means, entail an evaluation of the contents of that faith, just like, for example, an analysis of the changes of prices of Picasso's paintings does not, in itself, allow for a judgment of their esthetic value.

schism within the scientistic faith. It rejects the myth that a society can be rationally organized simply through knowledge distribution, and prioritizes a socialist revolution. Today, both scientific faith in general and its Marxist variant in particular undergo their own spiritual crises.

Losing the faithful because of the scientistic conversion has become so widespread in Catholicism that it transitioned to the phase of ecumenism. It is probably in that phase now. The concepts which are appearing within the framework of Catholicism also seem to predict future syncretic faiths: a Christian–scientistic one (Teilhard de Chardin's doctrine) or a Christian–Marxist one ('liberation theology'). However, if our model is true, then Catholicism is not becoming more expansive – on the contrary, it is in decline as a separate faith organized on the basis of a particular mythical set. Therefore, based on that model, we can make a long-term prediction that Catholicism will be assimilated by another faith, either one of the existing faiths or the result of a future schism of one of them. Such questions cannot be answered in a model in which only formal criteria are used and in which the content of particular faiths is not analyzed.

8.2 Historical Inaccuracies of the Model

In the idealizational theory of science, it is obvious that the explanations of phenomena offered by an idealized model must be imprecise because they refer to the activity of one factor (or a small number of factors), whereas the discussed phenomena are always a resultant of many factors. That is the case for model 1 sketched in this work – it only refers to one factor: the level of the struggle of spiritual classes, whereas all the above mentioned phenomena from the history of Christianity are the outcome of numerous and almost always different configurations of influences.

For example, the Orthodox Church did not come to existence only as a result of the spiritual oppression exercised by the church hierarchy but also because of the rivalry between the dissenting groups. We would probably obtain a fuller – even if still far from complete – explanation of the East–West Schism by concretizing model 1 with respect to institutional factors, especially the organization of the church.

Similarly, medieval religious movements were directed not only against the church hierarchy but also against the ally of that hierarchy: the great land ownership – after all, they sometimes assumed the form of people's utopias of anti-feudal movements. In order to take into account that additional dimension of medieval heresies, we would have to introduce into our model not only a division into classes of doctrinaires and the indoctrinated but also a division into classes of owners and direct producers.[19] Protestantism spread primarily as a reaction to the spiritual violence of the Roman Curia, but it also served the ideology of a new owners' class within the framework of feudalism – the class of bourgeoisie owners. Those processes took place under a significant influence of social and economic factors, so they can be explained more thoroughly in a concretization of model 1, which would take into account the struggle of economic classes and its ramifications.[20]

Model 1 is also too poor to properly explain the phenomenon of scientific conversion. After all, scientific faith did not come into existence only because the mind of the church, restricted by dogmas, turned to science which offers greater – though not absolute by any means – freedom. General civilizational processes also played a part in its birth. It is quite possible that if those civilizational aspects of social development – which go beyond any class divisions – were taken into account, model 1 could be concretized in such a way as would enable a fuller explanation of the laicization processes which have been accompanying the industrial civilization for so long.

8.3   A Certain Seemingly Falsifying Case

The factors mentioned above, although they have not been taken into account in model 1, operate in the direction indicated by it, which means that they strengthen the trends it describes. However, the prediction we have derived above from model 1 – about the absorption of Catholicism by another faith – is apparently at odds with the religious enlivening observed today. Let us briefly discuss this issue.

The common belief that there is a religious enlivening in contemporary world does not account for the entirely different meaning of that phenomenon in, for example, the countries of the capitalist West and socialist East. In the West, Christianity is on the wane, as evidenced by the number of the faithful, the intensity of religious practice, the number of new priests, etc. If there is any religious enlivening there, it is related to the influence of Eastern religions. Therefore, one can hardly overlook the fact that Christianity in the West is in a

---

19   Some remarks on that topic can be found in: Nowak (1983; 1991b).
20   Contrary to Marx's opinion, they are different class divisions – the priests' role cannot be reduced to that of ideologists of the economically ruling class. Considering the issue from the cultural point of view, capitalists and laborers alike need a meaning of life, and worldview doctrines satisfy that need, to a degree. When the priests who propagate such a doctrine spiritually incapacitate their believers, it applies to both economic classes in an equal measure because both of them function as the indoctrinated.

state which conforms to our model, namely, in the phase of ecumenism caused by its own weakness.

Meanwhile, in the socialist East – especially in Poland – there is, indeed, a real enlivening of Christian religions. That trend, admittedly, contradicts our model. However, we may ask if the contradiction is true – that is, if the trend cannot be explained in any concretization of that model – or if it is only seeming, and a certain concretization of our model could explain that counter-trend.[21] A careful analysis would be required to answer that question; nevertheless, we believe that we are dealing with the latter case here, as one of us writes elsewhere (Nowak 1984). A brief explanation would boil down to the social role of Christianity in socialism. In that system, the ruling apparatus, that is, the class of triple rulers, aspires to, among other things, the role of a doctrinaire, and it has a monopoly on the means of indoctrination. It is, then, ineluctably opposed to any religion – it competes with every church for the rule over souls. The class of triple rulers does not fight against Christianity on the grounds of its own atheism; rather, it professes Communist scientism in order to provide a rationale for its hostility toward religion. The experiences of the Catholic church in Poland show that there is but one way for it to survive: to go down, become a people's religion, give the masses not only support in the face of atheistic indoctrination but also an ideological basis for the struggle against the class of triple lords. That is probably the foundation of the religious enlivening in Poland and, to some extent, in other socialist states. Therefore, we can presume that when Catholicism – essentially in the phase of ecumenism – finds itself in a system of triple rule, it either disappears or – if it becomes a people's religion – becomes greatly invigorated. If a systematic concretization of model 1 confirmed such an initial assumption, we could say that the wave of heightened religious enthusiasm in the socialist states which appears to contradict model 1 only appears to be at odds with it because a certain concretization of that model – for the conditions of a system of triple rule – predicts that trend. That concretization also predicts that the religious enlivening will end when the social causes of it die out (Nowak 1984), and that Catholicism will then continue to develop in a normal, standard way: it will be subjected to fusions until it is absorbed by another faith, with a delay caused by the religious enlivening unintentionally triggered by the class of triple lords.

---

21   For a differentiation between the facts which actually contradict the idealizational theory and those which contradict *prima facie*, see: Nowak 1973, p. 97ff.

8.4 Gaps in the Explanatory Power of the Model

Apart from some inaccuracies in the explanations of the abovementioned phenomena from the history of Christianity, there are several gaps in model 1. It does not explain certain trends observed in the history of Christianity. Let us discuss a few examples.

The beginnings of Christianity are rife with divisions. From the point of view of the winning line, they were heresies. Model 1, however, does not take into account any such early schisms. Some of those heresies could, perhaps, be explained by factors related to the social sphere, in a more realistic model which would account for the owners' and rulers' classes in addition to the doctrinaires' class. Originally, Christianity included a radical social utopia, so the transition to the other side of the class barricade, related to the transformation of Christian social teaching from a people's utopia to an ideology of the state and private owners, inevitably brought about a doctrinal schism. This is one possible explanation of Pelagianism or Arianism.[22] It remains an open question, though, if the explanation could be applied to, say, monophysitism.

The so-called East–West schism can – although, as we have seen, in a very incomplete manner – be explained within the framework of model 1, but the so-called Western Schism cannot. Perhaps, such phenomena could be explained by taking into account inter-state relations[23] – that is, in a model in which the confessional community would be distributed among a number of states.

The phenomena associated with the internal organization of the Catholic church cannot be explained within the framework of model 1, either. Perhaps they could be explained by taking into consideration the institutional dimension of the class of the owners of the means of indoctrination.

8.5 The Problem of the Culture-Creating Role of Religion

We could easily find more such gaps. The most important one, however, is the gap we have indicated during the exposition of model 1, namely, that the model does not determine the conditions which a faith must fulfill in order to pass the phase of initial rejection. We suppose that the issue is related to the solidaristic dimension of religious phenomena, which is completely omitted in our antagonist model. Probably, a worldview can only become common if it satisfies the need to find the meaning of life to a degree not smaller than the existing alternatives, that is – generally speaking – if the tools it provides for endowing

---

22 An intuitive sketch: Nowak 1984.
23 A model which takes into account inter-state relations is presented in Nowak 1991a, 259–270.

human life with meaning are at least as less effective as those provided by the previously dominant faith. Only given such a worldview, can the division into spiritual classes be built and transform it into a faith. Indoctrination alone is not enough to force people to profess a worse alternative worldview than the one they have at the time (unless that indoctrination is supported with physical violence – in such a case, however, political power intervenes, and that subject falls outside the scope of the problem of the momentum of spiritual production). Within the framework of these reflections, we will not discuss the issue of what imbues an individual life with meaning[24]; let us just assert, however, that that problem – as well as the problem of the culture-creating function of faith – must be included in a comprehensive theory of religion. It is our belief, though, that such a theory should begin with an antagonicist model which takes into account the spiritual conflict among people.[25]

References

Bakunin, M. ([1867] 1971). Federalism, Socialism, Anti-Theologism (Critique of Rousseau's Theory of the State). In: *Bakunin on Anarchy: Selected Works by the Activist-Founder of World Anarchism*, edited and translated by Sam Dolgoff, pp. 102–147. New York: Vintage Books.

Bell, D. (1980). *The Winding Passage. Essays and Sociological Journeys, 1960–1980*. Cambridge, MA: ABT Books.

Berdyaev, N. (1937). *Problem komunizmu* [The Problem of Communism]. Warszawa: Rój.

---

24 Some such proposals are presented in Nowak 1985.
25 During a discussion of this text, at a conference organized in November 1984, in the Institute of Religion Studies of Jagiellonian University, an objection was raised that our model, in principle, does not reflect the Buddhist religion. Without entering into a discussion on the subject matter – since we are not competent in that field – we would like to make a methodological remark. That objection may – although it obviously does not have to – result from the fact that the commonly used concept of a religion is theoretically heterogeneous, just like – according to Petrażycki (1959, p. 97) the concept of a 'vegetable' in which a botanist cannot see a specific species of a plant. We use concepts of that type for practical reasons, but from a theoretical point of view, they point to an unnatural class. Obviously, we are not able to determine that that is the case in the said situation. We could only do so if our concept was sufficiently developed and tested in relation to religions other than Buddhism. However, it is not, so we may just as well treat that case as a falsifying one. We mention, however, the possibility of a reinterpretation of the concept of religion in order to show that a theoretician is not bound by the meaning given to the terms when they are used outside of theory.

Brzeziński, J. (1976). *Struktura procesu badawczego w naukach behawioralnych* [The Structure of Research Process in the Behavioural Sciences]. Warszawa-Poznań: PWN.

Buczkowski, P., A. Klawiter, L. Nowak (1987). Religia jako struktura klasowa. Przyczynek do nie-Marksowskiego materializmu historycznego [Religion as a Class Structure: A Contribution to Non-Marxian Historical Materialism] *Studia Religiogica* 20, 79–128.

Buczkowski, P., A. Klawiter, L. Nowak (1982). Historical Materialism as a Theory of the Social Whole. In: L. Nowak, (ed.) *Social Classes, Action and Historical Materialism. Poznań Studies in the Philosophy of the Sciences and the Humanities*, vol. 6, pp. 236–280. Amsterdam: Rodopi.

Eliade, M. (1966). *Traktat o historii religii* [A Treaty on the History of Religion]. Warszawa: KiW.

Eliade, M. (1959). *The Sacred and the Profane. The Nature of Religion.* Translated from the French by Willard R. Trask. New York: A Harvest Book.

Engels, F. ([1878] 1987). *Anty-Dühring.* In: K. Marx, F. Engels, *Collected Works*, vol 25. London: Lawrence & Wishart.

Falkiewicz, A. (1980). *Teatr-Społeczeństwo* [The Theatre – Society]. Wrocław: Ossolineum.

Fest, J. (1995). *The Face of the Third Reich.* Translated from the German by M. Bullock. London: Penguin.

Margul, T. (1983). *Jak umierały religie? Z zagadnień tanatalogii religii* [How did Religions Die]. Warszawa: KiW.

Marx, K. ([1843] 1970). *Contribution to the Critique of Hegel's Philosophy of Right.* Translated by J. O'Malley. Oxford: University Press.

Marx, K. ([1844] 1978). Economic and Philosophic Manuscripts. In: *The Marx-Engels Reader*, ed. by R. C. Tucker, pp. 66–125. New York/London: Norton Company.

Marx, K. ([1846] 1998). *The German Ideology.* New York: Prometheus Book.

Nowak, L. (1973). *Anatomia krytyki marksizmu* [An Anatomy of the Critique of Marxism]. Warszawa: KiW.

Nowak, L. (1977a). O wielości materializmów historycznych [On the Plurality of Historical Materialisms]. In: J. Kmita (ed.) *Założenia badań nad rozwojem historycznym,* pp. 250–256. Warszawa: PWN.

Nowak, L. (1977b). On the Structure of Marxist Dialectics: An Attempt Towards a Categorial Interpretation. *Erkenntnis*, 11, 341–363.

Nowak, L. (1977c). *U podstaw dialektyki Marksowskiej. Próba interpretacji kategorialnej.* [Foundations of Marxian Dialectics. Towards a Categorial Interpretation]. Warszawa: PWN.

Nowak, L. (1977d). *Wstęp do idealizacyjnej teorii nauki* [An Introduction to Idealizational Theory of Science]. Warszawa: PWN.

Nowak, L. (1979). Historical Momentums and Historical Epochs. An Attempt at a non-Marxian Historical Materialism. *Analyse und Kritik*, 1, 60–76.

Nowak, L. (1980). *The Structure of Idealization. Towards a Systematic Interpretation of the Marxian Idea of Science*. Dordrecht: Reidel.

Nowak, L. (1983). *Property and Power: Towards a Non-Marxian historical Materialism*. Dordrecht: Reidel.

Nowak, L. (1984). Kościół i lud ziemski [The Church and the Earthly People]. *Biuletyn Dolnośląski*, 5, 19–21.

Nowak, L. (1985). Człowiek i ludzie, czyli o tym, ile utopi społecznej da się wyrazić na obecnym poziomie konkretyzacji nie-Marksowskiego materializmu historycznego [A Person and People, that is, How Much of Social Utopia One May Derive at the Present Level of Concretization of non-Marxian Historical Materialism]. *Obecność. Niezależne Pismo Literackie*, 9, 45–54.

Nowak, L. (1986). Science, that is Domination through Truth. In: P. Buczkowski, A. Klawiter (eds.), *The Theories of Ideology and Ideology of Theories. Poznań Studies in the Philosophy of the Sciences and the Humanities*, vol. 9. Amsterdam: Rodopi.

Nowak L. (1991a). *Power and Civil Society. Toward a Dynamic Theory of Real Socialism*. New York: Greenwood Press.

Nowak, L. (1991b) *U podstaw teorii socjalizmu* [Foundations of the Theory of Socialism]; vol. 1: *Własność i władza. O konieczności socjalizmu* [Property and Power. On the Necessity of Socialism].

Nowak, L., I. Nowakowa (2000). *The Richness of Idealization X: Poznań Studies in the Philosophy of the Sciences and the Humanities*, vol. 69. Amsterdam/Atlanta: Rodopi.

Petrażycki, L. (1959). *Wstęp do nauki prawa i moralności* [An Introduction to the Sciences of Law and Morality]. Warszawa: PWN.

Rainko S. (1978). *Świadomość i historia* [Conscioussnes and History]. Warszawa: Czytelnik.

Wierusz-Kowalski, J. (1970). *Reformatorzy chrześcijaństwa* [The Reformers of Christianity]. Warszawa: KiW.

Wprowadzenie do zagadnień teologicznych. Dogmatyka [The Introduction to Theological Issues. Dogmatics]. Poznań-Warszawa-Lublin: Księgarnia Św. Wojciecha 1969.

Zielińska R. (1981) *Abstrakcja, idealizacja, generalizacja* [Abstraction, Generalization, Idealization]. Poznań: Wyd. UAM.

CHAPTER 2

The Truth Unbearable for All

Leszek Nowak

Abstract

The paper considers the Stalinist phase in the history of Soviet Union in three aspects: political, economic and cultural. From the point of view of the mechanisms of pure political power, Stalinism is a natural state of how the mechanism of political competition operates. From a purely economic point of view, Stalinism led to the elimination of private property and the market. However, the liberation of an individual from the market pressure entailed that people stopped working efficiently, and the economy became so ineffective that was unable to satisfy anyone's needs. From a cultural point of view Stalinism represents a kind of intellectual trap because it is enough morally condemn oppressive political system without any serious attempt at its theoretical explanation.

Keywords

communism – enslavement – free market economy – real socialism – satanization – Stalinism

Contrary to its name, which is derived from an individual, 'Stalinism' is a great historical process related, probably inevitably, in one form or another, with a certain developmental stage of the formation we are living in. Such processes always take place on all three basic levels of social life: political, economic, and spiritual. Let us say a few words about those levels, in that order.[1]

Stalinism is most commonly described in terms of 'pathology.' That classification is a typical example of normativism in social thought: something is evaluated (now) before it is (even) understood, whereas emotions should always depend on thoughts and not precede them. Since that is not the case,

---

[1] The paper appears in English translation for the first time. The Polish original „Prawda nieznośna dla wszystkich" has appeared in *Zdanie* 10, (1988), 16–18. The abstract and key words have been added by the editor.

the critics of Stalinism today begin to remind us too much of its apologists of yesterday. Sometimes we may have the impression that the two groups only differ in the emotional sign.

From the point of view of the mechanisms of political power, Stalinism is a totally natural and correct state – it is in line with the regularities of pure power. It would seem that in our civilization, this state was achieved in that way for the first time. Western civilization is based on the division of three ruling classes: the owners, the rulers, and the priests. Those three classes, which control the material foundations of social life (economy, coercion, means of communication), cooperate but also limit one another to a great degree so it becomes impossible for one of them to gain very disproportionate power over the masses. However, a revolution eliminates the bourgeoisie and the existing world view. The new power remains alone on the social battlefield: there is no significant social opposition. On that desert, the normal mechanism of competition for power, inherent in every political power, gains hurricane force. First, it destroys the resistance of the masses. Next, the state proceeds to regulate everything. For the first time in the history of Western civilization, rulers do not only rule but also manage the harvest action and catechizes.

In that extreme situation, new qualitative effects appear, just like new, special effects become apparent in especially high or low temperatures. This is how the mechanism of competition operates. It forces the members of the ruling class to expand their influence but there are no more spheres of social autonomy which could be subdued – virtually all that can be controlled at a given level of the means of control is already controlled. If the power system is not to disintegrate, there is only one solution: to eliminate the weakest rulers and, in that way, gain new social areas for subjugation. Indeed, that is what happens: positions are emptied by purges and, once more, the new power seekers soon maximize their control over their territories. For that reason, purges must be periodical.

It was not Stalin's madness or criminal tendencies but the mechanism of power in the conditions of a social vacuum that lead to a situation in which rulers turned 'against themselves.' If Stalin understood that, then he was a better theoretician of politics than Max Weber's epigones today, who repeat mantras about the credibility and legitimation of power, only to wonder or condemn later – since Weber's perspective does not allow for much more. In all likelihood, however, Stalin was just an outstanding leader of his class who knew instinctively that, at a certain point in time, terror should be directed against some of its sectors, in order to protect the whole. Still, he could truly have been a true madman or a criminal. No matter how he is classified, it does not exempt us from the effort of understanding. The qualifications themselves should not just be manifestations of our emotions but should have some cognitive meaning. Even if Stalin was, indeed, madman or a criminal, that only means that these features of his personality were, in those extreme conditions, functional for the system he was leading.

The political aspect of Stalinism, then, reveals an extreme situation of political power which, having eliminated all controllers, reaches the maximum of the technically possible regulation – and then must turn against itself. Such a power is not capable of extricating itself from this situation – only the rebellions of the masses were finally able to achieve that.

In the economic domain Stalinism reveals another boundary situation concerning the masses. That people maximize the degree to which their needs are satisfied is a central dogma of economics. Not even Marx or John Maynard Keynes freed themselves from it. Theoreticians have only begun to challenge it in recent years. Admittedly, counterexamples have long been known – we all remember the case of the Indian people whose salaries were raised in the hope of gaining greater efficiency and who stopped working for that very reason, saying they had earned enough – but those counterexamples have been treated as an exception to the rule established by the hard-working people of the West, a reason for a contemptuous shrug of the shoulders at the barbarians (another instance of a display of emotions before anything is understood). In reality, it is the Indians who represent the anthropological norm – it is not normal to strive to have as much as possible. When left to their own devices, human beings, as individual people, do not maximize their needs but satisfy them, which means that people who no longer feel the necessity to satisfy their needs begin to realize their values. Humans are thus beings that are forced to satisfy their needs, but who retain enough freedom to realize their values.

That only changes with capitalism. When it becomes technically feasible for the economy to flood a whole country with goods, and competition – in this case, among the owners – produces exactly that result, the production system must subdue human nature, if it is to continue to function. That is what the free market is: not a 'spontaneous expression' of human nature but violence against it. With the free market, people who prefer to contemplate rather than earn more than they need are pushed to the social margin. A new human being, better adapted to the new conditions, becomes prevalent: a *homo marketicus* (to travesty Zinoviev's term): a person who maximizes his or her needs beyond what is necessary and who, when those needs are too few, from the point of view of the market, can be talked into believing that there are more needs than is really the case. Those new needs, suggested by insistent advertising, are again maximized. However, in order to do be able to maximize their needs, the person must also accept a system of ethics which will tell that person to be hard-working and efficient – preferably the protestant work ethic. The production system becomes effective because of violence against inefficient human nature – and capable of flooding the market with goods again. Those are the mechanics at work.

That cycle is broken as the system of triple-rule comes into being. When private property is eliminated, so is the market. An individual who is liberated from the market pressure becomes a natural person who only satisfies his or her needs. However, as that person stops working efficiently, the economy becomes ineffective again, to such a degree that soon there are not enough products to satisfy needs.

Paradoxically, then, the system of triple-rule reflects, in its economic structure, human nature. It is not, by any means, 'state capitalism' because, although politically oppressive, economically it is 'too good' (in technical terms: it enslaves politically and satanizes economically, see Nowak 1988, in English Nowak 1991, pp. 12–13 [editorial note]). Today, voices are being raised for a return to capitalism. Perhaps they are right. One should, however, call things by their name: they are voices calling for renewed violence against our nature. We should call a spade a spade and not be fooled by ideological mirages – new ones are created before the old ones have even gone away – because only then will we have a chance to see some new possibilities. That is, if there exists such a possibility, if it is possible to think of an economy which is not subject to the political power or a few hundred families. When the sound of one kind of drums is replaced with that of a new one, the goal of which is also to magnify power and not to find arguments, and which also leads to standardized reactions and intellectual leveling down, then any such opportunities are the first to disappear.

On the spiritual level as well, Stalinism is a special situation: one in which the social status of the Marxist doctrine changes drastically. Marxist theory was, undoubtedly, a people's utopia written from the point of view of the lower social classes. The basic Marxist concepts concerned those classes: the value theory based on work, the additional value and exploitation theory, the theory of history understood as an incessant struggle against exploitation – a struggle for the liberation of labor. That is an entirely different outlook on social issues than the perspective of all kinds of social elites: political, economic, and spiritual ones. Thus, the creation of a system of three ruling classes leads to a situation in which a utopia becomes an ideology. That was possible thanks to Marx's basic error: the limitation of the materialist, class paradigm to the economic area and the perception of power as a kind of an accidental auxiliary measure in private owners' hands. Still, in its original form, Marxism was not a good material for an ideology. That is why it was reinterpreted and 'enriched' with various external, eclectic elements: political elitism, national solidarity, moralizing. Intellectuals probably did this with the best intentions, in order to blunt what they viewed as a sharp tool of the system. However, the result was the opposite: by transforming Marxism into an eclectic mash-up, they made Marxist critique of the system impossible and preserved its spiritual integrity. In a word, they acted precisely in the interest of the triple-power system.

Stalinism, one should add, is, in general, a trap for intellectuals – the enormousness of the crimes committed at that time tempts them to resort to theoretical shortcuts. Because of the shock experienced by every honest person upon learning about the vastness of the Gulag, even the mere appearance of an analysis is seized upon in the hope of gaining a sense of having an explanation. One example of that phenomenon is the theory of newspeak. Countless theoreticians have presented a frightful image of a system which controls our thoughts with the help of special syntax and vocabulary designed with the view to keeping them in predefined tracks. Well, just a few years have passed and it has turned out that the first – and only one, so far – *the* thing that the new reformist trend has completely destroyed is language. Despite that, social life continues intact and undisturbed.

It is the moralizing temptation that is responsible for such intellectual calamities, together with political ones – it is all too easy to attack an enemy by ascribing satanic intentions to it. Meanwhile, a little bit of critical reflection would bring about the awareness that the phenomenon of newspeak – of changing the meaning of words in the most powerful people's interest – is as old as the hills. After all, it is not so difficult to ask how the meaning of such words as 'love' or 'neighbor' changed when a church inquisitor said, when sending a heretic to the stake, that he was doing it in the interest of the condemned the burning of the body would save the heretic's soul and that he was just following the evangelical precepts of charity. Perhaps, though, the problem here is not the lack of reason but the lack of civil courage? Once more, the crux of the matter, as regards social analysis, is not to be afraid of the mighty people. Any of them.

References

Nowak, L. (1988). O podwójnej herezji w filozofii społecznej [On Double Heresy in Social Philosophy]. *Twórczość*, 11, 27–54.

Nowak, L. (1988). Prawda nieznośna dla wszystkich [The Truth Unbearable for All]. *Zdanie* 10, 16–18.

Nowak, L. (1991). *Power and Civil Society: Towards a Dynamic Theory of Real Socialism*. New York/ London: Greenwood Press.

CHAPTER 3

Hegel and Liberalism: On the Issue of the Nature of Historiosophy

Leszek Nowak

Abstract

The author analyzes the structure of the Hegelian philosophy of history, distinguishing the level of the humanity, nations and individuals. However, according to Nowak, the Hegelian vision of history is a mythologization of the historical process, not its theory. Mythologization consists in in the enrichment of a presupposed vision of history with properties it does not, possess (or which it possesses to a lesser degree). However, the mythologized images of history may be rational or irrational. The former are justified empirically, while the latter are not. According to Nowak, the Hegelian and liberal visions of history represent an irrational mythologization of history. The Marx's case is more sophisticated: the historiosophy of the young Marx represents an irrational mythologization, whereas later Marx's writings can be characterized as rational mythologization because it is supplemented with a theory of historical process.

Keywords

historiosophy – Hegel – idealization – Marx – liberalism – mythologization – philosophy of history

1 "The Hegelian Sting"[1]

It is a rather widespread opinion today that determining the laws of a historical process, in other words, practicing historiosophy, is a manifestation of not having overcome Hegelian prejudices, a testimony of – to quote Czesław Miłosz – "the Hegelian sting." That opinion is most often voiced from the liberal point

---

[1] The paper appears in English translation for the first time. The Polish original „Hegel i liberalizm: zagadnienie natury historiozofii" was published in: *Pismo* 1–2 (1989), pp. 126–146. The abstract and key words have been added by the editor.

of view. It is usually accompanied by two allegations: that it is not possible to detect the laws of a historical process, and that people who nevertheless — attempt that feat — in a Hegelian manner — are doing something dangerous.

Those allegations immediately come across as superficial. Off course, the human mind may be too weak to detect the regularities of a historical process. But how could the proponents of the liberal orientation know that? The proof from the failures of the undertaken attempts — let us, for the sake of simplicity, assume with the liberal theoreticians that, indeed, all those attempts have indeed failed — clearly misses the target. It is just as convincing as a proof of the failures of mechanics in the 16th century would be — before the founders of that domain of physics made their discoveries — would be. How, then, can we know that it is not possible to detect the regularities of social changes? How can we be self-confident enough to adamantly maintain that a standard scientific procedure — the construction of hypothetical images of the development of a typical society from a given class of societies, the verification of that model, the correction of it so that it differs as little as possible from the actual state of things — would not be effective in this domain? Surely not because of the ontological assumption that the successive changes of the stages of particular societies, that is, their historical paths, are not, themselves, irregular in any way. After all, how could such a thesis of historical indeterminism be justified? Definitely not by referring to historical facts. In order to realize that, one just has to remember how similar all forms of real socialism have been. Events in Cuba are very much like those in the German Democratic Republic, and Czechoslovakia has virtually the same system as Vietnam does. If, then, despite the enormous differences between the level of civilization development, cultural tradition, religion, etc., very similar processes can be observed in those countries, then it is clear proof of certain common, basic regularities operating there — just as a stone and a feather both fall in accordance with the law of gravity. The circumstances which differentiate those societies are the probable reason for the slightly different manifestations of those regularities — just like the different shapes of a stone and an ax influence their drag and make them fall slightly differently to the ground. Perhaps the human mind cannot understand those social laws. How can we know that, though? We can only learn about it in one way: by trying to find it out. Meanwhile, there are far fewer people who make that effort than those who declare in advance that it is impossible to do.

The second allegation, namely, that practicing historiosophy is socially dangerous because it tempts its proponents of it to shape reality according to a model, is equally unsubstantiated. After all, it is based on the assumption that the persuasive power of social ideas is so great that it can take precedence over demographic, economic, class, and other interests. Indeed, such a view exists — the thesis of historical idealism. However, that thesis itself belongs to historiosophy – the idealist strain of it, and the verity of it is not, by any means, unquestionable. Indeed, which historiosophers should be blamed for the creation of ancient oriental despotisms? Which historiosophical concept gave rise to the Inca Empire, which regulated individuals' lives to a greater degree than did even the 20th-century systems called (by liberalism) totalitarian did? Let us just carefully state that the thesis of historical idealism is as questionable as the thesis of materialism. Consequently, the second allegation is both shallow and confusing. It is shallow in that it presupposes a thesis as questionable as those against which it is aimed, and it is confusing because it draws our attention away from the hidden factors which, for thousands of years, have been leading various societies in the totalitarian direction while it emphasizes the role of the most spectacular elements (totalitarian ones) which only accompany some of them.

This much can be said about the systematic aspect of the dispute about the possibilities of historiosophy. As regards the historical aspect, Hegel is usually viewed as the main culprit. In this article, I would like to verify the validity of the supposition that Hegelian historiosophy is a paradigmatic example of the theory of the historical process and that one cannot, for that reason, practice historiosophy without inheriting the basic features of Hegel's historiosophical system.

2 The Hegelian Historiosophical Paradigm

According to an interpretation which I find reasonable, Hegel views the historical process as happening at three levels: of (i) humanity, (ii) nations, and (iii) individuals. In that model, the principle of the development of humanity as a certain whole is primary with respect to the principle of the development of nations, while the latter principle takes priority over the principle which defines the level of individuals. That is also the structure of Hegelian historiosophy: the image of the development of the human spirit imposes certain requirements on the image of the development of national spirits, while the latter image restricts the development of individual self-knowledge.

According to the basic principle which defines level (i),

> Universal history (...) shows the development of the consciousness of Freedom on the part of Spirit, and of the consequent realization of that Freedom. (...) But for spirit, the highest attainment is self-knowledge; an advance not only to the intuition, but to the thought – the clear conception of itself.
>
> HEGEL [1840] 1991, p. 79 and p. 88

Namely,

> Universal History exhibits the *gradation* in the development of that principle whose substantial *purport* is the consciousness of Freedom. (...) Here it is sufficient to state that the first step in the process presents that immersion of Spirit in Nature which has been already referred to; the second shows it as advancing to the consciousness of its freedom. But this initial separation from Nature is imperfect and partial, since it is derived immediately from the merely natural state, is consequently related to it, and is still encumbered with it as an essentially connected element. The third step is the elevation of the soul from this still limited and special form of freedom to its pure universal form; that state in which the spiritual essence attains the consciousness and feeling of itself.
> HEGEL [1840] 1991, p. 72–73

Those statements can, it seems, be interpreted as follows: People are free by nature. It does not follow, however, that they realize that fact, that they have self-knowledge about their freedom. The development of humanity is a process in which that self-knowledge expands, grows from the minimal level to the state of saturation.

Humanity consists of particular nations. Hegel distinguishes between historical and non-historical nations. A historical nation is a nation which contributes to the increase of the level of self-knowledge of humanity, or, rather, through which the self-knowledge of humanity rises to a higher level. We could interpret it as follows: a historical nation is defined as one whose self-knowledge of which shares some ground with the self-knowledge of humanity. Therefore, the spiritual development of a historical nation has three stages. At the initial stage, it is on the sidelines with regard to the spiritual development of mankind. Then, the self-knowledge of the nation grows until it reaches the peak stage at which it represents the self-knowledge of mankind:

> The highest point in the development of a people is this – to have gained a conception of its life and condition – to have reduced its laws, its ideas of justice and morality to a science. (...) In its work, it aims at having itself as the subject matter: a spirit only possesses itself as the subject in its existence when it includes itself in its thought.
> HEGEL [1840] 1991, p. 93

The third stage is that of decline:

> [when Nation] has attained full reality, has itself objectively present to it. But this having been attained, the activity displayed by the Spirit of the people in question is no longer needed;... The essential, supreme interest has consequently vanished from its life, for interest is present only where there is opposition. The nation lives the same kind of life as the individual when passing from maturity to old age – in the enjoyment of itself – in the satisfaction of being exactly what it desired and was able to attain.
> HEGEL [1840] 1991, p. 91.

A decline of the national spirit of a historical nation does not, however, mean a stagnation of the universal spirit because it develops constantly to an ever higher level of self-knowledge, except that another national spirit becomes the carrier of the progress of humanity, and another historical nation achieves a new, higher level of self-knowledge.

Apparently, it is essential for understanding the idea of development in Hegelian historiosophy that:

> The principles of the successive phases of Spirit that animate the Nations in a necessitated gradation, are themselves only steps in the development of the one universal Spirit, which through them elevates and completes itself to a self-comprehending *totality*.
> HEGEL [1840] 1991, p. 95–96

It might be understood as follows: each section of the curve which indicates the level of global self-knowledge is a sub-area of the highest self-knowledge of particular historical nations.

A nation, in turn, consists of particular individuals. Just as we can distinguish historical and non-historical nations, depending on whether their self-awareness introduces new elements to the self-knowledge of mankind, we can distinguish national figures and private persons among the individuals who constitute a nation.

An individual is a national figure if he or she contributes to the increase of national self-knowledge or, in other words, if the national spirit rises thanks to that person. Such an individual's awareness, in contrast to that of private individuals, partially overlaps with the self-knowledge of the nation. A national figure can be a historical figure if his or her awareness represents a historical nation at its peak stage, that is, the stage at which the nation represents humanity:

> Such are all great historical men – whose own particular aims involve those large issues which are the will of the World-Spirit. ... It was theirs to know this nascent principle; the necessary, directly sequent step in progress, which their world was to take; to make this their aim, and to expend their energy in promoting it. World-historical men – the Heroes of an epoch – must, therefore, be recognized as its clear-sighted ones; their deeds, their words are the best of that time.
>
> HEGEL [1840] 1991, pp. 44–45

Likewise, we can distinguish three stages (rising, peak, and declining) in national figures' lives, including great historical figures – just like in the development of a historical nation. Just as the development line of humanity is a combination of the peak stages of the development of successive historical nations, the line of the development of national self-knowledge is a combination of the peak stages of the development of the national figures' self-knowledge. Consequently, the development of the universal spirit is a combination of the peak stages of the development of great historical figures' awareness.

Let us summarize what has been said. Hegel opposes the individualist understanding of history as a set of individual actions directed by a subject's awareness. Instead, he says:

> in history an additional result is commonly produced by human actions beyond that which they aim at and obtain – that which they immediately recognize and desire. They gratify their own interest; but something further is thereby accomplished, latent in the actions in question, though not present to their consciousness, and not included in their design.
>
> HEGEL [1840] 1991, p. 42

That thing is the current state of the universal spirit which develops toward complete freedom:

> ... history is the exhibition of the divine, absolute development of Spirit in its highest forms – that gradation by which it attains its truth and consciousness of itself (...) Universal History is exclusively occupied with showing how Spirit comes to a recognition and adoption of the Truth: the dawn of knowledge appears; it begins to discover salient principles, and at last it arrives at full consciousness.
>
> HEGEL [1840] 1991, p. 69

A given level of universal self-knowledge manifests itself in the peak self-knowledge of a historical nation and, indirectly, in the highest achievements of the historical figures of that nation – the heroes, in Hegel's words. It is only in this way – from the universal spirit, through national spirits, toward individual awareness – that we can determine the meaning of history. A reverse procedure would not reveal anything but a chaos of accidental, disordered individual actions not governed by any sensible principle. That is why according to Hegel ([1840] 1991, p. 69) the spirit is not embodied in the form of an individual life but of collective life – the state.

3 Mythologization

The Hegelian construction is striking in that it does not take into account the actual courses of history – it is designed to introduce a new order to the world of historical facts rather than discover an order in that world. Facts are analyzed not to verify whether they confirm the hypothetically proposed explanatory model – and, in the case of a negative result, to reject that model – but rather to determine if they can be fit in that construction, if that construction gives them a meaning and makes it possible to perceive them as examples of the preestablished order. If it were not possible to line historical facts up in accordance with people's growing recognition of their freedom, that would not prove the falseness of the concept but rather its uselessness in assigning meaning to human history which is the history of the living creatures who have conquered the Earth. The Hegelian construction, then, is not an explanatory model but a kind of a measure of historical phenomena which contains an evaluative order.

Those historical facts which can be subsumed under the idea of growing self-knowledge become meaningful, whereas those which cannot be understood in that way are unreasonable or senseless. If we understand history, like Hegel does, as those trends which turn out to be meaningful in the light of his construction – that is, if historical equals meaningful – then those facts which cannot be interpreted can be classified as non-historical. The worse for them, in that they remain outside of the scope of meaningful history, or simply of history.

That last conclusion sounds absurd but only so long as we assume that Hegelian historiosophy is a theory of the historical process. If we do, then, it does indeed, it violates elementary cognitive rigors and can be viewed as an expression of dogmatism at odds with the ethos of science. The problem is that the assumption itself might be erroneous. I believe that we can interpret

Hegelian historiosophy as a theory which is not an explanatory theory – because it is not intended to be one.

There is an approach which suggests theories are built with the use of the idealization method. When we introduce idealizing assumptions, we presuppose that the parameters defined within their frameworks have values which do not influence the studied variables; in principle, idealizing assumptions postulate that appropriate parameters have zero values. In that way, a simplified – or depleted – ideal type of a phenomenon is constructed, about which idealizational hypotheses are made which are later concretized, while the initial simplifications are rejected.

A reverse procedure could be called mythologization. Mythologization does not consist in the depletion of an object through a thought process but in the enrichment of it with something it does not, *de facto*, possess. If we postulate zero dimensions of an object, we idealize it and construct an ideal type of a material point. If we postulate that a person accepts each true sentence, we mythologize and construct a mythical type of an omniscient being. Generally speaking, according to a mythologizing assumption, the appropriate parameter takes a value at which its influence on the studied variables is the highest. Idealizing assumptions ascribe certain properties to ideal types. Similarly, mythical theses ascribe properties to objects about which mythologizing assumptions have been made, that is, to mythical types. However, the aim of idealizing assumptions is to ascertain the influence exerted by the factors considered to be the main ones in the absence of other factors which are considered secondary; those additional influences are later taken into account within the course of concretization, and a better approximation of the complexity of the world is obtained. Therefore, they are to be true, although they can be false (in a particular, essential understanding). The role of a mythical thesis is to determine an evaluation standard on the basis of the maximization of a parameter (or a mythical core) which is considered to be basic and which is sublimated with the use of additional parameters – by introducing further mythologizing assumptions, we can make that initial standard more subtle or precise. It follows that mythical theses are neither true or false – they can just be more or less useful for the axiological qualification of facts within a given domain of knowledge. The basis for such a qualification is the degree of the divergence between a given fact and the accepted standard. The more sublimated such a standard is, the more facts it gives meaning to, that is, the more facts can be described as being sufficiently close to that standard.[1]

---

[1] A more detailed characteristic of the concepts which have been intuitively introduced in this text is provided in Nowak 1991b, 271–313; in English Nowak 2000; 2022 [editorial note].

We might suppose that Hegelian historiosophy is not only a theory but a mythologization – within the meaning sketched above – of a historical process. From among the various parameters of an actual historical process, it magnifies one: the human quest for freedom. It is to be the driving force of history, to be transformed into the basic manifestations of humans' collective life, such as the state and the law:

> freedom constitutes its [law] substance and destiny and the system of right is the realm of actualized freedom, the world of spirit produced from within itself.
> HEGEL [1821], 2003, p. 35

We are dealing here with the mythologization of freedom in history, and the abovementioned principle, which defines the three stages of the development of the universal spirit, can be interpreted as a mythical core which determines the basic standard which is subject to further sublimation.

The first sublimation consists in taking into account the level of nations, which makes it possible to distinguish between historical and non-historical nations, and to refine the idea of the realization of freedom in history. Historical nations, at peak stages of their development, are to be the carriers of progress. The second sublimation, which takes into account the individual level, allows for further refinement of that standard of history evaluation: progress turns out to be the work of great historical figures, that is, of heroes of historical nations. That construction provides a criterion for the evaluation of the history of humanity, nations, and individuals – a positive evaluation is made of the manifestations, more or less direct, of the development of the sense of freedom, and the greatest approval is expressed for the actions on which the development of freedom rests; instrumental approval is granted to actions which are not, themselves, a realization of the universal spirit but which contribute to the growth of the self-awareness of freedom.

4   Irrational and Rational Mythologization

Hegelian historiosophy, then, is a mythological construct which presents human history as a realization of the idea of freedom and provides standards for the evaluation of that history and, consequently, for giving it meaning – for those who are willing to accept those standards.

We should, however, distinguish between two types of mythologization, depending on what the initial decision to introduce particular parameters to the mythological construct is based on. Such a decision can only be justified with the constatation that the mythologization of specific variables will result in a mythical system which makes it possible to assign meaning to a given set of facts. There can be no substantive limitations here. Therefore, in such a situation, we will speak about arbitrary – or irrational – mythologization. It may also happen that while to assign meaning to a given set of facts we will impose on ourselves certain limitations as to the subject matter, in order to only take into account those factors which are indeed important in the given domain. Since, however, we never know in advance which factors have a basic impact and which are of the second order or even unimportant, that requirement is fulfilled by using the following procedure: we formulate significance hypotheses that certain factors are the main ones while other factors are secondary, we put forward idealizational hypotheses about the structure of the regularities which relate the main factors to the studied phenomena in the absence of secondary factors, and we check those hypotheses by means of concretization and/or approximation. That procedure is simply an idealization method of constructing a theory of a set of facts from a given domain. If we want a mythological construction not to be arbitrary but based on some justified image of facts from a given domain, we need to first create an idealizational model of that domain of knowledge.

Rational mythologization, then, operates on parameters derived from a theory of a domain of knowledge; in other words, it presupposes an idealization theory which has some empirical justification.

That expression is not, by any means, used to suggest that there is only one possible method of rational mythologization of a domain of knowledge (social history, individual life, etc.). On the contrary: many incompatible idealizational theories of a domain of knowledge can be, to a degree, empirically justified. Therefore, there are many possible ways of rational mythologization of every studied domain of knowledge.

The distinction between rational and irrational mythologization does not refer to the concept of truth but of justification. The essence of that distinction is the differentiation between, on the one hand, a mythological construction that assumes a certain image – which has an empirical justification – of the mythologized reality and, on the other hand, a mythological construction which is not preceded by any theoretical effort and which, for that reason, is only based on arbitrary decisions to take into account specific dimensions of collective life, the historical process, etc. Of course, mythologization which would not assume any knowledge at all about its subject matter would probably have to be based on a random draw, so it is virtually impossible – we always have some beliefs about what later becomes magnified in a myth. After all,

Hegel knew that in real history people follow their desire for freedom. The important question is if those judgments were accepted without reflection – for example, they were deemed common sense at the time – or if they were illuminated with some theoretical analysis.

The distinction between rational and irrational mythologization is precisely this: a rational mythologization of a given domain of knowledge logically presupposes an idealization of that domain.

5 Thesis 1: Hegelian Historiosophy is Irrational Mythologization

Hegelian historiosophy lacks precisely such an explanatory construction: it is neither built nor taken from somewhere. Hegel's procedure does not consist in proposing the hypothesis that striving for freedom is the main motif of social actions of human beings, building a theoretical model of a historical process on that basis, verifying that model in the light of facts, and making appropriate corrections of it – taking into account the influence of other, additional motifs or circumstances of actions, etc. Hegel does not explain – he decrees, and he needs facts not to verify the explanatory force of the construction but to show that it is that construction which gives them a meaning.

Hegelian historiosophy is not a theory of striving for freedom but a myth of freedom – a myth not based on any such kind of a theory. The base of the Hegelian myth is not illuminated with any theoretical analysis. Hegel does not make a theoretical effort in order to determine the essence of the historical process at the particular stages of its development and the manner in which that essence manifests – an effort marked with errors and corrections. He decrees the essence: he defines it as what fulfills his myth. The myth does not depend on the detection of the essence of the process – instead, the essence is to be determined by means of the myth. Hegelian mythologization, then, is irrational. It is also misleading because it is presented as something it is not – a theory of the historical process.

6 Liberal Historiosophy

There are, therefore, reasons for criticizing Hegel. However, the proponents of the liberal orientation do not criticize the "the father of modern historicism" (Popper 1966, vol. 2, p. 237) for that because they take seriously the appearance created by Hegelian historiosophy and try to view it as a theory which explains history. Next, having ascertained its obvious inadequacy – especially salient in the case of the thesis of the Prussian monarchy as a realization of reason – they conclude that a theory of the historical process cannot be constructed in a different way than Hegel's, so it cannot be built at all.

The particular arguments put forth by the proponents of the liberal orientation to support their position have already been discussed. Here, I would like to note the very fact of the wrong target of that critique. The liberal critique misses what should actually be criticized in Hegel's reflections – if the point of view sketched above is justified – that is, the lack of theoretical arguments to support his construction which gives meaning to facts, and it misses what definitely deserves a negative evaluation, namely, the creation of the false appearance of theoretical work in historiosophy. I will now try to show that the abovementioned state of things is not accidental, as liberalism also presupposes certain historiosophy. Here are its basic foundations. A human being, as an individual, has certain rights. The basic one is the right to freedom, followed by the rights implied by that primary requirement of the law of nature: to freedom of conscience, to private property, etc. However, the right to freedom conflicts with the right to safety. Therefore, people consciously waive a part of their rights and, in that way, agree to certain limitations of their freedom, to create a state organization the role of which is to ensure the safe existence of a society. Without a state, there is anarchy. Nevertheless, a state can go too far as it strives to protect citizens and may incapacitate them. Between the two extremes – anarchy and totalitarianism – there is the optimal solution: a democratic state. It respects an individual's natural rights because it is just an instrument created for the citizens' good, an effective instrument – any deviations from its proper role can be corrected in such a state through the use of democratic processes. Democracy is a self-regulating mechanism.

Historiosophical options are hidden in the liberal doctrine – usually at the level of assumptions rather than theses proposed *explicite*. Nevertheless, they are present in that doctrine:

> The progress of society like that of the individual depends, then, ultimately on choice. It is not "natural," in the sense in which a physical law is natural, that is, in the sense of going forward automatically from stage to stage without backward turnings, deflections to the left, or fallings away on the right. It is natural only in this sense, that it is the expression of deep-seated forces of human nature which come to their own only by an infinitely slow and cumbersome process of mutual adjustment.
> HOBHOUSE 1964, p. 36

As we can see, according to that thesis, an individual's natural rights are not only ethical imperatives but also "deeply rooted forces of human nature" which drive social progress leading toward a universally satisfying form of the organization of social life. Since the basis of those laws – and, at the same time, the most powerful component of human nature – is the quest for freedom, the most natural form of social organization must respect, first of all, individuals' freedom.

With that explanation, it becomes easy to identify a natural or optimal social system: it would be the democratic system of the Western states, which represents the historical model, and the degree of the democratization of a state is to be the measure of social progress. Here is an example of the use of that measure:

> In our part ... of the world, liberal ideas are still an unrealized but also undestroyed hope of progress. As regards the protection of individual and civil liberties, we have been living here, for nearly two centuries, as if in the era of feudal absolutism, as if time had stopped for us before the announcement of the great constitutional charters of the end of the 18th century.
>
> JEDLICKI 1981, p. 5

7 Thesis 2: Liberal Historiosophy is Irrational Mythologization

It becomes clear why the liberal critique of Hegelian historiosophy omits what deserves that critique the most: liberalism is based on the same assumptions as Hegelianism.

Liberal historiosophy is a mythologization of an individual's freedom, just like Hegelian historiosophy is a mythologization of collective freedom and its self-awareness. Hegelianism is a holism in which freedom is understood as a universal, while liberalism is an individualism which calls for individuals' freedom. Nevertheless, they have one basic thing in common: an arbitrary worldview unsupported by theoretical understanding of its subject matter. In liberalism, there is no theory of human nature which could, when properly expanded, be set side by side with facts and which could be abandoned if it turned out to be too weak to explain them. The catalog of human rights is a purely axiological project which, essentially, is not subject to falsification and which is misleading because, instead of a normative mode (people should be free), it makes use of a descriptive mode (a person has the right to freedom), just as if individuals were somehow objectively entitled to that natural right and as if it could, given sufficient perceptiveness, be discovered in them. The meaning of the liberal thesis:

> no power on earth is unlimited ... The limitations are justice and individual rights. The will of the whole nation cannot justify what is unjust. The representatives of a nation cannot do what the nation itself cannot do. No monarch, whatever he refers to ... has unlimited power.
> CONSTANT 1978, p. 204[2]

is of the same type as the meaning of the Hegelian thesis:

> [The state is] substantial unity is an absolute and unmoved end in itself, and in it, freedom enters into its highest right, just as this ultimate end possesses the highest right in relation to individuals [*die Einzelnen*], whose highest duty is to be members of the state.
> HEGEL [1821] 2003, p. 275

Both theses are equally indifferent to what happens in actual, existing legal and state systems, between actual rulers and citizens. They are projects – mutually contradictory – of world-view measures which make it possible to evaluate the phenomena of the social world as more or less distant from those norms. Therefore, those theses constitute mythologizations of the phenomenon of power. They are arbitrary, or irrational, mythologizations, in the sense of not explaining to us the actual world – they do not presuppose a theory which would explain the phenomenon of power, but they can be easily presented as such explanations.

8 Historiosophical Mythologization and the Theory of a Historical Process

Meanwhile, the crux of the matter is not to shout – while reading, for example, that: "all the worth which the human being possesses — all spiritual reality, he possesses only through the State" (Hegel [1840] 1991, p. 54) – that it is not true, and that, on the contrary, that the value of a state is its respect for human rights. The most important thing is to realize the equal status of those two

---

2 After Polish translation from: Constant 1837, p. 69 [editorial note].

theses, the fact that they are world-view projections, and their only connection with facts is that they serve the purpose of evaluating them; they do not contribute to the understanding of facts, just like a measuring bar makes it possible to evaluate lengths but does not explain the nature of the measured objects. Irrational mythologization should be replaced with rational mythologizations, that is, mythologizations based on a hypothetical model which explains the actual historical process.

People need mythologizations of history – as well as mythologizations of human life, human relationships, etc. – in order to have an evaluative point of reference for making evaluations and postulates. There is, however, a great difference between a situation in which we assume a model of the historical process – that is, a thought structure which can be refuted if it turns out to be inconsistent with facts – in order to explain actual trends and to predict the odds of particular courses of events in the future, and in which we construct the desired object in the light of that model, and a situation in which we begin from declaring how things should be without having first understood how things are and how they can be.

In the case of rational mythologization, which assumes an idealizational theory with some explanatory force as regards the given domain of study, the following condition, which limits the arbitrariness of that mythologization, applies. In a mythical core, we can only maximize that parameter (those parameters) which is (are) introduced in the initial model of the assumed idealizational theory, that is, which functions (function) in that theory as the main variable. In the course of the sublimation of the mythical core, we can only maximize those parameters which are introduced in the derivative models of the theory, within the framework of the concretization of its basic idealizational laws – that is, those which function in the theory as secondary variables. In short, that requirement of the structural appropriateness of mythologization, and of the idealizational theory it assumes, demands that value be assigned to phenomena on the basis of the recognition of their determinants, that is, only when one has formed a justified view on which factors have an impact on those phenomena and in what way. The requirement might seem trivial. In a way, it is – when one already makes use of the theory of a given domain of knowledge and knows (in the sense of having rational arguments for it) how the factors considered to be the main ones function and how their functioning is modified by secondary factors, then one chooses, automatically, so to speak, the basic evaluative parameter (parameters) from among the factors which essentially determine the phenomena in question. That is why, let us add, there are no 'disputes about values' in medicine or agricultural studies. The mere requirement for having a theory of a given domain of knowledge, however, is not trivial – even if it is yet to be constructed. That is why in such domains of study, typically humanistic ones, in which there are, as yet, no clear theoretical proposals, theoretical disputes often assume the form of alleged 'disputes about values'. The lack of a clear distinction between mythologization and a theory is one important reason for the confusion concerning axiological and theoretical discourses.

9 Thesis 3: Marxian Historiosophy is Rational Mythologization

There is a quite widespread belief that the whole difference between Marx's historiosophy and Hegelianism consists in the replacement of the Hegelian "spirit" with matter and with material and economic interests (Popper 1966, vol. 1, p. 61). Thus, as regards the nature of the understanding of the historical process, Marxian historical materialism is said to have inherited Hegelian assumptions, and it said is to differ from Hegel's theory in the same way as historical materialism differs from idealism, that is, by the type of the factors to which it refers, by content.

It is so, indeed, when we speak about the young Marx: the historiosophy in *Economic and Philosophic Manuscripts of 1844* is of the Hegelian type. The alienation of work replaces the "universal spirit," progress consists in the disappearance of the alienation instead of in the growth of self-knowledge, and the end of that progress, that is, communism, is defined as follows:

> Communism as fully-developed naturalism, equals humanism, and as fully-developed humanism equals naturalism; it is the genuine resolution of the conflict between man and nature and between man .and man-the true resolution of the strife between existence and essence, between objectification and self-confirmation, between freedom and necessity, between the individual and the species. Communism is the riddle of history solved, and it knows itself to be this solution.
>
> MARX [1844] 1978, p. 84

This mythical construction is completely in the Hegelian spirit – it is based on the projection of an ideal onto history and not on a theoretical explanation of history.

The mature Marx's historiosophy is entirely different. It does contain the obvious, mythological part, just like any other historiosophy. However, it is not the case that the philosopher's arbitrary project is based solely on his sense of the good and the evil. Instead of that, it is anchored in a construction which explains the existing course of history. Józef Tischner writes very perceptively about the mythological component of Marxian historical materialism:

> Marxism put forward ... a proposal of a particular ethos to which one could not remain indifferent. That ethos was shaped by the imperative of a consistent fight for freeing human work from the yoke of exploitation. The nature of the experience of Marxism was decidedly axiological ... The fundamental and absolute value was that special kind of ethical sensitivity to the issue of work, which underlies Marxism and which Marxism inspired in its recipients.
> TISCHNER 1980, p. 18–19.

However, most importantly, that axiological experience of Marxism was, in a sense, included in the model of the historical process proposed by Marxism. The ethos of Marxian historical materialism contains the myth of the exploited, but exploitation is, after all, also a theoretical concept: it means the difference between the value newly created by an employee and the value of the employee's work. The class of the exploited is not only an evaluative concept but also a theoretical one – the basic hypotheses of the Marxian theory of the historical process refer to that class, its interests, and its fight with the class of owners. The basic mythical cores of the ethos of Marxian historical materialism refer to parameters considered to be the main ones in Marx's theory. The myth of the exploited is subsequently sublimated as a result of the introduction of the myth of the dying of the state – the process of the abolition of the exploitation is to be accompanied by the process of the disappearance of political oppression. That is consistent because the state was only a superstructure for Marx, and it only appeared in the concretizations of the basic model. Further sublimation of the myth of the exploited takes place thanks to the introduction of the myth of the de-ideologization of social relations which, as class divisions (as understood by Marx, in other words as economic ones) disappear, are to become more and more transparent for their participants. That is also consistent because ideology is an even further side effect for Marx, and it appears in even further concretizations of Marx's basic laws. All in all, we can say that the mythologization of the historical process included in the Marxian historical materialism fulfills the condition of being structurally appropriate for the idealization of that process proposed in the theoretical component of that historiosophy. It is, then, a rational mythologization.

It is true that Marx was wrong concerning what he considered to be the superstructure – for a certain type of conditions, that superstructure appears to be an elementary component of the base, and, for that reason, his prognoses failed, and the myths turned out to be groundless, at least as regards the basic framework. Nevertheless, as was perceptively noted by Karl Popper, errors are for science what air is for the flight of a bird, that is, a natural and inevitable thing – as long as they are noticed and corrected. In the case of errors as important as those made by Marx, there can be no interdoctrinal corrections and error removal must lead to the creation of an alternative theory. Still, that theory must be constructed with Marx's errors as the starting point. Marx's doctrine must be transformed so that it has greater explanatory force than that of Marxian historical materialism, and so that it makes it possible to explain the phenomena which contradict Marx's theory.

10   Thesis 4: Neoliberalist Historiosophy is Going back to Hegelianism

If the three most important hypotheses presented in this text can be viewed as justified, then the map of the approaches in contemporary historiosophy is very different than commonly assumed. It is usually believed that the framework of seemingly scientific historiosophy was created by Hegel, while Marx just replaced idealism with historical materialism within the same thought structure. According to the modern neoliberal approach, the very thought concerning a theory of the historical process is erroneous, impracticable, and dangerous. If, however, I am right, the reality is quite different. It is liberalism that preserves the thought structure of Hegelian historiosophy, but it replaces holism with individualism: the myth of freedom realized in a state is replaced with the myth of freedom realized in human rights, and both cases are arbitrary axiological options unsupported with any explanatory models. That common thought foundation of Hegelianism and liberalism was already overcome in Marx's historiosophy.[3]

---

[3] I would like to make two Marxologist remarks here. We can see that the approach sketched in this text makes it possible to propose a certain interpretation of Marx's famous thesis that his historiosophy is "turning (Hegelian historiosophy) from standing on its head to standing on its feet." Usually, that is understood as a juxtaposition of historical materialism with historical idealism. Probably, though, it can also be understood in a different way: that Marx emphasizes the rational – within the meaning explained above – nature of his mythologization of history, as, in his words: "My dialectical method is, in its foundations, not only different from the Hegelian, but exactly opposite to it. For Hegel, the proccess of thinking, which he even transforms into an independent subject, under the name of 'the Idea', is the creator of the real world, and the real world is only the external appearance of the idea. With me the reverse is true: the ideal is nothing but the material world reflected in the mind of man, and translated into forms of thought" (Marx [1873] 1990, p. 102). From that statement, in my view, we can infer that Hegel equips his construction with an ideal which explains reality, while

The substantive erroneousness of Marx's historiosophy, as well as its axiological poverty – after all, it does not, on its own, sanction the fight against political oppression or spiritual enslavement – should not blind us to the fact that Marx took a step in the right direction and that we should go further – and more consistently – in that direction. A return to liberalism is a regression to – paradoxically – the Hegelian historiosophical paradigm.

References

Constant, B. ([1837] 1978). Wykłady z polityki konstytucyjnej [Lectures on Constitutional Politics]. In: B. Sobolewska, M. Sobolewski (eds.). *Myśl polityczna XIX i XX w. Liberalizm*, pp. 197- 204. Warszawa: PWN.

Constant, B. (1837). *Cours de politique constitutionnelle*. Bruxelles.

Hegel, G.W.F. ([1821] 2003). *Elements Philosophy of Law*. Translated by H. B. Nisbet. Cambridge: Cambridge University Press.

Hegel, G.W.F. ([1840] 1991). *Philosophy of History*. Translated by J. Sibree, Kitchener, Ontario: Batoche Books.

Hobhouse, L. (1964). *Liberalism*. London: Oxford University Press.

Jedlicki, J. (1981). Przedmowa [Preface]. In: *Liberalizm dzisiaj. Eseje Warszawskie*, pp. 5–9. Warsaw: NOW-a.

Marx, K. ([1844] 1978). Economic and Philosophic Manuscripts. In: *The Marx-Engels Reader*, ed. by R. C. Tucker, pp. 66–125. New York/London: Norton Company.

Marx claims that such an ideal cannot be anything more than a component of a real, material process and that that process ought to be evaluated not on the basis of arbitrary criteria but criteria derived from the theory of that process. Obviously, for the Marx-materialist, only a material factor could be such a criterion. Let us also note that if we view young Marx's philosophy as the key to his system, then, indeed, Marxian and Hegelian historiosophies cease to be separate. In such a case, it may really look like the former is a materialistic version of the latter. That observation cannot, off course, be treated as an argument for the position represented in the text; the thesis that Marx included the foundations of his system in *Economic and Philosophic Manuscripts of 1844* requires other counterarguments. They are not so difficult to find, though. For example, given that assumption, how should we understand the fact that *Manuscripts* remained a manuscript for nearly forty years? Why did Marx, although he agreed to republish *The Communist Manifesto* many times, not take care of the first printing of his supposedly foundational work? I believe that the young-Marxian interpretation of Marxism cannot be justified with historical arguments. It was, in essence, a political act – the point was to juxtapose Marx, even the young Marx, with the crimes of Stalinism. Actually, though, as we may assume, that interpretation played an exactly opposite historical role to the one intended by its well-meaning proponents; see: Nowak 1991a, pp. 165–198.

Marx, K. ([1873] 1990). *Capital. A Critique of Political Economy*, vol. I. Translated by B. Fowkes. London: Penguin Books.

Nowak, L. (1989). Hegel i liberalizm: zagadnienie natury historiozofii [Hegel and Liberalism: On the Issue of the Nature of Historiosophy]. *Pismo*, 1–2, 126–146.

Nowak, L. (1991a). *Power and Civil Society. Toward a Dynamic Theory of Real Socialism*. New York: Greenwood Press.

Nowak, L. (1991b). *U podstaw teorii socjalizmu [Foundation of Theory of Socialism]; vol. 1: Własność i władza. O konieczności socjalizmu [Property and Power. On the Necessity of Socialism]*. Poznań: Nakom.

Nowak, L. (2000). On the Common Structure of Science and Religion. In: A. Garcia de la Sienra (ed.), *The Rationality of Theism. Poznań Studies in the Philosophy of the Sciences and the Humanities*, vol. 69, pp. 317–343. Amsterdam/ Atlanta: Rodopi.

Nowak, L. (2022). Religion as a Class Structure: A Contribution to non-Marxian Historical Materialism. In: K. Brzechczyn (ed.). *New Developments in Theory of Historical Process. Contributions to non-Marxian Historical Materialism Poznań Studies in the Philosophy of the Sciences and the Humanities*, vol. 119, pp. 3–51. Leiden/Boston: Brill.

Popper, K. R. (1966). *The Open Society and its Enemies*, vol. 1–2. London: Routledge and Kegan.

Tischner, J. (1980). *Polski kształt dialogu* [Polish Shape of Dialoque]. Lublin: Spotkania.

CHAPTER 4

The Problem of the So-Called Social Transformation

Leszek Nowak

Abstract

One of the most surprising spiritual nowadays is the deep change of liberalism. For a long time, liberalism appeared to be a radically anti-utopian way of thinking, based on total refutation of any historiosophy; if it proclaimed any social reforms at all, it was just piecemeal social engineering. Recently, this doctrine has transformed into a utopia of the "end of history," based on a clear historiosophy, and it legitimizes a program of rapid and total systemic engineering, especially in Eastern Europe. A tentative conceptualization of this puzzle on the grounds of non-Marxian historical materialism requires a definite interpretation of the notion of chaos, which, in turn, allows us to closely inspect variations of the multilinearity of social development, especially in the conditions of so-called 'post-communist society'.

Keywords

Liberalism – non-Marxian historical materialism – philosophy of history – post-communism – transformation

1 Introduction[1]

Every person who treats social theory seriously is – I presume – somewhat embarrassed when seeing what theories are presented at numerous symposia and conferences on the so-called social transformation in our part of the world. After all, we have learned – and this fact is an elementary component of every scientist's consciousness – that science is probably the only area of human culture in which pluralism is not only a moral postulate but, as it were,

---

[1] The paper appears in English translation for the first time. The Polish original „O zagadnieniu tak zwanej transformacji ustrojowej" was published in: K. Zamiara (ed.), *Społeczna transformacja w refleksji humanistycznej* (Poznań: Wyd. UAM, 1994), pp. 117–129. The key words have been added by the editor.

an operational requirement – in science, many incongruent hypotheses compete to be selected by the scientific community, solely on the basis of cognitive arguments. If that is the case, how is the current astounding unanimity concerning the roadmap for the development of our country – and of other countries of Central and Eastern Europe – possible? There are no competing hypotheses, there is only one view: those countries are embarking on the path once trodden by Western Europe.

I spent 1989–90 – the year the consequences of which I will, discuss here – on a fellowship in a Berlin institute for advanced studies which invites, as a rule, both scientists and humanists. One day, a week before the election in the German Democratic Republic, the fellows decided to try and predict its outcome, for fun. It turned out the sociologists, political scientists, economists, and historians completely lost to a geophysicist who took first place far ahead of all the other competitors (including the present author): he was the only one from dozens of people to correctly indicate the winning party. However, the most interesting thing was the lesson he gave us, humanists, after having accepted the award: "I concluded that all humanists – with no exceptions – opt for the victory of the social democrats, and I thought that such great unanimity was suspicious, which is why I bet on the Christian democrats."

Indeed, such a consensus on the direction of the social transformation, on the part of economists, political scientists, or sociologists, is suspect. That is why I would like to take a look at the foundations of that historiosophical unanimity and to evaluate them, from a purely cognitive point of view.

2   Liberal Historiosophy

That unanimity is based on a certain historiosophy, which is embodied in the following principles:

(i) Human nature is egoistic by nature; egoism is a destructive force; in order to use it for public good, society establishes certain institutions: a parliamentary democracy and a free market based on private property.

(ii) Those institutions constitute a social system – liberal capitalism – which is a natural state of society within the meaning given below:
(LH) every society spontaneously heads toward liberal capitalism; this pursuit can be stopped by force, but it will only result in the arrival of the natural state being delayed.

(iii) When a given society reaches the stage of liberal capitalism, it simply remains in it; parliamentary democracy respects the rights of humans and citizens, a free market based on private property ensures the welfare not only of elites but also of the middle class, that is, the whole – if we omit the margins – society; it is no wonder that this natural state is the end point of social history.

It is easy to notice that this is liberal historiosophy, which became a dominant ideological form in the West in the 1980s and in Central and Eastern Europe in the 1990s. It is obvious – but worth reiterating – that the fact that (almost) everyone believes *p* does not mean that *p is true*. We should, then, take a look at the foundations of the faith in liberal historiosophy, especially at its crucial thesis (LH).

3 Is There No Alternative to Liberal Historiosophy?

First, we should give liberalism credit, where it is due. It is a very fruitful conception when it comes to normative constructions. The strongest point of liberal social philosophy can be found in its optimization models of how the human society should be organized if particular values are to be optimized. It is, indeed, difficult to find a serious alternative to models inspired by liberalism, such as Rawls's model (1971). However, those models belong to social policy, or broadly understood normative ethics, not to the theory of the historical process (historiosophy). Meanwhile, the principles (i)–(iii), which is always the basis of liberal thought and which was developed *explicite* in recent years, belongs *par excellence* to theory of the historical process. It is often presented as not having an alternative. In dozens of studies, we read that "History shows that liberal capitalism does not have a reasonable alternative." Therefore, liberal historiosophy is also deemed not to have a worthy competitor.

If we were to take those proclamations seriously, it would mean that liberal historiosophy ought to fulfill certain strict methodological requirements. Every scientific theory is expected to honor the principle of correspondence to its thought tradition, that is, roughly speaking, to explain (1) the facts which falsify the previous theory (in that tradition), and explain (2) all the facts which the predecessor was capable of explaining. A theory which is deemed to be without an alternative must fulfill a stricter requirement, namely, explain (1) the facts which falsify the current rivals from all competing traditions of thought, and explain (2) all the facts already explained by those theories. Let us, then, compare liberal historiosophy with, for example, Marxist historiosophy.

With some drastic simplification, we could say that social history comprises three lines of development: on the one hand, the line of primitive societies, from which the line of non-European civilizations (for example, Inca or Chinese) derives, and on the other hand, the line of the Western civilization. All of them endure to this day, in a more or less residual form (the so-called primitive societies which exist today or some societies of the 'third world'). At this point, we might ask what liberal historiosophy can say about the nature of primitive societies or of the Inca society. Well, liberal historiosophy can only say that neither primitive societies nor Asiatic despotisms have 'learned', as yet, that the optimal human institutions are parliamentary democracy and the free market. As the structures, mechanisms of change, etc. of those societies are drastically different, we must conclude that liberalism has nothing to about them. Whatever is claimed by liberalism refers to the societies of the Western civilization, more precisely: to the latest incarnation of those societies, namely, capitalism. Liberalism has nothing to say about feudalism, either. For a long time, capitalism itself could not be explained by the liberal model, because no liberal would view such events as the shooting down of a few thousand workers or the sending of a few thousand boys under the age of 16 to hard labor in Guiana by the French government after the suppression of the Paris Commune as 'respecting human rights'. Capitalism can only be considered within the framework of the liberal model after World War II when the fascist alternative disappeared. Today, the communist alternative is vanishing. There are, then, unquestionable and serious arguments for liberal historiosophy but that historiosophy is also obviously powerless when applied to the whole of the earlier social history of mankind. All in all, the range of the explanatory power of the liberal model is limited to one line of development of human societies, at the very end of the last of its known stages.

Liberalism explains those phenomena which have falsified Marxist historiosophy. That historiosophy turned out to be incapable of explaining the contemporary stage of the evolution of capitalism. Nevertheless, Marxism, managed to also explain the earlier stages of capitalism, the pre-capitalist formations of the European civilization, the Asiatic line of development (the very concept of an "Asiatic formation" was introduced by Marx, while the theory was created by Karl August Wittfogel (1957), who can also be considered to have worked in the Marxist tradition), and the nature of primitive societies. Maurice Godelier (1978) has created one of the most interesting concepts of those societies. It is not my claim that all those explanations are correct. I have actually questioned the Marxian explanations of the Western line of development (Nowak 1979; 1983). However, when we examine the correspondences among theories, we do not look for truth but want to compare the ranges of their explanatory power. That comparison does not favor liberal historiosophy – in fact, the range of the explanatory power of Marxist historiosophy is incomparably greater.[2] From the cognitive point of view, the declarations that there are no alternatives to liberalism are groundless. Whether they are justified from another perspective – for example, the normative and/or political one – is a question which must remain unanswered in a text which aspires to be scientific.

4   The Phenomenon of Doctrinal Renunciation

The most surprising thing about liberal historiosophy, though, is the mere fact of its existence, because the methodology of liberalism excludes the possibility of a historiosophy as a realm of reliable theoretical reflection. In every theoretical orientation, its methodology and the theories constructed on the basis of that methodology must remain in agreement – otherwise the inadequacies of a theory could always be explained away as resulting from the use of a wrong methodology, and the falsification of that theory would be postponed *ad calendas Graecas*. Meanwhile, liberal historiosophy is not, by any means, compliant

---

2   The weight of the issue of the relations among the explanatory powers of competing theories will become completely clear when one realizes that the greater the set of the facts explained (correctly or not) by a theory, the more credible it is. That rule is explained in various ways depending on the methodology. In Popper's hypothetism (Popper 1959), it is said that the more general a theory, the more controvertible it is, that is, the easier it is to refute it if it is really false. Another reason why we can say that the credibility of a theory grows in proportion to its generality concerns the interpretation of the cases which confirm the theory. Let fact s from field D be interpreted within the framework of theory T as its confirmation. When theory T', which is more general in the given field than theory T, is constructed, then the same fact s is, justifiably, interpreted differently, as a confirmation of T' but not of T. The wider the range of the explanations presented by a theory, the better that theory perceives the actual – for example, historical – role of facts. The generality of the theory makes it possible to avoid mistakes regarding the understanding of facts or the inevitable errors made when those facts are considered in the categories of a theory of more local range.

For example, within the framework of Marxian historical materialism, the success of socialist revolutions in Russia, China, or Yugoslavia was interpreted as a confirmation of the Marxian theory of revolution, or more precisely, of the thesis that socialism can be achieved by way of a revolution. The matter looks different from the point of view of the theory of revolution in non-Marxian historical materialism. The said revolutions are interpreted as civil loops in which the victory of the masses allows the revolutionary elites to enter the old structures of power, and the overthrowing of the bourgeoisie allows for their transformation into a class of triple lords. According to that concept, civil loops occur throughout history, not only during the transition to socialism. As they become an argument for a more general theory of revolution, the same events ease to prove the accuracy of the less general conceptualization – they even seem to contradict that framework.

with the methodology advocated by liberalism.[3] That methodology, as practiced by prominent proponents of liberalism, such as Isaiah Berlin (1984), Karl Popper (1957), or Leszek Kołakowski (1978), did not allow for the possibility of determining any laws of history, that is, for the possibility of constructing a theory of the historical process (historiosophy).

In Popper's words:

> we must reject the possibility of a *theoretical history*, that is, a historical social science which would be a counterpart of *theoretical physics*. There can be no scientific theory of historical development serving as a basis for historical prediction.
> POPPER 1957, p. VI[4]

The idea of the global engineering of forms of government was rejected because of such theses. Those issues were the leitmotif of countless studies critical of the historiosophy of Marxism and the political practice of communism, supposedly based on Marxism.[5] However, as soon as neoliberalism became a dominant ideological orientation, it transpired that the law of history (LH) which says that every society is developing in the direction of liberal capitalism and which makes it possible to predict history was possible; today, every journalist who announces that capitalism is the only self-developing form of government – and that whenever it is rejected, it is reborn, like the phoenix from its own ashes – makes such predictions. Also, the historiosophy of 'the

---

3 Within that meaning, Marxist historiosophy, for example, is methodologically consistent, at least according to one interpretation (see: Nowak 1971) which says that it is based on idealizational methodology postulating that a scientific theory be constructed as a series of models, from the most idealized one, through less idealized models which take into account more and more of the previously omitted factors, to a model which is considered to be sufficiently realistic and is tested against the accessible historical data. That is, indeed, the structure of Marxist historiosophy. The basic model comprises certain simple formulas – for example, about the adaptation of the relations of production to the achieved level of technology – which are binding for an isolated society with a constant level of technology, with only two economic classes, etc. It is only the later, more realistic models that take into account technological progress (Buczkowski 1981; 1982b; Łastowski 1978; 1982), intersocietal relations (Buczkowski 1982a), political power (Buczkowski, Klawiter, Nowak 1982), etc. That conceptual framework is – at least according to one interpretation – methodologically consistent: it is based on the declared methodology of 'going from the abstract to the concrete'.
4 I have made a critical analysis of the argumentation on which Popper based that thesis (see: Nowak 1991a, pp. 243–246, in English: Nowak 1987, pp. 4–6 [editorial note]).
5 I have presented my arguments for the thesis that the practice of systems of triple rule makes use of Marxism as an ideology and not a 'social technology' in Nowak 1991c, pp. 306–316.

end of history' (after the liberal ideal has been reached) has turned out to be possible. The popularity of this thesis put forth by Francis Fukuyama is doubtless attributable to the philosopher's attunement to the common sentiments of proponents of liberalism who had always silently assumed that this thesis was true.[6] Thus, it became apparent that liberal methodology involves double standards: "historiosophy is inadmissible, only my historiosophy is admissible." Liberalism proved to be a methodologically inconsistent theoretical orientation which uses various methodologies in different historical circumstances: first, it prohibits historiosophy, next, it admits one, namely, its own.

Only a person who knows the order of refutation in science will have a proper understanding of how enormously inconsistent liberalism has been. Whenever facts appear which contradict an established theory, they are initially reinterpreted so as to prevent a falsification of that theory; such an operation remains useful for as long as the theory is still weakly concretized. The theory is only rejected if, despite an advanced process of concretization, falsifiers are still being discovered, and/or a reinterpretation of old falsifiers leads to inconsistencies within the framework of that theory. Even at that stage, the methodology which constitutes the theoretical orientation remains undisturbed. The methodology is only rejected at the very end – when the theories generated by it are constantly falsified; it is only questioned at the end. Liberalism, however, questioned its own methodology at the outset.

That is undoubtedly a phenomenon of a cognitive nature, although it concerns a social theory. Let us note, however, that liberalism is not the only example of such phenomena – we can observe many of them. The dominant orientation of the Polish ideological sphere in the last two decades has undergone a surprising evolution. It began from the anarchism of the Workers' Defense Committee,[7] the ideological patron of which was Edward Abramowski, who propagated his idea of the "construction of a society outside of the state." It was that tradition that gave rise to the slogan "Let us not burn committees but create them!"[8] The next stage, in 1980–81, was the state-creating social

---

6 For a wider justification of the thesis that liberalism silently assumes a historiosophy see: Nowak 1991b, pp. 263–278; 2021 (editorial note).
7 The Workers' Defense Committee (*Komitet Obrony Robotników*, abbreviated to KOR) was a civil oppositional organization formed to provide aid to prisoners and their families after the workers protests in June 1976. In 1977 this structure was reorganized into the Committee for Social Self-Defense 'KOR' (*Komitet Samoobrony Społecznej KOR*) and during the I National Convention of Delegates of the Independent Self-Governing Trade Union "Solidarność" in 1981, the Committee was dissolved [editorial note].
8 This slogan, popular among Polish oppositional circles in the second half of 1970, was invented by Jacek Kuroń, one of the activists of the Workers' Defense Committee [editorial note].

democracy of that orientation. Here, the last echo of anarchism was the idea of a "Self-Governing Republic" from 1981[9]; that orientation remained within the widely understood socialist thought for many years to come, but in the fall of 1989, it turned to purely liberal monetarism, and it accepted liberal historiosophy: "the time for social democracy will come when we have constructed capitalism," said the author of the slogan about the creation of citizens' committees. All that happened without any public discussions which might reveal the reasons for those surprising turn-abouts. The circles of the Democratic Union[10] – to which I was referring – are not, obviously, an exception in that respect. In Poland – and probably also in the whole of Central and Eastern Europe – acts of disowning an ideology are an everyday occurrence. For example, the Catholic church initially proposed the socializing ideology of the 'third road' in which labor– that is, working people – and not ownership rights was viewed as the foundation of the human community, but today, the church hardly ever mentions work and the working masses, while it remembers its ownership rights very well. The road of the Church from *Laborem exercens* to contemporary conservatism – which is far to the right from liberalism, as exemplified by such groups as the Christian National Union[11] – is another example of a drastic disownment of an ideology. Needless to say, the communists had stopped taking their ideas seriously a long time before their fall.

In a word, we are living in the times of doctrinal renunciations. The liberal renunciation is just one of many. How can we explain this phenomenon?

The word 'explain' has two meanings. One of them is to derive (according to the principles of the assumed methodology) a description of a phenomenon from the accepted statements. The other, weaker meaning is to conceptualize a phenomenon by means of the used conceptual framework. We will call the second operation a clarification. A clarification presupposes a conceptualization, but it is not the other way round (if one does not have at one's disposal an explanatory theory). That is the case with non-Marxian historical materialism: it allows one to clarify the phenomenon of ideological renunciations, but – for reasons I will discuss below – does not explain it.

---

9   The popular and unofficial title of the program of the Independent Self-Governing Trade Union "Solidarność" adopted at the I National Convention of Delegates in October 1981 [editorial note].

10 The Democratic Union (*Unia Demokratyczna*, UD) was a centrist liberal Catholic party founded in 1991 by Tadeusz Mazowiecki. In 1994 the Democratic Union merged with the Liberal Democratic Congress into the Union of Freedom (*Unia Wolności*, UW).

11 The Christian National Union (*Zjednoczenie Chrześcijańsko-Narodowe*, ZChN) was a conservative, nationalist and Catholic party founded in October 1989 [editorial note].

5   The Basis of Conceptualization: Categorial Ontology

Since the conceptual framework I rely on in this article has already been published, it is not necessary to present it in this text. It constitutes a categorial ontology (discussed in greater detail in Nowak 1977; 1978) and will be assumed here. I will only discuss the very beginning because it was changed in later works (see, for example, Nowak 1989). The starting point is the concept of essentiality which is defined as follows:[12] magnitude B is essential on object x for magnitude A if and only if the fact that B adopts value b for object x excludes the possibility that A adopts values $a_1, ..., a_n$ on the object x (the range of the exclusion of A by B on x, in short, $excl_A(B, x)$). When $n = 0$, then the range of the exclusion $excl_A(B, x)$ is empty, and B is inessential for A on x; when n is equal to the power of the set of the values of magnitude A minus one, then that range of exclusion is maximal, and B is an unequivocal determinant of A on x. Usually, however, magnitudes are only partially significant for each other.

The ratio between the size of the range of the exclusion of A by B on x and the size of the set of all values of magnitude A is the degree of the impact B has on A on object x; in short, $W_A(B, x)$. Magnitude B is more essential for magnitude A on object x than magnitude C when the degree of the impact B has on magnitude A on object x is greater than the degree of the impact C has on magnitude A on that object.

Those definitions make it possible to recreate the typical notions of categorial ontology: the essential structure (the hierarchy of essential factors), the distinction between the real (consisting of at least two factors of various essentiality for the defined) and degenerate (consisting of a set of equally essential factors) essential structure of a phenomenon; the categorial transformation (the change of the value of a magnitude as a result of a transformation of the essential structure of that magnitude); the categorial process of a given phenomenon (the series of categorial transformations of that phenomenon); the categorial differentiation of the phenomenon (the class of objects on which the phenomenon occurs and which is divided into subclasses in which it is defined by different essential structures; a categorial differentiation is a set of simultaneous but different categorial transformations of a phenomenon); the categorial unification of a phenomenon (a process which is reverse to differentiation); and the categorial history of a phenomenon (a set of differentiations and/or unifications to which the phenomenon is subjected).

---

12   That definition contains a correction of Paprzycka, Paprzycki (1992), added to the initial definition from Nowak (1989). For other corrections, see: Kuokkanen, Tuomivaara (1992).

I would like to add some new notions to this conceptual apparatus. The starting point is the observation that a categorial transition from one real essential structure to another usually – perhaps always – takes place through leveling out the significance of factors, that is, through a degenerate essential structure. At that stage, the phenomenon is balanced with respect to essentiality – none of its determinants overpowers any other. Accidental circumstances determine what happens in that state, that is, what value a given magnitude will have. Typically, such circumstances do not have an influence on a magnitude; they only gain it when the significant magnitudes paralyze, in a way, the impact of one another. In such a situation, a 'small change' (a circumstance which is accidental with respect to a given phenomenon) has a 'great impact' (it causes a qualitative change, that is, the consolidation of the new essential structure for the appropriate magnitude), or, rather, 'small changes' lead to many 'great results'. In various realizations of a given phenomenon, various accidental circumstances can bring about various changes consisting in the consolidation of the diverse essential structures of the given magnitude. Obviously, those structures must have mutually exclusive ranges, otherwise they would not be contradictory. Therefore, the thesis that categorial transformations take place according to the scheme consisting of a real essential structure followed by a degenerate essential structure, followed by a real essential structure makes it possible to explain where categorial differentiations come from. They result from the fact that a given phenomenon loses its balance of significance (in various ways because it happens under the influence of various accidental circumstances). In such a state, the proverbial flapping of the wings of a butterfly can result in very serious consequences. Still, it will only happen in those special states. Accidents undeniably have an impact on objective processes – but only if they occur when there is a balance of the significance of the appropriate phenomena. Otherwise, they are irrelevant.

6   Regular Causality and Chaotic Causality

The notes above can be treated as a purely intuitive sketch of a correction of categorial ontology, which takes into account the idea that small causes lead to great results, which idea has recently gained the support of such theories as chaos theory. The very fruitfulness of the applications of that theory in scientific research appears to prove that ideas like 'small changes have a great impact' encompass an aspect of the causal relationship which has, indeed, been ignored in the classical approach to causality assumed in science. That does not mean that the classical approach must simply be rejected. What sane person, for example, would like to claim that the 'butterfly effect' can, let us say, reverse the current economic recession? It does, however, mean that the classical approach must somehow be corrected.

The concept of a cause is usually related to the intuition that from among all the determinants of a given phenomenon, the reason for its existence is the appearance of that determinant which, added to all the other determinants, transforms them into a condition which is sufficient for the occurrence of that phenomenon. In short, the cause is the determinant which completes the existing conditions in such a way that the phenomenon comes into existence. This concept can be explicated in the categorial apparatus in the following manner:

Let there be period of time T consisting of moments $t_1, ..., t_n$. Let the considered phenomenon F consists in the change of magnitude F on object a at moment t_n (in short: $\Delta_n F(a)$). Let there be a $m+1$ element set of factors, essential for magnitude F. Let suppose that m elements of that set on object a in the whole period of time T (they constitute the conditions of phenomenon F, in short, $U(a, T)$). We will now say that change $\Delta_{n-1} H(a)$ is the reason for change $\Delta_n F(a)$ in conditions $U(a, T)$ if and only if $excl_U (F, a) + excl_H (F, a) = Z_F - \{a\}$, where z_F is the range of the determined magnitude F. This means that adding the impact of H on F to the constant influence of conditions U on F results in the state of unequivocal determination of phenomenon F.

The considerations from the previous section make it possible to distinguish between two types of causes. Cause $\Delta_{n-1} H(a)$ is a regular cause of change $\Delta_n F(a)$ in conditions $U(a, T)$ where, with the established threshold ε, $\Delta_{n-1} H(a) \leq \varepsilon$ entails $\Delta_n F(a) \leq \varepsilon$. That condition assumes that $W_U (F, a) < W_H(F, a)$, that is, that the impact of H on F is greater than the total impact of all the remaining determinants (conditions). Cause $\Delta_{n-1} H(a)$ is a chaotic (accidental) cause of the change of $\Delta_n F(a)$ in conditions $U(a, T)$, when, with the established threshold ε, $\Delta_{n-1} H(a) \leq \varepsilon$ entails $\Delta_n F(a) >> \varepsilon$.

Given these assumptions, the thesis of categorial ontology which says that a qualitative transformation (of the essential structure of a phenomenon) always occurs through a state of balance of essential factors (degeneration of the essential structure) leads to the following image of causal relations:

a. during the existence of the real essential structure of a given phenomenon, causal relations are regular; in other words, the classical concept of causality applies: 'small changes have a small impact', and 'butterflies' can flap their wings to their hearts' content, without any serious effects;

b. in transitional periods of time, when the essential structure which influences the phenomenon is degenerate, and when accidental circumstances determine which possible actual essential structure will replace the existing one; only then do causal relations become chaotic, and only then do 'small changes have a great impact'; at those times, classical causality loses value;

c. when any accidental circumstance decides that this and not another one of the possible categorial transformations of the phenomenon will take place, and when the new essential structure solidifies, causal relations once again become regular, and the classical concept of causality regains its binding power.

Such a model of causal relations appears to be binding, at least in social history.

7 The Problem of the Laws of History

The extended in this way categorial ontology[13] makes it possible to present anew, in comparison to the initial approach (Nowak 1977), the issue of the laws of history in the following form: phenomenon Z leads to phenomenon Z' (where the essential structure of Z' is different to that of Z). The occurrence of a categorial differentiation does not, on its own, contradict the existence of laws of history, as long as that differentiation is subsequently unified. If, then, Z transforms into set of phenomena $Z, ..., Z_n$ (differentiation), and they, in turn, transform into phenomenon Z' (unification), we can say that the differentiation is balanced, and the law of history which transforms Z into Z' is preserved.

That observation allows us to distinguish the following views regarding the nature of the laws of history:

(i)   (t) every categorial history only contains balanced differentiations (historical determinism),

(ii) (tt) some categorial histories contain some unbalanced differentiations (historical indeterminism).

There are four varieties of the indeterministic view:

(tt_1) some categorial histories only contain unbalanced differentiations (extensionally moderate and intentionally radical historical indeterminism),

---

[13]   The fact that in this text, I work on the material of categorial ontology does not mean that I now treat this concept as the right philosophy. For some time, I have been inclined toward another concept, so-called unitarian metaphysics (Nowak 1991e; 1992; 1995). It is a different conceptual framework, but it retains certain ideas of categorial ontology, and, to a degree, constitutes a generalization of its conceptual structure (Nowak 1992, pp. 42–44, note 10). Since it is much simpler and since the basic metaphysical problems are irrelevant for the issues discussed in this article, I use that conceptual structure of categorial ontology here, in a somewhat instrumental manner.

(tt_2) all categorial histories contain balanced differentiations and unbalanced differentiations (extensionally radical and intentionally moderate historical indeterminism),

(tt_3) some categorial histories contain balanced differentiations and unbalanced differentiations (extensionally and intentionally moderate historical indeterminism),

(tt_4) all categorial histories only contain unbalanced differentiations (extensionally and intentionally radical historical indeterminism).

How can we choose one of those four positions? Referring to the so-called historical facts will not be helpful because we never make use of them, we only make use of their theoretical interpretations (Topolski 1968). It is better, then, to refer to a theory of the historical process – considered to be a credible one – from the start in order to determine which of the positions stated above it assumes. My basis for the comparison here is non-Marxian historical materialism (Nowak 1979; 1983; 1991a).

Some revolutions are an example of balanced differentiations. The thesis of Model I of the theory of power is that political revolutions of the first type invariably lead political systems to the stage of totalism, regardless of who wins – the authorities or the masses. In the latter case, of a civil loop, totalization is only postponed. A revolution, then, is a categorial differentiation because, in revolutionary conditions, both sides have a chance to win and, in that model, the victory of one side over the other is only determined by accidental factors, including the leaders' personality. In Model I, it is a balanced differentiation because each result of the revolution (political, of the first kind) lead to this same long term outcome. .

If one accepts non-Marxian historical materialism, that observation is enough to falsify the thesis of radical indeterminism (tt_4) and the thesis of extensionally moderate but intentionally radical indeterminism (tt_3). The remaining options are historical determinism (t) and variants of indeterminism (tt_2)–(tt_3).

Wars are an example of unbalanced differentiations in non-Marxian historical materialism (Model v of the theory of power, see: Nowak 1991c, pp. 187–194; Nowak 1991d, pp. 139–146). A war is a categorial differentiation, and the result of a war, in the case of societies with balanced potentials, depends (in Model v, see: Nowak 1991c, pp. 187–194) on accidental circumstances. That result, in turn, significantly differentiates the development paths of societies subject to aggression. When a society resists aggression, it stays on the standard road of development – determined by the relations among political classes. When a society is conquered, it transitions to the stage of totalization. In the theory of power discussed here, then, that differentiation is unbalanced.

Thus, non-Marxian historical materialism excludes the position of historical determinism. It also excludes position (tt_2) of extensionally radical and intentionally moderate radical indeterminism. There remains moderate indeterminism (tt_3), which is, indeed, tacitly assumed in the conceptual structure of non-Marxian historical materialism. The position of moderate indeterminism is credible insofar as that concept is credible.

8 Social Transformation in non-Marxian Historical Materialism

There remains the question as to what, in the light of non-Marxian historical materialism, is a political transformation in the conditions of an existing system of triple rule. Undoubtedly, it is a differentiation (Nowak 1993) because it is claimed that a triple rule can transform in the following ways:

(a) The first option is that the system of triple rule is restored. This can happen, for example, as a result of a victorious revolution against the power of the new elites. Like every revolution, it would only cause a change of the rulers' clothing. In a social void (especially without the bourgeoisie), it would lead to the new revolutionary authorities' triple rule. That possibility, particularly during an economic crisis, is not always excluded.

(b) It may also happen that the spiritual power will be separated, and that it will rest on the independence of the church – there will be double, political and economic rule. If the state does not yield to the church hierarchy and maintains – or, in the future, regains – economic power, such a turn of events is possible.

(c) Thirdly, the economic power can be separated from the state, and the bourgeoisie can come into existence, while political rulers will be subjected to spiritual power. The end result of such a process would be a system of double, political and spiritual rule.

(d) Finally, the economy and culture can be simultaneously separated from political power, which entails the emergence of a society of the Western type with separate political power, ownership, and culture.

The temporary interests of those social categories which – like workers in the big industries – have had certain relative privileges in socialism lead toward possibility (*a*). The interest of the state apparatus, which has incomparably greater power over citizens when it has the economic means of controlling their behavior, leads toward possibility (*b*). The interest of the church hierarchy leads toward possibility (*c*). Only the class of owners is interested in the creation of a class society, that is, in possibility (*d*).

As regards predicting the possible unification of those alternatives, the theoretical possibilities of non-Marxian historical materialism are rather limited. The range of the application of the last of the theories in that conceptual framework, that is, of the theory of triple rule, is restricted to a system which is happily becoming a thing of the past. As regards the way in which that happens, the prognostic possibilities of the said concept boil down to: alternative (*a*) leads to a restoration of the system of triple rule, perhaps under different ideological banners, and then, following the standard development path of such a system (civil revolution, civil loop, totalization, periodical lost civil revolutions), there is a return to the initial situation. The likelihood of either possibility (*b*) or (*d*) becoming a reality cannot be evaluated – at least, not in non-Marxian historical materialism, which is an insufficient tool for that purpose. Doubtless, the interests of the dominant social forces lead in direction (*b*) or (*c*). Unquestionably, too, the 'political class' consciously heads toward possibility (*d*), so one can only ascribe incompatible interests to it but not bad intentions. However, it does not follow that there should be the West in the East. There are still other possibilities.

All in all, in our conditions, a social transformation is an unbalanced differentiation. Therefore, the selection of the road of development depends on accidental circumstances – accidental from the perspective of non-Marxian historical materialism –. It does not mean, let us add, that we could not reduce the number of those possibilities, perhaps even to one, within the framework of a more general theory. In any case, non-Marxian historical materialism is too weak for that. From its point of view, accidental historical circumstances will decide about the direction of the development of such countries as Poland.

9 A Conceptualization of the Phenomenon of Doctrinal Renunciations

It becomes understandable why non-Marxian historical materialism cannot explain the phenomenon of doctrinal renunciations which are so characteristic of the time we are living in. We can, though, conceptualize that phenomenon. The actors on our political scene, such as the political elites which represent the church hierarchy, the bourgeoisie, or the state apparatus, appear to understand that they are in a new, unprecedented situation. Their actions so far can hardly be viewed as shaping history. The revolution of 1980–81 was not brought about by the creation of the Confederation of Independent Poland,[14]

---

14 Confederation of Independent Poland (*Konfederacja Polski Niepodległej*, KPN) was an oppositional political party founded on 1 September 1979 by Leszek Moczulski. In its

or the Pope's visit, or even the activity of the Workers' Defense Committee but by the efforts of millions of people, and then, when the strikes happened in 1988, the threat of a reignition of that revolution made the communist party relinquish power in 1989.[15] The elites were only significant insofar as they organized and doctrinally rationalized mass movements. Nowadays, the situation is different – the masses are a 'great mute'. Consequently, the elites, which used to be a decorative element in history, suddenly became instrumental in the course of events: it began to matter what they believed, which of them won which election in the world of great politics isolated from the rest of the society, etc.[16] In those circumstances, the 'flapping of the wings of a butterfly' can, indeed, be the critical determinant of the direction in which our country will move: toward a liberal class society or a Catholic system of double – political and spiritual – rule (a 'confessional state'). With such a historical value at stake, virtues like disciplined thinking, openly expressing and changing one's views, or being honest with one's proponents become less important. Much is excused when the goal is to increase the odds of that turn of events occurring which is considered to be beneficial to the country.

---

program, the party was committed to Poland regaining its independence, and it continued the political thought of Józef Piłsudski [editorial note].

15 Obviously, it is possible to explain the course of the events in Eastern Europe in a different way, for example, with the argument – which has been expressed for a long time – that the economy of socialist systems is inefficient (for example, Meissner 1976, Kornai 1983). Undoubtedly, that is a fact, but the historical role of that fact depends on the accepted historiosophical option. From the Marxist (or neo-Marxist, for example, Habermas 1976) perspective, that is a crucial fact. From the perspective of non-Marxian historical materialism, that is a secondary fact which can be derived from the internal regularities of political power (see: Nowak 1991c, 87–104), although it is also influential on its own, too (Tomczak 1988). One should add here that the results of empirical studies also indicate that economic development in the history of socialism depended on political events (Jermakowicz 1985).

16 That kind of abstraction is inadmissible within the framework of historical idealism, for which communism is the effect of the realization of a social utopia (for example, Berdyaev 1937). After all, the correctness of the direction of idealization should be verified on the basis of theoretical and not speculative arguments. That means that the accuracy of an ideological view can be confirmed if we can understand more of the actual history of socialism while we omit the nature of class interests and take into account the ideological content. If, then, we can understand more about that system while we omit what is written on communist banners and take into account the hidden interests of the triple rule, that constitutes an argument against idealism. I have already had an opportunity to present my arguments concerning that matter (Nowak 1991c).

10   Cognitive Rationality vs. Political Rationality

What does this prove? It shows the political rationality of the elites which change their views according to the circumstances. That is a normal and, to an extent, desirable characteristic in politics, at least from the point of view of the proponents of the final ideological transformation. However, political rationality is not cognitive rationality. Science should be more stable than politicians: instead of becoming more unanimous than political circles, it should present a spectrum of theoretical alternatives. The more so as – as I have been trying to show – in the described case, a plurality of views is required not only because of the very nature of the cognitive process but because of the nature of reality. Pluralism of thought in social science, then, is necessitated by not only epistemic but also ontological arguments. Still, those arguments are – in the here and for now – unanimous. Why? Because they are under the influence of politics dominated by liberal historiosophy. But science is not the same as politics – it is subservient to truth. And that 'trite but true' conclusion is what I would like to end this article with because what would have to be added, from this point on, would belong to the realm of publicism and not science.

References

Berdyaev, N. (1937). *Problem komunizmu* [The Problem of Communism]. Translated by M. Reutt. Warsaw: Rój.

Berlin, I. (1984). *Four Essays on Liberty*. Oxford: Oxford University Press.

Buczkowski, P. (1981). *Z teorii społeczeństw ekonomicznych* [From the Theory of Economic Societies]. Szczecin: Wyd. PAM.

Buczkowski, P. (1982a). International Relations in the Adaptive Interpretation of Historical Materialism. In: L. Nowak, ed. *Social Classes Action and Historical Materialism Poznań Studies in the Philosophy of the Sciences and the Humanities*, vol. 6, pp. 295–312. Amsterdam: Rodopi.

Buczkowski, P. (1982b). Toward a Theory of Economic Society: An Attempt at the Adaptive Interpretation. In: L. Nowak, ed. *Social Classes Action and Historical Materialism Poznań Studies in the Philosophy of the Sciences and the Humanities*, vol. 6, pp. 158–210, Amsterdam: Rodopi.

Buczkowski, P., A. Klawiter, and L. Nowak. (1982). Historical Materialism as a Theory of the Social Whole. In: L. Nowak (ed.) *Social Classes Action and Historical Materialism. Poznań Studies in the Philosophy of the Sciences and the Humanities,* vol. 6, pp. 236–280. Amsterdam: Rodopi.

Godelier, M. (1978). *Perspectives in Marxist Anthropology.* Cambridge: Cambridge University Press.

Habermas, J. (1976). *Legitimation Crisis.* London: Heinemann.

Jermakowicz, W. (1985). *Das wirtschaftliche Lenkungssystem Polens.* Marburg: Herder-Institut.

Kołakowski, L. (1978). *Main Currents of Marxism: Its Origins, Growth and Dissolution.* Oxford: Oxford University Press.

Kornai, J. (1983). *The Economics of Shortage.* Amsterdam: NHPC.

Kuokkanen, M., T. Tuomivaara (1992). On the Structure of Idealizations: Explorations in the Poznań School Methodology of Science. In: J. Brzeziński and L. Nowak (eds.). *Idealization III: Approximation and Truth. Poznań Studies in the Philosophy of the Sciences and the Humanities,* vol. 25, pp. 67–102. Amsterdam/Atlanta: Rodopi.

Łastowski, K. (1978). *Problem analogii teorii rozwoju gatunków i materializmu historycznego* [The Problem of the Analogy between the Theory of the Development of Species and of Historical Materialism]. *Warsaw – Poznań:* PWN.

Łastowski, K. (1982). The Theory of Development of Species and the Theory of Motion of Socio-Economic Formation. In: L. Nowak, ed., *Social Classes, Action and Historical Materialism Poznań Studies in the Philosophy of the Sciences and the Humanities,* vol. 6, pp. 122–157. Amsterdam: Rodopi.

Meissner, B. (1976). *Das Sowjetsystem und seine Wandlungsmöglichkeiten.* Bern: Schweizerisches Ost-Institut.

Nowak, L. (1971). *U podstaw Marksowskiej metodologii nauk* [The Foundations of Marxian Methodology of Science]. Warsaw: PWN.

Nowak, L. (1977). *U podstaw dialektyki Marksowskiej. Próba interpretacji kategorialnej* [The Foundations of Marxian Dialectics. An Attempt at a Categorial Interpretation]. Warsaw: PWN.

Nowak, L. (1978). *U podstaw ontologii kategorialnej* [The Foundations of Categorial Ontology]. Manuscript.

Nowak, L. (1979). Historical Momentums and Formations: A Contribution to non-Marxian Historical Materialism. *Kritik und Analyse* 1, 60–76.

Nowak, L. (1983). *Property and Power. Towards a non-Marxian Historical Materialism.* Dordrecht/Boston/Lancaster: Reidel.

Nowak, L. (1987). A Model of Socialist Society. *Studies in Soviet Thought,* 34 (1), 1–55.

Nowak, L. (1989). On the Idealizational Nature of Economic Theories, *Erkenntnis,* 30, 225–246.

Nowak, L. (1991abc). *U podstaw teorii socjalizmu* [The Foundations of the Theory of Socialism]; vol. 1: Własność i władza. O konieczności socjalizmu [Property and Power. On the Necessity of Socialism]; vol. 2: *Droga do socjalizmu. O konieczności socjalizmu w Rosji* [The Road to Socialism. On the Necessity of Socialism in Russia]; vol. 3: *Dynamika władzy. O strukturze i konieczności zaniku socjalizmu*

[The Dynamics of Power. On the Structure and Necessity of the Disappearance of Socialism]. Poznań: Nakom.

Nowak, L. (1991d). *Power and Civil Society: Toward a Dynamic Theory of Real Socialism*, translated by K. Sawala. New York: Greenwood Press.

Nowak, L. (1991e). Thoughts Are Facts in Possible Worlds, Truths Are Facts of a Given World. *Dialectica*, 45, 273–287.

Nowak, L. (1992). Myśl o czymś jest tym właśnie. Nie ma więc teorii bytu i teorii poznania: jest metafizyka [A Thought about Something is that Thing. Consequently, there is no Theory of Being and Theory of Cognition: There Is Metaphysics]. In: J. Brzeziński, K. Łastowski, T. Maruszewski (eds.) *O związkach teoretycznych w filozofii nauki i psychologii*, vol 12, pp. 17–63. Warsaw – Poznań: PWN.

Nowak, L. (1993). The Downfall of Real Socialism? An Analysis of a Myth. *Social Theory and Practice* 19 (4). 249–272.

Nowak, L. (1994). O zagadnieniu tak zwanej transformacji ustrojowej [The Problem of the So-Called Social Transformation]. In: K. Zamiara (ed.), *Społeczna transformacja w refleksji humanistycznej*, pp. 117-129. Poznań: Wyd. UAM.

Nowak, L. (1995). O pojęciu nicości [On the Concept of Nothingness]. In: J. Paśniczek (ed.) Między logiką a etyką. Studia z logiki, ontologii, epistemologii, metodologii, semiotyki i etyki. Prace ofiarowane Profesorowi Leonowi Kojowi, pp. 107–121. Lublin: Wyd. UMCS.

Nowak, L. (2022). Hegel and Liberalism: on the Issue of the Nature of Historiosophy. In: K. Brzechczyn (ed.), *New Developments in Theory of Historical Process. Polish Contributions to Non-Marxian Historical Materialism. Poznań Studies in the Philosophy of the Sciences and the Humanities*, vol. 119, pp. 57–76. Leiden/Boston: Brill.

Paprzycki, M. and K. Paprzycka (1992) A Note on the Unitarian Explication of Idealization. In: J. Brzeziński and L. Nowak (eds.) *Idealization III: Approximation and Truth. Poznań Studies in the Philosophy of the Sciences and the Humanities*, vol. 25, pp. 279–81. Amsterdam/Atlanta: Rodopi.

Popper, K. R. (1957). *The Poverty of Historicism*. London: Routledge and Kegan Paul.

Popper, K. R. (1959). *The Logic of Scientific Discovery*. London: Hutchinson.

Rawls, J. (1971). *A Theory of Justice*. Oxford: Oxford University Press.

Tomczak, G. (1988). The Economic Collapse in Two Models of Socio-economic Formation. In: L. Nowak (ed.) *Dimensions of the Historical Process. Poznań Studies in the Philosophy of the Sciences and the Humanities*, vol. 13, pp. 259–270. Amsterdam: Rodopi.

Topolski, J. (1968). *Metodologia historii* [The Methodology of History]. Warsaw: PWN.

Wittfogel, K. A. (1957). *Oriental Despotism*. New Haven: Yale University Press.

CHAPTER 5

The End of History or Its Repetition?

Leszek Nowak

Abstract

The aim of this paper is to reconstruct the hidden assumptions of the liberal philosophy of history. According to this philosophy, liberal democracy is the natural end of history. The author juxtaposes the liberal philosophy of history with Marxist historiosophy and the vision of the past presupposed by non-Marxian historical materialism, where the prognosis of the totalitarization of capitalism was propounded. The methodological status of this prognosis is considered in the last part of this paper.

Keywords

Capitalism – liberal philosophy of history – non-Marxian historical materialism – totalitarization

The dominant historiosophy in our part of the world today is the historiosophy of the liberal "end of history."[1] This asserts that liberal capitalism is a natural state of a society, in the sense that every society manifests a spontaneous tendency toward democracy and the free market. This trend can be restrained by force, but the result of such an effort will only slow down the arrival of this natural state. When a given society reaches the stage of liberal capitalism, it remains in it. Social history ends with this natural state.

However, contrary to this common belief, there is an alternative to liberal historiosophy, which becomes apparent when we compare it with Marxist historiosophy.[2] Put very briefly, we could say that social history comprises three lines of development: on the one hand, the line of primitive societies – from

---

[1] The paper appears in English translation for the first time. The Polish original „Koniec historii czy jej powtórka?" was published in: W. Heller (ed.), *Świat jako proces* (Poznań: Wydawnictwo Instytutu Filozofii UAM, 1996), pp. 31–40. The abstract and key words have been added by the editor.

[2] I discuss this issue in more detail in: Nowak (1994; in English: 2022 [editorial note]).

which the line of non-European civilizations (for example, Inca or Chinese) derives – and, on the other hand, the line of the Western civilization. All of them endure until now, in a more or less residual form (the so-called primitive societies which exist today or some societies of the 'third world'). As regards primitive societies, Asiatic despotisms, etc., liberal historiosophy can only say that neither the former nor the latter have learned, as yet, that the optimal human institutions are parliamentary democracy and the free market. Since those societies have various forms of government, economic relations, etc., the above statement has no value. Liberal historiosophy only applies to the third line of development – the Western civilization. Still, it does not, by any means, apply to the whole of it. For example, with regard to feudal societies or the societies of ancient Rome, liberal historiosophy can only say that although they did not figure out liberal capitalism, they were still 'going in that direction.' Incidentally, such a view of history is dangerously close to 'teleology' which is strongly condemned so much in Marxism. Liberal historiosophy, then, is only confirmed by capitalism – especially in the most modern times. Liberalism explains those phenomena which have falsified Marxist historiosophy. This historiosophy turned out to be incapable of explaining the contemporary stage of the evolution of capitalism. It did, however, also explain the pre-capitalist formations of the European civilization, the Asiatic line of development (the very concept of an 'Asiatic formation' was introduced by Marx, while the theory was created by Karl August Wittfogel (1957), who is also considered to have worked in the Marxist tradition), and the nature of primitive societies. Maurice Godelier (1978) authored one of the most interesting theories of those societies.[3] It is not my claim that all those explanations are correct. I have actually questioned the Marxian explanations of the Western line of development (Nowak 1981; 1983). At this moment, I am not focusing on the truth but on a comparison of the areas of explanatory power. That comparison does not favor liberal historiosophy – actually, the range of the explanatory power of Marxist historiosophy is incomparably greater.[4]

---

3   See also an interesting interpretation of the well-known Friedrich Engels's concept, put forth by Jolanta Burbelka (1980); Burbelka (1982).

4   Of course, when I speak of Marxian historical materialism, I mean a certain interpretation of it. According to that interpretation (see: Nowak 1977; in English: Nowak 1982 [editorial note]), the basic model of that theory consists of certain simple formulas – for example, about the adaptation of the relations of production to the achieved level of technology – which are binding for an isolated society with a constant level of technology and only two economic classes, etc. The influence of technological progress, inter-social relations (Buczkowski 1981: 1982a, etc. was only taken into account in subsequent, more realistic models (Buczkowski 1981; 1982b Łastowski 1981; in English 1982 [editorial note]). That interpretation is not the

The historiosophy of the 'end of history' is questioned not only in Marxian but also – in a different way – in non-Marxian historical materialism. In my work (Nowak 1981; 1983), I have proposed a hypothesis about the totalitarization of capitalism. I suggested that in the conditions of accelerated development of technology, a society with the classes of rulers, owners, and priests (that is, a class society described within the framework of non-Marxian historical materialism) gradually – by way of evolution – transforms into a society with a double class of rulers-owners (according to that concept – into a totalitarian society). That model, as well as several concretizations of it, can be found in the relevant literature (see below). At this point, I would like to discuss the conditions for the verifiability of that hypothesis.

That is all the more necessary as this hypothesis has been questioned several times (see my responses: Nowak 1986; 1987). Recently, Henryk Szabała (1994), while providing a clear report on the theoretical discussion which led, within the framework of the subsequent models of socio-economic formations, to the hypothesis of the totalitarization of capitalism, stated that thist hypothesis had merits within the framework of those theoretical assumptions and expressed doubts as to whether the course of events was, indeed, leading the West toward totalitarianism, to be followed by the rule of triple lords. I am not surprised at that; I myself have doubts about it. It would be difficult not to have them when the global press is writing suggesting the exact opposite: that the whole world is going in the direction of capitalism which prevails in the West now (and let it stay that way forever! – this wish forms the foundation of the commonly held opinion). Whatever the press is saying, *la théorie oblige*. If the hypothesis of the totalitarization of the West is a conclusion drawn from the assumed theory and if that theory has already been confirmed on other grounds (for example, the hypothesis regarding the impending fall of real socialism or on the priority of our country in that process, see: Nowak 1980), then there is no other choice but to also maintain that hypothesis, even if, *prima facie*, it seemed to be very doubtful. This must be done, due to the the fact that if this hypothesis ultimately turns out to be false, that will indicate – as I have already noted (1986, p. 141: 1991a, p. XI, and in other works) – the necessity of revising some basic assumptions of non-Marxian historical materialism, namely, those which generate this hypothesis. That is why I would like to give this matter some more attention.

---

only one; nor is it indisputable (see the critique of it in my books (1981; 1983). Nevertheless, Marxian historical materialism understood in that way is a serious theoretical alternative which clearly surpasses, as we have seen, liberal historiosophy.

The question I would like to consider is: to what degree, taking into account the entirety of the knowledge accessible to us today, has the hypothesis of the totalitarization of capitalism has been confirmed empirically? Although the question whether the West is going in the direction of capitalism is ideologically charged, to the highest degree – after all, that hypothesis is contrary to the dominant liberal historiosophy, according to which democratic capitalism is the 'end of history' – I will try, to the best of my ability, to discuss it in as rational a manner as possible.

Let us begin with the methodological criteria which ought to be considered when forming a hypothesis. The first one is quite obvious:

> (m) Let a certain set of facts be the area to be explained. The hypothesis is the better, the more factors – as different as possible – there are in that set, and the more of them can be explained within the framework of the theory from which the hypothesis has been derived.

According to Karl Popper's methodology, rule (m) must be supplemented with a rule which prohibits *clichés* in science, as rule (m) itself allows the inclusion of obvious, trivial concepts which appear to only be confirmed because they are generated by stereotypes. Hence, another rule is formed:

> (mm) The more unexpected a hypothesis is, within the context of the existing knowledge, the better it is.

Rules (m)–(mm) apply to all scientific hypotheses. For the purposes of our discussion, the rule which pertains to historical hypotheses is especially important:

> (mmm) Let a set of subsequent historical trends to which the system was subject in the course of history be the area to be explained. The more trends, as different as possible, there are in that set and the more of them can be explained by the theory from which the hypothesis has been derived, the stronger the confirmation of that hypothesis with regards to the system.

The theory of capitalism in non-Marxian historical materialism is constructed over the theory of socio-economic formation and consists of five models: a purely materialist model, VP (Nowak 1991a, pp. 221–239, extensions: Tomczak 1989, Brzechczyn 1995, chapter 6; English counterpart 2020, pp. 205–257 [editorial note]), a materialist-institutionalist model, VP*inp*, with political institutions (Nowak

1983, pp. 211–236; Nowak 1991a, pp. 346–353), a materialist-institutionalist model with economic institutions, VP*ine* (Niewiadomski 1989), a materialist- consciousness model, VP*c* (Nowak 1991b, pp. 273–283), and (partially) a model of inter-social relations, VP*m*, which comprises the relations between a capitalist metropolis and supra-class peripheries (Paprzycka and Nowak 1989).

The assumptions of the Model VP give rise to the hypothesis on the totalitarization of a capitalist society. As regards this hypothesis, it turns out that concretizations of that model with respect to the role of the political (model VP*inp*) and economic institutions (model VP*ine*), as well as social consciousness (model VP*c*) retain it, whereas a concretization of that model with respect to the relations between the metropolis and the peripheries (model VP*m*) is irrelevant for it.

In the works quoted above, we can find a rough explanation of a number of historical trends familiar from the history of capitalism. The Model VP makes it possible to explain, among other things:

(1) laborers' revolutions in early capitalism,
(2) the disappearance of the class struggle between the workers and the bourgeoisie,
(3) the reduction of the role of the state in early capitalism,
(4) the cyclical nature of the development of the capitalist economy in the 19th century,
(5) the great crisis of the 1930s,
(6) the coming into existence of the welfare state,
(7) the reduction of the economic cycle to slight variations of the economic situation in post-war capitalism,
(8) the fusion of big business and political structures,
(9) youth protests in the 1960s, and
(10) neoliberalism in the politics of the Western countries in the 1980s.

The Model VP*inp* additionally makes it possible to explain, among other things, that:

(11) a capitalist country assumes the form of a parliamentary democracy,
(12) for some time, there has been a transition of the actual political power, from the legislative to the executive branch.

The Model VP*ine* provides a more in-depth explanation of trends (6)–(8) because of the role of economic organizations, for both owners and laborers. The Model VP*c* additionally makes it possible to explain why:

(13) the consciousness of the working class was dominated by social utopias in the 19th century, and why
(14) it then fell under the influence of social-democratic reformism, and later – of social liberalism, and why

(15) the progressive irrationalization of Western thought in recent decades.
Finally, the Model VP*m* makes it possible to also understand why:
(16) "democracies are less warlike than other regimes" (Rudolph Rummel's thesis, 1985),
(17) capitalist countries of the West went through a stage of colonial conquests, and
(18) capitalist countries have now pulled out of colonialism.

Let us take a look at this collation from the point of view of rules (*m*)–(*mmm*). As shown in the works I refer to, the mere hypothesis of totalitarization makes it possible to explain trends (6)–(10), (12), and (15). Those trends are very diverse – as required by rule (*m*). It also seems to fulfill condition (*mm*), and it is derived from the theory which explains trends from (1) to (18), which are characteristic of the course of the development of capitalism so far.

Surely, the proposed explanations are not 'the only possible ones.' Each of trends (1) to (18) can be, and sometimes is, explained in alternative ways, as each fact can, obviously, be explained in various, non-equivalent ways. For example, the fact that Western countries have pulled out of colonialism (18) can be explained by the development of new techniques of production which require advanced infrastructure. That is a very factual explanation. The question arises, however, of how many phenomena can be explained with the 'development of new techniques of production.' For instance, can you explain in that manner why democracies do not wage wars with one another (16) or why there were students' protests in the 1960s?

Similarly, the coming into existence of a democratic state (11) could be explained, for example, by the influence of democratic political philosophy on the shape of political institutions. How much, though, can be explained by references to the influence of political philosophy? The reception of John Locke's, Jean Jacques Rousseau's, or John Stuart Mill's thought definitely has much in common with the wave of neoliberalism (10) but not with the students' protests (9) or the fusion of great property and the political structures of the West (8). If we combine the Marxist motif of the "development of new techniques of production" with the idealist motif of the influence of political philosophy, it will slightly expand the scope of the explained trends, but the combination itself is an eclectic set of completely different ideas which are difficult to reconcile. In contrast, non-Marxian historical materialism explains all those trends, starting from a uniform theoretical core, so it fulfills the requirements of rules (*m*)–(*mmm*).

Certainly, the list of important historical trends in capitalism, from (1) to (18), is not exhaustive. It would also be easy to find other well-known phenomena which have not, as yet, been explained in non-Marxian historical materialism.

For example, the already mentioned phenomenon of the development of productive forces is not explained by it, but it is entered into the Model VP as a separate assumption. It follows that non-Marxian historical materialism has, as I have written many times (for instance, Nowak 1991b, pp. 231–237), numerous theoretical gaps. That, however, pertains to all social theories.

The explanations of theses (1)–(18) are also, definitely, very perfunctory. Nevertheless, I would still venture to say that that is simply the case in the theory of historical processes. After all, the explanation that capitalism is permanent because it is "the only system which forms spontaneously" is not very subtle.

If I am not wrong, then, it seems that the hypothesis about the totalitarization of capitalism can compete with the hypothesis that capitalism is a natural social system which is the endpoint for all countries, in which they will remain, having once reached it. Then, we can ask about the list of historical trends which can be explained by the latter hypothesis. There surely exist such trends. The leading position on such a list would be occupied by the trend, observed in recent years in the countries of the former Soviet bloc, to imitate the system of parliamentary democracy and of private property. According to rule (mmm), that fact in itself does not suffice – it would have to be supported with explanations of possibly diverse trends from the whole history of capitalism. We can demand that liberal historiosophy find an explanation for the following facts: that a series of workers' revolts occurred in all leading Western countries in the 19th century; that there were regular crises of overproduction occurring through over a century in the leading capitalist countries – when a state was, indeed, but a 'night guard' and when the economy was almost solely a market economy; that there was a similarity between the etatization of economy in the West and the reduction of severe crises of overproduction to relatively mild oscillations in the economic situation; that there were students' movements in the 1960s, etc. I believe that if we required that the explanations be grounded in a theory – just like appropriate explanations in non-Marxian historical materialism – that is, that they refer to the core of liberal historiosophy and not to the theses appended to it *ad hoc*, then many of trends (1)–(18) would turn out to be difficult to explain within the framework of liberal historiosophy.

By that, I do not mean that the hypothesis on the totalitarization of capitalism has been substantiated to a greater degree than the one on the capitalist end of history. Any comparisons, if we were to take them seriously, would require a determination of some common, complete list of trends to be explained, of a comprehensive list of methodological rules of comparison, the acceptance of certain operationalizations of those trends respecting those methodological rules, etc. What I would like to say here is trivial: as there are certain factual arguments for the hypothesis on the totalitarization of capitalism, it is a possible approach to the processes which have been taking place in the West in recent decades. That viewpoint is so moderate that it might, I believe, be accepted by any person who does not mistake the criteria of scientific credibility for the criteria of ideological attractiveness.

References

Brzechczyn, K. (1995). *Procesy kaskadowe w rozwoju historycznym* [Cascade Processes in Historical Development]. A typescript of a doctoral dissertation. Poznań: Instytut Filozofii UAM.

Brzechczyn, K. (2020). *The Historical Distinctiveness of Central Europe: A Study in the Philosophy of History*. Berlin: Peter Lang.

Buczkowski, P. (1981). *Z teorii społeczeństw ekonomicznych* [From the Theory of Economic Societies]. Szczecin: Wyd. PAM.

Buczkowski, P. (1982a). Toward a Theory of Economic Society, An Attempt at the Adaptive Interpretation. In: L. Nowak, (ed.) *Social Classes, Action and Historical Materialism Poznań Studies in the Philosophy of the Sciences and the Humanities*, vol. 6, pp. 158–210, Amsterdam: Rodopi.

Buczkowski, P. (1982b). International Relations in the Adaptive Interpretation of Historical Materialism. In: L. Nowak, ed. *Social Classes, Action and Historical Materialism Poznań Studies in the Philosophy of the Sciences and the Humanities*, vol. 6, pp. 295–312. Amsterdam: Rodopi.

Burbelka, J. (1980). *Epoki i formacje. Próba interpretacji adaptacyjnej* [Epochs and Formations. An Attempt at an Adaptive Interpretation]. Wrocław: Ossolineum.

Burbelka, J. (1982). Historical Materialism. General Theory and Forms. In: L. Nowak (ed.), *Social Classes, Action and Historical Materialism. Poznań Studies in the Philosophy of the Sciences and the Humanities*, vol. 6, pp. 211- 235. Amsterdam: Rodopi.

Godelier, M. (1978). *Perspectives in Marxist Anthropology*. Cambridge: Cambridge University Press.

Klawiter, A. (1978). *Problem metodologicznego statusu materializmu historycznego* [The Problem of the Methodological Status of Historical Materialism]. Warszawa/ Poznań: PWN.

Łastowski, K. (1981). *Problem analogii teorii rozwoju gatunków i teorii formacji społeczno-ekonomicznej* [The Problem of the Analogy of the Theory of the Development of Species and the Theory of a Socio-Economic Formation]. Poznań: Wyd. UAM.

Łastowski, K. (1982). The Theory of Development of Species and the Theory of Motion of Socio-Economic Formation, In: L. Nowak, (ed.) *Social Classes, Action* and *Historical Materialism. Poznań Studies in the Philosophy of the Sciences and the Humanities*, vol. 6, pp. 122–157. Amsterdam: Rodopi.

Niewiadomski, M. (1989). Toward a Model of Economic Institutions. In: L. Nowak (ed.) *Dimensions of the Historical Process. Poznan Studies in the Philosophy of the Sciences and the Humanities*, vol 13, pp. 271–280. Amsterdam/Atlanta: Rodopi.

Nowak, L. (1977). Teoria formacji społeczno-ekonomicznej jako teoria adaptacyjna [The Theory of a Socio-Economic Formation as an Adaptive Theory]. In: L. Nowak (ed.) *Założenia materializmu historycznego.*, pp. 59–75. Warszawa/Poznań: PWN.

Nowak, L. (1980). *Polska droga od socjalizmu* [The Polish Road from Socialism]. Poznań: WiW.

Nowak, L. (1981). *Wolność i władza. Przyczynek do nie-Marksowskiego materializmu historycznego* [Freedom and Power. A Contribution to non-Marxian Historical Materialism]. Poznań: Wyd. Akademii Rolniczej.

Nowak, L. (1982). The Theory of Socio-Economic Formation as a Theory of Adaptation Process. In: L. Nowak (ed.), *Social Classes Action and Historical Materialism. Poznań Studies in the Philosophy of the Sciences and the Humanities*, vol. 6, pp. 110–121 Amsterdam: Rodopi.

Nowak, L. (1983). *Property and Power: Towards a Non-Marxian historical Materialism*. Dordrecht: Reidel.

Nowak, L. (1986). O historiozofii, antropologii, utopii i gnozie [On Historiosophy, Anthropology, Utopia, and Gnosis]. *Przegląd Polityczny* 8, 132–161.

Nowak, L. (1987). O teorii społecznej i faktach historycznych [On Social Theory and Historical Facts]. *Obecność* 17, 65–81.

Nowak, L. (1991a). *U podstaw teorii socjalizmu* [The Foundations of the Theory of Socialism]; vol. 1: *Własność i władza. O konieczności socjalizmu* [Property and Power. On the Necessity of Socialism].

Nowak, L. (1991b). *U podstaw teorii socjalizmu* [The Foundations of the Theory of Socialism]; vol. 3: *Dynamika władzy. O strukturze i konieczności zaniku socjalizmu* [The Dynamics of Power. On the Structure and Necessity of the Disappearance of Socialism]. Poznań: Nakom.

Nowak, L. (1994). O zagadnieniu tak zwanej transformacji ustrojowej [The Problem of the So-Called Social Transformation]. In: K. Zamiara (ed.). *Transformacja ustrojowa w refleksji humanistycznej*, pp. 117–129. Poznań: Wyd. UAM.

Nowak, L. (1996). Koniec historii czy jej powtórka? [The End of History or Its Repetition?]. In: W. Heller (ed.), *Świat jako proces*, pp. 31–40. Poznań: Wydawnictwo Instytutu Filozofii UAM.

Nowak, L. (2022). The Problem of the So-Called Social Transformation. In: K. Brzechczyn (ed.) *New Developments in Theory of Historical Process. Polish Contributions to Non-Marxian Historical Materialism. Poznań Studies in the Philosophy of the Sciences and the Humanities*, vol. 119, pp. 77–95. Leiden/Boston: Brill.

Paprzycka, K. and L. Nowak. (1989). On the Social Nature of Colonization. In: L. Nowak (ed.) *Dimensions of the Historical Process. Poznan Studies in the Philosophy of the Sciences and the Humanities*, vol. 13, pp. 299–312. Amsterdam/Atlanta: Rodopi.

Rummel, R. J. (1985). Libertarian Propositions on Violence Within and Between Nations. A Test Against Published Research Results. *Journal of Conflict Resolution*, 29, pp 419–455.

Szabała, H. (1994). Czy świat zmierza do socjalizmu? [Is the World Going in the Direction of Socialism?]. *Edukacja Filozoficzna* 17, 118–127.

Tomczak, G. (1989). The Economic Collapse in Two Models of Socio-economic Formation. In: L. Nowak (ed.) *Dimensions of the Historical Process. Poznań Studies in the Philosophy of the Sciences and the Humanities*, vol. 13, pp. 259–270. Amsterdam/Atlanta: Rodopi.

Wittfogel, K. A. (1957). *Oriental Despotism*. New Haven: Yale University Press.

CHAPTER 6

Marxism versus Liberalism: A Certain Paradox

Leszek Nowak

Abstract

The author compares Marxism with liberalism in terms of their programs and cognitive criteria. In the author's view, Marxism surpasses liberalism with regard to cognitive criteria, but liberalism surpasses Marxism with program criteria. If one preserves two criteria of truth: the criterion of practice and the criterion of explanatory power, one must accept the limited but real cognitive value of both theories. Hence, one needs to correct both Marxism and liberalism. As regards the third postulated theory, it would have to transition into error-free Marxism in one border case and into cleansed liberalism in another case. Such a theory, then, would preserve all the contributions of corrected Marxism and corrected liberalism. In the last part of the paper, the features of such theory are analyzed.

Keywords

analytical Marxism – liberalism – philosophy of history – truth

1   The First Problem[1]

[...] Nowadays – at least, in our part of the world – Marxism is not treated seriously. That reflex is somewhat understandable in the realm of politics, but is quite incomprehensible in the cognitive realm, because now is the time when the great cognitive successes of Marxism are coming to light. In the last two decades we have experienced a veritable renaissance of Marxism – called 'analytical' Marxism – especially in English-speaking countries. In our part of the

---

1 The paper is a part of introduction to the collected volume *Marksizm, liberalizm, próby wyjścia*. It appears in English translation for the first time. The Polish original „Marksizm versus liberalism. Pewien paradoks" was published in: L. Nowak, P. Przybysz (eds.), *Marksizm, liberalizm, próby wyjścia* (Poznań: Zysk i S-ka, 1997), pp. 7–19. The abstract and key words have been added by the editor.

world, at least in Poland, few people know about it. In truth, they do not really want to know about it. Postmodern thinkers are busy with themselves and their more or less subversive concepts. Liberals and Christian philosophers, on the other hand, have been so willing to believe that Marxism was the source of real socialism that they have linked the fall of the system with the fall of its ideology – a step as wise as blaming the injustice of feudalism or of capitalism (which was legitimized by liberalism) for the failure of Christ's ethics or of the doctrine of human rights. What about Marxists, who, until recently, had been coming to various conferences and meetings in such great numbers? Well, they have now moved on to postmodernism, liberalism, and Christian social science … However, if one is interested in the facts of the world, the only choice is to speak about the cognitive successes of analytical Marxism, to be absolutely honest […]

2 On Analytical Marxism

2.1 *A Handful of Basic Facts*

In the whole area in which Marxism has traditionally been interested, philosophers are currently conducting, sometimes with the use of highly sophisticated formal means, very fruitful and significant studies in a few scientific disciplines: economics, sociology, political science, and philosophy. I will only briefly discuss one typical example of theoretical work in analytical Marxism.

A classic statement of Karl Marx's economic theory is 'Marx's fundamental theorem' which states that employee exploitation is a necessary and sufficient condition for capitalist to have profit. In his renown book, Michio Morishima (1973), with the use of the standard apparatus of mathematical economy, wrote a proof of the standard set of basic Marxian statements, including the law of value and Marx's fundamental theorem. That proof is valid for numerous idealizing assumptions, constituting the so-called linear model of the value theory, which assert, among other things, that the technology of goods production is a given, that work is uniform, etc.

Morishima himself, in a later work (1974), demonstrated that the classical set of Marxian statements can be proven in an equally rigorous manner in a more realistic model which admits the phenomenon of the selection of an optimal technology of production. However, that proof was still based on the idealizing assumption that those optimal values depend on work in a linear fashion, as well as on the assumption, which had already been made in *Capital*, that a worker's work is uniform.

John Roemer (1981) constructed a more realistic model in which value depends on work but not necessarily in a linear fashion. In that model, he proved a generalization of Marx's fundamental theorem. However, that model is still based on the assumption of the uniformity of work.

That assumption was removed in Ulrich Krause's work (1981). In a new, even more realistic model, that author proved a more general form of Marx's fundamental theorem. In his newest monograph Garcia de la Sienra (1992) presents the most realistic of the mathematical models constructed so far which preserve the rigorous proofs of the classic body of Marxian economic statements, including Marx's fundamental theorem (Garcia de la Sienra 1992, p. 176f.). That is how a theory which is important but which remained at the intuitive level for one hundred years and which was partially unclear, and often criticized for that lack of clarity – let us remember that even some Marxists considered the value theory presented in *Capital* to be 'social metaphysics' unworthy of the rest of that work – became formulated in mathematical terms, with rigorous proofs of its basic theorems. Contemporary mathematical apparatus made it possible to demonstrate that Marx's perceptive intuitions were not wrong, and that a capitalist's profit does, indeed, always derive from his employee's unpaid work.

This is an example of the amazing development of just one aspect of Marxian theory. Gerald Allan Cohen's book, *Karl Marx's Theory of History: A Defence* (1978), which stirred many discussions in leading journals on analytical social philosophy, as well as Jon Elster's *Making Sense of Marx* (1985), Steven Lukes's *Power: A Radical View* (1981), Anthony Giddens's *Central Problems in Social Theory: Action, Structure and Contradiction in Social Analysis* (1981), and other authors' works are examples of a new wave of purely cognitive interest in Marxism in social philosophy, which is sweeping through English-speaking countries. That wave also encroaches on moral philosophy, as evidenced by many well-known books, some examples of which are Allen Wood's *Karl Marx* (1981), Steven Lukes's *Marxism and Morality* (1987), and the collection of articles entitled *Marx, Justice and History* (Cohen et al.1980,).

Likewise, there is growing interest in the epistemological and ontological aspects of Marxism or, more generally speaking, the dialectical tradition, which is seen in incisive interpretations of Marx's method (Rosdolsky 1977, Murray 1988, Garcia de la Sienra 1990, Moseley 1993) and the ontological assumptions of that method (Bhaskar 1978, Fisk 1979, 1981 et al.) discussed in literature on the subject. Also, systems of *explicite* paraconsistent logic have been created which formalized the ideas of dialectical contradiction, the 'unity of opposites,' the logical contradictions of movement, etc. (Routley, Meyer 1976, Da Costa, Wolf 1980, Priest 1982 et al.).

All this combines into an image of a great intellectual movement, mainly in the English-speaking world, which, on the one hand, modernizes Marxism by providing it with contemporary conceptual tools, while removing its outdated elements and enlivening the still current ones, and, on the other hand, gives analytical philosophy new material for reflections and new ideas which go beyond the empirical philosophical heritage with which that philosophy has been, so far, most often associated, *via* British empiricism and continental positivism. Conceptual techniques developed in the analytical tradition expand to areas which have traditionally been the subject matter of discussions in Marxism – this is how we could sum up the historical role of analytical Marxism. The fact that it is happening at a time when the global press monotonously repeats the cliché about the 'end of socialism' surely has something to do with the irony (and maybe even the cunning?) of the historical process.

The fact that this phenomenon is not known in Poland is surprising, at first, because it was our country that pioneered the development of analytical Marxism. It started with logic – Stanisław Jaśkowski created the first system of paraconsistent logic (Jaśkowski 1948) which clearly refers to Hegelian–Marxian inspirations, and Leonard Sławomir Rogowski (1964) built a system of quadrivalent logic which reconstructed the Hegelian thesis about the contradictoriness of change. Also, in the theory of cognition, Roman Suszko (1957) explicated the Marxist concepts of a partial, relative, and absolute truth, as well as the idea of the development of cognition by means of a semantic theory of models. In ontology, Oskar Lange (1965) conducted a systematic, formal reconstruction of dialectics. The list goes on. Among the further achievements of Polish analytical Marxism, allow me to mention, not without some pride, the concepts developed in the 1970s in the Poznań circles, which have also been presented in this publication series: the idealizational interpretation of Marx's methodology, historical epistemology, the categorial interpretation of dialectics, the adaptive interpretation of Marxian historical materialism, the socio-pragmatic theory of culture, and other concepts.

The astonishment at the fact that the great intellectual movement from the West not only was not propagated in Poland but is virtually unknown here diminishes, though, when we consider the historical moment in which we are now living. Poland was the only real-socialist country where non-Marxian philosophical orientations survived. Still, they were always marginalized by the ideology of the communist triple-rule system, and they were suppressed in the Stalinist periods. Nowadays, those orientations – logical empiricism, Christian philosophy, phenomenology – are slowly regaining strength. That also applies to those philosophic movements which only had Polish versions in the Polish Third Republic, like postmodernism or liberalism. It is simply not in their group interest to engage in that new form of Marxism. Quite the contrary, it is in their interest to accept the purely political dogma of the 'end of Marxism' as a cognitively valid concept. The fact that the most revered Western publishing houses publish books and whole publication series authored by analytical Marxists, that those philosophers' concepts are discussed in the most important journals on social philosophy or political philosophy, and that congresses on analytical Marxism in the United States attract 1.5 thousand participants – puts additional pressure on those orientations to use the most effective competitive strategy, namely, passing the subject over in silence. (To discuss something, even in the most critical manner, means to recognize the significance of that phenomenon. Ignoring the subject is more advantageous – in terms of spiritual power, not of truth). After all, a great intellectual movement in the center of the world is at stake here. Most of the time, spiritual phenomena of such rank have been very much recognized in Poland. However, if that were to happen this time as well, it would pose a threat to our newly formed relative strengths in philosophy, sociology, and political science – after the 'freeze' phase in real socialism. It is definitely much more convenient not to notice anything, to remain content with a few clichés about Marxism.

Nevertheless, like it or not, such are the facts. It is a surprising scientific fact, which will surely be noticed by historians of science in the next century, that Marxism has never had such a cognitive success as it did at the time of the collapse of the system which had (ab)used its name, bearing it on its dirtied banners. History likes such 'moments.' It is at those moments that we see it is perverse. However, perhaps history is just not aligned with our interests. Maybe this is a proof of the fact that those interests do not quite overlap with the purported values? That they are not so pure?

3   From the Cognitive Point of View, Marxism is Superior to Liberalism

Therefore, we cannot simply assume that Marxism is an outdated theory, and liberalism is, beyond a shadow of a doubt, true. Today, it makes sense to compare Marxism and liberalism. Let us take a look at the results of that comparison. Obviously, we cannot compare these two doctrines in their entirety here – they are too comprehensive, not to mention the shortcomings of the present author's competences. I will limit myself to a comparison of their core, that is, their historiosophies (my elaboration on this topic: Nowak 1994, in English 2022 [editorial note]).

These are the components of liberal historiosophy:
  (i)   human nature is egoistic by nature; egoism is a destructive force; in order to use it for public good, society establishes certain institutions: a parliamentary democracy and a free market based on private property;
  (ii) those institutions constitute a social system – liberal capitalism – which is the natural state of a society within the meaning given below: (L) every society spontaneously tends to orient itself toward liberal capitalism; this trend can be stopped by force, but the result will only be a delay of this drive toward this natural state;
  (iii) when a given society reaches the state of liberal capitalism, it simply remains in it; parliamentary democracy respects the rights of humans and citizens, a free market based on private property ensures the welfare not only of elites but also of the middle class, that is, the whole – if we omit the margins – society; it is no wonder that this natural state is the end point of social history.

Let us take a look at the foundations of the belief in liberal historiosophy, especially, its key thesis (L).

Components (i) – (iii) are often presented as one without an alternative. "History shows that liberal capitalism does not have a reasonable alternative" – this is what we read in tens of studies. Therefore, liberal historiosophy is also deemed not to have a worthy competitor. If we were to believe those proclamations, then liberal historiosophy would have to meet certain rigorous methodological criteria. We demand from every scientific theory that it respect the principle of correspondence in relation to its thought tradition, that is, roughly, that it (1) explain facts which falsify the previous theory (in that tradition) and that it (2) also explain all facts which its predecessor was not able to explain. A theory which is believed to be without an alternative has to fulfill stricter criteria, namely, (1) explain the facts which falsify the current rivals from all rival traditions of thought, and (2) explain all facts which have already been explained by those theories. Let us, then, compare liberal historiosophy to, for example, Marxist historiosophy.

Very briefly speaking, we could say that social history comprises three development lines: on the one hand, the line of primitive societies, from which the line of non-European civilizations (for example, Inca or Chinese) derives, and, on the other hand, the line of the Western civilization. All of them have endured until now, in a more or less residual form (the so-called primitive societies which exist today or some societies of the 'third world'). At this point, we might ask what liberal historiosophy can say about the nature of primitive societies or of the Inca society. Well, liberal historiosophy can only say that neither primitive societies nor Asiatic despotisms have 'learned,' as yet, that the optimal human institutions are parliamentary democracy and the free market. Since those societies have drastically different structures, mechanisms of change, etc., we must come to the conclusion that liberalism has nothing to say about them. Whatever is claimed within the framework of liberalism, refers to societies in the Western civilization or, more specifically, the latest incarnation of those societies, namely, the capitalist one – liberalism cannot tell us anything about, say, feudalism. For a long time, capitalism itself could not be explained by the liberal model, either, because no liberal would view such events as the shooting down of a few thousand workers, or sending a few thousand boys aged less than 16 to hard labor in Guiana by the French government after the suppression of the Paris Commune as 'respecting human rights.'

Capitalism can only be considered within the framework of the liberal model from the time of World War II when the fascist alternative disappeared. Today, the communist alternative is vanishing. There are, then, serious and incontrovertible arguments for liberal historiosophy but that historiosophy is also obviously powerless when applied to the whole earlier social history of mankind. All in all, the scope of the explanatory power of the liberal model is limited to one line of development of human societies; to that which is at the very end of the last of its known stages.

Liberalism explains those phenomena which have falsified Marxist historiosophy, as the latter turned out to be incapable of explaining the contemporary stage of the evolution of capitalism (I present a more comprehensive justification of that thesis in Nowak 1979; 1983). Marxism, however, managed to explain the earlier stages of capitalism and the pre-capitalist formations of the European civilization, and the Asiatic line of development (the very concept of an "Asiatic formation" was introduced by Marx, while the theory was created by Karl August Wittfogel (1957) who can also be considered to have worked in the Marxist tradition), and the nature of primitive societies (Maurice Godelier has authored one of the most interesting concepts of those societies [1978]). It is not my claim that all those explanations are correct. I have actually questioned the Marxian explanations of the Western line of development (Nowak 1983). However, when we examine the correspondences among theories, we do not look for truth, but rather want to compare the scopes of their explanatory power. That comparison does not favor liberal historiosophy – actually, the range of the explanatory power of Marxist historiosophy is incomparably greater.

4 In Terms of Their Programs, Liberalism is Superior to Marxism

This evaluation is based on a purely cognitive criterion. However, scientific theories are also evaluated from the point of view of their program power. The facts that physics provides conceptual means for very efficient engineering, that chemistry and biology lay the foundations for effective medicine or agriscience, or that theoretical economy can now program economic policies of states and international organizations are all very strong arguments for theories developed in appropriate basic sciences. There is no reason not to also apply that type of a criterion also to social philosophy. Let us, then, compare[1] liberalism and Marxism with respect to the criterion of programming power, although, obviously, we do not expect equally precise and indubitable applications here.

That collation makes it clear that those theories are incomparable, as the programming power of Marxism is negligible – not because it programmed too much and with disastrous practical effects but because it hardly ever programmed, or, at least, it did not program anything positive; at best, it created programs of struggles and not of construction. Marxism programmed the abolition of private property but did not say anything, except for commonalities ("an association of free producers"), about 'social property.' It programmed an abolition of the restrictions of "bourgeoisie democracy" but was silent on the postulated form of the government of the people. The list goes on. From the perspective of its program, Marxism was a negativism – it hardly designed anything.

The impression that this was not the case is linked to the confusion of the programmatic functions of the doctrine and the practical activity of communists in power. It is, however, obvious that those communists' activity was not necessarily motivated by their Marxist convictions but rather by their interest in power. After all, it is not difficult to understand that when an inquisitor sent a heretic to the stake, he was not following the principle of loving one's neighbor but rather the interest of the church, of the order, or, sometimes his own, private interest. We can hardly expect a different state of things in the case of a party chekist. Whatever is related to the form of government built by communists: the state ownership of industry and trade, the collectivization of farming, the state ownership of the means of indoctrination, the introduction of censorship, the rule of one party, reducing of parliamentary institutions to a sham, making Marxism the only acceptable ideology, etc. was a result of a revolutionary fight for power and the post-revolutionary practice of constructing the rule of triple lords – and not of a program left by the creators of Marxism or somehow derived by Marxists from Marxism. On the contrary, despite the constant calls for a "program for the party," somehow such a program could never be derived from Marxism. No one, by the way – except maybe in the first years of the "socialist construction" – earnestly made such calls. Marxism played the role of an ideology, not as a foundation for any 'social engineering.' Therefore, it simply had nothing to say about the social formation it recommended.

One of the reasons for this programmatic poverty of Marxism is, surely, Marx's and Engels's forbearance in this regard – the philosophers viewed such activity as proper only for "utopian socialism" and as inconsistent with the scientific nature of their theory. Still, that limitation does not explain why subsequent generations of Marxists could not derive any particular program for the construction of a new form of government from Marxism. Despite its great explanatory power, and effectiveness with regard to making predictions, Marxism turned out to be utterly useless for programming social changes.

The problem with liberalism is exactly the opposite. As we have seen, its explanatory power is very weak, while the power to create a program is very strong. Great Britain does not have a constitution, but it has classic political thinkers, such as John Stuart Mill, whose writings fulfill, in a way, the role of a constitution, as they explain the liberal principles respected in the political culture of the country. Contemporary liberal political philosophy provides additional justifications for those principles (for example, Rawls 1971).

One excellent illustration of the program-creating power of liberalism is the model of work distribution constructed by Bert Hamminga (1995). He provides a very simple and ingenious solution to one of the most troubling social problems by using a few basic principles of the liberal thought. First, the problem is explained in individualist terms – of decisions made by individuals on the basis of their preferences and their understanding of the situation. No limitations are imposed on those decisions because it is assumed that they are free of prejudice fed by any ideologies and that they are made by free people, who are unencumbered with the pressure of any social macro-structures such as the state, political parties, or the church. Neither are the people idealized, in the common meaning of the word – they are not presented as better than they are. Finally, not only are those people not motivated by any ideology but neither is the person modeling them motivated by any ideology concerning them. A liberal does not shy away from seeing that most people strive to acquire wealth and that most people, faced with the choice of either increasing their income or upholding their ideals, will not hesitate to trample on the ideals. Recognizing egoism as the fundamental flaw of human nature, the philosopher poses the question of how to organize a given part of the human world in such a way that that this flaw results in as few losses as possible and maximizes benefits.

This is the principal intention of liberalism: to think about human issues without humanistic illusions. The courage with which liberalism uncovers the uglier side of human nature and the great patience with which liberal thinkers reflect on the ways of minimizing the harm resulting from human imperfection – and, if possible, of even transforming individual harm into collective benefits – are admirable. In that theoretical perspective, ideals are not a given to which humans should subject themselves but a result of free individuals' free play; they are an optimal solution, which often simply means the least harmful – solution. They are not an outcome of the sentimental fascination we are all so prone to, but of an unflinching look at disillusioned outlook on the human world and of a persistent effort to make that world a little bit more bearable. Liberalism thinks bravely, which is probably the reason why it is unsurpassed when it comes to designing social solutions. Definitely, Marxism definitely does not compare in that regard, as it goes into Promethean hysterics in the face of human issues and turns out to be powerless in dealing with specific social problems.

5 The Second Problem

From the cognitive point of view, then, Marxism by far surpasses liberalism. From the point of view of program creation, however, liberalism is decidedly superior to Marxism. How is that possible? The surprise expressed in that question is a manifestation of the following reasoning.

(i) If Marxism can, in a consistent and uniform manner, explain a vast area of human history and, in that respect, it surpasses all alternative theories, that is a serious argument for the truthfulness of Marxism, even though it is hardly useful for creating a program; the explanatory power is the criterion of truth.

(ii) If liberalism provides the best known project of a social organization, that is, if it is practicable, that is a serious argument for its truthfulness, even though we can hardly explain the history of humanity with it; practice is the criterion of truth.

(iii) If we have two incompatible social theories of great scope, only one of them can be true.

There can be three solutions to that problem. One is that Marxism is true, and liberalism is false. The second one is that the opposite is true. The third one is that both theories are false.

The two first answers must be rejected. The first one requires us to drop the criterion of practice when evaluating social theories, while the second one – to give up the criterion of explanatory power. There is, however, no reason why we should adjust epistemology in accordance with a comparison of particular theories. On the contrary, such a change of the rules of the game during the game would give rise to the suspicion that that the comparison is unfair. What is more, the two competing theories are distinctive not because of their own methodological criteria but because of the criteria proper to the opponent. Pragmatic tendencies have always been strong in Marxism – after all, it was this theory that announced practice to be the criterion of truth, while it was somewhat skeptical about the classical concept of explanatory power. It is its very own criterion that speaks against Marxism and for liberalism. Liberalism, in turn – in John Stuart Mill's ([1843] 1974) or Karl Popper's methodology ([1934] 1959) – prioritizes the explanatory criterion of truth and is suspicious of the criterion of practice.[2] The criterion preferred by liberalism speaks against it and for Marxist historiosophy.

There is nothing left but the third solution – both theories are false, so we need a third theory. At the same time, if we preserve the criterion of practice as well as the criterion of explanatory power, we must accept the limited but real cognitive value of both compared theories. First, however, the fragments of both theories which have that value would have to be cleansed of errors. Those errors, as has been noted, are indubitable, as they are exposed by the criterion of practice (in the case of Marxism) and of explanatory power (in the case of liberalism). Hence, we need to correct both theories. As regards the third postulated theory, it would have to transition into error-free Marxism in one borderline case and into cleansed liberalism in another case[3]. Such a theory, then, would preserve all that speaks for corrected Marxism and corrected liberalism.

What would the postulated theory have to be like? Neither holistic, like Marxism – because then it would not be able to program holistic social institutions – nor individualist, like liberalism – because then it would not be sufficient to explain the history of great social structures. It could not be antagonistic, like Marxism – because in such a case it would be powerless in the face of the phenomenon of social solidarism which is, after all, a basic human fact – and it could not be solidaristic, like liberalism – because such a theory would not say a word about social revolutions, which are an equally essential element of social history. It could be neither purely materialist, like Marxism, nor

---

2 Popper (1957) limits that criterion to, for example, partial social engineering.
3 Non-Marxian historical materialism could be one such attempt, I believe. After all, attempts have been made in analytical Marxism to correct other aspects of Marx's Marxism. When it comes to liberalism, communitarianism could be viewed as one attempt at a significant correction of that theory.

purely idealistic, like liberalism, neither casuistically historical, like Marxism oftentimes was, nor overly formal, as is often the case with liberalism. The list goes on.

Is such a theory possible? It is difficult to say. We will not know that until someone creates it. However, there will be no serious attempt at creating such a theory as long as the topic has not been preliminarily explored. The studies included in the third part of this work are such initial attempts at exploring the area in which a theoretical synthesis could, perhaps, be made in the future. [...].

References

Bhaskar, R. (1978). *A Realist Theory of Science.* Brighton: Harvester Press.
Cohen, G.A. (1978). *Karl Marx's Theory of History: A Defence.* Princeton: Princeton University Press.
Cohen, M., Th. Nagel, and Th. Scanlon, eds. (1980). *Marx, Justice and History.* Princeton: Princeton University Press.
Da Costa, N.C., and R.A. Wolf. (1980). Studies in Paraconsistent Logic I: the Dialectical Principle of the Unity of Opposites. *Philosophia*, 9, 189–217.
Elster, J. (1985). *Making Sense of Marx.* Cambridge: Cambridge University Press.
Fisk, M. (1979). Materialism and Dialectic. *Critique* 12, 97–116.
Fisk, M. (1981). Determination and Dialectic. *Critique* 13, 79–102.
Garcia de la Sienra, A. (1990). Marx's Dialectical Method. *In:* J. Brzezinski, F. Coniglione, Th. A. F. Kuipers, and L. Nowak (eds.). *Idealization I. Poznań Studies in the Philosophy of the Sciences and the Humanities,* vol. 16, pp. 113–126. Amsterdam/Atlanta: Rodopi.
Garcia de la Sienra, A. (1992). *The Logical Foundations of the Marxian Theory of Value.* Dordreht/Boston/London: Kluwer.
Giddens, A. (1981). *Central Problems in Social Theory. Action, Structure and Contradiction in Social Analysis.* London: Macmillan.
Godelier, M. (1978). *Perspectives in Marxist Anthropology.* Cambridge: Cambridge University Press.
Hamminga, B. (1995). Demoralizing the Labour Market: Could Jobs be like Cars and Concerts? *Journal of Political Philosophy* 3, 22–35.
Jaśkowski, S. ([1948] 1969). The Propositional Calculus for Contradictory Deductive Systems. *Studia Logica*, 24, 143–157.
Krause, U. (1981). Heterogenous Labour and the Fundamental Marxian Theorem. *The Review of Economic Studies,* 48, 173–178.
Lange, O. (1965). Całość i rozwój w świetle cybernetyki [The Whole and Development in the Light of Cybernetics]. Warsaw: PWN.
Lukes, S. (1981). *Power: A Radical View.* London: Macmillan.

Lukes, S. (1987). *Marxism and Morality*. Oxford: Oxford University Press.
Mill, J. S. ([1843] 1974) *A System of Logic*. Toronto: Toronto University Press.
Morishima, M. (1973). *Marx's Economics*. Cambridge: Cambridge University Press.
Morishima, M. (1974). Marx in the Light of Modem Economic Theory. *Econometrica* 42, 611–632.
Moseley, F. (ed.) (1993). *Marx's Method in* Capital: *A Reexamination*. Atlantic Highlands, N.J.: Humanities Press.
Murray, P. (1988). *Marx's Theory of Scientific Knowledge*. Atlantic Highlands, N.J.: Humanities Press.
Nowak, L. (1979). Historical Momentums and Historical Epochs. An Attempt at a non-Marxian Historical Materialism. *Analyse und Kritik* 1, 60–76.
Nowak, L. (1983). Property and Power. Towards a non-Marxian Historical Materialism. Dordrecht/Boston/Lancaster: Reidel.
Nowak, L. (1994). O zagadnieniu tak zwanej transformacji ustrojowej [The Problem of the So-Called Social Transformation]. In: K. Zamiara (ed.) *Nauki społeczne wobec transformacji ustrojowej*, pp. 117–129. Poznań: Wyd. UAM.
Nowak, L. (1997). Marksizm versus liberalism. Pewien paradoks [Marxism versus Liberalism: A Certain Paradox]. In: L. Nowak, P. Przybysz (eds.), *Marksizm, libelarizm próby wyjścia*, pp. 7–19. Poznań: Zysk i S- ka.
Nowak, L. (2022). The Problem of the So-Called Social Transformation. In: K. Brzechczyn (ed.) *New Developments in Theory of Historical Process. Polish Contributions to Non-Marxian Historical Materialism. Poznań Studies in the Philosophy of the Sciences and the Humanities,* vol. 119, pp. 77–95. Leiden/Boston: Brill.
Popper, K. ([1934]1959). *The Logic of Scientific Discovery*. New York: Harper & Row.
Popper, K. (1957). *The Poverty of Historicism*. London: Routledge and Kegan Paul.
Priest, G. (1982). To Be and Not to Be: Dialectical Tense Logic. *Studia Logica*, 41 (2–3), 249–268.
Rawls, J. (1971). A *Theory of Justice*. Oxford: Oxford University Press.
Roemer, J. (1981). *Analytical Foundations of Marxian Economic Theory*. Cambridge: Cambridge University Press.
Rogowski, S. L. (1964). Logika kierunkowa a Heglowska teza o sprzeczności zmiany [Directional Logic and the Hegelian Thesis about the Contradictory Nature of Change]. Toruń: STNT.TNT.
Rosdolsky, R. (1977). *The Making of Marx's Capital*. London: Pluto Press.
Routley, R., and R. K. Meyer (1976). Dialectical Logic, Classical Logic, and the Consistency of the World. *Studies in Soviet Thought* 16 (1–2), 1–25.
Suszko, R. (1957). Logika formalna a niektóre zagadnienia teorii poznania [Formal Logics and Some Problems of the Theory of Knowledge]. *Myśl Filozoficzna* 2 (28), 27–56.
Wittfogel, K. (1957). *Oriental Despotism*. New Haven: Yale University Press.
Wood, A. (1981). *Karl Marx*. London: Routledge & Kegan Paul.

CHAPTER 7

On-the-Verge Effect in a Historical Process: An Attempt at an Interpretation in the Light of Non-Marxian Historical Materialism

Leszek Nowak

Abstract

The purpose of this paper is to incorporate the phenomenon of new social movements: peace, ecological and feminist into the conceptual apparatus of non-Marxian historical materialism. The explanation of these movements is possible owing to the fact that mechanisms of solidaristic social development have been incorporated into this theory. The solidaristic social development in the conditions of the so-called verge effect weakens the mechanisms of competition: both political and economic ones.

Keywords

capitalism – competition – ecologism – feminism – non-Marxian historical materialism – peace movement – solidarism – verge effect

1 The Problem of the Interpretation of New Social Movements[1]

One of the more troubling issues in an analysis of contemporary times is the conceptualization of the so-called *new social movements* – mainly the peace, ecological, and women's movements. This difficulty, like other problems of that kind, does not lie in the phenomenon but in its witnesses, in us – we do not understand the phenomenon, and it is simply because the old theoretical frameworks fail and new ones have not yet been created. One social researcher, then, is right when she says:

---

[1] The paper appears in English translation for the first time. The Polish original „Efekt kresowy w procesie historycznym" was published in: L. Nowak, P. Przybysz (eds.), *Marksizm, liberalizm, próby wyjścia* (Poznań: Zysk i S-ka, 1997), pp. 307–319. The abstract and key words have been added by the editor.

> None of the social groups which are active these days, neither women nor youth, neither 'alternativists', nor environmentalists, neither activists for peace no members of citizen's initiatives, can be defined as a class like the working men in the 19th century. ... In the ecological and peace movements people of all age groups, with varying degrees of education and from all walks of life, are participating. ... We cannot consider the new social protest groups as a new class; it is also a fact that they are not trying to associate themselves within class organizations. They do not establish unions or parties as the working men did in the 19th century. And they do not create a new, institutionalized elite leadership either.
>
> MOHL 1985, p. 263

Indeed, the patterns of Marxist historical materialism visibly fail here:

> The struggles of new social protest movements can no longer be explained as a consequence of a contradiction within capitalist production. For this reason there is no guarantee that it will occur at the base of society, in the sphere of production
>
> MOHL 1985, p. 263

Still, if a specific theory does not explain certain phenomena, it does not follow that one should not try to find alternative conceptualizations of those phenomena but just describe them in an impressionistic manner. We can easily imagine the results of the use of that cognitive strategy which is so frequently employed in sociology: when descriptions become well known – and the freshness of facts wears off – it will become manifest how useless they are as a tool for understanding the things for which they only provide new names. At that point, it will become necessary to understand what those names indicate, that is, to create a theory. Therefore, we had better undertake that task at once, not waiting for the time when volumes of empirical reports have bored us as much as we are now bored by the volumes of *Capital* (even though this boredom is not really justified).

2   Non-Marxian Historical Materialism

I will base my attempt at an interpretation of the new social movements on non-Marxian historical materialism. For obvious reasons, it cannot be presented here (for a full lecture, see: Nowak 1983, 1991a; 1991b; 1991c), but I will refer a few of its most important hypotheses (a summary: 1980).

(I) Class divisions do not only occur in the economy – because of the monopoly of a minority on the means of production (owners) – but also in politics and culture, because of the actual monopolies of minorities on the means of coercion (rulers) and the means of social communication (priests).

(II) Societies are divided into class societies – with separate classes of disposers of material means – and supra-class societies – with a double class of rulers-owners (totalitarianism) or rulers-priests (fascism), or with a triple class of rulers-owners-priests (socialism).

(III) From the theory of class societies (Model VP: Nowak 1981b, pp. 244–263; 1983, pp. 211–235), we can derive a thesis of the necessity of the totalitarization of capitalism. From the theory of supra-class societies (Nowak 1984, pp. 119–127 - Model I), we can derive a thesis of the necessity of the disappearance of socialism.

The question arises whether we can interpret the new social movements in the categories of the class theory proposed in non-Marxian historical materialism. The prospects are seemingly promising. Ecological movements could be interpreted as civil movements against blind economic development which is uncontrolled by either private owners or the state and which degrades the natural environment. The pacifist civic movement was directed against the alienation of state apparatuses which played their arcane and dangerous game in the field of international affairs. From that point of view, women's movements are, primarily, a protest against the indoctrination by the patriarchal culture – they are a form of a cultural rebellion.

That interpretation, although it is probably closer to the truth than an interpretation based on the economic categories of Marxian historical materialism, is still highly unsatisfactory, which becomes apparent when we ask what interests are to be realized by particular types of the new social movements. After all, people engaged in ecological movements have the same interest as their opponents – both groups should care about a clean environment. Likewise, pacifists do not represent their own, separate interest. On the contrary, peace is in everyone's interest. As regards the traditional antagonism of interests, it is the most visible in the feminist movement, but even there its presence is not indisputable. It looks, then, as if the *new social movements*, instead of being a protest of one part of the society against another (as was the case, for example, with such classic civic movements as the 'first' *Solidarność*), acted in in the interest of the whole society or, perhaps, on behalf of it. The activists are people who feel sufficiently responsible for everyone's fate that they to fight against the threats which they perceive more clearly than other people. That fight, however, is more against anonymous market forces, the international arena, and the cultural tradition than against distinctly contrary interests. This is how the new movements differ from the civic movements which led to revolutions in Eastern European countries and were directed against groups with contrary interests, gave rise to specific organizations, and created institutional elites – just like the 19th-century labor movement did.

In short, in the class interpretation of the new social movements – even if we generalize it in a non-Marxian manner – the element of social solidarity, which appears to be their distinctive feature, is missing.

3   Two Dimensions of Social Development

What is worse, in the existing version of non-Marxian historical materialism, we cannot even express that element of solidarism as the theory does not contain a model of civilizational development.

The thing is that social development encompasses two dimensions: the class dimension (economic, political, and cultural classes) and the civilizational one (respectively, in the same three aspects). Apart from being the area of social conflict, production improves people's living conditions. Apart from being the arena of fights for power, politics shapes permanent institutions, habits, and traditions. Culture, apart from being the field of rivalry for access to people's minds, creates values. Although a focus solely on the civilizational dimension can be rightly termed one of the more typical forms of ideological thinking, it remains a fact that this dimension exerts a great influence on social development and, at some point, should be taken into account during the development of a holistic theoretical construction. In non-Marxian historical materialism, the relationship between (narrow) class dimension and (narrow) civilizational one is not clear (Nowak, 1981b, pp. 28–61), however, they are both taken into account in the historiosophy of the author of *Capital*. In non-Marxian historical materialism, the class dimension of development is significantly expanded while the civilizational dimension is almost completely ignored[2]. In that respect, then, the former always has an advantage over the latter.

---

2   "Almost" – because Model I of the theory of a class society takes into account the adaptive mechanisms of the organization of production for the achieved technological level as well as the issue of the realization of the surplus product in Models II-VP or technological progress in Models III-VP of that theory (see: 1981a; 1983; 1991b). However, those "civilizational variables" are mainly considered from the point of view of their influence on inter-class relations.

In this text, it is not my intention to systematically reflect on the relations between those two dimensions of social development. Nevertheless, I will have to consider one aspect of that issue.

4 On-the-Verge Effect

It is a certain peculiar phenomenon which could be called the on-the-verge effect. Let us first take a look at an example.

Given the way in which international relations have been developing so far, the fact that it was possible to maintain peace between the antagonistic world powers for nearly half a century in the most recent history comes as a surprise. It appears even more astonishing when we realize that during all that time one of the parties was a 'totalitarian' – and economically backward – system; a circumstance which raises the odds of aggression. What is more, for a certain period of time within that half of a century, the totalitarian party was extremely repressive in its domestic affairs, which – as I have already argued (Nowak 1984; 1991b; 1991c) – significantly increases the propensity to be aggressive in international relations. Moreover, the Soviet Union – as this is, obviously, the state we are talking about – was the heir of one of the most aggressive political systems of the old world, and it added the idea of a global revolution to the Great Russian expansionism. It all happened when nuclear weapons and the means of transporting them made a global war technically possible. Still, there was no war, despite this unheard-of accumulation of factors conducive to aggression. Why?

The answer, of course, depends on the accepted theory of aggression. According to the concept I have already had an opportunity to present (1981a, 1991b; 1991c), the main reason for aggression is the interest which the rulers' class of a given state have in the increase of the area of regulation. In a two-state model, in which one of the parties is in the state of awakened aggression (mainly because of the type of its relations with its own citizens but also for other reasons, such as those enumerated above), acts of aggression are only committed when the potential for aggression of the said party is much higher than that of the other party, which means that the aggressor-ruler has a chance of realizing its interest.

If that approach is correct, then we owe the peace we enjoyed for half a century to nuclear weapons. Technology reached such a level that it made all the benefits of aggression illusory. The 'winner' could only take possession of unpopulated territories, now contaminated for dozens of years to come. It was probably also important that weapons of mass destruction put an end to the class nature of wars. Prior to the creation of nuclear weapons, political and military elites could always hide behind the simple soldier's back and survive. Nuclear weapons made war almost as risky for the rulers and their families as for their subjects. That technology led the wars between superpowers to a point at which no-one could have an interest in them, not even a despot, nor even a revolutionary despot, nor a revolutionary despot who was a despotic tsars' heir. In that situation even that despot – who had just added new territories to his country and subdued several other countries – evinced common sense.

The despot's successors were less and less expansive (in proportion, by the way, to the authorities' diminishing repressiveness in domestic affairs: Nowak 1981b). In the end, contrary to common expectations – which were based on delayed recognition of the state of affairs from half a century earlier – the 'empire of evil' transformed into a state which was willing to engage in peaceful conflict resolution. Quite obviously, a similar process was taking place on the other side of the Elbe, as democratic authorities are influenced by public opinion to a much greater degree, and the public was simply terrified at the prospect of mass destruction. In any case, the distinct aggressive trend observed a short time earlier subsided there as well, and Western politicians made genuine efforts to achieve international peace. We owe it all, in a large measure, to the invention of nuclear weapons. Had they not been invented, world wars would still be a rational means of increasing power, which would have been exploited in conducive circumstances. With the introduction of this technology, world wars no longer appeared sensible. In on-the-verge conditions, the authorities of superpowers began to behave quite reasonably, putting the interest of the whole society before their own.

That is the essence of the on-the-verge effect: in certain conditions, actions motivated by the self-interest of competing parties make the very mechanism of competition pointless; as a result, parties which used to be rivals, having lost their contradictory interests, begin to act in the common interest. When survival is at stake, even the eternal competition mechanisms in international politics change.

We are beginning to see the same on-the-verge effect in ecological processes. It is becoming increasingly clear that if we perpetuate the existing mechanisms of economic competition, we will bring about an ecological catastrophe. If we do not introduce other principles into the economy, apart from the maximization of profit, humanity will not survive.

5   A Model of Civilizational Paleo-Development

Let us try to describe the existing mechanism of *civilizational* development in general terms, and then consider the changes made to it by the on-the-verge effect mentioned above.[3]

Let us have the original conditions (or resources) pertaining to a specific social activity (practice), that is, conditions which have not been created by that practice but which are transformed by it into final conditions (or its products). Let us also assume that we are dealing with a free activity, that is, an activity for which there do not exist any limitations as to the set of the possible subjects of that practice. For the sake of simplicity, let us also assume that this practice consists of subsequent stages. The essential question is which of the individuals who participate in that practice, at a given stage, will survive to the next stage. According to the principle of free competition, those participants of a practice, from a set of active subjects, will survive as participants of that practice who act in a way which contributes to the greatest degree to the realization of their group interest. If that interest consists in gaining more power, then, according to the principle of free competition, those participants will survive – as rulers, that is, participants of a political process – who turn out to be the most effective at increasing their sphere of influence. If that interest consists in maximizing profit, then, according to the principle of free competition, those participants will survive – as owners, that is, participants of an economic process – who turn out to be the most effective at increasing their own assets.

Groups of people form a hierarchy in which a particular level comprises groups from the lower level and is included in a group of the higher level, up to the level of humanity as a whole. In the mechanism of free competition, participants of a process act to achieve their own partial results, which only maximizes the interest of the group of the first level, that is, the interest of the direct participants of that process (the bottom-up principle of interest realization). That mechanism of civilizational development has many advantages, rightly indicated in the liberal tradition. The most important one is effectiveness. First, without any restrictions as to who can be the subject of a practice, all talented people are allowed to participate in it – freedom is an essential source of effectiveness. Another source is a sanction in the form of a punishment for

---

[3] I have already argued that the model of civilizational changes is adaptive in nature (Nowak 1973; 1982); improvements and extensions of that model: Klawiter, 1978; 1982, Łastowski, 1981; 1982, Buczkowski, 1981; 1982. Strictly speaking, it is a special case of an adaptive process, based on the mechanism of competition.

the ineffective participants, which is built into the system of free competition. Ineffective people are simply eliminated, while the less effective ones are forced to self-improve. The system of free competition, ingrained in a society, produces individuals called rational by the social theory, that is, individuals who maximize their aims. Irrational people are pushed outside of the practice and later to the margins of the society – because, in time, free competition incorporates all practices.

This mechanism of free competition, however, does not have much in common with human nature. In that respect, liberalism is very wrong. Humans by themselves are not beings who maximize their interests. They must be forced to do that. The system of free competition is precisely such a mechanism which forces us to make constant efforts despite our natural love of comfort – so as not to be pushed to the side. Liberalism, however, considers the product of the system of free competition to be its supposedly natural and suprahistorical basis.

The presented above mechanism has also been beneficial in history. Actually, it has been constantly contributing to the development of civilization, and more and more comprehensive categories of people have been allowed to compete. The first selection criterion was birth. Then, in capitalism, birth barriers were abolished and everyone could, *de iure*, participate in competitive processes. Contrary to what the phrase means, competition did not become entirely free as there was no guarantee of the same opportunities for everyone – the former winners' heirs are, *de facto*, privileged here! Nevertheless, the mechanism of free competition, as long as it operated in the conditions of virtually unlimited resources, was the primary source of development.

The situation changes when the resources transformed by a given practice are nearly exhausted. When we reflect on an activity based on free competition, aimed at obtaining results which depend on the amount of the resources used to achieve them, and if those resources are not renewable, then it becomes clear that the resources will be depleted in the course of the process and, in the end, will reach a level at which it will no longer be possible to continue practices of that kind. At that point, it turns out that development based on free competition, with a minority furthering its own interests by ceaselessly transforming resources into products, leads to self-destruction. That is why it can be termed paleo-development.

There is, then, a natural end to the system of free competition: the moment when the critical value is reached. From that point in time on, further maximization of the global effect through free competition is not possible. Society – at least the idealized society we are considering here – faces the choice of either facing a catastrophe or transforming the mechanism of free competition.

6   Two Solutions

The mechanism of free competition is based on two principles: (1) freedom of an access for all participants of a given practice, (2) maximization of partial effects (rationality) by participants of a given practice. Therefore, the mechanism can be transformed in two ways. The first one is to replace the spontaneous, bottom-up process by a process which is managed from the top down and in which external controlling factors decide about the access to the group. That is how a social practice is totalitarized. Also, as freedom of action is restricted, the system ceases to be globally effective. As long as the resources are not exhausted, that solution is counterproductive. The situation changes in critical conditions. Then, the ineffectiveness which used to be a flaw becomes an advantage! It is in the interest of society to self-limit the practice to the level of simple reproduction. If the totalitarian control guarantees the achievement of that goal, then, through the restrictions of freedom, it is more in line with the social interest than free competition. The subjugation of a social practice to external leadership in critical conditions allows, because of that restriction of freedom, the regeneration of the possessed resources and staves off of the threat of self-destruction,

The second solution, let us call it a solidaristic one, consists in the preservation of the principle of freedom of participation but without the principle of the maximization of partial results by the participants of a given practice: every kind of practice is based on simple reproduction – the recreation of what is necessary, including the possessed resources – and not on extended reproduction. Instead of a group interest, people further the global interest, and only realize group interests to the degree to which those interests do not threaten the interest of the whole, at the higher level. The bottom-up realization of interests is replaced with a top-down rule: the interest of humanity as a whole is the highest priority. For that to happen, people need to change their behavior: instead of realizing egotistic partial results, they must be oriented toward the realization of global effects, and only realize those partial results which apply to them directly; in other words, people need to satisfy their needs instead of multiplying them. Metaphorically speaking, the expansionist pattern of civilizational development must be replaced with a pattern of 'acquiescent' development.

There is no need to explain that the totalitarian version of civilizational development has been practiced in history many times, whereas the solidaristic one has not. It follows that we are familiar with the former solution but have no major historical experience of the latter. Still, if one cannot explain how to avoid production which destroys the environment while simultaneously maintaining free-market mechanisms, and, at the same time, one does not like the totalitarian solution, one should not overlook the solidaristic proposition. Many a time have utopian and crazy ideas turned out to be the most realistic ones.

7 An Attempt at an Interpretation of 'New Social Movements'

But I digress. The important thing is that there are many signs that civilizational development is slowly coming to a crossroads. Free-market processes may continue for some time to come but probably not for too long. In any case, serious accusations have already been made:

> We are living on the threshold of a global crisis which will, perhaps, be the scariest in the history of mankind … The natural environment will only bear perhaps a few dozens of years of the economic growth in its current form.
> VON WEIZSAECKER, 1990, p. 20

If not today, then in a short time the issue of the end of free competition as the principle which organizes social life will have to be considered – or, rather, that time has already come, as proven by the new social movements. There is much hidden – one might say, instinctive – and often unverbalized wisdom in collective human actions, which are a spontaneous response to the impending threat the outlines of which have not, as yet, become equally clear to everyone. When there appears a massive social movement, its very existence is a testimony to the threat and its imminence.

That was the case with the nuclear war and the peace movement which was a response to the obvious threat of war and which, surprisingly, turned out to be effective. In on-the-verge conditions, a peaceful solution appeared to be realistic, even though it should certainly have been deemed utopian after thousands of years of wars – in our civilization, waged until virtually the last minute – in the history of mankind. In the face of the end, political elites manifested collective wisdom. However, there would not have been any collective wisdom were it not for the pressure exerted by public opinion for decades, were it not for the massive peace movements which made the issue of peace a crucial political problem. Even if some actions of those movements were rightly termed excessive, they were still valuable. Sometimes a society must become irrational if it is to enforce reasonable behavior on the part of its politicians.

The ecological movement, on the other hand, is a symptom of the fact that the organization of economic practice according to the principles of free competition is at an end and that further functioning of the economy according to the principle of the maximization of profits is no longer possible because the 'invisible hand' of the market, instead of benefits to the whole society, will bring about a general social, regional, or maybe even global cataclysm. It is hard to predict if that movement will turns out to be effective. What we do know – if I am not mistaken – is its historical significance: hindering further development of the free competition economy.

The meaning of the women's movement, on the other hand, becomes apparent when both political and economic conditions are based, with regard to individuals, on the principle of rationality which constitutes a typical and basic component of the 'masculine mentality' which dominates our culture. Whatever 'feminine mentality' is, it differs from the masculine one in that it is not oriented toward maximization – that is, the greatest possible success in partial activity. Rather, it is oriented toward global optimization – that is, satisfactory and not maximal effects which, moreover, pertain primarily to the whole and are not specialized. The 'feminine mentality' is, therefore, at least in its ideal type, oriented toward the principle of solidarity. That being the case, the significance of the feminist movement – together with the discovery of the 'feminist perspective' in philosophy, art, and so on – may lie in the introduction of the principle of solidarity into the rationalistic Western culture, as without solidarity it might be impossible to implement the new mechanisms of social practice. The feminist movement, then, supports the remaining new social movements; from the historical point of view, it could be seen as oriented toward an even more distant future. To use a metaphorical shortcut: the 'acquiescent' type of development can be more easily reconciled with the feminine mentality than with the masculine one because the latter was shaped by history with the view to the realization of an expansionist model of development.

8   Either Solidarism or the Triple-Rule System

In the end, it is difficult to refrain from making at least a rough estimate of the odds of success of the *new social movements* and, indirectly, of the transformations of which the new movements are, according to the hypothetically sketched interpretations, harbingers. Obviously, the evaluation depends on the assumed historiosophy. As regards this text, the starting point is the historiosophy of non-Marxian historical materialism, the main ideas of which have been expressed in points (I)–(III). Those ideas, however, are derived from the basic models of the theory of property (for class societies) and of the theory of power (for the system of triple rule), while those models – as has been said – leave the civilizational mechanisms of development completely aside. In particular, they do not take into account the on-the-verge effect discussed in this text. That is why those models should be carefully corrected after the introduction of that phenomenon.

Clearly, such a concretization is not possible in this short essay and it will have to be discussed elsewhere, on a different occasion. At this moment, I would just like to make a few preliminary observations.

(a) In the theoretical material sketched above, there is no mechanism which could direct further civilizational development toward totalitarian control or toward a search for a solidaristic manner of optimal growth. That being the case, both solutions are theoretically admissible in a model which is to illustrate the development of the states of the capitalist West. The considered correction of the theory of class societies, then, transforms the thesis of the Model VP (1981b, 1983; 1991b) about the necessity of the totalitarization of capitalism into a thesis about the possibility of totalitarization. In other words, the one-path Model VP based purely on class must be replaced with a two-path model which takes into account the on-the-verge effect (let us mark it as VPk).[4]

(b) That does not make the discussed theory less informative. We still know well enough – which does not equal 'true' knowledge – what that theory does not admit, namely, the thesis about 'the end of history': there will never be the end of history in the West, and capitalism based on the rule of three separate classes (as regards the class type of society) and on the mechanism of free competition (as regards the civilizational type of development) will evolve, either in the direction of totalitarianism or solidarity, because the maintenance of the *status quo*, that is, the ideological 'end of history,' carries the risk of an actual end of history.

(c) Although we cannot exclude the possibility of development in the solidaristic direction, we have to say that in the light of the Models IP–VP (see: Nowak 1981b; 1983; 1989; 1991b) and Model VPk of capitalism, such a line of development is not very likely. After all, factors from the

---

4 I would also like remind my readers that the Model IP is a two-path model (depending on the result of the laborers' revolution, there is a labor loop or a standard path of development); it is only the VP model that becomes a one-path model (1987; 1991a, 314–329). With another concretization, the VPk model becomes a two-path model again. By the way, those examples provide counterarguments to the frequently made objection to historiosophy, namely that the image of history it offers is, necessarily, unilinear (see: Nowak, Paprzycka, Paprzycki 1993).

Model VP – first and foremost, the fusion of political power and ownership – are still active, and the growing ecological threat only adds significance to them. Therefore, we are dealing with an accumulated effect of the class and civilizational factors of totalitarization. It is difficult to make any estimates in that regard – at least, non-Marxian historical materialism is an insufficient tool for that purpose. It does seem commonsensical, though, to assume that civic movements are too weak to counterbalance the top-down totalitarization trends in the Western countries.

(d) It is true that, thanks to the neoconservative wave in the politics of the West, those trends have definitely subsided in recent years (Nowak 1986). Nevertheless, let us note that neoconservatism strengthens the free-market mechanism of civilizational development. After a time, the problem of having to replace the expansive model with the model of acquiescent development will become more urgent. If, then, the theses presented in this sketch are accurate, then the impromptu effects which result from neoconservative politics and counteract totalitarization in the realm of class will give way to long-term pro-totalitarization effects in the realm of civilizations.

The circumstances mentioned above can be expressed in the theoretical terms assumed in this text. However, there are many circumstances which extend beyond that framework. I would like to mention two of them.

First, the integrational tendencies, for example, in Western Europe, could be a pro-totalitarization factor. Margaret Thatcher's fears about "bureaucrats from Brussels" imposing socialism top-down because they were not been able to implement it in their countries are not, in themselves, necessarily baseless. It also seems quite incontrovertible that a united Europe can turn to a totalitarian type of civilizational development if it is required for the sake of ecology.

A second pro-totalitarization factor for the West could be the transformations in the East, or, rather, their common interpretation as a proof of the thesis that capitalism –including the crisis-triggering free-competition mechanism – constitutes a natural form of government which is the destined final form of government for all states. If an ecological demon wanted to divert people's attention from the ecological calamity they were facing, he would not be able to think of a better ideology for that purpose. Also, it would be difficult for him to find a better opportunity for making that ideology credible than the revolutions in Central and Eastern Europe. As we all know, however, history is full of surprises, which is well worth remembering especially by those who only want it to confirm their wishful predictions.

References

Buczkowski, P. (1981). *Z teorii społeczeństw ekonomicznych* [From the Theory of Economic Societies]. Szczecin: Wyd. PAM.

Buczkowski, P. (1982). Toward a Theory of Economic Society. An Attempt at the Adaptive Interpretation. In: L. Nowak (ed.). *Social Classes Action and Historical Materialism. Poznań Studies in the Philosophy of the Sciences and the Humanities*, vol. 6, pp. 158–210. Amsterdam: Rodopi.

Klawiter, A. (1978). *Problem metodologicznego statusu materializmu historycznego* [The Issue of the Methodological Status of Historical Materialism]. Warsaw–Poznań: PWN.

Klawiter, A. (1982). The Theory of Social Formation in Historical Materialism. *In*: L. Nowak (ed.). *Social Classes Action and Historical Materialism. Poznań Studies in the Philosophy of the Sciences and the Humanities*, vol. 6, pp. 281–294. Amsterdam: Rodopi.

Łastowski, K. (1981). *Problem analogii teorii ewolucji i teorii formacji społeczno-ekonomicznej* [The Issue of the Analogy of the Theory of Evolution and the Theory of a Social-Economic Formation]. Poznań: Wyd. UAM.

Łastowski, K. (1982). The Theory of Development of Species and the Theory of Motion of Socio-Economic Formation. In: L. Nowak (ed.). *Social Classes Action and Historical Materialism. Poznań Studies in the Philosophy of the Sciences and the Humanities*, vol. 6, pp. 122–157. Amsterdam: Rodopi.

Mohl, A. (1985). Marx's Theory of Emancipation and the Analysis of Modem Social Movements, pp. 261–275. In: B. Chavance (ed.) *Marx en perspective*. Paris: EHESS.

Nowak, L. (1973). Teoria formacji społecznej jako teoria adaptacyjna [Theory of Social Formation as a Adaptive Theory]. *Studia Socjologiczne*, 4, 5–21.

Nowak, L. (1980). *Głos klasy ludowej: polska droga od socjalizmu* [The Voice of the People Class: The Polish Road from Socialism Onward]. Poznań: WiW.

Nowak, L. (1981a). *Dwa szkice z nie-Marksowskiego materializmu historycznego* [Two Essays from non-Marxian Historical Materialism]. Poznań: WiW.

Nowak, L. (1981b). *Wolność i władza. Przyczynek do nie-Marksowskiego materializmu historycznego* [Property and Power. A Contribution to non-Marxian Historical Materialism]. Poznań: AR NZS.

Nowak, L. (1982). The Theory of Socio-Economic Formation as Theory of Adaptation Processes. In: L. Nowak (ed.). *Social Classes Action and Historical Materialism. Poznań Studies in the Philosophy of the Sciences and the Humanities*, vol. 6, pp. 110–121. Amsterdam: Rodopi.

Nowak, L. (1983). *Property and Power. Towards a non-Marxian Historical Materialism*. Dordrecht/Boston/London: Kluwer.

Nowak, L. (1984). O konieczności socjalizmu i konieczności jego zaniku [On the Necessity of Socialism and the Necessity of its Disappearance]. *Przyjaciel Nauk* 1–2, 105–150.

Nowak, L. (1986). O historiozofii, antropologii, utopii i gnozie [On Historiosophy, Utopia, and Gnosis]. *Przegląd Polityczny* 8, 132–161.

Nowak, L. (1987). Pętla pracownicza i kontr-pętla ideowa. Próba konkretyzacji modelu kapitalizmu [Labor Loop and the Ideological Counter-Loop. An Attempt at a Concretization of a Model of Capitalism]. *Przyjaciel Nauk*, 3–4, 41–55.

Nowak, L. (1989). An Idealizational Model of Capitalist Society. In: L. Nowak (ed.). *Dimensions of the Historical Process. Poznań Studies in the Philosophy of the Sciences and the Humanities,* vol. 13, pp. 217–258. Amsterdam: Rodopi.

Nowak, L. (1991a). *Power and Civil Society: Towards a Dynamic Theory of Real Socialism.* New York: Greenwood Press.

Nowak, L. (1991b). *U podstaw teorii socjalizmu* [The Foundations of the Theory of Socialism]; vol. 1: *Własność i władza. O konieczności socjalizmu* [Property and Power. On the Necessity of Socialism]. Poznań: Nakom.

Nowak, L. (1997). Efekt kresowy w procesie historycznym [On-the-Verge Effect in a Historical Process: An Attempt at an Interpretation in the Light of Non-Marxian Historical Materialism]. In: L. Nowak, P. Przybysz (eds.), *Marksizm, liberalizm, próby wyjścia,* pp. 307–319. Poznań: Zysk i S-ka.

Nowak, L. (1991c). *U podstaw teorii socjalizmu* [The Foundations of the Theory of Socialism]; vol. 3: *Dynamika władzy. O strukturze i konieczności zaniku socjalizmu* [The Dynamics of Power. On the Structure and Necessity of the Disappearance of Socialism]. Poznań: Nakom.

Nowak, L. M. Paprzycki, K. Paprzycka (1993). On Multilinearity of the Historical Process. In: L. Nowak and M. Paprzycki (eds.) *Social Systems, Revolution and Rationality. Poznań Studies in the Philosophy of the Sciences and the Humanities* vol. 33, pp. 355–370. Amsterdam: Rodopi.

Weizsaecker, C. F. von (1990). O kryzysie [On Crisis]. In: K. Michalski (ed.), *O kryzysie,* pp. 11–28. Warsaw: Idee.

CHAPTER 8

Hegel's Chuckle, That is, Marxism and Liberalism in Polish Politics

Leszek Nowak

Abstract

The purpose of this paper is to analyze the process of transformation in Poland from point of view of Marxist and liberal vision of social philosophy. According to this analysis, under the surface of the Polish politics of the period of transformation, a phenomenon significantly present in Hegelian dialectics, namely, the ideological "reversal of oppositions" has appeared. Namely, the liberal right assumes historiosophical assumptions of Marxist historical materialism in restoration of capitalism, and the left wing declares faith in liberal values.

Keywords

capitalism – historiosophy – liberalism – Marxism – Polish politics – transformation

According to a well-known thesis, 'communism' originated from the 'Hegelian sting.'[1] The very commonness of that view suggests it should be taken with a grain of salt. If everybody says so … A theoretician's – and maybe even every creator's – elementary experience is that if everyone claims the same about some (non-trivial) matter, then that claim must be fundamentally false.

Following that instinctive principle – supported with stronger or weaker arguments – I have, a few times, polemicized that that thesis was false (see: Nowak 1980; 1981; 1991b, pp. 251–256; 1991c, pp. 290–305; 1997a), so I do not intend to present further arguments against it here. Instead, I would like to show that there has appeared, under the surface of the Polish politics of the

---

[1] The paper appears in English translation for the first time. The Polish original „Chichot heglowski, czyli marksizm i liberalizm w polityce polskiej" was published in: K.T. Toeplitz (ed.), *Człowiek rynek sprawiedliwość* (Warszawa: Towarzystwo Wydawnictwa Literackiego, 2001), pp. 62–85. The abstract and key words have been added by the editor.

era of the so-called transformation, a figure significantly present in Hegelian dialectics, namely, the ideological "reversal of oppositions." To connoisseurs of more fancy phrases, we could also say that the recent decade of the political scene of the Polish Third Republic has been filled with Hegel's chuckle.

We must, however, begin with the question why it is the contemporary left, the enlightened and intelligent formation – on which a growing number of people, including those from the circles of the former democratic opposition, pins their hope for a change of the gloomy state of economy, state, and culture after the rule of the Solidarity Electoral Action – Freedom Union coalition[2] – quietly accepts the accusations that it has been poisoned by the "Hegelian-Marxist sting." It might be because the left is still under the influence of the right-wing historiosophical myths.

The main one is that myth of the "Marxist roots of socialism": Marx's historiosophical project is to be responsible for the injustice of the system of triple rule in real socialism. However, that thesis is clearly untrue. Teutonic Knights' form of government was a closer approximation to the pure triple rule than the form of the government of the Polish People's Republic – in those two systems, a similar degree of political and economic power was in the hands of minorities, but the Teutonic Order imposed the Christian worldview on Prussia much more forcefully than the communist government pushed dialectical materialism on Poles; it was also incomparably more effective in its efforts. The unfortunate Prussians were murdered, and their culture was destroyed, to the point at which only the name remained. If Marx's thought is to be responsible for the structural injustice of real socialism, then we should ask whose thought was responsible for the structural injustice in the state of The Order of Brothers of the German House of Saint Mary in Jerusalem.

Is Christ's thought responsible for the genocide and the destruction of culture in Prussia? According to the logic of Czesław Miłosz's or Leszek Kołakowski's reflections – yes, it is. But that is a blatant falsehood! The knights murdered Prussians in order to subject them to their rule and make them their workhorses, and destroyed their culture because cultural tradition binds individuals, which makes the community stronger. In the end, the Teutonic Order achieved its goal and obtained an atomized crowd of subjects. The fact that they utilized Christ's phraseology for that purpose (just like NKVD availed itself of Marxist phraseology) is an entirely different matter, ideological one.

---

2   The coalition between Solidarity Electoral Action (*Akcja Wyborcza Solidarność*, abbreviated to AWS) and Freedom Union (*Unia Wolności,* UW) formed a government in Poland in the years 1997–2001. These two parties originated from Solidarity movement of 1980–1981 [editorial note].

Social injustice must always be masked with some ideology, and any inconvenient elements (for example, the postulate of common property in the case of Christian thought or the doctrine of the gradual death of the state in Marxism) are always weeded from that ideology. Moreover, there will always be some silver-tongued orators who will present those meager remnants of a consistent concept as the banners of a new idea, and will even blow on them to make them flap. The ideologists of the other side will always accept the act of the self-disgrace of the opponent's doctrine at face value, except that they will supplement it with a sign of objection motivated by more or less putative damages claimed to have been caused by that thought of the opposing side because such acceptance makes it possible to cut the opponents off from their own tradition of thought. And that is the political-cultural function of the myth of the 'Marxist roots of (real) socialism': the cutting off of the left from its theoretical and axiological sources – preventing it from working on them in order to profit from a new variety of materialist social thought – and, in the realm of politics, the denigration of its values so that it lacks the civil courage to refer to them in public.

The myth, reinforced with a media campaign, deafening at first and just persistent later on,[3] turned out to be highly effective.[4] Devoid of its own spiritual heritage, the left – solidaristic as well as from the Democratic Left Alliance – simply took over the liberal historiosophy of the 'capitalist end of history.' Immediately after the victory of Marxism, liberalism, which has, for over 100 years, with the pens of John Stuart Mill, Friedrich Hayek, Karl Popper, or Raymond Aron – in Poland, of Leszek Kołakowski or Andrzej Walicki – criticized Hegelianism/Marxism for the supposedly invalid faith in the 'laws of history,' that is, in historiosophy, simply put forth its own historiosophy which had, by the way, always been inherent in it (Karl Marx himself criticized it), but it became manifest to the world without the (pseudo-)methodological cover of Fukuyama's 'claim about the end of history.' The historiosophy says that: human nature is, in principle, egoistic; in order to use that egoism for the public good, society founds certain institutions: a parliamentary democracy

---

3   In "Gazeta Wyborcza", the campaign is so comprehensive that it includes, for example, notes in TV shows. See: Nowak 2001b.

4   Symptoms of that abound. The newest one is the fact that it was possible to sum up the position of the left in the re-privatization debate in the following manner: "No-one dares to question the very principle of the return of nationalized landed assets included in the (agricultural) reform to their old owners' descendants (...). Even the people's movement does not dare to put forth the argument that most of the great landownership in Poland was the result of class exploitation of the country, and that the agricultural reform (...) was to be an act of social justice" (Toeplitz, 2001, 53).

and a free market based on private property; liberal capitalism is a natural state for people in the sense that every society either disappears or learns free-market economy and democracy – that process of learning can be stopped by means of violence, but the result will only be a delay, that is, a waste of historical time; when society finally reaches the state of liberal capitalism, it simply remains in it; that natural state ends social history.

That is the dominant right-wing vision of history. Surprisingly, it is also ashamedly accepted by the contemporary left, not only the Polish one, by the way. I write "ashamedly" because the left hides, in phrases like 'contemporary society,' 'modern civilization,' or 'post-industrialism,' the fact that they all refer to capitalism – the capitalism it has always wanted to overcome, either by way of revolution (communists) or evolution (socialists), in order to establish a new, juster form of government, worthy of human beings. By the way, when the matter is considered from a philosopher's and not a politician's point of view, the feeling of shame is quite justified.

From a purely cognitive point of view, the most serious theoretical foundation of left-wing thought, that is, Marxism, was abandoned decidedly too early. Admittedly, Marx's theory contains serious theoretical errors and Marxist explanations of social history have a number of gaps – I know something about it because I once had written hundreds of pages about them. Nevertheless, one has to state clearly that even with *those errors and gaps the explanatory power of Marxism is incomparably greater than that of liberalism*.

I cannot conduct a whole comparison of those orientations here as they are too complex. Let us, then, just compare – and that in a sketchy manner[5] – the core of the two doctrines, namely, their historiosophy. We will also remember the basics of methodology which require that when we choose from two theories which try to explain the same discipline (here: social history), we should ascribe greater cognitive credibility to the one which explains a more numerous set of facts.

To put it simply, social history comprises three development lines: on the one hand, the line of primitive societies – from which the line of non-European civilizations (for example, Inca or Chinese) derives – and, on the other hand, the line of the Western civilization. All those lines continue until today, in a more or less residual form. At this point, we might ask what liberal historiosophy can say about the nature of primitive societies or of the Inca society. Well, liberal historiosophy can only say that neither primitive societies nor Asiatic

---

5 I present a more detailed comparison, which also points to the practical advantages of liberalism over Marxism, in: Nowak (1997b) in English Nowak (2022) [editorial note].

despotisms have 'learned', as yet, that the optimal human institutions are parliamentary democracy and free market. As the social structures of those societies are drastically different from each other, what liberalism says about them is actually almost nothing. All liberal claims refer to the Western civilization or, more precisely, to the latest incarnation of those societies, namely, capitalism. Likewise, liberalism can hardly say anything about feudalism. For a long time, even capitalism was not included in the liberal model – after all, there is no liberal theory of revolution, and revolutions were a typical phenomenon of the 19th century in the world of Western civilization.

Capitalism only began to fall within the scope of the liberal model after World War II. The disappearance of the fascist alternative and, nowadays, also of the 'communist' one is an indubitable, serious argument for liberal historiosophy. Equally unquestionable, however, is the helplessness of that historiosophy when it is applied to the whole previous social history of mankind. The scope of the explanatory power of the liberal model is, then, limited to one development line of human societies, at the very end of the last of its known stages.

Marxist historiosophy cannot explain the contemporary stage of the evolution of capitalism, and liberalism explains the phenomena which contradict that historiosophy. Marxism, however, managed to also explain the earlier stages of capitalism, the pre-capitalist formations of the European civilization, and the Asiatic line of development (the very concept of an "Asiatic formation" was introduced by Marx, while the theory was created by Karl August Wittfogel who can also be considered to have worked in the Marxist tradition), as well as the nature of primitive societies (Maurice Godelier has created one of the most interesting concepts of those societies). It is not my claim that all those explanations are correct. I have actually questioned some Marxist theses about the Western line of development. When we compare the two theories, however, we do not refer to the category of truth – which cannot be determined by mortals – but to their ranges of explanatory power. To put it mildly, that comparison does not favor liberal historiosophy – actually, the range of the explanatory power of Marxist historiosophy is incomparably greater.[6] The left

---

6   I do realize that that phrase sounds strange in our country where Kołakowski's work, titled *Main Current of Marxism: its Origins, Growth and Dissolution* (1978), which heralds the "disintegration of Marxism" is considered to be the 'last word' about Marxism. The irony of the history of ideas is that it was precisely in the years in which those Kołakowski's volumes were published that the classical books on so-called 'analytical Marxism' – which became very well-known and influential in the whole Western intellectual world – were also published, mainly in England. Works such as Morishima (1973), Cohen (1978), or Elster (1985) belong to the leading, most often discussed publications on social philosophy of the English-speaking

was too quick to believe liberals. It simply yielded in the face of the clamor of global and national liberal press.

The left was also too quick to believe liberalism because, despite its own claims, it never legitimizes capitalism in our part of the world.

If liberalism opts for capitalism, making it almost the Aristotelian 'natural place' for which human societies are destined, then we might expect that, with the help of its own thought categories, it would be easy to justify a process so important as the 'construction of capitalism' (we will see below why the phrase is in inverted commas here). The basic category of contemporary liberal thought is the idea of human rights. Let us, then, ask who and by what right can decide about so basic a matter as the selection of a form of social government? The significance of that question will be easily seen by any person who realizes that it was a dilemma faced by Poland, in 1989, for probably the first time in human history. Before that time, capitalism in its initial stages arose spontaneously wherever it occurred: centers of social gravity formed around slowly growing capitals; as the owners of those capitals were becoming a significant social power, they gained the favor of state apparatuses willing to liberate themselves from their subjugation to the feudal class; therefore, even the violence of absolute monarchies was used to further develop capitalism, until it turned out that most of the working people who create a great majority of the domestic product were already circling around those centers; thus, it turned out that capitalism had already emerged. On the Vistula River, where there were no significant private capitals, it was, in 1989, in a way, a matter of a conscious decision. Who and on the basis of what right was to make it?

---

world in recent decades. Even such an accomplished liberal thinker as Raymond Aron wondered at that phenomenon ('Marxist systems' are at an end, and the Marxist theory flourishes in an entirely new way). Meanwhile, Kołakowski has been repeating that Marxism has ended. I present a critique of that idea from the quoted work, which is the most important one for the issues discussed in Nowak (1991a, pp. 252–255). That can only be understood as taking advantage of the ambiguity of the word because, although it is a truth for state ideology, it is an obvious falsehood for Marxism as a scientific theory. The latter statement is proven by the great cognitive successes of 'analytical Marxism' in recent decades (for example, the mathematization of the theory of surplus value from *Capital*, the formalizations of dialectical logic, rational reconstructions of Marxist historical materialism). For more information on that topic, see: Nowak (1997b [2022 editorial note]). Historical truth is even stranger – 'analytical Marxism' was not created in the 1970s in Cambridge or London but at the end of the 1950s in …Poland, where it evolved to a very sophisticated formal and logical system in Roman Suszko's epistemology and Leonard Sławomir Rogowski's or Oskar Lange's metaphysics. Still, the topic is virtually unknown in Poland… To sum the situation up by saying, with a sigh, "That is all so typically Polish" would not be accurate. A better explanation would be that it is all representative of provincialism in thinking.

Not only was that question not asked, but it was then that liberal newspapers started an uproar about the "lack of an alternative solution to capitalism."[7]

The problem is of basic doctrinal significance: do people have the right to make decisions about the form of government in which they are to live, that is, about the inescapable inconveniences and injustices of it which they are to bear?

If they do, then capitalism has been introduced in Poland illegally because no one has asked people who live here about their opinion on the matter, for example, in a referendum. Not only have the people not been offered an opportunity to say what they think, but they were also denied the freedom of the form of government. They would have that freedom if all the forms of ownership which had existed or which might, more or less spontaneously, be created were allowed in economic practice in an equal measure. For example, the option of employee companies was quantitatively dominant in the enterprises the ownership of which was changed from public to private, and the liberal elites did not even care to use honest terms – they gave that purely socialist form of ownership the name of the 'path to privatization'. Most importantly, the state only assisted – in terms of finances, organization, and ideology – one option: private capitalist ownership.

Who gave the elites of Solidarność the right to do that? Definitely, it was not liberalism because it is (significantly) silent on the 'human right to choose the form of ownership'. Neither can it have been the earlier, anarchizing tradition of the opposition of the Workers' Defense Committee in the Polish People's Republic, nor the ideology of the first Solidarność, which remained socialist from its very beginnings to the oppositional end. Not one person who knew the programs of Solidarity or, at least, read the newspapers which informed about the views of the 'social side' of the Round Table Agreement could guess that voting on that side on June 4, 1989 meant voting for private ownership as the basis for the form of government. Having voted for one thing, those people received, starting from January 1, 1990, something completely different, without a word of explanation. Solidarity, dominated by the circles of the Freedom Union of today, misled citizens as to its convictions about the form of government.

If, then, a civil society has the right to decide about its form of government, then that right was clearly not given to Poles – actually, that right was, in practice, violated, and the society was duped. Until now, none of the political forces

---

7   Meanwhile, as shown by Tadeusz Kowalik (2000), there were alternative solutions in Poland. The elites of Solidarity did not see them because their "views did a 180 degree turn."

responsible for that fact has revealed the nature or even the mere fact of that manipulation concerning the form of government in Poland.

Perhaps, however, society does not have the right to decide about its form of government? Perhaps that is not a voting matter? Perhaps. Admittedly, in contemporary conditions it only means that when the right to decide about those matters is taken away from citizens, they are voted on during the meetings of political offices, episcopates, or – at best – parliaments. When the right to decide is granted to elites, then the purported sovereign, the will of which is invoked in all constitutions, is refused that right. Therefore, even if one agreed – contrary to the spirit of democratic constitutions – that people should be refused the right to choose forms of ownership, even though the effects of that choice will be suffered by the people (not the great owners who fare quite well within the framework of those constitutions), then that principle ought to apply to all forms of government, not only to capitalism. If, then, the majority of voting citizens in Poland are refused the right to select the form of ownership, how did it actually happen that those same citizens have so recently brought down (not without a significant contribution of the reformists from the Polish United Workers' Party, let us remember) 'communism' based on state ownership? In the Polish People's Republic, the 'democratic opposition' which refuses citizens the right to a referendum on the form of government should, it seems, have supported the form of government of the Polish People's Republic. At the very least, it should not have encouraged citizens to rebel against the 'inviolable state ownership'. After all, if we allow someone to choose between *A* and *B*, we accept the rejection of *A* for the sake of *B* as well as the rejection of *B* for the sake of *A*. In this case, however, it looks like the 'democratic opposition' has granted the Polish society the right to reject real socialism, but the same elites, once in power, refused the society the right to possibly reject capitalism. Why? Because they know better? Because they have the only true historiosophy? Can one be so complacent as to think that anyone has truly credible knowledge about such matters? Not to mention the fact that every citizen of the Polish Third Republic has learned that only communists always know better and want to make people happy without asking their opinion ... Meanwhile, liberals have just behaved like communists, right before our eyes.

That is not, by any means, a word play designed to put down the 'new liberal people'[8] from the Freedom Union. It remains a fact that people who call

---

8 I have described (Nowak 1996) the numerous doctrinal about-turns of that political circle and the possible reasons for them.

themselves democrats have treated 'their sovereign' like numbskulls incapable of deciding their own fate, the way communists used to do. However, communists, when doing so, acted in accordance with their doctrine about the 'bourgeoisie democracy' – they were consistent or, at least, not hypocritical.

Later, things continued the same way – *in political practice, Polish 'new liberals' applied the schemes of Marxism.* For decades, we have been reading, in emigration or opposition publications, that capitalism is the only form of government which is created spontaneously because it reflects the 'natural tendencies' of human egoistic nature. We may 'construct,' on the basis of projects, totalitarian forms of government, but capitalism 'creates itself'. Obviously, if we believe that capitalism is a natural form of government, and if we want to maintain congruity in our thinking, we must accept those precepts which lead to the conclusion that 'construction of capitalism' is a self-contradictory term. Never mind that all those deductions could hardly survive a confrontation with obvious historical facts (it was not on the basis of speculations but on the basis of those facts that Marx showed that state force is the midwife of capitalism). From our point of view, the most important thing is that as soon as the elite from the Freedom Union eagerly forgot its socialist origins and, immediately after taking over power, transitioned to monetarist liberalism, the party also forgot all deductions from the concept of a 'natural form of government' and announced a state program of the 'construction of capitalism,' which simply confirmed Marx's thesis. Once more, state coercion – fortunately, without violence (since the Enlightenment, moral progress has been an unquestionable fact in the Atlantic civilization) – turned out to be indispensable for the introduction of capitalist relations of production.

Marx's shadow was cast over the whole Polish transformation. After all, it was Marx who authored a historiosophy according to which technological progress determines the form of government – a form of government which hinders that progress is historically reactive and collapses. Those were also the typical arguments of the right wing of Solidarność against real socialism: that no important inventions were made in it, that it obstructed technological progress while they had pinned their hopes for that progress on the new form of government. It was Marx who introduced the concept of an economic base determined by the type of ownership relations. And then, when it came to the 'construction of capitalism,' it turned out that privatization was necessary precisely because the type of ownership relations (and not the scope of 'freedom' or the type of 'human rights', or the level at which they were perceived) was the foundation of forms of government, and that there could be no technological progress or a democratic political superstructure, characteristic of capitalism, or the appropriate liberal mentality, without private ownership. It would be difficult to find more Marxist ideas!

'New liberals' from the Freedom Union only bit their tongues so as not to use Marxist jargon (partly because of public reasons – after all, Marxism was the subject of almost two decades of their ideological critique – and partly, probably, because of private shame ...). As I have neither public nor private reasons to be ashamed of my former views, I will express the real doctrine constituting the foundations of the 'construction of capitalism' in terms of Marxist historical materialism: ownership relations adjust to the level of productive forces; those relations are historically progressive when they allow the increase of productive forces; progress in the organization of the process of production adjusts to that increase, and the work of the direct producers' class leads to the growth of the surplus product of the owners' class; appropriate political and legal superstructure is needed for the maintenance and additional stimulation of economic growth; the whole of it functions even better when liberal consciousness – including the ethics of dutiful work on one's own account – is popularized among citizens. Had Poland chosen the Chinese road and 'constructed capitalism' under the auspices of a communist party, the doctrine described above could be repeated during (internal) trainings for the management of the Polish United Workers' Party by the employees of an Institute for Basic Problems of Marxism-Leninism ...

Not only the principles of the 'construction of capitalism' but also local deviations from the 'universal teachings of Marxism' were determined along the lines of Marxist reasoning (not to be confused with speaking). How else could we explain that the former 'lay left' has moved, en masse, in the direction of, to put it mildly, the Catholic Church in Poland? No social phenomenon can be explained by 'summing up the units.' It is a well-known fact that spontaneous conversions to a faith do happen, however, the problem is why they have become so common and so sudden, why atheists convert to Catholicism (after all, there are many alternative choices for the seekers), why even the few atheists who have not converted do not call themselves atheists but choose a less radical expression ('agnostics'), why even the brave 'agnostics' hasten to declare that they feel something is missing and that they actually envy believers, and, last but not least, why the former 'lay left' so often overlooks the actions of the haughty institution of the Catholic Church. What can be understood at the level of an individual and his or her personal biography becomes incomprehensible as a social phenomenon. Still, the change of the world view of a whole political formation – seemingly undisturbed by the open nationalism or antisemitism which are so prevalent among the hierarchs of the Catholic Church in Poland – can be easily explained with the help of one premise – one just has to assume the prevalence, in the circles of the 'new liberals', of the faith – sometimes unconscious that the problem will be resolved on its own when the capitalist economy is fully established in Poland (and Poland enters the lay European Union). The temples of that church (let us not call it by its name yet) will become empty, the church will become weak, the market will easily cope with the sanctimonious baloney which will not be read by anyone, and the church will turn into what it is in the West: a component of the cultural tradition, devoid of serious impact on human attitudes. The capitalist base will manage the ideologically incongruent superstructure by reducing it to the role of a traditional ornament. The whole effort must, therefore, be put into economic politics, and the superstructure must be left to the Christian National Union or Solidarity Electoral Action – they will not do much, anyway. Actually, one could hardly imagine more Marxist reasoning ...

I would not, obviously, like to claim that all elements of the politically active liberal thought (that is, thought which motivates political activity) derive from Marxism. For example, the resistance against an 'overprotective state' in real socialism is motivated by *purely liberal reasons*.

Let me first speak about a certain political inconsistency related to that. In the times of Solidarity, the 'new liberals' of today from the Freedom Union called the state-owner an exploiter – hence the proud and, at the time, merited name of the Workers' Defense Committee. We also remember the wave of accusations made by Solidarność in 1980–1981, which, in the language of *Gazeta Wyborcza*, only deserve one word-insult: populism ... However, when the form of government changed, it turned out that the state was not so much an oppressor of the people as its blithe benefactor.[9] The side is unimportant – the point is to kick the opponent ... Thus, the matter is clear: neither in the past, nor now have the circles of the current Freedom Union (not to be confused with particular individuals who sometimes deserve authentic respect) cared about the 'point of view' – they only cared about their own prospects. The fact that the actual situation is accompanied by the drums of (subsequent) ethoses is not surprising for a historical materialist – on the contrary, it is expected.

However, the basic liberal motif of the politics of the solidarity government was a conviction, derived from global liberalism, that contemporary capitalist economy is no longer capable of carrying the financial burden of social welfare which it had put upon itself in the 1950s. That is a truly liberal explanation, but two things here are not clear.

---

9 J. Zychowicz drew my attention to it in one of his publicistic texts.

First, the explanation is not easy to understand. Let us consider that for decades, capitalist economy has been able to provide the means for social welfare but now it can no longer do that. Surely, the effectiveness of capitalist economy must have decreased? If a horse carries a burden and, after some time, stops, it means that the animal has fallen ill, does it not? However, common sense contradicts that notion – in recent years, capitalist economy has been bolstered with tremendous development of production technologies ('new technologies'), organizational technologies ('informatization'), and economic knowledge ('monetarism') ... How is it possible that it has nevertheless become so weak that it can no longer contribute to the equalization of opportunities in the conditions of allegedly free competition?

Second, we do not know how exactly the 'welfare state' wasted money. The waste must have been due to administrative overgrowth, usual for states. Yet, in the past, many people were receiving large parts of those huge funds and had the means to buy bread, modest clothes, maybe even a used car. The social welfare system was not 'wasteful' because it created demand for goods, even if elementary ones. Instead of looking for things in dumpsters, people bought them in small stores, helping local store owners – and, indirectly, entrepreneurs, who are supposedly the cornerstone of capitalism – to survive. Who, then, was actually losing in that situation?

The currency of (some of) Marx's ideas has been revealed in this text so many times that I will take the risk of thinking in the Marxist way:

> were the beneficiaries of the spending reduction of the 'welfare state' not those who do not sow, do not plough, and yet their capital is growing? Perhaps it was them – the owners of the capitals which were fruitlessly circulating between New York, London, Frankfurt, Tokyo, and back and which multiplied on their own, for themselves, and without much import for the rest of the human world – that increased those capitals even more in that way. Could it be, then, that free-market economy, profit-oriented and, within that meaning, 'effective' – increasingly so under the liberals' auspices – is not rational, in spite of the way it presents itself? In reality, the "huge economic success of the United States" in the last quarter of the century consisted in ... a decrease of the average American's real wage of by 18%, with a simultaneous increase of the richest 1% of Americans' wealth from 20% to 36% of the national property of the USA. Even a satirist would not come up with such a 'criterion of progress'. Perhaps, then, that inability of capitalism to maintain a social welfare system is a testimony to the progressing parasitism of the once free-market economy.

Perhaps equating profitability with rationality should – in a world which cannot feed hundreds of millions of children or manage mass illnesses, even in the most civilized countries, and in which global natural environment is being destroyed – simply be viewed as fairy-tale wishful thinking.

I am not an economist, and those sentences are intended as questions rather than statements. To be honest, though, I am convinced that there exist purely liberal elements in the thought of the (serious!) Polish right wing. One example is the decision to close all state-owned farms which brought extreme poverty on a large part of Polish rural areas. The decision was made by a person who has somehow disappeared from the Polish political scene, which is rife with politically assigned positions, and who cannot, even after over a decade has passed, simply say: "I was wrong, I am sorry."

Nevertheless, it is easy to see that all those elements are of secondary importance for historiosophy. The core of the assumptions which legitimize the construction of capitalism in Poland are Marx's theoretical ideas (not to be confused with a social program), sometimes merely expressed with words which sound neoliberal. Those ideas constitute a framework supplemented, in some areas, by liberal theses and filled in by liberal program postulates ("privatize!," "re-privatize!," etc.). Still, whoever has spent a little time studying the methodological structure of social doctrines, knows that it is their theoretical frameworks that play an absolutely crucial role. The filling in of that thought model with particular postulates may be politically troubling but is theoretically trivial; in particular, the so-called 'disputes about values' are usually covert disputes about the truthfulness of the assumed theoretical theses, that is, the way in which we conceptualize the social world. That is why the fact that the 'new liberals' from the Freedom Union applied Marxist thought to their construction of capitalism is significant.

Can we, in such a case, justify the conclusion that it is capitalism that has *'Marxist roots' in Poland?* It depends on who we are talking about. That conclusion is inevitable for those who believe in historical idealism, that is, in the dependence of social processes chiefly on social ideas. Miłosz, Kołakowski, and their countless imitators, then, would actually have to accept the thesis about Marxist sources of capitalism in our country. As those thinkers accept capitalism in the form it assumes in Poland, they must also admit that one of its accomplished fathers-founders was Marx. I am serious about it. The reasoning is as follows:

(1) social processes mainly depend on social ideas,
(2) 'new liberals' pursued a transformation policy – they founded Marxist historical materialism and filled in the Marxist theoretical model with liberal values,

(3) capitalism in Poland is a good, hence:
(4) we owe the introduction of capitalism to our country to, primarily, Marx's theory and to liberal ideology.

After all, conclusion (4) results from – assuming the usual meaning of the concepts included in our reasoning – premises (1), (2), and (3); from the formal point of view, the reasoning looks correct. Premises (1) and (3) are proclaimed by the mentioned authors quite explicitly. Only premise (2) may be contentious from their perspective; nevertheless, it concerns facts so it is also somehow empirically verifiable. If one cannot factually reject the arguments which speak for it and which have been quoted above and replace them with the alternative explanations of the facts referred to in those arguments, one should accept it. A liberal, then, should consider Marx to have been the father (the first one – because a thought model is more important than its ideological interpretation) of the form of government in which "everything is great", to refer to the well-known phrase from the quoted circles. For a *historical materialist*, the quoted reasoning is not, by any means, compelling because he decidedly rejects the premise of historical idealism (1), so there is no reason for him to consider the 'new liberals" arguments for their decisions to have been that important; therefore, a historical materialist will not refer to premise (2) at all, nor to any other premise of that kind. Consequently, he will absolve Marx from another absurd allegation, just like he absolves Christ from the responsibility for the numerous horrors his followers have caused their fellow beings.

Instead, a historical materialist will be trying to find out what interests the 'new liberals' were realizing during the so-called transformation and what the strange Marxist-liberal thought mixture mentioned in this text hides. "What interests might those be, actually, if there were no capitalists yet in 1989 – whose interests should those 'new liberals' actually have expressed?" – one could ask. That question sounds natural, does it not? That, precisely, is the proof of how deeply ingrained Marx's thought models have become in our subconsciousness. Marx would have to ask that question today. Perhaps, though, it would be worthwhile to think of a new question?

This is how, then – if the reflections sketched in this text are, indeed, correct – the *situation in Poland looks like from the ideological perspective*. The liberal right wing assumes Marxist historical materialism, and the left wing declares liberalism. It is a truly Hegelian "reversal of opposites". Both sides also believe they have built democratic capitalism which should only be improved here and there in order to measure up to the model of the union. That evaluation is – let us repeat that – founded on Marxist theory (not to be mistaken with the Leninist political program of one party representing proletariat, of the leading role of that party in a socialist state, and so on; see: Nowak 1991b, pp. 10–13).

Meanwhile, Marx's theory, despite its respect – in my case, great respect – for the historical role played by the author of *Capital* in the foundation of general social science, is based on a number of theoretical errors (Nowak 1991a, pp. 11–24, 167–199; in English: Nowak 1983, pp. 18–32, 137–187 [editorial note]). Those errors still have an impact on the Polish politics. They make it impossible to notice, both for liberals thinking in a Marxist way and leftists trying to reason in a liberal way, what is actually happening in our country, which has a bearing on social consciousness and on very real – and disadvantageous – social actions. That broad topic, however, belongs to a different discussion.

References

Cohen, G.A. (1978). *Karl Marx's Theory of History: A Defense.* Oxford: Princeton University Press.

Elster, J. (1985). *Making Sense of Marx.* Cambridge: Cambridge University Press.

Kołakowski, L. (1978). *Main Currents of Marxism: Its Origins, Growth and Dissolution.* Oxford: Oxford University Press.

Kowalik, T. (2000). Nowy ład społeczny: ani konieczny, ani pożądany [New Social Order: Neither Necessary Nor Desirable]. *Barometr Społeczno-Ekonomiczny 1999. Polska przed nowymi problemami*, pp. 35–36. Warsaw: ISIS.

Morishima, M. (1973). *Marx's Economics.* (Cambridge: Cambridge University Press).

Nowak, L. (1980). *Głos klasy ludowej: polska droga od socjalizmu* [The Voice of the People Class: The Polish Road from Socialism Onward]. Poznań: WiW.

Nowak, L. (1981). *Nie wiemy z dziejów akurat tego, co jest konieczne, aby zrozumieć świat, w którym żyjemy* [We Do Not Know from History Just It What Is Necessary to Understand World We Live]. Kraków: NZS UJ.

Nowak L. (1983). *Property and Power. Towards a non-Marxian Historical Materialism.* Dordrecht/Boston/Lancaster: Reidel.

Nowak, L. (1991abc). *U podstaw teorii socjalizmu* [The Foundations of the Theory of Socialism]; vol. 1: *Własność i władza. O konieczności socjalizmu* [Property and Power. On the Necessity of Socialism]; vol. 2: *Droga do socjalizmu. O konieczności socjalizmu w Rosji* [The Road to Socialism. On the Necessity of Socialism in Russia]; vol. 3: *Dynamika władzy. O strukturze i konieczności zaniku socjalizmu* [The Dynamics of Power. On the Structure and Necessity of the Disappearance of Socialism]. Poznań: Nakom.

Nowak, L. (1996). O polskich paradoksach [On Polish Paradoxes]. *Myśl Socjaldemokratyczna* 4, 7–20.

Nowak, L. (1997a). Historyczna wina, histeryczna gęba i materializm historyczny [Historical Fault, Histerical *Mouth*, and Historical Materialism]. *Bez Dogmatu* 32, 1–3.

Nowak, L. (1997b). Marksizm versus liberalizm. Pewien paradoks [Marxism versus Liberalism: A Certain Paradox]. In: L. Nowak, P. Przybysz (eds.) *Marksizm, liberalizm, próby wyjścia*, pp. 7–19. Poznań: Zysk & S-ka.

Nowak, L. (2001a). Chichot heglowski, czyli marksizm i liberalizm w polityce polskiej" In: K.T. Toeplitz (ed.), *Człowiek rynek sprawiedliwość*, pp. 62–85. Warszawa: Towarzystwo Wydawnictwa Literackiego.

Nowak, L. (2001b). Chwiejny filar demokracji. Kryzys polityczny jako choroba przenoszona drogą niedomyślanych aliansów [The Wobbly Pillar of Democracy: Political Crisis as a Disease Transmitted by Reckless Alliances]. *Dziś*, 4, 32–40.

Nowak, L. (2022). Marxism versus Liberalism: A Certain Paradox. In: K. Brzechczyn (ed.), *New Developments in Theory of Historical Process. Polish Contributions to Non-Marxian Historical Materialism,* vol. 119, pp. 106–118. Leiden/Boston: Brill.

Toeplitz, K. T. (2001). Lewica a polityka kulturalna [The Left and Cultural Policy]. *Myśl Socjaldemokratyczna* 1, 51–56.

CHAPTER 9

On the Prediction of the Totalitarization of Capitalism: An Attempt at an Evaluation after Twenty Years Later

Leszek Nowak

Abstract

In the paper, the methodological status of the prediction of totalitarization of capitalism is considered. The author of this paper made such prognosis in 1979. However, the neo-liberal policies of Margaret Thatcher and Ronald Reagan in the 1980 of previous century seemed to block the processes of cumulation of power and property. The author considers the directions in which non-Marxian historical materialism can be extended in order to accommodate the socio-political development of Western societies which do not confirm this prediction

Keywords

capitalism – idealization – liberal democracy – non-Marxian historical materialism – prediction – totalitarization

1 The Problem[1]

Non-Marxian historical materialism[2] is a set of a few theories of various scopes, of which two, having great scope, are the most important: the theory of

---

[1] The paper appears in English translation for the first time. The Polish original „O prognozie totalitaryzacji kapitalizmu. Próba oceny po dwudziestu latach" was published in: K. Brzechczyn (ed.), Ścieżki transformacji. Ujęcia teoretyczne i opisy empiryczne (Poznań: Zysk i S-ka, 2003), pp. 361–401. The abstract and key words have been added by the editor.

[2] I first formulated it in two articles: (Nowak 1979a; 1979b); my most important monographs on that topic were published in Nowak 1981; 1983b, 1988 and 1991d. I write about the genesis of that concept in the so-called adaptive interpretation of Marxian historical materialism developed in Piotr Buczkowski's, Jolanta Burbelka's, Andrzej Klawiter's, Krzysztof Łastowski's, Niedźwiadek's, mine, and other authors' works in my review articles: Nowak 1997; 1998a [editorial note].

property or economic power (see: Nowak 1979a; 1983b; 1991a) and the theory of political power (see: Nowak 1980a, 1985, 1991c; 1991d). Model VP of the first theory leads to a prediction of the totalitarization of capitalism. However, when one observes what has been happening in the last twenty years – especially the formation of neoliberal politics in the West and the later 'transformations' which, from the economic point of view, are considered, not without reason, to be a restitution of capitalism in the West – it is difficult not to have doubts as to the truthfulness of that prediction. I have expressed them many times in articles (Nowak 1986a, pp. 139–141; 1991a, pp. 340–342; 1996; English counterpart 2022a [editorial note]). In my book (Nowak 2000a, p. 84) I determined the prediction to be decidedly false. However, this conclusion – purely from the cognitive point of view – is the least important aspect of the issue.

The thing to bear in mind is that the prediction was not a prophecy – it was theoretical prediction, which means that it:

(i) was formulated in the technical terms of non-Marxian historical materialism, which were determined according to the standard principles of social theories in their current state: a few concepts were accepted as original – and explained by means of examples or postulates – and other concepts were clearly defined with the use of the ones introduced earlier (the original or previously defined ones);

(ii) was derived from the principles of one of the models of the already mentioned theory of property – Model VP – with idealizing assumptions accepted at the level of abstraction proper to that model and determined *explicite*;

(iii) was shown to be retained in a few subsequent concretizations of the Model VP – taking into account that the subsequent introduced in those models did not paralyze the trend predicted in the Model VP (although some of those factors did weaken the trend); therefore, the prediction is not only a thesis of that idealized model but also of some of its more realistic extensions.

I will elaborate a little[3] on those conditions further in the text; at this moment, I will just emphasize that, despite the suppositions of some polemicists,[4] the

---

A summary of non-Marxian historical materialism is presented in Nowak 1991abc. Of all the later developments of that concept, the most notable is Krzysztof Brzechczyn's theoretical-historical monograph (Brzechczyn 1998; English counterpart: Brzechczyn 2020 [editorial note]).

3 Just a 'little' because those issues have been explained a long time ago, in literature cited in footnote 1.

4 See, for example, Iem (1985, 1986), Wigorska (1986).

prediction was not a political act of attempting the impossible but – when appropriate proportions or, rather, disproportions between constantly backward social sciences and developed life sciences are preserved – a relatively normal theoretical prediction. The prediction was made, then, without references to theoretically insignificant, empty ideological ('freedom,' 'democracy,' 'civil rights,' 'free market') or moral ('human being,' 'dignity,' 'human rights') slogans.[5] For that reason, on the one hand, it lost persuasive power, but on the other hand, it could be confronted with facts. The result of that confrontation appears to be negative. If, then, that prediction fails, and if it is not an accidental perception but a consequence of the initial assumptions of non-Marxian historical materialism, then the error must be located in the foundations of that concept. Let us, then, take a closer look at the issue.

There is one more thing. I assume that readers of this article know the basics of the idealizational theory of science (Nowak 1977 and Nowak 1980b, or the summary written by Nowakowa and Nowak 2000). It is not possible to present it in greater detail in this work due to length limitations. A perfunctory presentation could be misleading when we have to refer to technical concepts and not only rely on intuitions.

2 Certain Reservations

To 'take a closer look' does not mean a 'thorough' look, though. Having worked in a completely different domain of philosophy for a few years, I cannot allow myself to indulge an exact analysis of the matter. Probably, it would not lead to interesting results anyway because that field of study – metaphysics – is very distant from social philosophy. I have, therefore, 'due to lack of use,' lost theoretical intuitions in the field of social theory and got very much out of touch with literature on the topic. In my willingness to nonetheless cursorily address that matter, I am actuated simply by a sense of professional duty because it is not proper to first claim something and then not account for it before readers, especially since on account of some circumstances which were entirely independent of me, I had many such intuitions in the 1980s. Hence, I will now try to discuss where the error might lie and what it might consist in. Perhaps a social theorist might find some of these explanations useful in the future.

---

5 If someone views that sentence as a proof of my disdain for values, I would recommend that person to take a look at chapter 6 of my book (Nowak 1974, p. 75–80) where values are presented as one of the most important sources of inspiration (but not justification!) in the humanities.

3 An Incorrect Prediction (of the End of Capitalism) and a Correct Prediction of the End of Real Socialism)

Is it, however, sensible to reflect on a theory which – to all intents and purposes (from our contemporary perspective) – was false with regard to such a basic issue? I think it is because the same theory made predictions about another basic issue which came true. Intuitively at first (in an article published in 1980a), and later (Nowak 1983b; 1985, and my other works) in a standard manner – that is, in accordance with the rules accepted in non-Marxian historical materialism (hereinafter I will abbreviate it to n-Mhm) – I predicted the fall of the system of triple-rule, which has been confirmed by the course of events. That prediction, which derives from Model I of pure power, is retained in the subsequent seven – more and more realistic – models of real socialism (Nowak 1988; 1991c; 1991d).

Granted, it only turned out to be true in its general outlines (I have already had the opportunity to intuitively identify certain specific factors which had to be additionally included in the justification of the prediction – see Nowak 2000b)[6]. Still, n-Mhm was capable of correctly determining at least one direction of the process which – as was noted in the global press for many years, with sarcasm flavored with journalistic satisfaction – completely surprised the official Western Sovietology[7] as well as both official and unofficial Eastern European sociology.

---

6 Krzysztof Brzechczyn indicates these and other circumstances related to the international affairs within the framework of the block of real socialist states (Brzechczyn 2003; English counterpart: 2007b [editorial note]).

7 It must have been the greatest surprise to the most prominent Sovietologist here, who co-created the theory of the 'totalitarian syndrome' (which presented the form of government of the Union of Soviet Socialist Republics as one which always renews itself and eternally atomizes the subjects of the party) and then, at the very end of 1970s – the theory of the 'convergence of capitalism and socialism,' and who, when asked in an interview about the perspectives of the Eastern form of government, gave the following answer: "Well, such forms of government – the Byzantine Empire is one proof of that – can rot for a few hundred years." Still, that did not prevent him from hastily writing, in the middle of the 1980s, about the "grand failure" of communism – following journalist sparrows which had already been reporting, from every rooftop, what was happening in the East. In that context, we should also mention a positive example. Probably the first author who indicated the actual direction of the development of 'real socialism' in a rationally motivated way (that is, not on the basis of a 'prediction' similar to: 'Without private property, sir, it will not hold!') was Witold Gombrowicz. That issue is discussed in my works (Nowak 2000a, 169 and in other publications).

  However, more important than anecdotes is finding the explanation why Sovietology turned out to be helpless. In point of fact, the phenomenon of social resistance in 'communist totalitarianism' was not interpreted in Sovietologist descriptions. Although Sovietologists knew about the workers and soldiers' rebellion in Kronstadt in 1921, the simultaneous peasants' rebellion in the Tambov Governorate, which lasted over a year, the wave of uprisings

I would like to apologize to the reader for my pettiness. My only excuse is that this is the first time I have written about that matter, and that I am doing it after many years. I do not see why, while openly admitting the falsity of one of the two basic predictions of my concept, I should be silent about the correctness of the other one.

4   A Non-Marxian Model of the Development of a Socio-Economic Formation

The Marxian model of the development of a socio-economic formation contains the following tenets:

(M1) Human civilizational development depends on the progress of technology ('productive forces'). Those societies which do not use technological progress lose the competition with other societies. Those which can achieve higher effectiveness of work prevail.

(M2) Work efficiency in a given society grows as follows: from a set of historically given systems of the organization of work ('relations of production'), the owners of the means of production choose those which, at a particular level of the development of technology, bring them the highest profit ('surplus product').

(M3) Every form of ownership, however, stagnates and becomes incapable of generating technological progress. At that point, there occurs the 'epoch of a social revolution' – social revolts enabled a new class of owners,

---

and strikes in the Gulag at the turn of the 1940s and 1950s, the wave of strikes and riots in 14 cites of the Union of Soviet Socialist Republics at the turn of the 1950s and 1960s, and about further strikes and riots in the 1970s, they did not grasp their historical significance. Even postwar history of Poland, where peasant rebellions took place almost every decade, did not open their eyes. The reason was obvious – after all, a proper interpretation of that resistance entails a theory lying dangerously close to the main enemy of Sovietology, namely, Marxism. That is why the categories of Sovietological thought could not encompass a mass movement like Solidarity. The same pertained to the near, at that time, end of the system. Generally speaking, Sovietology did not build a dynamic theory of real socialism – that would have meant the necessity of working in a paradigm similar to Marxism, since it was Karl Marx who introduced thinking in categories of dynamics into the theory of society. That could be done by Gombrowicz, who emphasized the closeness of his position to those of Hegel and Marx, but not by a liberalizing Sovietologists. Neither could the Sovietologists build developmental models of real socialism. Sovietology was decidedly too close to the ideology of a capitalist system. Even the most venerable ideologies – after all, liberalism is a serious and wise doctrine (see Nowak 1986a) – are still ideologies, thus, from the cognitive perspective, they make one blind.

which is more open to technological progress, to take over the ownership. Mechanism (M2) can operate again.

(M4) The highest form of ownership is capitalist ownership. When even that form of ownership begins to hinder technological progress, a proletariat revolution allows for a change of power and a transfer of property to society; at that point, unlimited generation of technical progress is possible.

It is very easy to criticize those theses today, so I will avoid this and just refer the interested readers to my earlier works (Nowak 1979a; 1983b, pp. 3–63; 1991a, pp. 11–52). I will only highlight three of Marx's theoretical errors which have been identified by non-Marxian historical materialism, since that is necessary in order to explain the model of the development of a socio-economic formation proposed within the framework of that concept. First of all, Marx assumes that technical progress occurs automatically, which is a historical falsehood (that type of progress only grew and became significant in modernity) and is theoretically incomprehensible within the framework of the philosopher's assumptions because it is not clear why the working class should be interested in it. Second, the mechanism of the appearance of new ownership relations is not clear in Marx's thought: it is not true that there always appears a new class of owners' (what kind of a 'new class of owners' appeared in feudalism?), and when – as is the case in capitalism – a new class of owners does, indeed, come into existence, then the mechanism of that appearance is not clear (how does technical progress relate to the principles of product division into profit and workers' remuneration?). Third, Marx presupposes a common sense but entirely false model of a revolution: a rebellion is to happen in conditions of extreme destitution caused by that unclear "conflict of productive forces and ownership relations." If that was the case, then neither German concentration camps nor Soviet labor camps would have been possible. Let us not, however, dwell any longer on the errors in Marx's theses about the "socialist revolution" – in that regard, we can clearly see very commonplace and naive moralism in Marx's reflections, the conviction that "truth (moral truth, here: the rationale of the oppressed) must prevail in history." In Marx's defense, we can add here that Christianity has been unashamedly avowing such things until today and, on top of that, it has been calling them "social science."

That is enough to grasp the meaning of the model of a social formation proposed by n-Mhm. That model is based on certain idealizing assumptions:

i. technical progress is constant;
ii. the society in question is economic and two-class (it consists of the class of owners and the working class) – the division of a society into political (rulers/citizens) and spiritual (priests/followers) classes is omitted here;

iii. it is assumed that there is no division of labor in that society (that is, no new sectors of economy come into existence);
iv. the institutional superstructure of that society in the sphere of economic, political, and spiritual power is omitted here, on the side of the dominating and the dominated classes;
v. the influence of social ideologies/utopias on the social processes in the spheres of economy, politics, and world view is omitted;
vi. also omitted are international affairs, in all three areas of social life.

Three factual principles are assumed for that abstract society, namely:

(R) [*a non-standard mechanism of a revolution*] the class struggle has the form of a bell curve: workers do not rebel when the level of exploitation is low (because they are satisfied with having work which pays for their everyday needs) or when it is high (because destitution causes rivalry among the workers themselves, for the elementary means of survival), revolutions only happen when exploitation is at an average level (when it is already felt but does not paralyze the solidarity of the exploited);

(E) [*the principle of the moral egalitarianism of classes*] in every sufficiently numerous population of people, both from the ruling classes and from the classes of subjects, competition leads to the victory of those individuals who are the most willing to exploit and/or rule over others, and/or spiritually subjugate them.

Instead of the groundless belief in unlimited demand for goods produced in the economy, as demonstrated by Rosa Luxemburg in her critique of Marx's *Capital*, it is also assumed that:

(L) [*Luxemburg's condition of economic balance*] the increase of real social demand (grounded in actual income) is a necessary condition of economic reproduction.

From principles (R), (E), and (L) – with assumptions (i)–(vi) – it is concluded that the discussed abstract society develops in the following way:

I. *the phase of class peace*: given the lack of workers' resistance, the mechanism of competition leads to growing exploitation and, in turn, to the appearance of that resistance;

II. *the revolution phase*: resistance becomes general (a peaceful or violent revolution); should the masses win, the leadership elites eliminate the former owners and become the new economically ruling class; then, there is a return to phase 1: competition among the rulers leads to greater exploitation and, finally, a new revolution directed against 'their own' elites (the labor loop[8]);

---

8 The idea of a workers' loop has been present in n-Mhm since the monograph of Nowak 1981; 1983b, whereas the concept and term were introduced in Nowak 1987.

III. *the phase of the evolution of ownership relations*: in the case of a lost revolution, the owners – in order to avoid new social upheavals – modify ownership relations (the principles of product division into their profit and employees' remuneration) to the benefit of the working class; they become a 'new class' of owners because the ownership relations have changed, and the newly achieved class peace becomes the first stage of the next socio-economic formation.

In order to emphasize the historiosophical meaning of this model, let us note certain conclusions which contradict both most important historiosophies: Marxian and liberal. Contrary to what Marx wrote, relations among economic classes are not a 'zero-sum game' because classes must cooperate. However, contrary to what is proposed in liberalism, that game must lead to revolutions which are not historical accidents but an inescapable result of the mechanism of free competition among owners. However, and again, contrary to Marxism, a revolution is not an 'engine of progress.' If it wins, it is actually a driving force of social regression. The mechanism of competition among the winners always brings about a restitution of exploitation, which means another upheaval, while a repetition of the workers' loop under the control of 'their own' elites may even constitute a threat to the condition of balance (L)[9]; elites which derive from the lower strata of society are always more voracious than old elites, who are materially grounded and stable. A revolution only leads to progress if it is lost, but economic effectiveness is improved by the class of old owners ('exploiters') who, afraid of further losses, alleviate the situation of the masses by introducing new ownership relations which are also more beneficial for themselves. That is how, under the (again expected) influence of the subjugated, the victorious class of owners transforms, in an evolutionary manner, the old socio-economic formation into a new formation which is better from the point of view of general social interests. That is another anti-Marxian conclusion. Admittedly, that conclusion is made with intentions which are close to Marxian intentions. I have never tried to hide that, nor do I attempt to deny it today.

---

[9] In certain, special circumstances, a lost revolution can even bring about an economic catastrophe (Tomczak 1985; 1989).

5   The Peculiarity of Capitalism and the Prediction of Totalitarianism

After some insignificant modifications, Model I, sketched above, is used for the slave formation (Model II), and after some more serious modifications, related to the rejection of assumption (iii), it is transformed into Model IV, which applies to feudalism. In both formations, the growing consumption (including the construction of palaces, pyramids, etc.) of the ruling class played the role of a driving force of consumption which created social demand (see condition (L)) as well as more modest but real mass demand of the class of direct producers. In the first two formations, then, the issue raised by Luxemburg – of how a society creates consumer demand – was solved by the parasitism of the rulers whose excessive and constantly growing consumption (with respect to cost), combined with the derivative consumption of workers who satisfied their rulers' ever more sophisticated requirements, allowed for the fulfillment of Luxemburg's condition (L).

The peculiarity of capitalism consists in the inclusion of the mechanism of technical progress. When we reject condition (i) as clearly unrealistic for modern conditions, we are dealing with a society which constantly increases its product because of the incessantly improving efficiency of work (the growing technical surplus of goods). Here, the rate at which demand grows due to rulers' love of luxury is no longer fast enough (especially since capitalism eliminates the feudal barriers between social classes and everyone can become an owner, even a person from the bottom of the social ladder). Therefore, it is not possible to construct a purely economic Model V of the development of a capitalist formation – fashioned after Marxism or liberalism. The Model I have been trying to present (1983b; 1991a) does not fulfill the conditions of economic balance (L).

A closer analysis reveals that the state apparatus creates additional consumer demand – that is, guarantees the fulfillment of Luxemburg's condition (L). Knowing that, we can explain the correctness of Marx's historical analyses which demonstrated that state violence helped bring capitalism to life (on the other hand, those analyses undermined his doctrine about the state as an "eternal superstructure" of the economy). In order to construct a theoretical model of a capitalist formation, then, one has to reject assumption (ii) by introducing the division into political classes. Three major corrections of Model I can be formed as a result of the mutual game of both pairs of classes, economic and political, the rules of which it would be hard to present here, even briefly (for a more detailed discussion see: Nowak 1983b; 1991c; 1991d):
- Incessant, increasing technical surplus accelerates the formative cycle (a phase of class peace followed by a phase of a revolution, followed by a phase

of concessions on the part of owners). Owners, as they retreat in the face of a social threat, increase workers' remuneration from technical surplus, that is, from the expected profit, and, as a result, they no longer have to revise the ownership relations. That cycle, interpreted purely in economic terms, appears to be a business cycle of the market-capitalist economy.
- After a certain number of such cycles, permanent class peace is achieved: the working class enjoys stable welfare and its revolutionary tendencies disappear.
- The whole process occurred differently than in previous class formations – at the prize of makeshift concessions without revisions (increasing socialization) of ownership relations. Capitalism, considered in Marxism to be a classic socio-economic formation, is the first formation in which class struggle within the meaning assigned to it by Marx disappears.

That does not mean that capitalism becomes the liberal 'end of history.'[10] Due to purely economic necessities – the creation of effective demand for products of a dynamic economy – supra-class relations between owners and rulers become more and more important. By way of evolution, a class of rulers-owners is formed which gradually subjugates private economy (like in tsarist Russia: Nowak 1983b, pp. 239–371; 1991b). Citizens' masses are stirred to resist the growing power of the rulers-owners class; however, because of certain peculiarities of the mechanisms of the struggle of political classes, which cannot be elaborated upon in this perfunctory summary, it does not matter if the citizens' class wins or loses – the result is the same: the creation of a system of double, political and economic, rule. The only difference – a very small one, which results from principle (E)[11] – between the two scenarios is that in the case of citizens' victory, the rulers-owners come from the revolutionary elites. Capitalism ends in totalitarianism which, in turn, leads to an accumulation of the third, spiritual kind of power, so it transforms into a system of triple rule.[12] That was the prediction (intuitive in 1980a, expressed in greater detail in 1981, 1983b).

---

10 That thesis, which is now associated with Fukuyama, has been present in liberalism almost since its very beginnings – its critique is one of the main motifs of Marx's *Theories of Surplus Value*.
11 In 'our capitalism' today, we can observe examples of that, too.
12 The postulate of that last step was purely intuitive because no general theory of a spiritual power could be developed on the grounds of n-Mhm; only two special cases of it were presented (power in a religious community: Buczkowski, Klawiter, Nowak 1987; English counterpart: Nowak 2022b [editorial note] and power in a scientific community: Nowak 1986b; 2000a, pp. 212–227). I have reported that (see, for example, 1991a, preface).

In n-Mhm, the theory of capitalism is superimposed on the very roughly sketched Model VP of a theory of the socio-economic formation and is comprised of five models:
- purely materialist Model VP (Nowak 1981, pp. 144–189; 1991a, pp. 221–239 and 314–329)[13],
- materialist-institutionalist Model VP*inp* with political institutions (Nowak 1991a, pp. 346–353; English counterpart 1989 [edtiorial note]),
- materialist-institutionalist Model VP*ine* with economic institutions (Niewiadomski 1989),
- materialist-consciousness Model VP*c* (Nowak 1991a, pp. 314–329),
- (partially) a model of inter-social relations, VP*m*, which encompasses the relations between a capitalist metropolis and its supra-class peripheries (Paprzycka, Nowak 1987, reprint in: 1991a, pp. 330–339; English counterpart 1989 (editorial note), also see: 1991a, pp. 343–345).[14]

The assumptions of the Model VP give rise to the hypothesis on the totalitarization of a capitalist society. A concretization of that model with respect to the role of political (Model VP*inp*) institutions, economic (Model VP*ine*) institutions, and social consciousness (model VP*c*) retains that hypothesis, while a concretization with respect to the relations between a metropolis and its peripheries (Model VP*m*) is irrelevant for it.

As has already been said, it looks like that prediction was wrong. Yet, was it, in fact, wrong? And if it was, how can we explain that failure?

6   Conditions of Falsity of a Historiosophical Prediction

The simplest explanation would be the one most often reached for by unworthy defenders of predictions belied by facts: a reinterpretation of the data which contradict the prediction.[15] I am not going to resort to that solution. At

---

13   This model could be somewhat expanded with the use of Brzechczyn's (1998; English counterpart Brzechczyn 2020 [editorial note]) application of the two-bell model of revolution, based on a non-Christian model of man, to the economy.

14   A number of models more or less alternative to the indicated core of the theory of a social-economic formation was also developed. In those models, various restrictions of the "core sequence" were removed in different ways. See, for example, Brzechczyn (1998, English counterpart Brzechczyn 2020, pp. 219–235 [editorial note]) or Banaszak (1997; 2022 [editorial note]).

15   A classic example of that type of 'defense' is the explanation Isaac Deutscher – an accomplished Trotskyist theorist of real socialism – provides an answer for the question why "it seems to us, one hundred years after *The Communist Manifesto*" (published in 1848), that Marx's prediction of a socialist revolution failed (Deutscher 1971, *Introduction*): we think

this point, however, it would be good to fully realize what the problem situation is, and especially, in what conditions a prediction can be declared to be definitely false.

The hypothesis that the West might be heading toward totalitarianism, however, is ideologically charged, to the highest degree – after all, it is contrary to the liberal historiosophy dominant in right-wing and left-wing thought, according to which democratic capitalism is the natural state of historical development. I will try, to the best of my ability, to discuss that hypothesis in as rational a manner as possible.

Let us begin with the methodological criteria which ought to be considered when forming a scientific hypothesis:

(*m*) Let a certain set of facts be the area to be explained. The hypothesis is the better, the more factors – as different as possible – there are in that set and the more of them can be explained within the framework of the theory from which the hypothesis has been derived.

According to Karl Popper's methodology (1964), rule (*m*) must be completed with a rule which prohibits clichés in science, as rule (m) itself allows for obvious, trivial concepts which appear to only be confirmed because they are generated by stereotypes. Hence, another rule is formed:

(*mm*) The more unexpected a hypothesis is, within the context of the existing knowledge, the better it is.

Both rules apply to all scientific hypotheses. For the purposes of our discussion, the rule which pertains to historical hypotheses is especially important:

(*mmm*) Let a set of subsequent historical trends to which the system was subject in the course of history be the area to be explained. The more trends, as different as possible, there are in that set, and the more of them can be explained by the theory from which the hypothesis has been derived, the stronger the confirmation of that hypothesis about the system.

7 Arguments for the Prediction of the Totalitarization of Capitalism

If we accept rules (*m*)–(*mmm*) – which are methodologically obvious – then, first of all, we have to say that the cognitive situation of the prediction about the totalitarization of capitalism is not as bad as it might appear to people who

---

this so simply because our time perspective is too short – from a sufficiently long time perspective, the whole of the 20th century will appear to have been a series of socialist revolutions in various places all over the world …

blindly accept the world view presented in newspapers. In the works quoted above, we can find a perfunctory but theoretically uniform – that is, referring to the concepts and hypotheses of n-Mhm, and only to them – explanation of many historical trends known from the history of capitalism. The Model VP makes it possible to explain, among other things:

(T1) workers' revolutions in the 19th-century capitalism;
(T2) the disappearance of the working class struggle against the bourgeoisie in the 20th century;
(T3) the reduction of the role of the state to that of a 'night guard' in early capitalism;
(T4) the cyclical nature of the development of the capitalist economy in the 19th century;
(T5) the sudden and great crisis of the 1930s (including its suddenness and greatness),
(T6) the coming into existence of the welfare state,
(T7) the reduction of the economic cycle to slight variations of the economic situation in post-war capitalism,
(T8) the fusion of great business and political structures (Galbraith's thesis);
(T9) the youth protests in the 1960s;
(T10) the wave of neoliberal politics in the Western countries in the 1980s (additionally see: Nowak 1987; 1993[16]).

The Model VP*inp* also makes it possible to explain, among other things, that:

(T11) a capitalist state assumes the form of a parliamentary democracy;
(T12) for some time, there has been a transition of the actual political power, from the legislative to the executive branch, even outside of the legal system.

The Model VP*ine* provides more detailed explanations of trends (T6)–(T8) because of the role of economic organizations on both – the owners' and the workers' – sides. The Model VPc also makes it possible to also explain why

(T13) in the 19th century, the consciousness of the working class was dominated by social utopias, and
(T14) later, contrary to György Lukács's predictions, it yielded to the influence of, first, social democratic reformism and, nowadays, of social liberalism.

Moreover, the Model VP makes it possible to explain

(T15) the ongoing irrationalization of the Western thought in recent decades (also see Nowak 1993; 1997b).

Finally, the Model VP*m* makes it possible to understand why

---

16 "Additionally" here means apart from the basic works referred to above, in which appropriate models are discussed.

(T16) "democracies are less warlike than other regimes" (Rudolph Rummel's thesis),
(T17) capitalist countries of the West went through a stage of colonial conquests, and
(T18) capitalist countries have now pulled out of colonialism.

Theory consisted from Models: VP, VP*inp*, ..., VP*m* also make it possible to explain many other trends, as well as particular facts; however, let us stop at that enumeration. Let us take a look at it from the point of view of rules (m)–(mmm). As shown in the works I refer to, the mere hypothesis of totalitarization makes it possible to explain trends (T6)–(T10), (T2), and (T5). Those trends are very diverse – as required by rule (m). It also seems to fulfill condition (mm) and it is derived from the theory which explains the trends from (T1) to (T18), which are characteristic of the historical course of the development of capitalism.

Surely, the proposed explanations are not 'the only possible ones.' After all, each of the trends (T1) to (T18) can be, and sometimes is, explained in alternative ways, as each fact can, obviously, be explained in various ways. For example, the fact that Western countries have pulled out of colonialism (T18) can be explained by the development of new techniques of production which require advanced infrastructure. That is a very factual explanation. The question arises, however, as to how many phenomena can be explained with the development of new techniques of production. Can we, for example, explain the student demonstrations in the 1960s (T9) in this way? Similarly, the coming into existence of a democratic state (T11) could be explained, for example, with the influence of democratic political philosophy on the shape of political institutions. How much, though, can be explained by references to the influence of political philosophy? The reception of John Locke's, Jean Jacques Rousseau's, or John Stuart Mill's thought is definitely connected to the wave of neoliberalism (T10) – even if we might question the direction of that influence – but not to the students' protests (T9) or the fusion of great property and the political structures of the West (T8). As regards the relationship between the Marxist motif of the "development of new techniques of production" with the idealist motif of the influence of political philosophy, it will slightly expand the scope of the explained trends, but that combination in itself is an eclectic set of completely different ideas which are difficult to reconcile.

In contrast, n-Mhm explains all those trends, starting from a uniform theoretical core, so it fulfills the requirements of rules (m)–(mmm).

The (T1)–(T18) list of important historical trends in capitalism is certainly not exhaustive. Also, it would not be difficult to find other well-known phenomena which have not, as yet, been explained in n-Mhm. For example, the already mentioned phenomenon of the development of productive forces is not explained by it, but it is entered into the vp model as a separate assumption. It follows that non-Marxian historical materialism has, as I have written many times (for instance, 1991c, 231–237) numerous theoretical gaps. However, all social theories have them.

Admittedly, the explanations of theses (T1)–(T18) are very perfunctory and rough. However, I would venture to say that that is simply a constant characteristic of the theory of historical processes. After all, the explanation that capitalism is permanent because it is "the only system which forms spontaneously" is not very subtle, either.

8 A Basic Fact

I am writing about it all in order to show that the prediction about the totalitarization of capitalism is not simply made up; it is derived from a theory with an empirical justification – a weak one, in absolute terms, but relatively not the worst one in relative terms, I believe. I am also discussing that issue to demonstrate that the fact that that prediction goes against the grain of accepted political (and, hence, journalist) thinking does not matter at all – it is not up to politicians (let alone journalists) to discuss basic social mechanisms. The fact that their opinions are all too often seconded by scientists – who have been yoked to political chariots – is not a testament to the charioteers' skills but a dishonor to the scientific (not to be confused with titular!) rank of 'fellow runners.'

I do not intend to deny the basic fact that twenty years after the announcement of the prediction about the evolutionary totalitarization of a typical capitalist society, not many trends have appeared which confirm that prediction, and it definitely has not stirred citizens' protests within particular capitalist societies – the masses do not protest much against the accumulation of economic, political, and media power in Italy (where, symbolically, it seems, the greatest media mogul became the prime minister), Great Britain, France, or Germany. The processes of the accumulation of class power are real, but they are not a basic fact of capitalism today; most importantly, they have not stimulated citizens' resistance. We must, therefore, admit that, apart from the basically (approximately) correct prediction that:

> (n-Mhm-I) real socialism will fall as a result of citizens' pressure against the triple rule (in classical cases – because of concessions of the triple rule, necessitated by subsequent lost revolutions), a basically incorrect

(that is, not even close to the actual course of events) prediction has also been made within the framework of non-Marxian historical materialism, namely, that (n-Mhm-II) the processes of class accumulation in capitalism will result in citizens' resistance which, however, will not be capable of stopping them;[17] consequently, capitalism will transform into totalitarianism, and then into a system of triple rule.[18]

Therefore, we should gradually begin to think about the renovation of non-Marxian historical materialism. For the already mentioned reasons, I will probably not be able to do that in the foreseeable future, but who knows, maybe these remarks will be helpful for another thinker who will undertake that task – or for another purpose. After all, wrong predictions have been made in other theories as well. Actually, the rate of the correct predictions made within the framework of non-Marxian historical materialism – that is, half of them – is rather decent.

The main claim to scientific pride here, though, is the very possibility of making some clear predictions on the basis of that theory – predictions which could later be proved wrong by the course of events. That theory was not limited to vague prognoses like "things might develop in various ways" or to more or less pompous generalities consisting of a mixture of normative ("human and citizens' rights," "the good is victorious in history," "democracy and capitalism are the end of history," etc.) and descriptive discourse. Once more, I would like to apologize to the reader for the perhaps too personal tone of my reflections. My only justification is this: I do believe that humility is required in the case of such an effective, inter-human cognitive mechanism as science (for a more elaborate justification, see 2000a, pp. 217ff.). I am not, however, the least inclined to be humble before many people who practice social science (especially those who owe their positions to mass media). I have lost – only with regard to a half of my predictions! – but at least I have played the game. I do not see any reason to be humble before those who have not even tried to join that cognitive game.

---

17 To put it more precisely, possible revolutions (possible in reality, necessary in the model) end in totalitarization, whether citizens lose or win (via the mechanism of a revolutionary loop). A theoretical justification is given by the already discussed model VP.
18 See note 11.

9 The Most Obvious Method of 'Modern' (Neoliberal) Renovation is Very Doubtful

As is frequently the case, what we consider to be the simplest – in the light of contemporary stereotypes, especially those of Eastern Europe – course of action is doubtful: it is not that easy to renounce non-Marxian historical materialism and replace it with 'what everyone believes,' namely, with liberal historiosophy in the style of Friedrich Hayek, Popper, Isaiah Berlin, or Leszek Kołakowski.

Let us compare the hypothesis of the evolutionary totalitarization of capitalism with the competing hypothesis, always present in liberalism, of capitalism being a natural social system which is the last and final stage of development of all countries. Then, we can ask about the list of historical trends which can be explained by the latter hypothesis. There surely exist such trends. The leading position on such a list would be occupied by the trend, observed in recent years in the countries of the former Soviet bloc, to imitate the system of parliamentary democracy and of private property. According to rule (mmm), that fact in itself does not suffice – it would have to be supported with explanations of possibly diverse trends from the whole history of capitalism. We can demand that liberal historiosophy find an explanation for the following facts: that there were series of workers' revolts in all the leading Western countries in the 19th century (T1), that regular crises of overproduction were occurring for over a century in leading capitalist countries (T4) – at a time when the state was, indeed, but a 'night guard,' and when the economy was almost solely a market economy; that 'welfare state' was introduced in the main countries of the West for half a century (T6); that there was a similarity – which was odd from the point of view of liberalism – between, on the one hand, the etatization of economy in the West and, on the other hand, the reduction of severe crises of overproduction to relatively mild oscillations in the economic situation and a simultaneous growth of welfare (T7); that there was a fusion of great business and great political power (T8), which contradicted the liberal theory of capitalism; that there were students' movements in the 1960s, (T9), and so on. I suspect that if one demanded that those explanations be somehow theoretically grounded – just like appropriate explanations within the framework of n-Mhm – that is, that they refer to the core of liberal historiosophy and not to the theses or even banalities (for example, about the imperfection of human nature) appended to it *ad hoc*, then many of the (T1)–(T18) trends would turn out to be hard to explain on the grounds of liberal historiosophy.[19]

---

19   That does not mean that n-Mhm cannot benefit from adopting liberal ideas for self-improvement in the mode of dialectic correspondence. Especially recommended

By that, I do not wish to say that the hypothesis on the liberal end of history is impossible. Such a hypothesis could be true because virtually anything can be true, including the hypothesis (n-Mhm-II) about the evolutionary totalitarization of capitalism. I only wish to say that if someone wanted to impel a rational being – a being who respects methodological rules (m)–(mmm) – to renounce n-Mhm for the sake of liberal historiosophy on the basis of the falsity of the prediction of non-Marxian historical materialism which has been discussed here, that person would have to:
- either present consistent and conceptually uniform explanations of trends (T1)–(T18) and some additional trends,
- or – if that person only managed to explain the majority of those trends – to compensate for that lack with a uniform explanation of a large number of those additional trends which, in turn, cannot be explained by n-Mhm.

On the other hand, if that person only managed to explain a few of the (T1)–(T18) trends and did compensate for that by explaining at least about a dozen of the trends unexplained by n-Mhm, then, even if the few explained trends

---

here – Tomasz Zarębski (2003; English counterpart Zarębski 2022 [editorial note]) is right about that – is the creation of an institutional concept proper to liberalism in order to enrich institutional models in n-Mhm. Tomasz Banaszak (1997; English counterpart Banaszak 2022 [editorial note]), for example, significantly expanded the n-Mhm theory of a state, including in it the role of political parties. Of similar interest is Zarębski's attempt at an incorporation of Adam Przeworski's ideas in n-Mhm. Those contributions are interesting attempts at creating new derivative models in the framework of non-Marxian historical materialism. I do not, however, agree with those authors' declarations that their corrections make it possible to cancel the prediction about the totalitarization and to 'save,' in that way, n-Mhm from the accusation of having generated a false prediction. In my view, the corrections they propose are too weak for that. In n-Mhm, the mere fact of the replacement of a state apparatus controlled by voters with a political corporation divided into two parts: the apparatus and people waiting for the election opportunity (Banaszak 1997; 2022) – which is actually worth trying because the model of a state which I have proposed included democracy, in a special case, but did not take into account the phenomenon of inter-party play (Nowak 1991c, pp. 81–86; Nowak 1991d, pp. 49–54) – is only a superficial, conceptual operation. For that fact to be able to thwart such a significant trend as a fusion of power and property, n-Mhm would have to be enriched with an assumption which is essentially alien to it (the assumption that the influence of a political ideology can outweigh the influence of the interests of a political corporation). Had that been done, however, the result would no longer be historical materialism but an eclectic amalgam of materialism and political idealism. Zarębski's attempt (2003; 2022 [editorial note]) at including the "reasonings of the proletariat (a typical proletarian?) on the forms of government" into the theory of a socio-economic formation is a similar case. It is difficult to incorporate one approach in the other without a paraphrase. Another problem is that I do not know how to carry out such a paraphrase in the language of n-Mhm – and if that is at all feasible.

were of the greatest importance for politicians (and 'serious newspapers'), it would not be significant from the scientific point of view. Such a person had better not aspire to scholarly recognition, especially if it is a person recognized in politics and in the media. Scientists are like soldiers: everyone must know their place in the line, and, in a respectable army, popularity in the canteen has no bearing on a charge.[20]

10   What Future Theory of Social Development Can I Imagine?

Only a conceptually uniform idealizational theory with the first model containing a few factors of a particular type and with the subsequent concretizations enriching that model with new factors – which can be of different types but are always interpreted ('paraphrased') in the language of the first model – can predict the future, and that always in a rough manner. The concepts of the postulated theory must, therefore, be uniform enough to grasp the deep structure of the studied phenomena. At the same time, that theory must do justice to the surface world and take into account the variety of factors which have an influence on those phenomena. Such a theory is not constructed by registering and multiplying trends of the kind enumerated, by way of example, above. There should, however, be as many such theories – alternative and, therefore, incompatible with one another – as possible so that the one with the greatest explanatory power can be found. A theory which could not explain the trends listed above should be removed or, preferably, withdrawn. It should not be artificially saved, by way of eclectic enrichment with elements of other theories – that is, by adding those elements to the body of the theory literally, without an appropriate paraphrase. It is better to sink in a well-constructed ship than abandon that ship in the hour of need, by taking over a common boat. Any master mariner knows that.

But how exactly can we imagine such a future theory? Quoting Tevye the dairyman from *Fiddler on the Roof*, I will tell the truth: I do not know. Describing such things in advance would, in Popper's words (1967, *Introduction*), be akin to making a discovery before it has been made. Discoveries, however, are not made easily. One has to work for them for many years. That work is not on

---

20   As the reader may have noticed, I am making a conscious effort not to mix the normative and descriptive modes here. That is how it should be in the social sciences. The actual state of affairs in that respect is lamentable, as I already had an opportunity to note (Nowak 1998c [English counterpart Nowak 2012, editorial note]; Nowak 2000a 212ff.) and prefer not to repeat in this text so as not to lose the civil courage needed to finish it.

facts – the time for a discovery comes when the main outlines of the thought image of the structure of a given process are ready, and if that image is good, trends roll onto the right shelves on their own. That work is work on oneself: one has to get rid of stereotypes and replace them with something that used to seem improbable, or even unimaginable. I, for one, cannot imagine even an outline of a new theory of historical processes. I will not begin such work in the foreseeable future, either – I have enough hard work on my plate, which is related to an entirely different and much more difficult topic (difficult for me, at least) topic.

11 'Conservative' (Neo-Marxist) Renovation is Also Doubtful

The second possibility of sanation is of directly opposite origins – after all, the following argumentation is also possible. The changes in capitalism in the last two decades, which have gone against the prediction of totalitarization derived from non-Marxian historical materialism – a prediction which seemed fairly accurate as recently as the turn of the 1970s and 1980s – are related to the new, neoliberal turn in the politics of Western countries. It would be quite reasonable to assume that economic policy – at least the kind which 'conquers the world' as it reappears, state after state, regardless of the victorious political orientation – is not accidental but a response to a certain need of the economy. In the case in question – according to neo-Marxism – the economy simply had to prepare for the introduction of the technical progress related to the revolution of information technology. The old, social democratic welfare state, with its inefficient public sector and social burdens, was not able to cope with the new wave of technical progress. Therefore, in the 1950s, enterprises were privatized, and the economic policy of the state was once more employed to serve the effective private sector. According to neo-Marxism, what happened was in agreement with the Marxian theory: the relations of the organization of production became adapted to the new level of productive forces, and the state superstructure to the – once again private – economic base.[21]

In the meantime, non-Marxian historical materialism began to reject the very foundations of Marxian historical materialism. For that reason, it does

---

21 It is probably worth explaining that that refers to Marx's theory – as it has been presented above – and not to his ideological or political views. A Marxist theoretical explanation of the transformations in the recent decades of capitalism is, then, quite possible, however, it ignores what he wished for as an ideologist, not to mention what he advocated as a politician.

not understand – I am continuing the neo-Marxist train of thought here – the recent course of events in contemporary capitalism. What is happening is in alignment with Marx's theory: the economy and its immanent demands still determine the direction of historical development, and the state is just a political superstructure which adjusts to the condition of the economy, while consciousness continues to sanction what objectively surfaces. The theses about spontaneous divisions into the classes of rulers and citizens, priests and believers are simply an old a fairy tale.

It is not my intention to disrespect that train of thought – not many thinkers would want to do that, at least in our part of the world (certainly not the ex-Marxists who are now zealous followers of neoliberalism or Christian social science). Still, I do not find that neo-Marxist road worth traveling today – even if that would be proof, in contemporary cultural circumstances, of great civil courage which should be respected at any time, in anyone. Courageous thinking is a necessary attribute of the mind but not a sufficient one, as evidenced – if I am not mistaken – also by this case. Clearly, to restore Marxian historical materialism today is a very difficult task, rife with problems with no easy solutions.

It is, indeed, possible to explain the 'neoliberal breakthrough' in Marxian terms, and it sounds quite reasonable. However, such an explanation is very risky for the author of that theory – it calls into question the theoretical theses about "the contradiction between social production and private appropriation." If, in order to absorb the new wave of technical progress, the economy must resort to privatization, then that contradiction must have disappeared in the 1980s of the 20th century – or could it be that it had never existed, in the first place? The former solution is wrong because it invalidates the generality of the theory. The latter is even worse because it completely discredits the whole theory.

What is more, the problems with Marx's theory did not begin at the time of Margaret Thatcher and Ronald Reagan. Can we even explain the half of a century of welfare, now social democratic capitalism now – after the makeshift acceptance of the Marxist explanation of the neoliberal breakthrough, quoted above? Can it be that the same thing which used to obstruct – let us say – the development of productive forces is now conducive to it, and what used to be beneficial for that development has turned into an obstacle? Those are clearly *ad hoc* explanations! We could, indeed, avoid that methodological error by referring to the content of the dominant state ideologies: for half a century, social democratic ideology was dominant, so the economy was nationalized, social welfare was developed, and workers were allowed to co-manage enterprises; now, when liberal ideology has become dominant, all that is all reversed. The problem is that when we use that line of thought as a crutch, we cut Marxism at the roots – it turns out that historical idealism is right. Everything depends on the contents of human minds, and the state is not a superstructure on an economic base but an enforcer of human views on the proper type of management ('beneficial for all,' 'as efficient as possible while ethically admissible,' or maybe 'morally right'?). Historical idealism might be the truth, but a Marxist defending in that way ceases to be a Marxist ...

The attempt at explaining the 'neoliberal breakthrough' in purely Marxist terms also, typically, lacks any explanations of that kind coming from Marx. Technological progress itself remains unexplained. The obvious fact that inventions are born from creative thought immediately gives rise to a suspicion that a turn is being made toward historical idealism, while any attempts at taking into account – from the very beginning – the 'reciprocal influence' of relations of production on productive forces makes Marx's basic statement (M_1) about the priority of the latter with respect to the former self-contradictory. There is, obviously, 'reciprocal influence' here – in social matters, it is quite common – however, where the theory declares the priority of A with respect to B, there simple influence (of A on B) must be of greater significance than reciprocal influence (of B on A); consequently, the first model of the theory must contain a statement about the priority, and the statement about the reciprocal influence can only be included in a derivative model. The Neo-Marxism of the English-speaking world has not, as yet, digested the old, Marxian method of idealization, as used in the Marxist theory of the bourgeoisie method of production.

Capitalism is not the only phenomenon which is problematic for Marx's theory. How can fascism in the Third Reich be explained within the framework of Marxism, that is, if we only use the core of that theory and not the alternative – *ad hoc* – additions to it? As great capital with its interests? It was absent in the Teutonic Order but there still was fascism – aggregated political power and a 'reign over souls' – there. Later, that fascism evolved very near to triple rule (Brzechczyn 1993). In the first place, it becomes unclear what actually happened – from the Marxist point of view – in Russia in 1917, in Yugoslavia in 1945, in China in 1949, and so on ... Why did the executives of communist parties have at their disposal incomparably greater means than the bourgeoisie in the West and how (according to Marxian conceptualizations) did those systems fall?

Let us stop at that. While Marxian historical materialism cannot cope at all with quite a number of great problems – as I tried to show in my earlier works – non-Marxian historical materialism explains all of them, more or less accurately. The relatively apparent success of Marx's theory in explaining the neoliberal breakthrough does not seem to be worth those difficulties. Surely, that explanation has earned the right to be included in any instruction book titled *Contemporary Attempts at Understanding Neoliberal Economic Policy*, but it does not – if I am not mistaken – have the 'cognitive ability' to be referenced in a (sufficiently comprehensive) course book on the history of social thought in a chapter on Marxism. That is because Marx, like any great person in human history, deserves respect regardless of the turn that history is taking and of the current travelers' direction of thoughts.

12 On Certain Development Trends and Their Interpretation

Having reviewed the solutions discussed above, dictated by stereotypes of both the right wing (including 'social democratic' ones, within the contemporary meaning of the word) and the left wing, we can see that there are no cognitive gains (not to be confused with ideological ones) gains without cognitive losses in theoretical work. In both cases, there appear to be more losses. However, if neither has succeeded, then how can we explain the fact that there was no totalitarization of capitalism for a quarter of a century? Contrary to all appearances, it is very easy to answer that question. There was no totalitarization of capitalism – not even a harbinger of it anywhere – because, in recent decades:

(C1.1) the internationalization of capital has created economic forces which are independent from political power – which remains at the level of national states – and shape an autonomous global market governed by its own, non-political laws;

(C1.2) that market, in accordance with economic laws, favors the Atlantic center of the world, which results in migration pressure from the peripheral countries and, consequently, increased disproportion of power between peripheral countries and global private potentates of the world market;

(C1.3) the pressure of structural unemployment in the democratic center of the world operates in the same direction, that of growing disproportion of power between economic and political rulers – after all, the unemployed will not turn against the flow of anonymous capitals, but they can, in democratic conditions, refuse their votes, so the state is tied to its voting citizens and, in this way, weakened in its relations with international capital;

(C2) as a result of globalization, the capitalist economy becomes ever more efficient, which has made it – as well as the institutions which support it, such as democratic structures of political power or liberal ideals – a model for general imitation, which, in turn, additionally bolsters the acceptance of the global center by the citizens;

(C3) the cultural and religious differences between the center and the peripheries pose a risk of conflicts between civilizations, one symptom of that threat being terrorism;

(C4) new communication technologies have been developed (the Internet!) which make it more difficult to control citizens, if the elites were inclined to do that;

...

(Cn) the conditions of contemporary civilization atomize citizens and make it very difficult for them to organize any kind of a mass protest – the crisis of the union movement is a symptom of the gradual disappearance of civil society.

A person whose bookshelves are filled with current literature on the subject would easily add to the list (and maybe even determine the value of that n), enriching all items with a plethora of data and crowding them together in a more or less suggestive narration. However, an answer given in that way: the totalitarization of capitalism did not happen because (C1.1–3) and/or (C2) and/or ... and/or (Cn) would be worth as much as analogous (with respect to the lack of a proper methodological structure) answers to the question why 'communism' persists[22] – which I found on my bookshelves a quarter of a century ago. It is also possible that their approach to future facts will be quite similar to Sovietologist descriptions which consistently ignored the basic fact of real socialism: social opposition to that system.

Indeed. Trend (C 1.1) is based on a wish that the 'global market' will turn out to be a free market; the role of auxiliary trends (C1.2–3) is to strengthen that main tendency. Yet, the very occurrence of the main trend is doubtful – it is quite as possible to interpret the predominance of international capital with respect to state capital the other way round, as the formation of a new, international class of owners-rulers who subjugate local (state) political authorities – that is, as what has been termed (Nowak 1981, p. 221, pp. 230–233; 1983b, pp. 191–196) economic totalitarianism. I do not claim that I have predicted that – in the quoted works, I predicted rulers-owners' symbiotic political totalitarianism, with political and not economic interest being dominant. Nor do I claim that the abovementioned interpretation is more accurate than the one concealed in description (C1) – I have not put enough effort in that alternative interpretation for such an opinion to be warranted. My only claim is that this

---

[22] I would like to remind the readers that at that time, Sovietology was dominated by the convenient doctrine of the convergence of the two forms of government. When citizens' masses began to openly protest against the triple rule, sovietologists became more determined in their paper critiques of real socialism.

interpretation of the phenomenon is also admissible. The conclusion is that assertions like (C1.1) are not theoretically compelling in any way.

The situation is similar with regard to statement (C2). Is the capitalist economy really becoming more effective? In what sense? If within the standard meaning of the term, then even common knowledge about the economic facts of recent decades would make one doubt that supposition. After all, the basic motif of governmental neoliberal politics is the conviction that the contemporary capitalist economy is no longer capable of bearing the burden – accepted in the 1950s – of financing social welfare. That is, indeed, a liberal explanation. However, two questions arise in this context.

First, that explanation is not very clear. Let us consider that: for decades, the capitalist economy was capable of providing the means for social welfare, and now it cannot do that anymore. Surely, the effectiveness of the capitalist economy must have diminished? If a horse pulling a burden stops after some time, it must have become weak, must it not? Yet, according to statement (C2), the economic effectiveness of capitalism has increased. That seems to confirm the Marxian style of thinking: in recent decades, the economy was bolstered by enormous development of technologies of production ('new technologies'!) and of organization ('informatization'!); a liberal would probably add the development of economic knowledge to that list ('monetarism'!). Has the economy, in spite of everything, become so weak that it is no longer able to level opportunities in the conditions of supposedly free competition? It seems that either (C2) is true – and the liberal explanation of the politics of the destruction of 'welfare state' is unjustified – or it is not true, in which case, instead of the triumphalism expressed in that condition, we should announce a progressive decline of the capitalist economy. Either way, liberal thought is not consistent with respect to this matter.

The second problem is the uncertainty as to the way in which the 'welfare state' wasted money. The state must have overspent on administration, as it is apt to do, but still many people received a large part of those huge funds, so they could buy bread, modest apparel, or even a used car. The social welfare system was not 'wasteful' because it created demand for goods, even if elementary ones, and allowed for the survival of small traders and, indirectly, entrepreneurs. The poor, through their demand for goods, supported the 'middle class' which, according to the liberal ideology, constitutes the very core of capitalism. It is hard to say if there were any losers there.

Maybe the problem is not the ineffectiveness of the economy within the standard meaning of the word – the ability of the economy to satisfy human needs – but within some special meaning. Perhaps the goal in politics is not to satisfy the needs of all the participants of the market game but only to make the rich even richer, and it should be left up to the stronger people if they will pull the weaker ones behind them. Such a reframing could also allow for a clarification of the origins of the abovementioned inconsistency of neoliberal thought. Have not those who do not sow and do not plough but who reap the harvest benefited from the reduction of the expenses of the 'welfare state'? Perhaps it is them, the owners of capitals – which circulate, unproductive, between New York, London, Frankfurt, and Tokyo, multiply on their own, for themselves, without putting down the roots in the real economy – that have made those capitals even greater in that way. Perhaps a free-market economy – profit-oriented and, within that meaning, 'effective,' and coming under the auspices of liberals – is not rational for most people, despite what is said about it. Perhaps, then, that inability of capitalism to maintain the social welfare system is a proof of the increasing parasitism of the formerly free-market economy. Perhaps, in a world which cannot feed a hundred million children, cope with mass illnesses – even in the most civilized countries – or with the destruction of the global natural environment, the identification of profitability with rationality should simply be seen as an ideological fairy tale.

Indeed, the historiosophical content of the supposedly descriptive (C2) is undebatable. Similarly, each of the other trends which have been enumerated by way of example can be interpreted theoretically in various ways. I claim nothing more. I do not favor a particular interpretation, nor do I make one. That is not even my intention because I will be professionally occupied with other topics for many years to come.

13   The Illusory Power of 'Complex Explanations'

I will only add one reservation. The critique presented above does not mean that collecting such trends, not to mention reliable – or, at least, professional – finding of facts associated with those trends is worthless from the cognitive point of view. It may be just the opposite. One only needs to understand what one is doing. In any case, creating those collections does not mean forming a social theory. A social theory is not constructed even when the occurrence of each trend in a given collection is empirically justified in a thorough manner. The doubts are not dispelled when questionable interpretations of trends are combined – rather, they become more pronounced, unless one begins with a construction of a theory of social dynamics – or makes use of an existing one – and explains all those trends at once. That is not, however, the case when type (C1.1) and other descriptions are made. I have written so many times about what constructing a social theory entails – and those expositions have been elaborated upon by my collaborators, also in this publication series – that I will not repeat myself here; a curious reader will find much information about this topic. I will only limit myself to three conclusions about it based on the idealizational concept of social theory.

The first one is that collections of trends of the type described above are just material to be explained by a future theory within the framework of which a new, unimaginable now, conceptualization of the social world will be proposed. The discovery we do not have today will consist precisely in someone redirecting his abstract imagination and not in analyzing new statistics. That person will break the existing thought patterns and propose a new categorization of phenomena, which will not begin with a conceptualization of 'technological progress,' 'conflict of civilizations,' 'structural unemployment,' etc. but end with it, and that only in advanced models. At this moment, we do not understand those categories and, therefore, do not understand the meaning of trends ($C_{1.1-3}$), (C_2), etc., precisely because they are so frequently discussed by all the world's media that they have been reduced to conceptual shreds which arouse many strong feelings (of either solidarity or enmity – it does not matter) but no thoughts worthy of the name.

Second, such a conceptualization, true or false, will only be constructed by a person who will risk ostracism by speaking, out of necessity, against the prevailing 'scientific' and/or journalistic opinion (in the humanities those two types of opinion are not, unfortunately, separate – on the contrary, they are increasingly conflated, and the inverted commas around the former term are becoming more and more deserved). I wrote "out of necessity" because a discovery is always directed against stereotypes in which many smart but shallow-minded – and, therefore, not creative – people have built their 'scientific' and/or media nests.

My third remark is that such a person will have to renounce presentism which is so common (within both meanings of the word) among the practitioners of social science. Just like the past development of species on the Galápagos Islands was of the same cognitive importance for Darwin as selective breeding on the British Islands in his time, so too the explanation of the past workers' revolutions in capitalism should be of the same cognitive importance for a sociologist-theoretician as the modern explanation of the miracles of mass communication. If that theoretician attaches greater importance to the latter phenomenon only because 'the whole serious press' is enthusing (not always seriously) about it, then it should come as no surprise that 'modern empirical sociology' remains at the level of (at best) Carl Linnaeus's biology, since that very subservience to the priests of mass culture contributes to the sad state of matters. As a result, the author of that future, more adequate theory will have to explain in it not only civilizational news but also what will have already been explained in earlier theoretical attempts (that is, fulfill the requirements of dialectical correspondence as well as dialectical refutation). That theory should, then, provide better explanations of such issues as the failures of the prediction about the transformation of capitalism into a 'community of free producers' or the prediction about the totalitarization of capitalism. The news must also be explained because they are obviously not simply made up, as has been discussed above. It is just unwise to believe that holding onto them equals holding the future.

14   A Factual Conclusion

One of my friends tried very hard to dissuade me from publishing this text:

> As regards social theory, you have done what you had to do; the socialist part has already come true, the capitalist one – not yet, but strange things are, indeed, happening, things which no-one would have believed even five years ago. A few years ago, who knew what 'creative accounting' was and that it was common in the 'most serious companies,' on the 'freest market,' under the protective umbrella of old, model democracy? Who knows what the future fate of your prediction of the totalitarization of that system will be?

Well, the prediction that:

(K) the capitalist form of government will fall

might turn out to be true; we will see. However, the prediction of non-Marxian historical materialism is different – it is phrased as formula (n-Mhm-II). That prediction is not confirmed by any – or, at least, not by every – 'fall of a form of government' but by a precisely defined sequence of catastrophic trends:

> (s) accumulation of property and power for the sake of multiplying power – the restriction of civil liberties and of the effectiveness of the economy – growing citizens' resistance resulting in mass movements, the failure of which has the same effect as a victory: accumulation of power and property in the hands of either old or new elite.

There is no such sequence of events within the framework of classic capitalist societies[23]. Maybe such a sequence will happen in global capitalism, but no-one has built a model of global capitalism in non-Marxian historical materialism yet, so we cannot make such a statement.

And since a catastrophe can befall capitalism ... First, let me make an ideological declaration: we should not, by any means, wish for such an occurrence. After all, capitalism has been the first form of government in history which enabled hundreds of millions of people to live comfortably and granted them considerable civil rights. One could only wish for further reforms of such a system, including reforms pertaining to the form of government, which would, at least, limit the evil created in the system (the disproportions of assets in particular states and on a global level, the accumulation of avarice and pride at the 'top' and the paralyzing hopelessness at the 'bottom' resulting in, among other things, criminality and terrorism, and so on), and not for a fall of the system, especially not for a fall followed by another period of consternation as to what could replace that system because no alternative concept would be on hand. Be that as it may, those are ideological-political matters which I only mention in order to avoid unnecessary misunderstandings.

From the cognitive point of view, the problem is obvious. Surely, capitalism may fall, but if it does today, the factors influencing that process would be different than those predicted in non-Marxian historical materialism (cf. (s)) in its present shape. Well, *la théorie oblige*...

15 A Methodological Conclusion

By admitting the falsity of prediction (n-Mhm-II), I assumed the idealization approach to science, with its concept of empirical verification, which is only a correction of Popper's concept of testing, because I did not want to, as I was

---

23 Perhaps they will appear at the global level. It is, off course, possible that the global class of rulers-owners will provoke – actually, it has already done so – citizens' resistance, and that the end result will be a kind of a supraclass society. At best, however, that will mean a confirmation not of prediction (n-Mhm-II) but of a concretization of it, so far unformulated, resulting from a VP*glob* model which does not exist yet and which takes into account the influence of globalization (that is, a thing which is yet to be conceptualized) on all variables considered in earlier models of capitalism, beginning from vp; such a model would dialectically correspond to series {vp ... ,vp*m*}. I wrote "at best" because it is not certain at all if the empirical content of the actual concretization would be the expected content desirable from the point of view of that theory – although rather undesirable as regards the people to whom it would pertain.

analyzing the predictions, depart from the methodology declared to be the basis of the construction of the theory from which those predictions were derived – obviously, such a 'change of the rules during the game' might look suspicious.

At the end, however, I would like to say that unitarian metaphysics generates a different model of scientific verification, within the framework of which the discussed prediction of totalitarization admittedly remains unaccepted by science but, at least, it is not false. Let us first note that prediction (n-Mhm-II), as it is derived from Model VP, is binding within the framework of the assumptions of that model (let us mark them collectively Z_{VP}). Among those assumptions, there are idealizing assumptions, including assumptions which have not been discarded in any of the existing concretizations of Model VP, for example, the assumption about the isolation of the analyzed class society, that is, about the lack of other societies (class, supraclass, and mixed ones[24] comprising the so-called third world), or the assumption about the lack of stratified hierarchization of that society, that is, about the lack of substructures of each of the already admitted class divisions, and so on. It follows that the described prediction does not actually have the (n-Mhm-II) form but the form of implication:

> (n-Mhm-II*): if conditions Z_{VP} are fulfilled, then the processes of class accumulation result in civil resistance which, however, will not be capable of stopping them; consequently, capitalism will transform into totalitarianism, and then into a system of triple rule.

In the meantime, conditions Z_{VP} are obviously not fulfilled in the 'actual world,' and it is not even possible to fulfill their idealizational components in it. That is, as they say in course books on logic, a true conditional but emptily fulfilled.

This distinction between falsehood and truth emptily fulfilled is not used in the standard theory of empirical testing (including, unfortunately, its modification in the current idealizational theory of science assumed in this text). That is not, however, because of the influence of classical logic – which unambiguously says that an implication with a false antecedent is a truth – but because of the widespread understanding of that logic which presupposes standard metaphysics according to which there is only one 'actual world,' and that is all. The difference between a falsehood and empty fulfillment is hard to grasp within the framework of classical metaphysics (not logic!), which means that

---

24 An analysis of those societies in terms of appropriately expanded non-Marxian historical materialism is presented in Brzechczyn 2004 (English counterpart 2007a [editorial note]).

it is difficult to express in strictly metaphysical terms. Leaving aside the trouble with the ontic criteria of that world, we can thus postulate – as it is done in possibilism – a multiplicity of worlds. That is radicalized even further by unitarian metaphysics which postulates a negative-positive-neutralist universe of plurality-of-worlds (beingness) and, instead of assuming it outright, as is done in possibilism, it (re)constructs the traditional metaphysical categories (being, significance, causality, change, time, etc.) on the foundation of that universe, and those categories have very different properties than the ones ascribed to them in standard metaphysics. Let us, then, assume a unitarian universe.[25]

In that universe, there is a sphere of worlds and there is a sphere of enigma. Tautological situations (within the meaning of classical logic) take place in every world of the first sphere; all (such) counter-tautologies take place in the enigma. Normal situations occur in non-empty strict subsets of the sphere of worlds. That makes it possible to invest the logical distinction between a falsehood and an empty fulfillment with metaphysical meaning. A false implication 'states' a situation from an empty set (the completion of beingness to a universe, which is by definition empty). A true implication 'states' a situation from at least one world of the world sphere of beingness. An implication fulfilled non-emptily 'states' a normal situation from the 'actual world' of that sphere. An implication fulfilled emptily 'states' a normal situation from at least one world of that sphere, which situation, however, is not a situation of the 'actual world.' It follows that all (classical) tautologies are truths, whereas (such) counter-tautologies are neither truths nor falsehoods. It also follows that all emptily fulfilled implications are truths, as required by classical logic. Also, contrary to the (mis)interpretations of classical metaphysics, that is not 'paradoxical' at all but accurate and deep because it follows that in some worlds of beingness, things are in accordance with the implication emptily fulfilled, but none of those worlds is the 'actual world.' Nevertheless, some 'objective' regularity from beingness has been discovered in that way.

By definition, an idealizing condition is neither tautological nor counter-tautological. An idealizational statement is always fulfilled emptily; only its final concretization can be fulfilled non-emptily. So there exists at least one world in beingness in which things happen exactly as described in the idealizational statement. That applies especially to those idealizational statements which are predictions.

---

25 I do not explain unitarian concepts but refer the interested readers to my book (1998b) or the condensed description in the introduction to the second volume of my book (Nowak 2004).

Obviously, all this pertains to every prediction based on an idealization theory, not only to the prediction discussed in this article. As regards cognitive value, a theoretician's effort is never in vain. If it sometimes appears virtually useless to 'featherless two-legged creatures,' they can be happy or unhappy about it – to each their own. Actually, both reactions can turn out to be premature – in fact, there is no 'actual world' in beingness, there is only a trajectory of worlds through which we travel. No-one can say in advance if that trajectory achieves, at a certain time, the 'epistemic field' (the area of approximation) of the world, in which the old idealizational prediction, which used to be fulfilled emptily in that trajectory, becomes, before our eyes, fulfilled (almost) non-emptily.

Examples of that are not hard to find. Who knows, maybe that is what will happen to the Marxian predictions of a disintegration of the capitalist system into the bourgeoisie and the proletariat, or of the absolute pauperization of proletariat? Admittedly, those predictions failed in an obvious way in capitalist national societies (see Nowak 1971, 239–246), as they have never provided a proper approximation for the countries of the capitalist center, but that might change as globalization continues to be a growing trend. Noteworthily, in the global capitalist world, the Marxian 'bourgeoisie' is the center, and peripheral societies are the 'proletariat.' That is probably not what Marx had in mind, but his theory – like any other theory – allows for many interpretations (i.e. it is fulfilled in many worlds of beingness), including this one in question. We have even long known it for a fact because that is how the matter was interpreted by a Marxist named Mao Zedong. Can anyone today exclude the possibility that 'our development trajectory' is nearing Marx's or Zedong's epistemic field? I am not saying it is – because I have no reason to say so; what I am saying is that it is not impossible, that it may be the case. The horror that overtakes the 'terrible scientific bourgeoisie' (it seems that ex-Marxists excel in eliciting that horror) at the very sound of Marx's name can be an argument for the worthiness of the endeavor of studying that possibility *sine ire et studio*. After all, we know that the truth can usually be found far from the beaten track, especially one which is frequented by herds.

That is the methodological conclusion of these reflections. No idealizational theory – that is, no theory worthy of that name – commits a falsehood because that category ought to be reserved for half-baked thoughts which are not to be found in any world of beingness. Whoever has worked hard to construct an idealizational theory, has the right to the truth. The worst-case scenario would be truths fulfilled emptily. Such truths may be useless for individuals, classes, nations, cultures, and perhaps even the whole of humanity, but they are still very much truths, ontically speaking.

References

Banaszak, T. (1997). Problem autokratyzacji ustroju demokratycznego [The Problem of the Autocratization of a Democratic System]. In: L. Nowak and P. Przybysz (eds.) *Marksizm, liberalizm, próby wyjścia*, pp. 381–398. Poznań: Zysk i S-ka.

Banaszak, T. (2022). *How Democracy does Evolve into Autocracy.* In: K. Brzechczyn (ed.) *New Developments in Theory of Historical Process. Polish Contributions to Non-Marxian Historical Materialism. Poznań Studies in the Philosophy of the Sciences and the Humanities*, vol. 119, pp. 239–255. Leiden/Boston: Brill.

Brzechczyn, K. (1993). The State of the Teutonic Order as a Socialist Society. In: L. Nowak and M. Paprzycki *Social System, Revolutions and Rationality. Poznań Studies in the Philosophy of the Sciences and the Humanities,* vol. 33, pp. 397–417. Amsterdam/Atlanta: Rodopi.

Brzechczyn, K. (1998). *Odrębność historyczna Europy Środkowej. Studium metodologiczne* [The Historical Distinctiveness of Central Europe. A Methodological Study]. Poznań: Humaniora.

Brzechczyn, K. (2003). Upadek imperium socjalistycznego. Próba modelu. In: K. Brzechczyn (ed.), *Ścieżki transformacji. Ujęcia teoretyczne i opisy empiryczne*, pp. 135–169. Poznań: Zysk i S-ka.

Brzechczyn, K. (2004). *O wielości linii rozwojowych w procesie historycznym* [On the Multitude of the Lines of Developments in the Historical Process. An Attempt at Interpretation of the Evolution of the Mexican Society]. Poznań: Wyd. UAM.

Brzechczyn, K. (2007a). On the Application of Non-Marxian Historical Materialism to Development of Non-European Societies. In: J. Brzeziński, A. Klawiter, T. A. F. Kuipers, K. Łastowski, K. Paprzycka, P. Przybysz (eds.), *The Courage of Doing Philosophy. Essays Presented to Leszek Nowak,* pp. 235–254. Amsterdam-Atlanta: Rodopi.

Brzechczyn, K. (2007b). Paths to Democracy of the Post-Soviet Republics: Attempt At Conceptualization. In: E. Czerwińska-Schupp, (ed.) *Values and Norms In the Age of Globalization.* pp. 529–571. Berlin: Peter Lang.

Brzechczyn, K. (2020). *The Historical Distinctiveness of Central Europe: A Study in Philosophy of History,* Berlin: Peter Lang.

Buczkowski, P., A. Klawiter, and L. Nowak (1987). Religia jako struktura klasowa [Religion as a Class Structure]. *Studia Religiologica* 20, 79–128.

Deutscher, I. (1971). *Trotsky,* vol. 1: *The Prophet.* Penguin Books.

Iem. (1985). Teoria nowego totalitaryzmu [The Theory of New Totalitarianism]. *Przegląd Polityczny* 6, 77–111.

Iem. (1986). Między totalitarną groźbą a zacną socjalistyczno-liberalno-konserwatywną kompanią [Between a Totalitarian Threat and the 'Honorable Socialist-Liberal-Conservative Campaign']. *Przegląd Polityczny,* 8, 62–179.

Niewiadomski, M. (1989). Toward a Model of Economic Institutions. In: L. Nowak (ed.) *Dimensions of the Historical Process. Poznań Studies in the Philosophy of the Sciences and the Humanities vol. 13, pp.* 371–380. Amsterdam: Rodopi.

Nowak, L. (1971). *U podstaw Marksowskiej metodologii nauk* [The Foundations of Marxian Methodology of Science]. Warsaw: PWN.

Nowak, L. (1974). *U podstaw marksistowskiej aksjologii* [The Foundations of Marxist Axiology]. Warsaw: PWN.

Nowak, L. (1977). *Wstęp do idealizacyjnej teorii nauki* [An Introduction to the Idealizational Theory of Science]. Warsaw: PWN.

Nowak, L. (1979a). Epochs and Formations: an Attempt at a non-Marxian Generalization of Historical Materialism. In: E. Leinfellner, A. Hübner, and W. Leinfellner (eds.) *Wittgenstein, the Vienna Circle, Critical Rationalism, Proceedings of 3rd Wittgenstein Symposium, 13–18 August 1978*, pp. 435–444. Vienna: Holder-Pichler-Tempsky.

Nowak, L. (1979b). Historical Momentums and Historical Epochs. An Attempt at a non-Marxian Historical Materialism. *Analyse und Kritik*, 1, 60–76.

Nowak, L. (1980a). *Polska droga od socjalizmu* [The Polish Road from Socialism]. Poznań: Wielkopolska Inicjatywa Wydawnicza.

Nowak, L. (1980b). *The Structure of Idealization. Towards a Systematic Interpretation of the Marxian Idea of Science.* Dordrecht/Boston/London: Kluwer.

Nowak, L. (1981). *Wolność i władza. Przyczynek do nie-Marksowskiego materializmu historycznego* [Freedom and Power. A Contribution to non-Marxian Historical Materialism]. Poznań: Wyd. NZS Akademii Rolniczej.

Nowak, L. (1983a). Kilka tez o współczesnym społeczeństwie polskim [A Few Theses on Contemporary Polish Society]. *Veto* 9, 68–77.

Nowak, L. (1983b). *Property and Power. Towards a non-Marxian Historical Materialism.* Dordrecht/Boston/London: Kluwer.

Nowak, L. (1985). O konieczności socjalizmu i konieczności jego zaniku [On the Necessity of Socialism and Necessity of its Disappearance]. *Przyjaciel Nauk. Studia z teorii i krytyki społecznej*, 1–2, 105–151.

Nowak, L. (1986a). O historiozofii, antropologii, utopii i gnozie [On Historiosophy, Anthropology, Utopia, and Gnosis]. *Przegląd Polityczny* 8, 32–61.

Nowak, L. (1986b). Science, that is, Domination through Truth. In: P. Buczkowski and A. Klawiter (eds.), *Theories of Ideology and Ideology of Theories. Poznań Studies in the Philosophy of the Sciences and the Humanities*, vol. 9, pp. 106–122. Amsterdam: Rodopi.

Nowak, L. (1987). Pętla pracownicza i kontrpętla ideowa. Próba konkretyzacji modelu kapitalizmu [Workers' Loop and Ideological Counter-Loop. An Attempt at a Concretization of a Model of Capitalism]. *Przyjaciel Nauk. Studia z Teorii i Krytyki Społecznej* 3–4, 41–55.

Nowak, L. (1988). *Władza. Próba teorii idealizacyjnej* [Power: An Attempt at an Idealizational Theory]. Warsaw: In Plus.

Nowak, L. (1989). An Idealizational Model of Capitalist Society. In. : L. Nowak (ed.), *Dimensions of the Historical Process. Poznań Studies in the Philosophy of the Sciences and the Humanities*, vol. 13, pp. 217–257. Amsterdam: Rodopi.

Nowak, L. (1991abc). *U podstaw teorii socjalizmu* [The Foundations of the Theory of Socialism]; vol. 1: *Własność i władza. O konieczności socjalizmu* [Property and Power. On the Necessity of Socialism]; vol. 2: *Droga do socjalizmu. O konieczności socjalizmu w Rosji* [The Road to Socialism. On the Necessity of Socialism in Russia]; vol. 3: *Dynamika władzy. O strukturze i konieczności zaniku socjalizmu* [The Dynamics of Power. On the Structure and Necessity of the Disappearance of Socialism]. Poznań: Nakom.

Nowak, L. (1991d). *Power and Civil Society: Towards a Dynamic Theory of Real Socialism*. New York: Greenwood Press.

Nowak, L. (1993). Postmodernizm: Próba wykładni metafizycznej i interpretacji sensu historycznego [Postmodernism: an Attempt at a Metaphysical Interpretation and an Interpretation of its Historical Meaning]. In: L. Grudziński (ed). *Wobec kryzysu kultury*, pp. 39–51. Gdańsk: Wyd. UG.

Nowak, L. (1996). Koniec historii czy jej powtórka? [The End of History or its Repetition]. In: W. Heller (ed.) *Świat jako proces*, pp. 31–40. Poznań: Wyd. IF UAM.

Nowak, L. (1997a). Adaptacyjna interpretacja materializmu historycznego: przegląd. Przyczynek do polskiego marksizmu analitycznego [An Adaptive Interpretation of Historical Materialism: a Review. A Contribution to Polish Analytical Marxism]. In: P. Przybysz, L. Nowak (eds.) *Marksizm, liberalizm, próby wyjścia*, pp. 29–69. Poznań: Zysk i S-ka.

Nowak, L. (1997b). On Postmodernist Philosophy: An Attempt to Identify its Historical Sense. In: S-E Liedman (ed.) *The Postmodernist Critique of the Project of Enlightenment. Poznań Studies in the Philosophy of the Sciences and the Humanities*, vol. 58, pp. 123–134. Amsterdam: Rodopi.

Nowak, L. (1998a). The Adaptive Interpretation of Historical Materialism: A Survey. On a Contribution to Polish Analytical Marxism. In: L. Nowak, R. Panasiuk (eds.) *Marx's Theories Today. Poznań Studies in the Philosophy of the Sciences and the Humanities*, vol. 60, pp. 201–236. Amsterdam/Atlanta: Rodopi.

Nowak, L. (1998b). *Byt i myśl* [Being and Thought], vol. 1: *Nicość i istnienie* [Nothingness and Existence]. Poznań: Zysk i S-ka Wydawnictwo.

Nowak, L. (1998c). O skrytej jedności nauk przyrodniczych i nauk społecznych [On the Hidden Unity of Social and Natural Sciences]. *Nauka* 1, 11–42.

Nowak, L. (2000a). *Człowiek i ludzie. Modele z Gombrowicza* [Man and People. Models from Gombrowicz]. Warsaw: Prószyński i S-ka.

Nowak, L. (2000b). Współczesne mity o PZPR [Contemporary Myths about the Polish United Workers' Party]. In: M.F. Rakowski (ed.) *Polska pod rządami PZPR.*, pp. 91–103. Warsaw: Profit.

Nowak, L. (2004). *Byt i myśl* [Being and Thought], vol. II: *Wieczność i zmiana* [Eternity and Change]. Poznań: Zysk i S-ka.

Nowak, L. (2012). On the Hidden Unity of Social and Natural Sciences. In: K. Brzechczyn, K. Paprzycka (eds.). *Thinking about Provincialism in Thinking. Poznań Studies in the Philosophy of the Sciences and the Humanities*, vol. 69, pp. 13–50. Amsterdam/Atlanta: Rodopi.

Nowak, L. (2022a). The End of History or its Repetition? In: K. Brzechczyn (ed.) *New Developments in Theory of Historical Process. Polish Contributions to Non-Marxian Historical Materialism. Poznań Studies in the Philosophy of the Sciences and the Humanities*, vol. 119, pp. 96–105. Leiden/Boston: Brill.

Nowak, L. (2022b). Religion as a Class Structure: A Contribution to Non-Marxian Historical Materialism. In: K. Brzechczyn (ed.) *New Developments in Theory of Historical Process. Polish Contributions to non-Marxian Historical Materialism. Poznań Studies in the Philosophy of the Sciences and the Humanities*, vol. 119, pp. 3–51. Leiden/Boston: Brill.

Nowakowa, I., L. Nowak (2000). *Idealization X: The Richness of Idealization. Poznań Studies in the Philosophy of the Sciences and the Humanities*, vol. 69. Amsterdam/Atlanta: Rodopi.

Nowak, L. (2003). O prognozie totalitaryzacji kapitalizmu. Próba oceny po dwudziestu latach [On the Prediction of the Totalitarization of Capitalism: An Attempt at an Evaluation after Twenty Years Later]. pp. 361–401. In: K. Brzechczyn (ed.), *Ścieżki transformacji. Ujęcia teoretyczne i opisy empiryczne*. Poznań: Zysk i S-ka.

Paprzycka, K., L. Nowak (1987). Kilka uwag o naturze społeczeństw Trzeciego Świata (A Few Notes on the Nature of Third-World Societies). *Przyjaciel Nauk* 3–4, 57–66.

Paprzycka, K. L. Nowak (1989) On the Social Nature of Colonization. In: L. Nowak (ed.), *Dimensions of the Historical Process. Poznań Studies in the Philosophy of the Sciences and the Humanities,* vol. 13, pp. 299–312. Amsterdam: Rodopi.

Popper, K.R. (1964). *Conjectures and Refutations*. London: Routledge & Kegan Paul.

Popper, K.R. (1967). *The Poverty of Historicism*. London: Routledge & Kegan Paul.

Tomczak, G. (1985). Modele zaburzonego rozwoju społecznego: załamanie i katastrofa ekonomiczna [Models of Disturbed Social Development: a Breakdown and an Economic Catastrophe]. In: P. Buczkowski and A. Klawiter (eds.) *Klasy, światopogląd, idealizacja*, pp. 47–71.Warsaw-Poznań: PWN.

Tomczak, G. (1989). The Economic Collapse in Two Models of Socio-Economic Formation. In: L. Nowak (ed.) *Dimensions of the Historical Process. Poznań Studies in the Philosophy of the Sciences and the Humanities*, vol. 13, pp. 259–270. Amsterdam/Atlanta: Rodopi.

Wigorska, N. (1985). W obronie wygranych rewolucji [In Defense of Victorious Revolutions]. *Niepodległość* 2, 17–19.

Zarębski, T. (2003). Problem totalitaryzacji kapitalizmu [*The Problem of Totalitarization of Capitalism*]. In: K. Brzechczyn (ed.). *Ścieżki transformacji. Ujęcia teoretyczne i opisy empiryczne*, pp. 229–260. Poznań: Zysk i S-ka.

Zarębski, T. (2022). *The Problem of Totalitarization of Capitalism*. In: K. Brzechczyn (ed.). *New Developments in Theory of Historical Process. Polish Contributions to Non-Marxian Historical Materialism. Poznań Studies in the Philosophy of the Sciences and the Humanities*, vol. 119, pp. 189–216. Leiden/Boston: Brill.

PART 2

*On Totalitarization of Capitalism,
Democratization of Real Socialism and
Development of Non-European Societies*

∴

CHAPTER 10

The Problem of Totalitarization of the Capitalist Society

Tomasz Zarębski

Abstract

The paper is an attempt to juxtapose the research results achieved by Polish and Anglo-Saxon analytical Marxism in regard to the evolution of late capitalism. Two theories are compared: Leszek Nowak's non-Marxian historical materialism and Adam Przeworski's concept of class compromise. On the base of the first theory, the hypothesis of the totalitarization of capitalism was put forward, being the transformation of the capitalist class system into a supra-class system where the class of owners was merged with the class of rulers. The second concept presents a different vision of the evolution of capitalist society, namely the stabilization of economic social relations through institutional support of the class of direct producers' interests. This hypothesis – according to author – is supported by better empirical evidence. It the last part of the paper, a modification of Nowak's model of capitalist society is proposed. This improvement should take into account the factors involved in making a group-decision which are differentia specifica of the Anglo-Saxon kind of analytical Marxism.

Keywords

Adam Przeworski – analytical Marxism – capitalism – class compromise – group decision – Leszek Nowak – non-Marxian historical materialism – totalitarianism

1 Foreword

In this article, I will try to compare two theories of the development of capitalism, which can be classified as belonging to the broad contemporary current of social research called analytical Marxism. One of them is Leszek Nowak's model of the capitalist society developed in non-Marxian historical materialism (hereinafter referred to as n-Mhm) and second one – Adam Przeworski's concept of class conflict.

I begin with a sketch of the more important problems and positions in analytical Marxism. Next, I present models of the dynamics of capitalism built with the use of the assumptions of n-Mhm, and subject their basic hypotheses to critique. I also attempt to provide theoretical justifications for the critical arguments, by referring to Przeworski's concept which is reconstructed in the last part of the article.

2 Analytical Marxism. The Most Important Information

In the introduction to a collection of articles published in 1986, entitled *Analytical Marxism*, John E. Roemer writes:

> The past decade, what now appears as a new species in social theory has been forming: analytically sophisticated Marxism. Its practitioners are largely inspired by Marxian questions, which they pursue with contemporary tools of logic, mathematics, and model building.
> ROEMER 1986a, p. 3.

Indeed, as early as in the 1960s and 1970s many researchers from the English-speaking world began working on the 'translation' of selected ideas of classical Marxism to the language of contemporary social science and on their critical evaluation. Authors such as Gerald Cohen, Jon Elster, Roemer, Eric Wright, and Adam Przeworski, educated in the analytical tradition, understood their task – naturally, as it were – as an attempt at constructing a modern Marxist social theory which would use the analytical techniques developed within the framework of broadly defined analytical philosophy.[1]

Cohen's book, entitled *Karl Marx' Theory of History: A Defence,* (Cohen 1978) was a breakthrough in that respect.. It was an attempt at a methodological defense of the theory of historical materialism, which highlighted to the functional nature of explaining posited, according to Cohen, by Marx himself.

---

[1] Marxists from the English-speaking world were inspired by game theory, decision theory, expected utility hypothesis, and other similar tools of analytically sophisticated social science. A bibliography of the more important works on game theory can be found in Malawski, Wieczorek, and Sosnowska (1997). The set of titles from that book can be complemented with Kenneth Arrow's (1963) and Amartya Sen's (1970) works on decision theory. Herbert A. Simon (1997, pp. 3–23) presents a valuable review of the history of the rationalistic model of action, and Alfred N. Page (1968) – a review of the classic articles on the expected utility hypothesis. Gary Becker (1990) uses the tools of rational choice in neoclassical economy.

However, this approach was subjected to critique. Jon Elster rejected with the general reasonableness of explaining social facts functionally, and instead opted for a kind of intentional explaining. This approach is usually called methodological individualism:

> By this I mean a doctrine that all social phenomena – their structure and their change – are in principle explicable in ways that only involve individuals – their properties, their goals, their beliefs, and their actions. Methodological individualism thus conceived is a form of reductionism. To go from social institutions and aggregate patterns of behavior to individuals is the same kind of operation as going from cells to molecules.
> ELSTER 1985, p. 5

Most analytical Marxists from the English-speaking world have followed the same train of thought. An increasingly frequent postulate was to precisely define the so-called micro-foundations of social phenomena under consideration. The researchers, equipped with the tools of rational choice, reflected on the traditional problems of Marxism, such as capitalist oppression and social and economic inequalities, especially class divisions. It also seems that new research is being conducted within the framework of the ethical theory of social order – the researchers are developing concepts of an ideal social democratic order which are alternatives to the liberal ones.[2]

In the 1980s, Roemer developed a general microeconomic concept, intended as a new theoretical foundation for the Marxist analysis of the phenomenon of oppression.[3] Based on the findings of that theory, Erik Olin Wright (1986) tried to describe the class structure of contemporary capitalist societies within the framework of theoretical sociology. He focused especially on the issue of the so-called middle class as a group which oppresses and is oppressed.[4]

One example of normative modeling in the analytical Marxism of the Anglosphere is Bert Hamminga's (1995) model of the distribution of work. He develops the idea of a utopian society of so-called market socialism, in which a centralist institution broadens the scope of the functioning of market

---

2 See mainly James M. Buchanan, Gordon Tullock (1962), John Rawls (1999), Robert Nozick (2013).
3 Roemer (1982b) presents that theory in a systematic manner. A less formal presentation can be found in Roemer (1982a; 1986b; 1988).
4 That special position of the middle class results from the contradictory interests of that part of society with respect to the remaining antagonistic classes. The middle class is oppressed by capitalists, but, as a manager class, it oppresses direct producers.

mechanisms by adding to it the sphere of employment, in a manner which the author believed is more just than in the liberal solutions.

As we can see, Western analytical Marxism is a broad and internally varied movement. What particular researchers have in common is their interest in the same issues and their general conviction that the analytical approach is right, but it seems they have not formed a research school.

Polish analytical Marxism is different – and here the Poznań School of Methodology (Coniglione 2010; Borbone 2016; 2021) occupies a distinguished position in it. It is worth noting that both varieties of analytical Marxism have strong roots in the analytical approach. In Poland, that genesis has determined the style of research for decades to come.

The Poznań School of Methodology was particularly active in the reconstruction of Marxian methodology. It also tried to interpret historical materialism in a consistent manner and factually corrected Marx's theory. Since the works of the representatives of that school have been widely available in Polish and extensively discussed by Polish philosophical circles, I will only give some basic information here.

The fruit of that methodological research was the publication, by Nowak (1980) and his colleagues, of the Idealizational Theory of Science (ITS; summary: Nowak, Nowakowa 2000). That theory had many applications, in such disciplines as the methodology of physics, biology, psychology, and linguistics.[5] Next, based on the findings of ITS, the Adaptive Interpretation of Historical Materialism (AIHM) was proposed[6]. According to this interpretation, three laws of determination:
1) of the relations of production by the forces of production,
2) of the superstructure by the base, and
3) of social consciousness by socio-economic conditions

were explicated as relations analogous to the adaptive mechanisms described in biology.[7] Nowak's n-Mhm – a theory which overcomes Marx's theory while preserving some of its premises – also presupposes such an understanding of global social dependencies. Below, I present and subject to critique that part of n-Mhm which relates to the dynamics of a capitalist system.

---

5 Nowak (1977) contains a systematic presentation of ITS. As regards applications and developments, see especially Nowak, Nowakowa (2000), pp. 109–182.
6 AIHM is presented in, among other works, Nowak (1997; 1998).
7 See especially Andrzej Klawiter (1978) and Krzysztof Łastowski (1981).

3 The Dynamics of Capitalism According to n-Mhm

Because of the limited length of this article, I will not present the general assumptions of n-Mhm or the analyses of the real socialism system carried out in it; the reader will find them in the relevant literature.[8] Instead, I will focus on two models linked by the relation of concretization and constructed according to the assumptions of n-Mhm, in order to explain the development of Western capitalism and to propose a general hypothesis as to its future development. In Model I, the line of development of capitalist class relations of capitalism is conceptualized in purely materialist terms. Model II is the outcome of an institutional concretization of Model I. It complements the basic concept and expresses the previously described trend in appropriate categories relating to the type of state system.

I will begin with the exposition of the assumptions which constitute a model capitalist society and move on to a discussion of an idealized image of its dynamics.

3.1 *The Assumptions of Model I*

Model I is based on a number of idealizing assumptions:

A: society S only consists of the class of owners, the class of rulers, and the people's class;
B: the classes of society S are not organized in any institutional structures;
C: society S is isolated from all other societies;
D: the progress of the productive forces in society S is continuous and uniformly accelerated;
E: in society S, the number of the areas of production does not grow;
F: in society S, expanded reproduction takes place.

As we can see, the base of the society in question contains an element of political power. That means that political factors are included among the basic determinants of social development, alongside economic ones. After all, in abstract society S, the momentum of spiritual production is missing – the possible influence of a conflict of spiritual classes on the development of the system is (in an idealizing manner) omitted. In this society, there is expanded reproduction, and the aim of the owners of the means of production is accumulation. Both phenomena are commonly believed to be basic characteristics of a capitalist system.

---

8 For a systematic presentation of that theory, see Nowak (1983; pp. 32–62; 1991a).

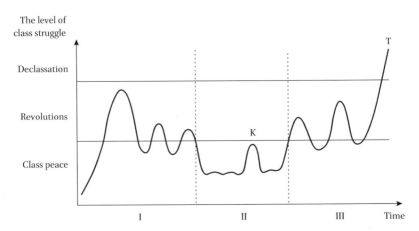

FIGURE 10.1 The development of a model capitalist society in the n-Mhm. Explanations: The areas marked with Roman letters correspond to three historical stages of the development of capitalism: I – from the beginning of the industrial revolution to the end of the 19th century, II – contemporary times, III – the foreseeable future. The remaining designations: K – the great crisis of the 1930s, T – totalitarianism.

3.2 A Description of Model 1

The model development of capitalism is presented in a graphic form in Figure 10.1. The dashed vertical lines divide the curve into three areas. Historically they appear to roughly correspond to three stages of the history of capitalism:

1) from the beginning of the industrial revolution until now,
2) contemporary capitalism, and
3) the predicted future of that system.

In total, Model 1 distinguishes six phases of the development of capitalism within such a historical framework; I discuss them below.

3.2.1 The Increase of the Alienation of Work

Let us assume that initially the level of the alienation of work and the level of civil alienation are in the area of class peace (see Figure 10.1). Individual owners, who aim to maximize profit and who yield to the pressure of competition, begin to introduce systems of appropriation which are increasingly disadvantageous to workers.

As a result, the efficiency of production admittedly grows, but at the same time direct producers are impoverished because earnings are being gradually lowered. In time, workers' consumption decreases, which leads to a crisis of overproduction. With further impoverishment of workers, the economic class struggle enters the realm of revolutionary unrest – the curve on the chart jumps up.

3.2.2 A People's Revolution

The class of rulers becomes engaged in the conflict on the owners' side, and workers have to fight not only against the owners but also against those who have at their disposal the means of coercion. In those conditions, the odds of a victory are admittedly small, but the struggle does not have to end in the declassation of the people because the owners are capable of effectively solving the class conflict through with their 'own' means. They can do that thanks to the so-called technical surplus (see assumption C) which enables the increase of workers' wages and, consequently, a return to a stable economic situation. The society emerges from the first phase of revolutionary unrest, and the curve returns to the area of class peace. There is no sudden growth in the power of the state authority.

3.2.3 Autonomous Cyclical Development and Decreasing Trend of the Alienation of Work

The society in question begins to 'repeat,' as it were, its standard path of development. Owners once more heighten the oppression of workers, which, on the macroscale, leads to another increase of the alienation of work in Model 1. The system re-enters the area of revolution. The solution to the conflict is identical to the case of the first disturbances, except that the process is faster, and the role of the state apparatus is even smaller, so this revolution is less violent. This mechanism occurs in each subsequent cycle of the current phase of social development. What is more, new cycles bring about ever lower levels of the alienation of work, whereas the economic class conflict gradually loses its historical significance. The two phenomena are illustrated by the figure 10.1. Each new rise in the curve of the class conflict is less dramatic. At some point, for a relatively long period of time the curve does not reach the area of revolution for a relatively long time. It seems that this phase is a kind of a 'turning point' in the history of capitalism.

3.2.4 Economic Crisis

In the phases described above, the struggle between owners and direct producers, which ends in concessions to the benefit of the latter group, stabilizes the economic system by solving subsequent overproduction crises. However, due to the autonomous cyclical development and the gradual lowering of the alienation of work, that tool de facto ceases to exist. In their safe class positions, owners are not forced to increase workers' wages. There is a slight growth in demand, but it is accompanied by an increase in the amount of unsold stock, which is the main cause of the approaching overproduction crisis. Workers, lulled by owners' concessions made in previous phases, cannot organize a revolution 'on cue.' The crisis deepens. On the figure, the curve of the class conflict rises, but it does not reach the area of revolution. From the historical point of view, that appears to correspond to the situation of the great crisis of the 1930s. The only force capable of stopping the economic slump in that situation is the class of rulers.

3.2.5 The Etatization of the Economy

The state apparatus begins to play a bigger role in the economy. Members of that class consume more, mainly because of increasing armaments. As a result, the society can overcome the most serious overproduction crisis it has experienced so far. At the same time, the authorities incite demand among workers by means of income redistribution. However, neither of those methods is neutral – after all, the rulers' interest is to expand their sphere of regulation. The economy becomes increasingly dependent on them, and they no longer try to maximize their profits, unlike capitalists. Moreover, due to the bureaucratization of the system of production, the authorities can create a technological base for enslaving people, and they become more and more effective at extending their power over citizens. Notwithstanding, they continue to occasionally raise citizens' welfare; the curve of the class conflict stabilizes at a low level of the area of class peace.

3.2.6 Civil Revolutions and Totalitarianism

Nonetheless, the class of citizens opposes the growth of the power of the state authority. Initially that opposition is limited in scope, chiefly because direct producers' economic needs are efficiently met. Small-scale revolutionary disturbances must end in the rebellious citizens' defeat. The concessions made by the state authority do not weaken it. On the contrary, they offer another possibility of growing in power. The class of rulers broadens its sphere of influence and incorporates more and more members, and the whole system is enriched with new financial means. However, the economy becomes less effective because of its entanglement with politics. Greater numbers of citizens experience economic hardships and take part in new disturbances. Still, the historical trend appears to be irreversible regardless of the outcome of revolutions. After each lost revolution, state authority gains power. If a revolution is victorious, a new political elite forms which is only capable of one thing: replacing the overthrown rulers and taking over their sphere of influence. The social system transitions to P-totalitarianism.

3.3 The Hypotheses of Model I

There are, it seems, two main hypotheses of the model presented above:
(T_1) that the disappearance of the struggle of economic classes was a significant factor for social development in contemporary capitalism;
(T_2) that capitalism must transition to P-totalitarianism.
Both hypotheses appear to be questionable. Let us, however, first consider Model II which is a concretization of model I because of the cancellation of one of its previously binding idealizing assumptions.

3.4 The Assumptions of Model II

According to Idealizational Theory of Science:

> The concretization of a model of phenomenon (phenomena) F determining the dependence of F on factor(s) considered to be main H is a two-step process. At the beginning, a model of the factor(s) considered to be secondary p is built. Next, that model is introduced to the original model for the purpose of determining if and how the influence of factor p modifies the relationships between F and H.
> NOWAK, 1991b, p. 346

> Model II retains all assumptions of Model I, except for condition
> B: classes of society S are not organized in any institutional structures.

Henceforth, it is assumed that the class of rulers from Model I is organized in a hierarchical institutional structure called the state, while the economic sphere remains institutionally disorganized. It follows that we are dealing here with a partial institutional concretization of Model I.

That understanding of the said methodological procedure implies we should first define more closely what the institutional organization of political power is. As regards that issue, Model II presupposes the existence of the following elements of the hierarchy of the class of rulers:
(w) the highest ruler,
(ww) the power elite,
(www) the power apparatus.
The lowest rank in that hierarchy is civil society. Indeed, it is the politically weakest class of society S because it has the smallest share in the disposal of the means of coercion (which is omitted in the model conditions for idealizational reasons).

Various state systems (see Table 10.1 on the page 198) turn out to be optimal from the point of view of the realization of the material interest of the

TABLE 10.1   Types of State Systems (Nowak 1991a, p. 75)

Institutional channels of control of	the official authority by the civil society	the leadership by the apparatus of power	The supreme ruler by the elite of power
Democracy	yes	yes	yes
Autocracy	no	yes	yes
Dictatorship	no	no	yes
Despotism	no	no	no

authorities, depending on the state of the political class struggle. During the period of class peace, democracy is the optimal form of state system because it guarantees the smallest obstacles to the growth of the so-called power regulation with respect to the relatively strong – because it augments interpersonal relationships independent from the state authority – civil society.

However, when the scope of power regulation has grown, and the state of the political class struggle slightly exceeds the threshold of class peace, the state authority is forced to tame citizens' control – otherwise it could easily lose the achieved advantage. At such a time, an autocratic state system is optimal for the state authority.

When the level of class struggle reaches the area of a revolution, dictatorship becomes the best solution. It is necessitated by the authorities' need to mobilize in the face of the global threat. Still, the power elite continues to control the dictator so that it can, should he make any errors, effectively change the leader.

In the case of declassation, that is, when citizens cease to pose a threat to rulers, a dictatorship can easily be transformed into a despotism which, in turn, becomes the optimal state system for the authorities.

Those arrangements are the minimal theoretical foundation for the institutional correction of Model I. The main hypothesis is: various types of state systems which are optimal from the point of view of the realization of the interests of the authorities correspond to particular phases of the political class struggle. Therefore, the evolution of political and economic class relations in Model II must be accompanied by an analogous evolution of particular types of state systems.

3.5   Model II: The Natural Sequence of State Systems

The stipulated starting point in the development of a society from Model I is the state of class peace. Therefore, in Model II, the initial assumption is that the optimal state system for the authorities in such a case is democracy. However, when oppression increases, the system enters the phase of economically conditioned revolutionary unrest. If the scale of the rebellion forces the owners to ask the authorities to intervene with the use of the means of coercion, the democratic system can change into an autocratic one, and later – into a dictatorship. If the people's revolution wins, then the optimal form of state system for the new double class of rulers-owners will be a despotism; a victory of the allied but separated classes of owners and rulers will bring about an autocracy. Therefore, we obtain the following sequence of the state systems:

democracy → autocracy → dictatorship → [despotism or autocracy]

However, in the conditions of the model, there is the so-called technical surplus which allows the class of owners to resolve their conflict with the workers with the use of 'their own means' which, in the long run, weakens the revolutionary moods and leads to a long period of class peace. The sequence described above is initially modified by the exclusion of the possibility of a dictatorship, and later also of autocracy. In Nowak's words, "social peace can be ensured without the need of changing the state system" (Nowak 1991b, p. 351). Democracy, which is optimal in the conditions of class peace, becomes a long-lasting type of state system. Still, in accordance with hypothesis (T_1) (about the disappearance of classes as a historically significant factor for social development), a serious economic crisis occurs, and the overcoming of this crisis is accompanied by unparalleled growth of the power of the state. Then, capitalism changes into political (P-)totalitarianism. That process has its counterpart in the evolution of state systems. Faced with revolutionary unrest, democracy changes into an autocracy, and when the unrest becomes stronger – into a dictatorship. People's victory leads to despotism with origins in the revolution; people's defeat augments rulers-owners' power and generates a conservative despotism.

It becomes obvious that the introduction of an institutional correction, does not contradict the hypothesis – formed in Model I – on the necessity of the totalitarization of capitalism. It does, however, make that prediction more precise, as it points to the political aspect of phenomena which have previously only been described in materialist terms. The discussion of Model II, then, leads to a prediction of the necessary autocratization of democratic Western societies.

4 A Critique of the Predictions[9]

However, the hypotheses proposed in those models appear to be incongruent with the facts known from the recent history of most – if not all – Western European states. Still, before we dispute those predictions, we should take a closer look at a methodological difficulty emphasized by their author[10].

All the analyses mentioned above have been conducted with the use of many idealizing assumptions. This means that the image of the dynamics of capitalism is drastically simplified in comparison to the countless facts from the actual histories of capitalist societies. In order to avoid the error of the reification of idealizing assumptions, one should first define the most important actual consequences of the methodology of n-Mhm.

The necessity related to the prediction of totalitarization and capitalism made in Model I and to the prediction of the autocratization of the democratic system which is its counterpart in Model II only refers to a counterfactual, model social system. In the real world, it becomes but one possible trend

> which can, in many cases, be stopped, although it will usually be realized; however, even where it is realized, one pattern will not be replicated in all realizations – instead, there will be many different systems deviating, to a lesser or greater extent, from that ideal pattern of totalitarianism.
> NOWAK 1991C, p. 341

Therefore, an empirical confirmation of the abovementioned hypotheses can only be obtained by statistical approximation – since the gained theoretical knowledge only roughly corresponds to a phenomenon from the empirical world, it is the more difficult to verify.

Nevertheless, the empirical hypotheses of n-Mhm can be controlled because every historical trend shown by the model can encounter a countertrend in real life – for instance, factors omitted in the idealized model can sometimes, in certain circumstances, balance or even reverse the predicted course of events.

Taking that into account, I propose the following plan for the critique of the predictions of totalitarization and autocratization:

---

9   We should note that the reflections presented in this article are not the first attempt at a critique of the prediction of the totalitarization of capitalism made within the framework of n-Mhm. The issue has been discussed in other texts, for example, Ciesielski (2022) and Szabała (1994). General overview of various theories of totalitarianism can be found in Bäcker (2012, p. 31–70).
10 His arguments can be found in Nowak (1991), vol. 1, 340–342.

1) indicating that they are contradicted by facts,
2) recognizing the developmental countertrend which turned out to be stronger than the trend described by n-Mhm,
3) indicating a concept capable of explaining that countertrend.

A rejection of the hypotheses of the idealized model must be based on something more than a simple breakdown of theories and phenomena. An empirical critique must be followed by a theoretical critique – determining the countertrends – and by a theoretical analysis which proves that those hypotheses have not been rejected *ad hoc*.

4.1 The Empirical Critique

However, let us begin by trying to determine the degree to which the predictions about totalitarization and autocratization are indeed reflected in some trends in the current political and economic development of Western European societies.

According to Model II, the gradual transformation of capitalism into a system of double totalitarian rule manifests itself on the institutional level in the form of the autocratization of the democratic political system. Nevertheless, it seems that the disappearance of the institutional channels of the grassroots control of the hierarchy of power by citizens, required by n-Mhm, has not taken place in any Western state in the last few decades. The democracies in those states appear to be strengthening their structures rather than transforming into autocracies. There is no evidence whatsoever that the institution of free parliamentary elections and, consequently, the principle of the separation of powers, has been endangered in any Western state. That does not mean that there are no phenomena in European capitalism which would support the hypothesis on autocratization – one example to the contrary, pointed out by worried neoliberals, are the excessively centralist trends in the economic politics of European Union. However, models of n-Mhm omit, because of the idealization, the influence of international affairs on the internal situation of the analyzed social structure. For that reason, those phenomena which are outside of the realm – delimited by the predetermined set of assumptions – of the explanatory applications of both models cannot support the predictions. It is difficult to obtain an empirical confirmation of the predicted autocratic processes, which can also mean that the predictions made within the framework of Model I are false.

Let us elaborate this issue. Model I predicted further revolutions in response to the worsening of living conditions caused by the processes of the amalgamation of power and ownership in late capitalism. The expected result was a totalitarian system with a double class of rulers-owners class. However, in actual Western societies, riots motivated by economic factors never resulted in a real danger of a change of ownership relations. Political power was not capable of marginalizing capitalists. The etatization of economic life did not reach the level at which there would be a threat to the long-term inefficiency of the economic system[11]. As regards political class relations, we can see that in Western societies, the sphere of power regulation – even though it is more complex than in the United States of America, especially in terms of the economy – has never encroached on the area of basic personal freedoms and civil liberties to a degree comparable to the milder forms of the systems of the accumulation of class rule, such as the Polish People's Republic. A comparison with a system classified within the framework of n-Mhm as a triple rule society appears to be appropriate here insofar as the next step of the evolution of capitalism – after the phase of totalitarianism – suggested by Model 1 is socialism. I believe, though, that the premises for the construction of the image of the evolution of a capitalist system proposed in n-Mhm – especially in the period from the great crisis to contemporary times – are too limited to properly explain the current developmental trend of capitalist societies, which, in my opinion, does not lead to totalitarianism at all.

4.2 A Theoretical Explanation of the Prognostic Failures of n-Mhm

I believe that the basic reason for the inaccuracy of the predictions of n-Mhm concerning the development of capitalism is that the concept of political institutions introduced in model 2 of that theory is limited. The assumptions formed in that model conceptualize the institutions of the class of rulers in a rudimentary manner and completely omit both the structure and social role of citizens' institutions.

The institutional concretization of Model 1 intentionally omits the influence of economic institutions as well as, in a less controlled manner, the significance of citizens' institutions, such as unions, associations, or political

---

11 The effectiveness of an economic system is by no means a simple matter. In particular, it is hard to select appropriate criteria for evaluation – one has to reach beyond the usual statistical data concerning economic growth, employment, or income. We can find an interesting presentation of various ethical criteria of the evaluation of an individual's position in an economic system in Sen's works (1995; 1998). Nevertheless, it is worth noting that, as stated in *European Economy. 2001 Broad Economic Policy Guidelines* no. 72, 312–313, during the 1990s, the 'fifteen states' only saw a negative rate of economic growth (-0.4) in 1993. In recent years, that rate has been oscillating around 2.5–3.0. Employment is increasing: the unemployment rate fell from 11.1 in 1994 to 7.4 this year.

parties.[12] That results in one-sided perception of the process of the transformation of a state system as oriented toward the determination of the best way to realize the material interest of the class of rulers. In Model II, democracy is characterized with the use of the rather vague concept of a "channel of the institutional control of the hierarchy of power through citizens", but those channels are not defined in greater detail; free elections, which come to mind at that point, are not taken into account in Model II. Meanwhile, actual democratic societies differ from autocratic and despotic regimes in that they allow the free appointment of citizens' political representatives. The real influence of citizens on the authorities in a democracy can hardly be evaluated without having made at least provisional assumptions about the phenomenon of citizens' collective actions.

Late capitalism is characterized by the ability to channel social and economic conflicts through institutions while preserving the institutional function of restoring the economic stability of the system. Both the collective pacts which engage the authorities and the agreements between employers' organizations and trade unions in which the authorities do not participate directly can be seen as outcomes of the negotiatory form of class struggle. The disappearance of revolutions is not, in itself, a sign of the solidarism of economic classes in capitalism – they still fight, although without violence.

Therefore, I think that what can hypothetically be juxtaposed to the trend described in Models I and II, as a developmental countertrend, is political and economic stability based on institutions, which improves the situation of all classes. In my view, Przeworski's theory of class conflict is an attempt at a theoretical approach to that trend.

Przeworski defended the hypothesis of the totalitarization of capitalism by arguing that it is derived from theory of the historical process which has greater explanatory power than the so-called liberal historiosophy of the end of history.[13] However, Przeworski's proposal goes beyond the naive teleological visions ascribed to liberals, even if it surely cannot explain as many historical trends in capitalism as n-Mhm. Przeworski's conception, although not comprehensive, is a theoretical alternative to both liberal historiosophy and n-Mhm, at least with respect to the development of the 20th-century capitalism.

---

12 Banaszak (1997; 2022) has analyzed the influence of political parties on the development of a political society.
13 This argument is developed by Nowak (1996; 2022).

5 Przeworski's Approach to the Nature of the Historical Process and Class Conflict

Przeworski's approach, just like n-Mhm, is rooted in the critique of Marx's theory, and it is an attempt at taking a fresh look at the mechanisms of the development of a capitalist social system. Marx claimed that the conflict between economic classes wanting to realize their material interests must lead to the erosion of capitalism and then cause a transition to socialism as a system in which the exploitation will end and class divisions will disappear.[14]

However, that did not happen in Western European states. Przeworski's goal is to show why Marx's predictions turned out to be false. Przeworski tries to propose his own model of class conflict, in which he abandons the belief, nearly universally held by classic Marxists, that there are so-called internal contradictions of capitalism which will lead to the liberation of mankind by the working class.

Before I discuss Przeworski's conception, I owe the reader an explanation of a certain methodological issue, namely, that I will not attempt to present the whole of the author's scientific views in the fragments below, but only reconstruct what I consider to be the most important in his conceptual framework. I deliberately omit a few apparently significant elements of Przeworski's argument,[15] and I may slightly distort the remaining ones.

5.1 The Nature of the Historical Process

The theoretical assumptions which have to be made in probably every theory of historical development appear to pertain primarily to two problems:

---

14   In the Marxian approach, socialism means that: "In place of the old bourgeois society, with its classes and class antagonisms, we shall have an association, in which the free development of each is the condition for the free development of all." (Marx, Engels [1848] 1978, p. 491). However, the intersocietal liberation is only one aspect of the emergence of a new, socialist social order: "In proportion as the exploitation of one individual by another is put an end to, the exploitation of one nation by another will also be put an end to." (Marx, Engels [1848] 1978, p. 488). As regards the nature of Marx's socialism, also see Leszek Kołakowski (1978, chapter 13).

15   That pertains especially to the interesting model analysis of the development of the workers' movement from the beginning of the 20th century on the basis of the election results in the Western states in that time period. Also, I have omitted many elements of Przeworski's formal and mathematical analyses. For a more complete discussion of the issue of class compromise, see: Przeworski (1985; 1986), Przeworski, Wallerstein (1988). One of the author's more recent works presents a model of balance of a democratic system (see Przeworski 2005).

1) what kind of beings ought to be classified as the subjects of the historical process, and
2) what kind of mechanisms underlie the historical development of societies.

I believe that Przeworski's assumptions concerning (2) are a consequence of the nature of the assumptions regarding (1). Let us take a closer look at this issue.

Similarly to Marx, Przeworski sees direct producers and the owners of the means of production as the subjects of history. However, unlike Marx, he treats those classes as rational decision-making entities. What is more, he ascribes a great amount of autonomy to those classes – as is the case with the model individuals of liberalism – because they consider the long-term results of their actions[16]. Przeworski justifies it as follows: "Classes must thus be viewed as effects of struggles structured by objective conditions that are simultaneously economic, political, and ideological." (Przeworski 1985, p. 47). This means that:

> Class analysis is a form of analysis that links social development to struggles among concrete historical actors. Such actors, collectivities-in-struggle at a particular moment of history, are not determined uniquely by objective conditions, not even by the totality of economic, political, and ideological conditions. Precisely because class formation is an effect of struggles, outcomes of this process are at each moment of history to some extent indeterminate.
> PRZEWORSKI 1985, p. 47

This particular lack of the determination of class actions justifies the necessity of decision-making factors being present in the social process. Przeworski states that:

> Social relations are treated here as structures of choices available to the historical actors, individual and collective, at each moment of history, and in turn as the outcomes of strategies adopted earlier by some political forces. Behavior is thus analyzed as strategic action, oriented toward goals, based on deliberations, responding to perceived alternatives, resulting from decisions.
> PRZEWORSKI 1985, p. 5

---

16   Cf. See Przeworski (1986, p. 162). Rawls (1999) and Nozick (2013) present models of a liberal individual. For a systematic reconstruction of that model, see: Przybysz (1997).

Therefore, social dynamics should be considered from the point of view of model class decision makers – their preferences and strategies of action which are adopted in a particular historical situation.

Hence, in assumption (1), the subjects of the historical process are economic classes, understood as decision-making entities. That is of crucial importance for Przeworski's position on matter (2). In his conception, just like in Marx's theory, class antagonisms determine social development. Thus, the assumption that classes should be treated like model decision makers means that the mechanisms of social development are, to an extent, voluntary in nature.[17]

The assumptions made on account of (1) and (2) are, it seems, primarily methodological as they allow Przeworski to analyze historical phenomena from the perspective of the theory of decision making. That analysis is mainly applicable to the research on the development of contemporary capitalism because it is this stage of system development that 'necessitates' the rationality of actions of all its participants[18]. The set of tools of rational choice, then, is used on the premise that the organization of social life in capitalism is, in principle, rational.

5.2 A Model of Class Conflict

The main research problem in Przeworski's conceptual framework is the explanation of the development of Western societies in the period of more or less the last one hundred years. The special phenomena observed during that time were: the improved welfare of the working class, the improvement of the conditions and safety of work, and, most importantly, a gradual disappearance of revolutionary moods among the Western proletariat. We could say that there had never been a time when all social groups had such good material conditions as during the past few decades.

For traditional Marxism, that means a theoretical failure. How is it possible that the working class which was expected

> will use its political supremacy to wrest, by degrees, all capital from the bourgeoisie, to centralize all instruments of production in the hands of the State, i.e., of the proletariat organized as the ruling class; and to increase the total of productive forces as rapidly as possible.
> MARX, ENGELS, p. 490

---

17   The issue of a voluntary vs structuralist concept of a social revolution is discussed in Taylor (1988).

18   For a discussion of the so-called enforcement of rational behavior by the social milieu, see Nowak (1993, pp. 216–217).

became a model example of a conformist approach to such a deeply degenerated system as capitalism? That issue is the Achilles heel of Marx's Marxism.

In his model, Przeworski tries to reject Marx's delusions in order to correctly explain those phenomena. I will begin the reconstruction of the system by determining the assumptions concerning the parties of the class conflict.

5.2.1 Antagonistic Classes and Their Material Interests

In the system analyzed by Przeworski, there are only two social classes. The first one, the working class, wants to fulfill "those needs which can be satisfied by consumption or by the use of those products of the socially organized activity of nature processing which are available in capitalism, that is, goods" (Przeworski 1986, p. 163). In capitalism, the realization of that interest depends on the payment which workers receive for the work they do for the second economic class of the system: capitalists. Capitalists, in turn, benefit from – among other things – the lowering of the costs of the factors of production, a significant part of which are the so-called costs of work. Obviously, the interests of the two classes are conflict.

Przeworski formulates the following problem: "will the attempts of the working class to realize its material interests necessarily lead it to choose socialism" (Przeworski, 1986, p. 162). The alternatives here are naturally, in a way, ascribed to the working class because that class is economically dependent on capitalists, so it is in its interest, at least potentially, to fight against capitalists in order to change the ownership relations. Capitalists, on the other hand – by definition, as it were – do not have any rational reasons for leaving a system which gives them a high social and economic status.

Models (M I) and (M II) of the two decision-making situations of the working class give answers to those questions. Przeworski's model of a class conflict (M) is a system of models (M1) and (M2) which are, as I will try to demonstrate below, connected by the relation of concretization.

5.2.2 Model (M1)

Model I is an analysis of a very simple decision-making situation. The working class wants to realize its material interest, understood as a systematic increase of the level of its welfare which is related to its wages. Therefore, it has two options:
1) it can stay in the capitalist system,
2) it can transition to socialism.

When he asks the question whether workers who want to improve their welfare will choose socialism or capitalism, Przeworski formulates two conditions of a rational transition of that class to socialism:

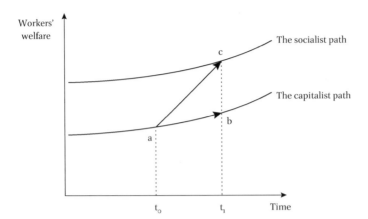

FIGURE 10.2   An illustration of the decision-making possibilities of the working class if conditions (W_1), (W_2) are fulfilled.

(W_1) the greater effectiveness – in comparison to capitalism – of a socialist economy in terms of meeting workers' material needs;

(W_2) immediate and lasting improvement of workers' welfare if they choose socialism.

The possibilities which exist when conditions (W_1) and (W_2) are fulfilled are shown in Figure 10.2. As the mutual positioning of the paths of socialism and capitalism shows, condition (W_1) is fulfilled – the first path is always lower (according to the Marxist ideology) than the second one, which means the economic advantage of socialism over capitalism. The line which joins points a and c shows that condition (W_2) is fulfilled. Indeed, whenever workers decide to organize the economy in a socialist manner, their situation immediately improves. The statements of Model (M I) can be formulated in the following manner:

Statement (M I): If conditions (W_1) and (W_2) are fulfilled, then rational workers decide to choose the socialist path.

5.2.3   Model (M II)

Let us now consider the situation in which condition (W_2) is not fulfilled. The reasons for this appear to be quite realistic. After all, we can predict something quite opposite to condition (W_2), that is, a temporary worsening of the workers' situation when they attempt to implement socialism. Let us distinguish two cases.

If a sufficiently strong political group which represents the workers' interests nationalizes, effectively and democratically, the means of production, then, for some time to come, the workers' situation will be worse anyway. Production management requires qualifications that are only possessed, in a capitalist system, by capitalists. Workers cannot acquire such qualifications overnight. What is more, the mere probability of nationalization can trigger a serious economic crisis. According to Przeworski:

> financial panic can break out even before elections, that is, before a socialist government has nationalized anything. [...] In an Italian industrialist's words said just before the 1976 elections: "We should stay here and fight, but our money is already in Switzerland."
> PRZEWORSKI 1986, p. 179

Needless to say, the crisis would hurt mainly workers.

As for the second case, let us assume that workers decide to size the means of production by way of a revolution. In such a scenario, they must take into account the worsening of their situation because of the costs of their participation in the revolutionary movement[19] – just by leaving their jobs they will lose their remuneration from capitalists. Demonstrations, strikes, and armed struggle are very costly; they require great funds and human resources.

If we take those arguments seriously and maintain the validity of condition (W_1), we should, it seems, change condition (W_2) into a more realistic one:

(W'_2) transformations leading toward socialism will worsen the situation of the working class, at least temporarily.

Figure 10.3 illustrates Model (M2). Therefore, socialism is a more efficient alternative to remaining in the capitalist system, but with the caveat that the material quality of life will temporarily deteriorate. In the figure, this is visualized as the 'valley' between points a and c. Let us note that, in this somewhat stalemate situation, the workers' decision to remain on the capitalist path does not only depend on the truthfulness of condition (W'_2). After all, in accordance with (W_1), socialism guarantees a higher satisfaction of the needs of the working class. Importantly, both analyzed decision-making situations have so far been based on the *implicit* assumption that capitalism is capable of systematically and permanently improving the workers' welfare.

That is clearly visible in figures 10.2 and 10.3: regardless of the lower economic efficiency of capitalism in comparison to socialism, the curve which illustrates the change of workers' welfare in time is constantly rising in the

---

19 Tullock (1979) presents analyses of individual costs of participation in a revolution from the perspective of liberalism.

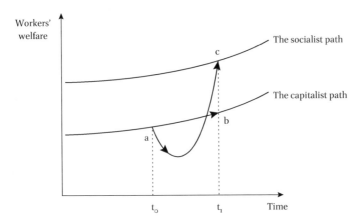

FIGURE 10.3 An illustration of the decision-making possibilities of the working class when conditions (W_1) and (W'_2) are fulfilled.

capitalist system. Apparently, rational workers decide whether to stay in capitalism on the basis of the degree of certainty as to whether that curve will have that shape. The conditions in which that is possible constitute the foundation for the class compromise with capitalists.

5.2.4 The Conditions for a Class Compromise

The actual improvement of workers' welfare can be ensured by making their wages grow systematically in proportion to the profits gained by capitalists. This means that a certain part of the profits must be immediately transformed into an increase of wages. How big should that increase be? We can automatically exclude two cases:

1) when it is equal to zero and
2) when it is equal to the whole profit achieved by capitalists.

Situation (1) means a lack of a compromise on the part of capitalists – workers would not gain anything in return for abstaining from radical actions. Situation (2) means a lack of a compromise on the workers' part. In those circumstances, capitalists do not have any grounds for making an agreement because it would eliminate profit as an institution of the economic system.

Let us mark the level of workers' welfare, related to a particular level of their economic militancy (r) and the rate of capitalists' profit (s) as D. Coefficient r expresses the economic aspect of workers' revolutionary moods, that is, what part of capitalists' profits they desire to seize. In Przeworski's words: "employees will select level r, which constitutes a compromise only when that level maximizes D given a particular response on the part of capitalists" (Przeworski

1986, p. 174). Capitalists will select a such level of s as maximizes their own welfare W given a particular level of r and a particular response on the part of workers. The decisions of both parties constitute a non-zero-sum game, the result of which is the determination of optimal values of both elements of pair $\{r, i\}$ in given conditions. Any kind of interclass cooperation will depend on the degree of workers' confidence about whether capitalists keep the conditions of the agreement.[20] That entails the necessity of taking into account the possibility that capitalism might be generally incapable of creating economic growth which would ensure a systematic increase of workers' wages.[21]

In order to ensure that, a part of the capitalists' control over economic investments is to be taken from them and given to state institutions. What is more, workers must be confident that capitalists will not break the compromise. According to Przeworski, that is where the institutionalization of work and capital plays an important role. Antagonistic classes function in a system of mutual institutional control in which the state plays the role of a mediator of social conflicts. The best examples here are probably workers and employers' collective negotiations and the political parties which represent the interests of both groups. Therefore:

Statement (M2): If conditions (W_1) and (W_2) are fulfilled and if the level of the institutionalization of the relations between work and capital is high, then rational workers prefer a capitalist system.

5.3   Conclusion

In my view, the recognition of the negotiatory nature of the struggle of economic classes in contemporary capitalism as well as the realization that a compromise solution to that struggle is possible, are the greatest achievements of Przeworski's conceptualization. Another advantage of that framework is that it shows how important social institutions are in contemporary capitalism: on the one hand, they are the arena for class conflicts, on the other hand, they guarantee that promises will be kept. I believe that Przeworski's model leads to the following theoretical conclusion.

(*T*) In conditions of democratic capitalism, the negotiatory-institutional conflict of economic classes stabilizes the social system and ensures a gradual increase of the material interests of the participants of the system.

---

20   The term 'certainty' is here used in its colloquial meaning. Howard Raiffa and Duncan Luce (1964, Chapter 2) explain the technical meaning of that term within the theory of decision making (1964, Chapter 2).
21   For example, because of a wrong investment policy; see Przeworski (1986, p. 172).

That thesis, therefore, is incongruent with the hypotheses of Models I and II of non-Marxian historical materialism. Admittedly, a revolution does not take place, but the institutional channels of the realization of class interests allow for ongoing regulation of mutual obligations. Contrary to the predictions of non-Marxian historical materialism, the struggle of economic classes can continue to restore the stability of the economic system, albeit in a different form. Consequently, the conditions of all social groups improves, and rational workers – contrary to Marx's predictions – have no reason to undertake the risky struggle for the introduction of socialism.

6   Final Remarks

I believe that the concept of the development of capitalism put forth in non-Marxian historical materialism is too limited to explain the path of the development of Western capitalism in the last century. Consequently, the predictions concerning the totalitarization of the system have not been empirically confirmed, and democratic capitalism appears to be able to remain politically and economically balanced for a long time.

Przeworski subjected the economic balance to a theoretical-historical analysis. However, the issue of the political balance of Western democracies, which is important from the perspective of non-Marxian historical materialism, is outside of the scope of the applications of his model. The reference to the functions of political institutions of contemporary capitalism is intended to help explain the more basic phenomenon of the relations among economic classes. The paradigm which leads to such an approach is easy to identify – it is Marxian historical materialism, modified as regards the function of the state in a capitalist system. Traditionally, Marxists believed that the only role of a state is to realize the interests of the class of the owners of the means of production. Przeworski's theory shows that in some conditions, a state and its institutions can create a kind of a 'space' for the economic classes, for the rational reconciliation of their interests, and be a warrantor of any agreements which may be made.

From the point of view of non-Marxian historical materialism, however, a state is not independent from either the class of capitalists or the class of direct producers. It has its own material interest, namely, increasing the so-called sphere of power regulation, that is, subjecting as possibly a great number of citizens' autonomous actions as possible to its control. Indeed, when Przeworski tries to solve the problem of a proletarian revolution which-has-never-been, he indicates mechanisms based on premises which themselves require explanations. Why does a state which is not, in any way, reminiscent of the "night janitor" of 19th-century capitalism, not constitute a threat to the freedom and ownership of the citizens of contemporary Western societies? Within the framework of Marxism, the very formulation of such a question is difficult although it is quite justified in non-Marxian historical materialism.

We can see, then, that the erroneous elements of the theory of capitalism in non-Marxian historical materialism cannot be simply replaced by Przeworski's conception. In order to create of a theoretical synthesis of the Polish and English varieties of analytical Marxism, many methodological and material issues must be critically considered. However, if we accept Przeworski's suggestions, we can indicate the direction of potentially promising research even now. I believe that non-Marxian historical materialism should be complemented with certain ideas of Przeworski's conceptual framework in order to shift the focus of the analysis of social conflicts from the theory of revolution to the class social contract.

References

Arrow, K. J. (1963). *Social Choce and Individual Values*. New York, London, Sydney: John Wiley & Sons, Second Edition.

Banaszak, T. (1997). Problem autokratyzacji ustroju demokratycznego [The Problem of the Autocratization of a Democratic System]. In: L. Nowak, P. Przybysz (eds.) *Marksizm, liberalizm, próby wyjścia*, pp. 381–398. Poznań: Zysk i S-ka Wydawnictwo.

Banaszak, T. (2022). How does Democracy Evolve into Autocracy?. In: K. Brzechczyn (ed.) *New Developments in Theory of Historical Process. Polish Contributions to Non-Marxian Historical Materialism. Poznań Studies in the Philosophy of the Sciences and the Humanities*, vol. 119, pp. 239–255 Leiden/Boston: Brill.

Bäcker, R. (2012). *Nietradycyjne teorie polityki* [Non-traditional Theories of Politics]. Toruń: Wydawnictwo Naukowe Uniwersytetu Mikołaja Kopernika.

Becker, G. S. (1978). *The Economic Approach to Human Behavior*. Chicago: Chicago University Press.

Borbone, G. (2016). *Questioni di Metodo. Leszek Nowak e la scienza come idealizzazione*. Roma: Acireale.

Borbone, G. (2021). *The Relevance of Models. Idealization and Concretization in Leszek Nowak*. Műnchen: Grin Verlag.

Buchanan, J. M., and G. Tullock (1962). *The Calculus of Consent*. Ann Arbor: The University of Michigan Press.

Ciesielski, M. (2022). The Problem of the Accumulation of Class Divisions in Contemporary Capitalism. An Attempt at a Theoretical Interpretation. In:

K. Brzechczyn (ed.) *New Developments in Theory of Historical Process. Polish Contributions to Non-Marxian Historical Materialism*. Poznań Studies in the Philosophy of the Sciences and the Humanities, vol. 119, pp. 217–238. Leiden/Boston: Brill.

Coniglione, F. (2010). *Realtà e astrazione. Scuola polacca ed epistemologia post-positivista*. Roma: Bonanno Editore.

Elster, J. (1985). *Making Sense of Marx*. Cambridge: Cambridge University Press.

Hamminga, B. (1995). Demoralizing the Labour Market: Could Jobs be like Cars and Concerts? *Journal of Political Philosophy* 3, 22–35.

Klawiter, A. (1978). *Problem metodologicznego statusu materializmu historycznego* [The Problem of the Methodological Status of Historical Materialism]. Warsaw–Poznań: PWN.

Kołakowski, L. (1978). *Main Currents of Marxism: Its Origins, Growth and Dissolution*. Oxford: Oxford University Press.

Łastowski, K. (1981). *Problem analogii teorii ewolucji i teorii formacji społeczno-ekonomicznej* [The Problem of the Analogy of the Theory of Evolution and the Theory of Socio-Economic Formation]. Warsaw –Poznań: PWN.

Malawski, M, A. Wieczorek and H. Sosnowska (1997). *Konkurencja i kooperacja. Teoria gier w ekonomii i naukach społecznych* [Competition and Cooperation. Game Theory in Ekonomy and Social Science]. Warszawa: PWN.

Marx, K. F. Engels ([1848] 1978). Manifesto of the Communist Party. In: *The Marx-Engels Reader*, ed. by R.C. Tucker, pp. 469–500. New York/London: Norton Company.

Nowak, L. (1977). *Wstęp do idealizacyjnej teorii nauki* [An Introduction to the Idealizational Theory of Science]. Warsaw: PWN.

Nowak, L. (1980). *The Structure of Idealization. Towards a Systematic Interpretation of the Marxian Idea of Science*. Dordrecht: Reidel.

Nowak L. (1983). *Property and Power. Towards a non-Marxian Historical Materialism* (Theory and Decision Library, t. 27). Dordrecht/Boston/Lancaster: Reidel.

Nowak L. (1991a). *Power and Civil Society. Toward a Dynamic Theory of Real Socialism*. New York: Greenwood Press.

Nowak, L. (1991b). *U podstaw teorii socjalizmu* [The Foundations of the Theory of Socialism]; vol. 1: *Własność i władza. O konieczności socjalizmu* [Property and Power. On the Necessity of Socialism]. Poznań: Nakom.

Nowak, L. (1991c). *U podstaw teorii socjalizmu* [The Foundations of the Theory of Socialism]; vol. 3: *Dynamika władzy. O strukturze i konieczności zaniku socjalizmu* [The Dynamics of Power. On the Structure and Necessity of the Disappearance of Socialism]. Poznań: Nakom.

Nowak, L (1993). O granicach paradygmatu racjonalistycznego [On the Boundaries of the Rationalistic Paradigm]. In: K. Zamiara (ed.). *Humanistyka jako autorefleksja kultury* Poznań: CIA Books.

Nowak, L. (1996). Koniec historii czy jej powtórka? [The End of History or its Repetition?]. In: W. Heller *Świat jako Proces*, pp. 31–40. Poznań: Wydawnictwo Naukowe IF UAM.

Nowak, L. (1997). Adaptacyjna interpretacja materializmu historycznego: przegląd. Przyczynek do polskiego marksizmu analitycznego [An Adaptive Interpretation of Historical Materialism: a Review. A Contribution to Polish Analytical Marxism]. In: L. Nowak, P. Przybysz (eds.) *Marksizm, liberalizm, próby wyjścia*, pp. 29–69. Poznań: Zysk i S-ka Wydawnictwo.

Nowak, L. (1998). The Adaptive Interpretation of Historical Materialism: A Survey. On a Contribution to Polish Analytical Marxism. In: L. Nowak, R. Panasiuk (eds.) *Marx's Theories Today. Poznań Studies in the Philosophy of the Sciences and the Humanities*, vol. 60, pp. 201–236. Amsterdam/Atlanta: Rodopi.

Nowak, L. (2022). The End of History or its Repetition? In: K. Brzechczyn (ed.) *New Developments in Theory of Historical Process. Polish Contributions to non-Marxian Historical Materialism. Poznań Studies in the Philosophy of the Sciences and the Humanities*, vol. 119, pp. 96–105. Leiden/Boston: Brill.

Nowak, L., Nowakowa, I. (2000). *Idealization X: The Richness of Idealization. Poznań Studies in the Philosophy of the Sciences and the Humanities*, vol. 69. Amsterdam/Atlanta: Rodopi.

Nozick, R. (2013). *Anarchy, State and Utopia*. Basic Books.

Page, A. N. (1968). *Utility Theory: A Book of Readings*. New York, London, Sydney: John Wiley & Sons.

Przeworski, A. (1985). *Capitalism and Social Democracy*. Cambridge: Cambridge University Press.

Przeworski, A. (1986). Material Interests, Class Compromise, and the Transition to Socialism. In: J. E. Roemer (ed.) *Analytical Marxism*, pp. 162–188 Cambridge: Cambridge University Press.

Przeworski, A. and M. Wallerstein (1988). Workers Welfare and Socialization of Capital. In: M. Taylor (ed.) *Rationality and Revolution*, pp. 179–205. Cambridge: Cambridge University Press.

Przeworski, A. (2005). "Democracy as An Equilibrium." *Public Choice*, 123 (3–4), 253–273.

Przybysz, P. (1997). Liberalna koncepcja jednostki a marksizm [A Liberal Concept of the Individual and Marxism]. In: L. Nowak, P. Przybysz (eds.). *Marksizm, liberalizm, próby wyjścia*, pp. 135–158. Poznań: Zysk i S-ka Wydawnictwo.

Raiffa, H, and R. Duncan Luce (1964). *Games and Decisions*. Dover Publications.

Rawls, J. (1999). *A Theory of Justice. Revised Edition*. Cambridge Massachusetts: The Belknap Press of Harvard University Press.

Roemer, J.E. (1982a). Exploitation, Alternatives and Socialism. *The Economic Journal*, 92, 87–107.

Roemer, J.E. (1982b). *A General Theory of Exploitation and Class.* Cambridge, Massachusetts, and London, England: Harvard University Press.

Roemer, J.E. (1986a). Introduction. In: J. E. Roemer (ed.) *Analytical Marxism*, pp. 3–8. Cambridge: Cambridge University Press.

Roemer, J.E. (1986b). New Directions in the Marxian Theory of Exploitation and Class. In: J.E. Roemer (ed.) *Analytical Marxism,* pp. 81–113. Cambridge: Cambridge University Press.

Roemer, J.E. (1988). *Free to Lose. An Introduction to Marxist Economic Philosophy.* Cambridge, Massachusetts: Harvard University Press.

Sen, A.K. (1970). *Collective Choice and Social Welfare.* Holden Day: San Francisco.

Sen, A.K. (1995). *Inequalities Reexamined.* Cambridge Massachusetts: Harvard University Press.

Sen, A.K. (1998). *Development and Freedom.* New York: Knopf.

Simon, H.A. (1997). *An Empirically Based Microeconomics.* Cambridge: Cambridge University Press.

Szabała, H. (1994). Czy świat zmierza do socjalizmu? [Is the World Heading Toward Socialism?]. *Edukacja Filozoficzna,* 17, 286–295.

Taylor, M. (1988). Rationality and Revolutionary Collective Action. In: M. Taylor (ed.), *Rationality and Revolution,* pp. 63–97. Cambridge: Cambridge University Press.

Tullock, G. (1979). The Economics of Revolution. In: H.J. Johnson, J. Leach, R. Muehlman.(eds.) *Revolutions, Systems and Theories,* pp. 47–61. Dordrecht: Reidel.

Wright, E.O. (1986). What is Middle about the Middle Class? In: J.E. Roemer (ed.) *Analytical Marxism,* pp. 115–140. Cambridge: Cambridge University Press.

CHAPTER 11

The Problem of the Accumulation of Class Divisions in Contemporary Capitalism: An Attempt at a Theoretical Analysis

Mieszko Ciesielski

Abstract

The author elaborates on Leszek Nowak's theory of non-Marxian historical materialism. The typology of societies developed so far on the basis of the theory included types with only one class which had the combined possession of various kinds of material social means (coercion, production, indoctrination). The author presents an extended typology which includes societies where two or three classes simultaneously jointly possess various material means. This expanded typology of non-Marxian historical materialism allows the author to suggest a more adequate description of the contemporary tendencies in the interpenetration of politics and the media, as well as the economy and the media.

Keywords

Benjamin Barber – Leszek Nowak – non-Marxian historical materialism – social development – typology of societies

1   Foreword

At the end of the 20th century and in the 21st century, we can observe greater interest in the issue of the future of capitalism and of the liberal democratic form of government. Many researchers describe phenomena which occur in contemporary societies of the Euro-Atlantic civilization and present optimistic or pessimistic visions of their further development. Two such researchers are Immanuel Wallerstein and Francis Fukuyama. The former predicts the demise of the world system of capitalist economy. In his view, capitalism has entered a phase in which cheap labor force is running out, while the cost of production of goods, associated with environmental protection, is growing, which will soon lead to a final breakdown of the current system.[1] Fukuyama predicts a very different fate for of the democratic form of government and of the capitalist system. In his vision of the future of democratic capitalist societies, there emerges "the end of history," that is, a stable social reality in which no fundamental ideological, political, or economic changes take place.[2]

Leszek Nowak, a Polish philosopher, also presented a prediction about the future. In his theory, non-Marxian historical materialism (n-Mhm), he put forth a hypothesis about the transformation of capitalist societies – in which the political class and the capitalist class are separate – into totalitarian societies in which the political and economic authorities are combined. In the institutional dimension, this translates into a transformation of a democratic state system into an authoritarian rule.

Nowak's prediction, published in the late 1970s, concerned the last decades of the 20th century. It seems that the course of events in the 1980s and 1990s, especially the growth of neoliberal trends, halted the processes of totalitarization. Nowak, then, came to the obvious conclusion that the hypothesis was false.[3] This has led some authors to the belief that – given that the process of totalitarianism is halted and that according to n-Mhm, that process is the only threat to democracy and the capitalist system – Western societies will continue to enjoy, uninterruptedly, the current form of government.[4]

---

[1] In Wallerstein's words: "the modern world-system, as a historical system, has entered into a terminal crisis and is unlikely to exist in fifty years. However, since its outcome is uncertain, we do not know whether the resulting system (or systems) will be better or worse than the one in which we are living, but we do know that the period of transition will be a terrible time of troubles" (Wallerstein 1999, p. 1).

[2] "What we may be witnessing is not just the ... passing of a particular period of postwar history, but the end of history as such: that is, the end point of mankind's ideological evolution and the universalization of Western liberal democracy as the final form of human government. This is not to say that there will no longer be events to fill the pages of Foreign Affair's yearly summaries of international relations, for the victory of liberalism has occurred primarily in the realm of ideas or consciousness and is as yet incomplete in the real or material world. But there are powerful reasons for believing that it is the ideal that will govern the material world in the long run." (Fukuyama 1989, p. 3).

[3] See Nowak 2003; 2022a. It should be noted that the theory of n-Mhm is constructed on the basis of the assumptions of the method of idealization and concretizations, which influences the form of particular research procedures, including the disconfirmation of the theses of the theory. Izabella Nowakowa (1976) discusses the question of the truthfulness of statements and theories in the perspective of the idealizational theory of science. A systematic overview of the idealizational theory of science can be found in Nowak 1977; 1980, also see Nowak, Nowakowa 2000. On methodology of Poznań School, and Leszek Nowak's approach, see: Coniglione 2010; Borbone 2016; 2021; Brzechczyn 2017.

[4] Researchers also tried to discover the reasons why the predictions about the totalitarization of contemporary capitalism turned out to be wrong. One explanation was that the role of

After all, though, it seems that the conclusion about the stability of democracy and capitalism in Western societies, based on the observation of the weakening of the totalitarization process – that is, of the interfusion of political and economic power – was premature. Even if we agree that the process has been very much stalled in contemporary capitalism, it does not automatically entail the further uninterrupted functioning of the democratic form of government. It is worth asking the question about other possible directions in which various social spheres can merge, which may result in the erosion of the functioning of democracies.

2 The Thesis on the Totalitarization of Capitalism

In n-Mhm, three social momentums are distinguished: economic, political, and spiritual. Each of them consists of three levels: material, institutional, and axiological.[5] The basic one is the material dimension. There are also three class divisions, dependent on the disposal of the means of: production in the economy, coercion in politics, and spiritual production in the spiritual realm. Within each of the three divisions, there are two antagonistic social classes, respectively: the owners and the direct producers, the rulers and the citizens, and the priests and the followers.

Two principal types of societies can be distinguished in the theoretical apparatus of n-Mhm: class and supraclass. A society is classified as belonging to one of those types by the separateness of the groups of people who have at their disposal particular material social means. In a class society, those groups are separate, that is, three different groups of people have at their disposal the means of production, coercion, and spiritual production. None of the groups has access to two or three types of material means at the same time. Those societies are called three-momentum societies. In supraclass societies, two or three types of material social means are at the disposal of one person or group of people. This is called an accumulation of various types of material means. If

---

institutional factors – which can effectively counteract the appropriation of economy by the rulers' class – may have been underestimated. Henryk Szabała (1994) addressed the issue of parliamentary representation and of the political competition between parties, Tomasz Banaszak (1997; 2022) emphasized the role of party organizations, and Tomasz Zarębski (2003; 2022) pointed to, among other factors, the institution of trade unions.

5   In this text, I will only present the main ideas of n-Mhm. For a systematic overview of that theory, see Nowak 1983; 1989; 1991a; 1991bcd and further extensions: Brzechczyn 2003; 2004a; 2004b; 2007; 2020; Ciesielski 2012.

two types of material means are accumulated, we speak of a two-momentum society, and in the case of three – of an one-momentum society.

In the light of n-Mhm, the functioning of a democratic state system depends on the manner in which class conflicts are solved. According to Brzechczyn:

> In the democratic variant of the three-momentum society, the social conflict between the rulers and the citizens in politics, between the owners and the direct producers in economy, and between the priests and the followers in culture, is solved by way of concessions made by the 'higher' classes to the 'lower' ones.
> BRZECHCZYN 2004b, p. 92

Thus, in a democratic society:
i. there is no accumulation of class divisions – there are only single classes;
ii. there is class peace in all three social momentums (politics, the economy, and the spiritual realm);
iii. the classes which have at their disposal material means in a given social momentum support the autonomy of the 'lower' classes in the other two momentums; in particular, the owners support the citizens' efforts to maintain political autonomy, and the rulers help the direct producers in their disputes with the owners (Brzechczyn 2004b, p. 92).

The existence of the democratic form of government, as defined above, is threatened when one class of oppressors comes to have a monopoly on the disposal of two or three types of material means.[6] One such threat, predicted within n-Mhm, is the process of totalitarization, which consists in a transformation of a democratic class society into a supraclass (p-totalitarian) society in which there emerges a double class of owners and rulers.[7]

The transition from the class society to the p-totalitarian society can be presented graphically, as in Figure 11.1 (on p. 221).

As already mentioned, in the light of the assumptions of the discussed theory, the trend toward totalitarization has been significantly weakened. That does not, however, preclude other threats, related to the emergence of double or triple classes. Some authors' reflections on social phenomena in contemporary Western democracies prompt the formulation of the following assumption:

---

6   The n-Mhm theory also points to the phenomenon of the so-called class alliance, that is, 'cooperation' of the oppressors' classes for the purpose of declassing the people's class. See more in Brzechczyn 2004b, p. 93.
7   See more in Nowak 1991b, pp. 237–239.

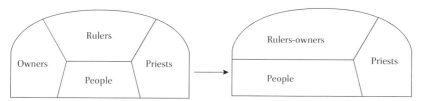

FIGURE 11.1 The transition from the class society to the p-totalitarian society. Abbreviations used: rulers – the class of rulers, owners – the class of owners, priests – the class of priests, people – the people class; the people means the three classes which do not have the material social means at their disposal, that is: the citizens, the direct producers, and the followers.

H: in contemporary democratic societies, we can observe two directions of the accumulation of class divisions, namely, combining the disposal of the means of production and indoctrination and combining the disposal of the means of coercion and of indoctrination.

Below, I present an expanded typology of n-Mhm societies, which makes it possible to conceptualize societies with more than one direction of the accumulation of class divisions, which I believe will enable a more adequate interpretation of selected researchers' visions of contemporary democratic societies.

3   The Expanded Typology of Societies in Non-Marxian Historical Materialism

As regards the number of double or triple classes, the typology of societies in n-Mhm has so far only accounted for the existence of one double or triple class of oppressors in a society (Nowak 1991b, pp. 178–180). In this work, I would like to expand that typology by adding societies with two or three double or triple classes.

For that purpose, I will avail myself of two terms defined within the framework of n-Mhm, namely, class domination and class interest. I will quote those definitions following Brzechczyn:

> The domination of class A over class B means that in the case of conflict between them, in the long-run, the interest of class A is maximized. A social class, which dominates over the rest of society this way, is called the main class.
>
> BRZECHCZYN 2007, p. 244

The class which dominates over all other classes is the main class in the given society. The priority interest term refers to double and triple classes:

> The priority of the class interest of type A over the class interest of type B means that in the situation in which the maximization of interest of B excludes the maximization of class interest of A, in the long-run the interest of A is maximized.
> BRZECHCZYN 2007, p. 244

Thus, we can distinguish the main interest and the derivative interest (instrumentally subordinated to the main interest). In the case of the triple class, there are two derivative interests.

The typology proposed here is based on two criteria:

(i) the nature of the dominant class (whether it is a single, double, or triple class); and
(ii) the nature of the classes subordinated to the main class (the remaining classes of the disposers of material social means).

Criterion (i) makes it possible to distinguish three types of societies: three-momentum (with three single main classes), two-momentum (with a double dominant class), and one-momentum (with a triple main class).[8] Criterion (ii) makes it possible to distinguish two varieties of the types of societies: pure and mixed. In the pure variety, the nature of all oppressors' classes is the same: single, double, or triple. In the mixed variety, the subordinated classes differ in that regard from the dominant class. If, for example, the main class is a triple one, then the subordinated classes are single or double.

I will now move to a more detailed presentation of particular variants of societies in pure and mixed societies. For the sake of simplicity, I will only consider the versions of societies in which the main class is the class of rulers and the priority interest of the dominant class is the maximization of political power. The expanded typology of n-Mhm societies can be presented as follows (Figure 11.2 on p. 223).

3.1 Three-Momentum Societies

According to the proposed typology, there are two varieties of three-momentum societies: pure and mixed. A pure three-momentum society consists of

---

8 That criterion differs from the one used by Nowak because he distinguishes the three types by the mere fact of the existence of a single, double, or triple class. I use the 'stronger' criterion of the domination of a particular single, double, or triple class.

THE PROBLEM OF THE ACCUMULATION OF CLASS DIVISIONS 223

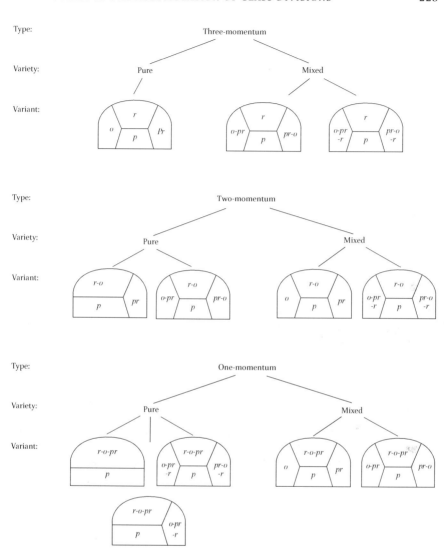

FIGURE 11.2 The expanded typology of societies of non-Marxian historical materialism. On the figure, I assume that the societies are in the political version. Abbreviations used: r – the class of rulers, o – the class of owners, pr – the class of priests, p – the people's class; the people means the three classes which do not have the material social means at their disposal, that is: the citizens, the direct producers, and the followers.

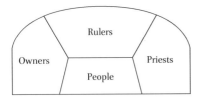

FIGURE 11.3 A pure three-momentum society

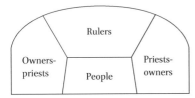

FIGURE 11.4 A mixed three-momentum society, the variant with two double derivative classes

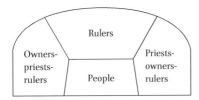

FIGURE 11.5 A mixed three-momentum society, the variant with two triple derivative classes

three classes of single oppressors and of the people's class, so it is a class society (Figure 11.3).

As regards the mixed three-momentum society, it has two variants:

(1) a variant with two double derivative classes (rulers, owners-priests, priests-owners, and the people, Figure 11.4); in that society, the dominant class is a single class of rulers, and there are also: a double class of owners-priests, a double class of priests-owners, and a people's class; and

(2) a variant with two triple derivative classes (rulers, owners-priests-rulers, priests-owners-rulers, people, Figure 11.5); in that society, the main class is a single class of rulers, and there are also: a triple class of owners-priests-rulers, a triple class of priests-owners-rulers, and a people's class.

3.2   Two-Momentum Societies

Two-momentum societies also have the pure and mixed varieties. There are two variants of the pure variety.

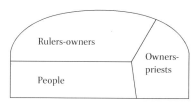

FIGURE 11.6 A pure two-momentum society, the variant with one derivative class

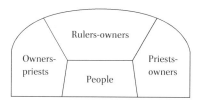

FIGURE 11.7 A pure two-momentum society, the variant with two derivative classes

(1) a variant with one derivative class (rulers-owners, owners-priests, people, Figure 11.6); in that society, the main class is a double class of rulers-owners, and there are also: a double class of owners-priests, and a people's class; and

(2) a variant with two derivative classes (rulers-owners, owners-priests, priests-owners, people, Figure 11.7); in that society, the dominant class is the double class of rulers–owners, and there are also: a double class of owners–priests, a double class of priests–owners, and a people's class.

In the mixed variety of the two-momentum society, there are two variants:

(1) a variant with two single derivative classes (rulers–owners, owners, priests, and people, Figure 11.8); in that society, the main class is a double class of rulers–owners, and there are also: a single class of owners, a single class of priests, and a people's class.

(2) a variant with two triple derivative classes (rulers-owners, owners-priests-rulers, priests-owners-rulers, people, Figure 11.9 on p. 226); in that society, the dominant class is a double class of rulers–owners, and

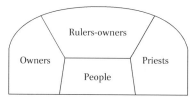

FIGURE 11.8 A mixed two-momentum society, the variant with two single derivative classes

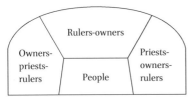

FIGURE 11.9 A mixed two-momentum society, the variant with two triple derivative classes

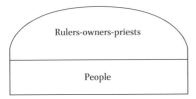

FIGURE 11.10 A pure one-momentum society, the variant without derivative classes

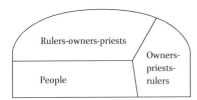

FIGURE 11.11 A pure one-momentum society, the variant with one derivative class

there are also: a triple class of owners–priests–rulers, a triple class of priests–owners–rulers, and a people's class.

3.3 One-Momentum Societies

One-momentum societies also have the pure and mixed varieties. There are three variants of the pure variety:

(1) a variant without derivative classes (rulers-owners-priests, people, Figure 11.10); that society consists of one class of oppressors – which has at its disposal three kinds of material social means – and a people's class; it is a *socialist* society;

(2) a variant with one derivative class (rulers-owners-priests, owners-priests-rulers, people, Figure 11.11); that society consist of a people's class and two triple classes: a dominant class of rulers–owners–priests and a class of owners–priests–rulers; and

(3) a variant with two derivative classes (rulers-owners-priests, owners-priests-rulers, priests-owners-rulers and the people, Figure 11.12 on

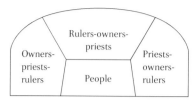

FIGURE 11.12 A pure one-momentum society, the variant with two derivative classes

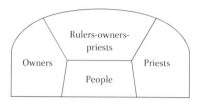

FIGURE 11.13 A mixed one-momentum society, the variant with two single derivative classes

p. 227); in that society, the dominant class is the triple class of rulers–owners–priests; and there are also: a triple class of owners–priests–rulers, a triple class of priests–owners–rulers, and a people's class.

In the mixed variety of the one-momentum society, we can distinguish two variants:

(1) a variant with two single derivative classes (rulers-owners-priests, owners, priests, people, Figure 11.13); that society consists of a dominant triple class of rulers–owners–priests, a single class of owners, a single class of priests, and a people's class;

(2) a variant with two double derivative classes (rulers-owners-priests, owners-priests, priests-owners, people, Figure 11.14); in that society, the main class is the triple class of rulers–owners-priests, and there are also: a double class of owners–priests, a double class of priests–owners, and a people's class.

Those are the three-, two-, and one-momentum classes, with their pure and mixed varieties, in the proposed typology. A complete presentation of them

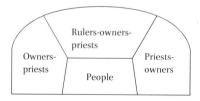

FIGURE 11.14 A mixed one-momentum society, the variant with two double derivative classes

would contain the versions with the owners or priests as the dominant class, as well as subversions based on the relations between the two subordinated classes. For the purposes of this work, though, the theory does not have to be honed to that degree.

The typology proposed in this work posits societies which contain two or three double or triple classes. The supraclass societies conceptualized in the existing n-Mhm typology are only two-momentum societies with one double class and one-momentum societies with one triple class. We could say, then, that the societies with two or three double or triple classes which are introduced here constitute a group of supraclass societies. In order to distinguish them from the previously defined supraclass societies, I will call them polysupraclass societies. Thus, the group of supraclass societies can be divided into two categories:

monosupraclass societies – with one double or triple class:
- mixed two-momentum societies, the variant with two single derivative classes (Figure 11.8 on p. 225),
- pure one-momentum societies, the variant without derivative classes (Figure 11.10 on p. 226),
- mixed one-momentum societies, the variant with two single derivative classes (Figure 11.13 on p. 227); and

poly-supraclass societies – in which there are two or three double or triple classes:
- mixed three-momentum societies, the variant with two double derivative classes (Figure 11.4 on p. 224),
- mixed three-momentum societies, the variant with two triple derivative classes (Figure 11.5 on p. 224),
- pure two-momentum societies, the variant with one derivative class (Figure 11.6 on p. 225),
- pure two-momentum societies, the variant with two derivative classes (Figure 11.7 on p. 225),
- mixed two-momentum societies, the variant with two triple derivative classes (Figure 11.9 on p. 226),
- pure one-momentum societies, the variant with one derivative class (Figure 11.11 on p. 226),
- pure one-momentum societies, the variant with two derivative classes (Figure 11.2 on p. 223),
- mixed one-momentum societies, the variant with two double derivative classes (Figure 11.14 on p. 227).

In the light of n-Mhm, a democratic system can only function in a class society, that is, a society with single classes of oppressors. The polysupraclass societies mentioned above do not fulfill that condition because they contain double or triple classes. Therefore, we can say that the social processes which lead, in the long run, to the creation of a polysupraclass society, may weaken or even eliminate the democratic system.

4 The Processes of the Accumulation of Class Divisions in Contemporary Capitalism

So far, authors working in n-Mhm paradigm have been focusing on the phenomena of the fusion of politics and economics because they predicted that Western societies would be increasingly totalitarized.[9] In this text, I would like to also highlight other processes accompanying the emergence of double and triple classes. Below, I present descriptions of certain social processes in which we can discern the phenomenon of the accumulation of social divisions.

4.1 The Accumulation of Economic and Spiritual Authority

In his book titled *Jihad vs. McWorld*, Benjamin Barber devotes the most attention to the phenomenon he calls "McWorld." In his opinion, this is one of the main trends which are shaping the contemporary Western society. The author created the term "McWorld" from the names of famous – symbolic – American companies "that mesmerize people everywhere with fast music, fast computers, and fast food – MTV, Macintosh, and McDonald's" (Barber 1995, p. 5) and the word "World," which is signifies the global nature of the discussed phenomenon.

Barber notes that capitalism has changed from a system which satisfied needs into one that creates them and manipulates them (Barber 1995, p. 268), which, in turn, has led to a huge transformation in the nature of the economy. Production used to be a response to particular demands and customers' tastes which were external to the process of goods manufacturing. Nowadays, the economic system has engulfed the process of need creation, and it can stimulate consumer behaviors:

> Much of "McWorld's" strategy for creating global markets depends on a systematic rejection of any genuine consumer autonomy or any costly program variety – deftly coupled, however, with the appearance of

---

9 That is also the reason why the spiritual realm has been studied the least in n-Mhm. Some of the few attempts at conceptualizing the spiritual area as a class structure are the works of Niedźwiadek (1985; 1989), Buczkowski, Klawiter, Nowak (1987) and Nowak (1988; 2022a).

> infinite variety. Selling depends on fixed tastes (tastes fixed by sellers) and focused desires (desires focused by merchandisers).
>
> BARBER 1995, p. 116.

That phenomenon is also described by Zygmunt Bauman who claims that today:

> The traditional relationship between a need and the satisfaction of that need is reversed: the promise and hope of the satisfaction of a need appears before the need itself, and it is always more intense and compelling than other promises.
>
> BAUMAN 2000, p. 98

At the beginning of capitalism, introducing changes in the area of production was the only method of optimizing the functioning of economy, that is, to adapt production to the demand for goods (to achieve a balance supply and demand). Nowadays, economic optimization is achieved not only by regulating production but also – if not primarily – by changing the demand.

Barber writes about "churches" of a new faith with economic dogmas related to consumerist values. "To create the cultural values necessary to material consumption is McWorld's first operating imperative" (Barber 1995, p. 109; also see Ritzer 2005).

The contemporary capitalist economy does not only meet the needs of the body but also of the soul (Barber 1995, pp. 59–60). "Our enormously productive economy ... demands that we make consumption our way of life, that we convert the buying and selling of goods into rituals, that we seek our spiritual satisfaction, our ego satisfaction, in consumption" (Victor Lebow, as cited in Barber 1995, p. 223).

The essence of the McWorld trend is not internal economic or cultural transformations but the taking over of the disposal of the material means of indoctrination by the owners' class:

> The concept that drives the new media merger frenzy carries the fashionable name "synergy," which describes what is supposed to be the cultural creativity and economic productivity that arise out of conglomerating the disparate industries that once, quite separately, controlled all three segments of the infotainment telesector: the software programming, the conduits and pipes that distribute it, and the hardware on which it is displayed. The production companies turning out product, the phone and cable and satellite companies and the companies manufacturing

or controlling television sets and computers and multiplexes all, in McWorld's ideal economy, belong in the hands of one global company

BARBER 1995, p. 137.

Barber defines the concept of synergy very broadly – it encompasses sometimes very different phenomena. For example, he writes about the "close cooperation" of a company which produces beverages with an agency which creates and promotes the *image* of the beverage producer, and he calls the relationship synergistic (Barber 1995, pp. 61–62). He also quotes Walt Disney's licensing of products related to the movies of the company as an example of synergy (Barber 1995, pp. 65–66). Another illustration of synergistic operations (Barber 1995, pp. 66–67) are the promotion activities of shoe companies which advertise their brands and trademarks in such a way that they are associated with a lifestyle rather than the mere fact of possessing a particular type of shoes. Clearly, Barber's definition of synergy includes various phenomena consisting in a fusion or, at least, close cooperation of companies or corporations from various areas of production and services, aimed at increasing their profits and economic effectiveness.

However, I would like to draw the readers' attention to a particular meaning of synergy, namely, that of a fusion of mass media and private companies or the whole economic sector. In that merger, a few corporations take control over, among other things, the creation and distribution of network and cable television programs, the production of technical means of communication (cables, telephones, satellites) and equipment (television sets and computers) (Barber 1995, p. 114). In Barber's words:

> If you own movies, buy book companies and theme parks and sports teams (Paramount acquiring Simon&Schuster, Viacom buying Paramount). If you own hardware, buy software (Sony swallowing Columbia). If you own television stations, buy film libraries (Turner imbibing MGM's library).
>
> BARBER 1995, pp. 124–125

The author also takes a look at the press market: After World War II, 80 percent of American newspapers were independent; by 1989, 80 percent were owned by chains (Barber 1995, p. 124). By controlling media content creation, economic corporations can rule individuals-consumers. The power described by Barber is power over images, information, and ideas which, in the contemporary capitalist society, are the tools for indoctrinating individuals so that they become oriented toward consumption.

At this point, I would like to emphasize that the principal meaning of "synergy" and, at the same time, the essence of the "McWorld" trend is the fact that the media are controlled by large companies. The owners of financial corporations use mass media for economic purposes. In the contemporary capitalist economy, economic interest is threatened if consumption is too low. If new media propagate consumerist lifestyles, it is easier to multiply profits.

The phenomenon described by Barber in *Jihad vs. McWorld* consists in, first of all, a fusion of the economic and spiritual spheres. According to the author, financial corporations take control over the new media in order to maximize their economic profits. They can sell more goods and services when they impose a specific set of consumerist values on individuals. The trend of McWorld can be interpreted in n-Mhm as the owners' class taking over the disposal of the means of mass communication. When economic and spiritual power is accumulated in the hands of the owners' class, the single owners' class can transform into a double class of owners-priests.

4.2 *The Accumulation of Political and Spiritual Authority*

In democratic countries, political success depends on the extent of voters' support, which explains why the media are used for distributing propaganda. Particular political parties must effectively win citizens to their value systems and political programs, not only during elections but also while their members are in political and state offices. Mass media become an indispensable instrument of power, so politicians try to control them in various ways. Piotr Żuk writes:

> The media pressure in so-called liberal-democratic orders assumes a different form than the primitive coercion used in authoritarian regimes – and it is more effective, for that very reason. It seduces the potential customer, voter, or buyer, and the majority of the consumerist market does not see it as manipulation but as, at best, a specialist's or an expert's recommendation
>
> ŻUK 2006, pp. 10.

The attempts at controlling the transmission of public information by the authorities assume various forms in democratic states, such as: one radio and television broadcaster's monopoly on the media market, a restrictive policy on concessions and permits for other broadcasters, or informal relations between politicians and media people. The researchers who study the associations between mass media and politicians note the strong influence of the authorities on the means of mass communication.

Italy is one example of a country where the use of the media for political struggle is very salient. Silvio Berlusconi, a media potentate who has been the prime minister of Italy three times since the 1990s, used the means of mass communication very skillfully for political goals. In his article, Francesco Amoretti rightly notes that the success of Berlusconi and his political formation, *Forza Italia* "is not based on the support of the party organization and specific political subculture but on strategically and systematically engaging the media in the efforts to win votes" (Amoretti 2003, p. 179). Internal political mechanisms, such as competent political alliance building or a convincing political program, were not the main reasons for the political victory of Berlusconi's party. The most effective tool of success was the propaganda spread through the means of mass communication. It could be done easily because Berlusconi owns 90% of the media market. That fact also explains his simultaneous appearances as a prime minister on all television programs and his frequent invitations to popular talk shows (Amoretti 2003, p. 191).

Another country where political elites are clearly inclined to control the mass media is Germany. Beata Ociepka and Magdalena Ratajczak write:

> Since the political parties in the federal states are also represented in the radio and television councils, those councils frequently reflect party connections. Thus, radio and television stations can be called "black" or "red" depending on whether they are dominated by the Christian Democratic Union of Germany or the Social Democratic Party of Germany
>
> OCIEPKA, RATAJCZAK 2000, p. 59.

After every election, the positions the management boards of the two greatest German television stations, ARD and ZDF, are distributed in proportion to the power relations between the greatest parties, with media influence frequently looking like spoils to be shared (Ociepka, Ratajczak 2000, p. 61).

In Austria, it is evident that the state television stations have a monopoly on the mass media market. From its very beginnings in the 1950s, ORF television was a state medium treated as a governmental institution. Political parties decide about the filling of the crucial management positions in ORF, in proportion to their representations in the parliament. The media became an instrument of the authorities, and their messages are strongly politicized. The state had a monopoly on radio and television stations until the end of the 1990s. Then, new laws were passed, enforced by the European Union, which allowed the establishment of private stations.

The politicization of the media in various countries assumes different forms but its essence is always the same – the goal is to harness the media to political advantage. In her article, Bogusława Dobek-Ostrowska describes the role of the media in a democratic system in the following way:

> The media are increasingly used as a tool for furthering economic and political interests ... As a result of the politicization of the media and the integration of political and media elites, the media lose their independence for the sake of being at the disposal of the ruling groups.
>
> DOBEK-OSTROWSKA 2003, p. 39

The means of mass communication are a useful instrument of state institutions – they can create the image of the ruling party and present the actions of the government in an appropriate light, which greatly facilitates the implementation of political aims. Thus, it is in politicians' interest to gain the influence over and control of the mass media.

Within the framework of n-Mhm, that process can be interpreted as a trend toward the transformation of a single class of rulers into a double class of rulers and priests. The political elites try to subordinate the mass media to have an impact on the content of media messages. It is easier to wield power when the flow of the information which is inconvenient to the authorities is stifled. In contemporary democratic societies, the ruling class broadens its scope of power with the use of not only the means of coercion but also of the means of indoctrination.

5 Conclusions

In the theory of n-Mhm, the thesis on the totalitarization of contemporary capitalism – a process of the transformation of a single class of rulers into a double class of rulers-owners – is put forth. According to n-Mhm, that trend is the only threat to contemporary democratic societies. When the totalitarization process was stalled – as the neoliberal movements intensified in the last decades of the 20th century – some authors accepted the thesis on the stabilization of the democratic state system.

The broadened typology of n-Mhm societies, with the category of polysupraclass societies, makes it possible to characterize a few simultaneous directions in which the disposal of various kinds of material social means is combined in a given society. Contemporary researchers of social phenomena point to certain trends which can be interpreted in n-Mhm as processes involved in the creation of double classes. The specific economic phenomena of economic corporations taking control over the media, called "McWorld" by

Barber, appear to be an argument for the thesis that single classes of owners are changing into double classes of owners-priests in contemporary democratic societies. In Barber's view, that trend is the basic pattern of transformation in those societies.

The research on the intersections of the political and media realms in recent years, in various European countries shows that political parties tend to take over the media (to various degrees). In the light of n-Mhm, that process can be presented as a transformation of the single class of rulers into a double class of rulers-priests.

In the proposed typology of polysupraclass societies, a society in which the two trends described above would lead to the emergence of double classes could be classified as a pure variety of the two-momentum variant with one double class and with the double class of owners-priests being the dominant class. A graphic representation of this type of society in on Figure 11.15.

If, then, we assume that the recent trend toward totalitarization (the accumulation of power and property) in capitalist societies has been stalled, it does not automatically follow that other processes of the accumulation of class divisions are not taking place there.

The typology of polysupraclass societies presented above and the quoted descriptions of the fusion of the economic, political, and cultural spheres make it possible to identify the directions in which the disposal of various kinds of material social means is combined in the hands of a single group of people. Those phenomena are frequently restricted in scope, but they are salient enough for us to speak about the symptoms of certain social trends which can pose a threat to the continued functioning of democratic capitalist societies in their current form.

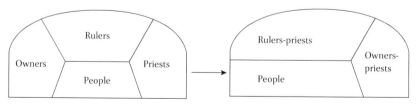

FIGURE 11.15 A transition from a class society to a society with a tendency toward the accumulation of class divisions (economic with spiritual one and political with spiritual)

References

Amoretti, F. (2003). Silvio Berlusconi. Od kampanii typu prezydenckiego do prezydenckiego rządu [Silvio Berlusconi. From a Presidential-Type Campaign to a Presidential Government]. In: B. Dobek-Ostrowska (ed.), *Media masowe w systemach demokratycznych*, pp. 171–198. Wrocław: Dolnośląska Szkoła Wyższa Edukacji TWP.

Barber, B. R. (1995). *Jihad vs. McWorld*. New York: Ballantine Books.

Banaszak, T. (1997). Problem autokratyzacji ustroju demokratycznego [The Problem of the Autocratization of the Democratic System]. In: L. Nowak and P. Przybysz (eds.), *Marksizm, liberalizm, próby wyjścia*, pp. 381–398. Poznań: Zysk i S-ka.

Banaszak, T. (2022) How does Democracy Evolves into Autocracy? In: K. Brzechczyn (ed.) *New Developments in Theory of Historical Process. Polish Contributions to Non-Marxian Historical Materialism. Poznań Studies in the Philosophy of the Sciences and the Humanities*, vol. 119, pp. 240–255. Leiden/Boston: Brill.

Bauman, Z. (2000). *Globalizacja. I co z tego dla ludzi wynika* [Globalization. Its Ramifications for People]. Warszawa: PIW.

Borbone, G. (2016). *Questioni di Metodo. Leszek Nowak e la scienza come idealizzazione*. Roma: Acireale.

Borbone, G. (2021). *The Relevance of Models. Idealization and Concretization in Leszek Nowak*. München: Grin Verlag.

Brzechczyn, K. (2003). Upadek realnego socjalizmu w Europie Wschodniej a załamanie się hiszpańskiego imperium kolonialnego w Ameryce Łacińskiej. Próba analizy porównawczej [The Fall of Real Socialism in Eastern Europe and the Breakdown of the Spanish Colonial Empire in Latin America]. In: K. Brzechczyn (ed.), *Ścieżki transformacji. Ujęcia teoretyczne i opisy empiryczne*, pp. 37–80. Poznań: Zysk i S-ka.

Brzechczyn, K. (2004a). The Collapse of Real Socialism in Eastern Europe versus the Overthrow of the Spanish Colonial Empire in Latin America: An Attempt at Comparative Analysis. *Journal of Interdisciplinary Studies in History and Archaeology*, 1 (2), 105–133.

Brzechczyn, K. (2004b). *O wielości linii rozwojowych w procesie historycznym. Próba interpretacji ewolucji społeczeństwa meksykańskiego* [On the Multitude of the Lines of Developments in the Historical Process. An Attempt at Interpretation of the Evolution of the Mexican Society]. Poznań: Wydawnictwo Naukowe UAM.

Brzechczyn, K. (2007). On the Application of Non-Marxian Historical Materialism to Development of Non-European Societies. In: J. Brzeziński, A. Klawiter, T.A.F. Kuipers, K. Łastowski, K. Paprzycka, P. Przybysz (ed.), *The Courage of Doing Philosophy. Essays Presented to Leszek Nowak*, pp. 235–254. Amsterdam – New York, NY: Rodopi.

Brzechczyn, K. (2017). From Interpretation to Refutation of Marxism. On Leszek Nowak's non-Marxian Historical Materialism. *Hybris*, 37, 141–178.

Brzechczyn, K. (2020). *The Historical Distinctiveness of Central Europe: A Study in Philosophy of History*, Berlin: Peter Lang.

Buczkowski, P, A. Klawiter, and L. Nowak (1987). Religia jako struktura klasowa [Religion as a Class Structure]. *Studia Religiologica* 20, 79–128.

Ciesielski, M. (2012). *Zagadnienie ograniczeń racjonalnego modelu działań ludzkich. Próba ujęcia działania nawykowo-racjonalnego* [The Issue of Limitations of the Rational Model of Human Activities: an Attempt to Grasp a Habitual-Rational Action]. Poznań: Wydawnictwo Poznańskie.

Coniglione, F. (2010). *Realtà e astrazione. Scuola polacca ed epistemologia post-positivista.* Roma: Bonanno Editore.

Dobek-Ostrowska, B. (2003). Miejsce i rola mediów masowych w systemach demokratycznych [The Place and the Role of Mass-Media in Democracy]. In: B. Dobek-Ostrowska (ed.), *Media masowe w systemach demokratycznych*, pp. 14–41. Wrocław: Dolnośląska Szkoła Wyższa Edukacji TWP.

Fukuyama, F. (1989). The End of History? *The National Interest* 16, 3–18.

Niedźwiadek, K. (1985). Struktura i rozwój momentu produkcji duchowej [The Structure and Development of the Momentum of Spiritual Production]. In: J. Brzeziński (ed.), *Klasy – światopogląd – idealizacja*, pp. 17–45. Warszawa – Poznań: PWN.

Niedźwiadek K. (1989). The Structure and Development of the Society's Mode of Spiritual Production. In: L. Nowak (ed.). *Dimensions of Historical Process. Poznań Studies in the Philosophy of the Sciences and the Humanities*, vol. 13, pp. 157–181, Amsterdam: Rodopi.

Nowak, L. (1977). *Wstęp do idealizacyjnej teorii nauki* [The Introduction to the Idealizational Theory of Science]. Warszawa: PWN.

Nowak, L. (1980). *The Structure of Idealization. Towards a Systematic Interpretation of the Marxian Idea of Science.* Dordrecht: Reidel.

Nowak, L. (1983). *Property and Power: Towards a non-Marxian Historical Materialism.* Dordrecht: Reidel.

Nowak, L. (1988). Spiritual Domination as a Class Oppression: A Contribution to the Theory of Culture in non-Marxian Historical Materialism. *Philosophy of the Social Sciences,* 18 (2), pp. 231–238.

Nowak, L. (1989). An Idealizational Model of Capitalist Society. In: L. Nowak (ed.), *Dimensions of the Historical Process. Poznań Studies in the Philosophy of the Sciences and the Humanities*, vol. 13, pp. 217–258. Amsterdam: Rodopi.

Nowak, L. (1991a). *Power and Civil Society. Towards a Dynamic Theory of Real Socialism.* New York: Greenwood Press.

Nowak, L. (1991bcd). *U podstaw teorii socjalizmu* [The Foundations of the Theory of Socialism]; vol. 1: *Własność i władza. O konieczności socjalizmu* [Property and Power. On the Necessity of Socialism]; vol. 2: *Droga do socjalizmu. O konieczności socjalizmu w Rosji* [The Road to Socialism. On the Necessity of Socialism in Russia]; vol.

3: *Dynamika władzy. O strukturze i konieczności zaniku socjalizmu* [The Dynamics of Power. On the Structure of Socialism and the Necessity of its Disappearance]. Poznań: Nakom.

Nowak, L. (2003). O prognozie totalitaryzacji kapitalizmu. Próba oceny po dwudziestu latach [On the Prognosis about the Totalitarization of Capitalism. An Attempt at an Evaluation after Twenty Years]. In: K. Brzechczyn (ed.), *Ścieżki transformacji. Ujęcia teoretyczne i opisy empiryczne,* pp. 361–400. Poznań: Zysk i S-ka.

Nowak, L. (2022a). On the Prediction of the Totalitarization of Capitalism: An Attempt at an Evaluation after Twenty Years Later. In: K. Brzechczyn (ed.) *New Developments in Theory of Historical Process. Polish Contributions to Non-Marxian Historical Materialism. Poznań Studies in the Philosophy of the Sciences and the Humanities*, vol. 119, pp. 150–185. Leiden/Boston: Brill.

Nowak, L. (2022b). Religion as a Class Structure: A Contribution to non-Marxian Historical Materialism. In: K. Brzechczyn (ed.) *New Developments in Theory of Historical Process. The Contributions to Non-Marxian Historical Materialism. Poznań Studies in the Philosophy of the Sciences and the Humanities*, vol. 119, pp. 3–51. Leiden/Boston: Brill.

Nowakowa, I. (1976). Prawda cząstkowa – prawda względna – prawda absolutna. Próba wprowadzenia porządkującego pojęcia prawdziwości esencjalnej [Partial Truth, Relative Truth, Absolute Truth. An Attempt at Introducing the Ordering Notion of Essential Truth]. In: L. Nowak (ed.), *Teoria a rzeczywistość*, pp. 225–255. Warszawa – Poznań: PWN.

Ociepka, B., M. Ratajczak (2000). *Media i komunikowanie polityczne. Niemcy, Austria, Szwajcaria* [The Media and Political Communicating. Germany, Austria, Switzerland]. Wrocław: Arboretum.

Ritzer, G. (2005). *Enchanting a Disenchanted World. Revolutionizing the Means of Consumption.* Thousand Oaks-London-New Delhi: Pine Forge Press.

Szabała, H. (1994). Czy świat zmierza do socjalizmu? [Does the World Go to Socialism?]. *Edukacja Filozoficzna* 17, pp. 286–295.

Wallerstein, I. (1999). *The end of the World as we know it. Social Science for the Twenty-First Century.* London: University of Minnesota Press.

Zarębski, T. (2003). Problem totalitaryzacji kapitalizmu [The Problem of the Totalitarization of Capitalism]. In: K. Brzechczyn (ed.), *Ścieżki transformacji. Ujęcia teoretyczne i opisy empiryczne,* pp. 229–260. Poznań: Zysk i S-ka.

Zarębski T. (2022). The Problem of Totalitarization of the Capitalist Society. In: K. Brzechczyn (ed.) *New Developments in Theory of Historical Process. Polizh Contributions to Non-Marxian Historical Materialism. Poznań Studies in the Philosophy of the Sciences and the Humanities*, vol. 119, pp. 189–216. Leiden/Boston: Brill.

Żuk, P. (2006). Wstęp [Introduction]. In: P. Żuk (ed.), *Media i władza*, pp. 9–14. Warszawa: Scholar.

CHAPTER 12

How Does Democracy Evolve in Autocracy?

Tomasz Banaszak

Abstract

In her works Hannah Arendt distinguishes between two-party and multi-party political systems. According to her thesis, multi-party systems, connected strictly to continental Europe, tend to evolve into autocracy, while two-party systems, established in the United States by the Founding Fathers, are safeguarded from this danger. The following paper tries to describe this difference, using the non-Marxian materialism of Leszek Nowak as one of the descriptive and explanatory tools to explain the phenomena.

Keywords

autocracy – democracy – Hannah Arendt – Leszek Nowak – non-Marxian historical materialism – political party

One of the fundamental problems associated with the phenomenon of democracy is the issue of the stability and survival ability of this form of the system. The following attempt to answer this question is based on two concepts: the theory of power formulated by Leszek Nowak (1983; 1991a; 1991b) in non-Marxian historical materialism and the concept of party systems proposed by Hannah Arendt (1963).

1   The Theory of Power in non-Marxian Historical Materialism

The theory of power in non-Marxian historical materialism can be described as idiogenic antagonistic materialism (Nowak 1991a; 1991b). Idiogenic, because this theory seeks constitutive properties for describing the phenomenon of power within the sphere of politics, and not – as in the case with allogenic theories – in the non-political extent, e. g. in the economy or culture of a given society. The materialist nature of the discussed theory is determined by the fact that, from among the various characteristics of power, it espouses the basic materialist feature: the disposal of the means of coercion. Therefore, it omits the features of power which are usually referred to by theories of idealism, linked, for example, to the community of values and beliefs of the people who make up the given society. The theory of power in non-Marxian historical materialism is an antagonistic theory, and in turn it is decided that the relations of power and civil society are reflected in the terms of non-uniformity towards the means of coercion. The interest of power, which commands the means of coercion, in accordance with the given theory, remains in conflict with the interests of civil society, which do not have such means. In solidarity theories, however, power does not create contradictions by itself but it integrates society into a unified whole. The basic task of this theory is to capture the dynamic features of the phenomenon of power. The method used for this purpose is the method of idealization. Thus, the theory is composed of sequences of models that arise as a result of revealing the following idealizing assumptions. For my purposes, Model I and II of this theory are of dominant importance. So let me introduce their main ideas.

1.1 Purely Materialist Model I and a Materialist-Institutionalist Model II

The basic model of the theory of power in non-Marxian historical materialism is the materialist model. It consists of six idealizing assumptions.

Z-1. Society S is completely isolated from other societies.

Z-2. There are only two classes in S: the rulers (holder of coercive means) and citizens (the rest of the population).

Z-3. The means of coercion that are at the disposal of the S-class rulers have constant technical efficiency. This assumption abstracts from technical progress in this field.

Z-4. The rulers of society S not only have the means of coercion, but they apply it directly. This assumption allows the relationship between the rulers and their forces of coercion to be omitted.

Z-5. The rulers and citizens are not ordered in any institutional hierarchy.

Z-6. Lack of ideological doctrines in S. This assumption omits the influence of doctrines professed by particular classes of society S and the fact that these doctrines organize the individual's consciousness into a collective one.

Every ruler has a certain sphere of influence, and the sum of the spheres of influence of all rulers is the extent of the ruling regulation of the class of rulers. Civil alienation is defined as the ratio between the number of regulated actions to the total number of actions undertaken by citizens. In the extreme case, when all social action are controlled by the authorities, we say that the society is in a state of totalization.

In the relevant theory of power, the relationship between civil society and the class of rulers is described as an antagonistic one. That is to say, the ruling class is mainly seeking to expand its sphere of influence, whereas civil society is trying to counter it and to win the maximum area of independence. Without going into a detailed description of the following phases of this conflict, it is sufficient to state that none of its stages is of a final character. On the contrary, it fluctuates between the two extremes: the total enslavement of civil society and its total freedom.[1]

The materialist-institutionalist Model II is formed as the result of revealing of the Z-5 ideology, bypassing the institutional structure of power. The starting point for model II is the distinction between the actual hierarchy of power and the institutional structure of power – the state pyramid. The hierarchy of power is constituted by the relation of higher social force and relation of domination over citizens (Nowak 1991a, p. 70). Rulers are direct holders of the means of coercion. At the same time, every ruler will master some people (of the first ranks rulers) who become subjected to enslavement, in order to be able to enslave others. The latter, however, will enslave the next rulers of further ranks, until the citizens, who can no longer enslave anyone, are enslaved themselves. In the class of rulers, the further levels of power can be identified, consisting of rulers of a similar sphere of influence. To the first level belong the rulers who have the largest, mutually similar spheres of influence. The second circle of power is made up of those rulers who are comparable among themselves but smaller than the first sphere of influence of power, etc. In this way, the core of the hierarchy of power is formed, consisting of successive levels of domination, from the strongest rulers with the greatest sphere of influence to the weakest rulers, with the smallest sphere of influence. The sequence of these levels is the hierarchy of power.

The institutional structure of power is represented by the notion of a state pyramid. This pyramid consists of the supreme ruler, the elite of power and the apparatus of power. The supreme ruler is the position which is institutionally assigned to the greatest sphere of influence. The elite of power are the positions whom are assigned the smaller spheres of influence than the supreme ruler, but at the same time larger than all other rulers. The rest of the ruling positions are the lower rank of the state administration.

The specific types of state pyramid differ from each other, creating a classification of state systems. The criterion of their distinction is the kind of control that takes place within a given pyramid of political power. On this basis, three

---

1 For a more detailed description, compare: Nowak 1991a, p. 49–69; 1991b, p. 87–105.

main variants of the democratic system were distinguished. In one-component democracy, only one element of the pyramid of political power is controlled by civil society. It may be either the supreme ruler (presidential democracy), or the elite of power (government democracy), or the apparatus of power (committee democracy). Two-component democracy (e. g. presidential-government) involves two of the elements of the pyramid of power being controlled by civil society. Three-component democracy (or full) is a type of democratic system in which all the levels of the state pyramid are controlled by civil society.

1.2 *The Primary Thesis and Its Criticism*

The fundamental thesis of the theory of non-Marxian historical materialism with regards to democracy states that in an isolated purely political society, democratic state system must disappear and transform into an autocratic state system. Thus, the interest of authority is to maximize its own sphere of regulation. The realization of this interest depends, however, on the current state of civil society and power relations. There is a different way to realize the royal interest in the case of full control of the state pyramid by civil society, and another when, for example, only the highest ruler is controlled by the elite of power. Therefore, in every state of class relations there is an optimal state system for the interests of power, which introduces the maximum increase in the sphere of power regulation. Democracy is in a state of balance between political authorities and civil society. In this state there is a vast area of civil society that is autonomous with respect to state power, and any increase in the sphere of imperial regulation causes the resistance of the citizenry. In this situation, the democratic system is most beneficial from the point of view of power, since it allows the elimination of non-operational officers, and the efficient ones, under threat of dismissal, are forced to be even more efficient.

The authorities, reinforced as a result of this process – as the theory holds – can allow for a more complete realization of its interests and bottom-up control channels are liquidated. In the above theories of power, democracy is thus doomed to failure, as the result of working class actions.

The argument that democracy needs to be transformed into autocracy is, however, inconsistent with reality. Undoubtedly, there are many examples that the democratic state system, by virtue of its internal dynamics, tends to transform itself into an autocratic system. This happened to the ancient Greek and Roman democracies, in which the tyranny of government finally prevailed. This was also the case for the Weimar Republic, which, after Hitler's rise to power, turned into a fascist state. However, there are also counter-examples: American democracy, English democracy and contemporary European democracies. So the question arises: what makes certain types of democratic system transform into autocracy while others exhibit resistance to autocratic tendencies deriving from the nature of power? Certain intuitions related to this issue are provided by Hannah Arendt's theory of party systems.

2 Hannah Arendt's Theory of Party Systems

From Arendt's views it is possible to identify, for these considerations, basic conclusions concerning party systems. Arendt's fundamental idea is that multi-party democracy is inevitably bound to transform into an autocratic or dictatorial system, whereas dual-party systems are effectively capable of representing the interests of civil society.

Arendt distinguished two types of democracy: based on a two-party system (the Anglo-Saxon system) and based on a multi-party system (the continental system).

> Faced with the stability of political institutions in the British Isles and the simultaneous decline of all nation-states on the Continent, one can hardly avoid concluding that the difference between the Anglo-Saxon and the Continental party system must be an important factor.
> ARENDT 1962, p. 252

> It has frequently been noted that the United States and Great Britain are among the few countries where the party system has worked sufficiently well to assure stability and authority. It so happens that the two-party system coincides with a constitution that rests on the division of power among the various branches of government, and the chief reason for its stability is, of course, the recognition of the opposition as an institution of government.
> ARENDT 1963, p. 267.

The factors that make democracies able to effectively oppose the threat of autocratization can be found, according to Arendt, in the institutional structure of a given society, such as in the form of a party system.[2] The two-party system is defined by Arendt as follows:

---

[2] Intuitions on the resilience of two-party democracies to totalitarian tendencies in the 20th century were also expressed by other researchers, i.e. Simon (1951). However, Arendt attempted to explain this fact theoretically.

> In the two-party system one party always represents the government and actually rules the country, so that, temporarily, the party in power becomes identical with the state (...) As the two parties are planned and organized for alternate rule, all branches of the administration are planned and organized for alternation.
>
> ARENDT 1962, p. 252

Civil society is organized in this situation into two parties. One of them is in power, while the other is in opposition to her. In contrast, it is in multi-party continental systems, where there are many parties, and each of them only serves as a representative of particular interests.

The different positions of the parties also results in a different function of the state in both systems. According to Arendt, in the Anglo-Saxon system, the state means only the institutions guaranteeing the unity of the country, and the rest of the scope of government regulation is subject to party play. In contrast, in multi-party systems, the parties only serve the role of representative of particular interests with regard to state institutions, whose positions are not – as opposed to the two-party systems – exchangeable as a result of cross-party play. This entails that the government party functions on behalf of a small group of citizens. Thus, in multi-party systems there is a state structure that is independent of the mechanism of cross-party competition, whose size goes beyond the institutions guaranteeing the unity of the country, and which represent individual interests. These are the ideas of Arendt that I will try to paraphrase in notion apparatus of non-Marxian historical materialism.

3   Power versus Politically Organized Civil Society

Democracy is the only type of political system in which civic masses can achieve lasting participation in exercising power. However, according to the theory of power from non-Marxian historical materialism, even the strongest civil society will be enslaved after some time by state power, and the democratic system will be transformed into an autocratic one.

The thesis on the necessary transformation of the democratic system into the autocratic one is, as was mentioned, incompatible with reality. The adoption of this thesis by non-Marxian historical materialism is the result of the fact that it does not take into account the internal diversity of civil society and the existing conflicts within it. The consequence of this step is that the concept of a democratic system is treated too vaguely. For it is not known how and if the organization of civic masses allows the sphere of regulation of state power to be stopped. Therefore, it is questionable whether civil society can self-organize in such a way that it can sufficiently represent the interests of civilian masses in the face of state power. The democratic model that I would like to continue outlining is, based on the ideas of Arendt, an attempt to answer the above question.

3.1 Methodological Assumptions

In order to analyze the internal structure of civil society at all, it is necessary to replace the Z-5 idealizing assumption of the Model I of the political society with an idealizing assumption Z^*-5. The assumption Z-5 stipulates that the political authorities and civil society are not organized in any political institution. According to the assumption Z^*-5 society S is divided into state power and political parties organized by civil society. The latter assumption is still idealizing, as it omits the non-political forms of civil society.

3.2 The Concept of Political Party

The concept of a political party does not exist in non-Marxian historical materialism. As has been mentioned, this means that the materialist-institutionalist Model II that I have discussed is too poor to capture the internal diversity of civil society. However, the concept of a political party can be introduced into the language of non-Marxian historical materialism, using the concepts that appear in this theory. A political party, at least as we know it from history and the present political reality, is always divided into the sphere of party power and, somehow dependent on it, the grassroot members of the party; together these categories make up the given party sub-society. This fact, based on non-Marxian historical materialism, can be explained as follows. In each sufficiently large population, there are individuals maximizing their influences. This goal can be achieved through a mechanism of competition existing in a given society. Therefore, party power is the part of the sub-society party, which, thanks to the mechanism of competition, has the greatest influence in it. According to the assumed nature of power, party power seeks to broaden its own scope of power regulation. The concept of a political party can thus be introduced into the conceptual apparatus of non- Marxian historical materialism, creating, by analogy with the concept of the state pyramid, the notion of the party pyramid. This consists of the party leader (equivalent to the highest ruler in the state pyramid), the party elite (equivalent to the state elite), party apparatus (equivalent to the governing body) and the members. The first three levels of the party pyramid (party leader, party elite and party apparatus) form the party power. The scope of regulation of party power over the party members can be called the sphere of party regulation.

The question arises of why the party sub-society reproduces the subordinate structure analogous to the state pyramid. This, as it seems, results not from some flaw in civil society, but from the nature of the democratic system of state power. Scattered and unorganized civil masses can at the very least tolerate this power, which results in anomie, i.e. complete disorganization of social life. Whereas if, a party system is formed in a society, the conflict of state power and civil society is not so much a matter of eliminating state power as of replacing it. And that requires a strong, internally hierarchical organization – party power. Thus, the inception of a political party is an expression of the readiness of a certain part of civil society to reject the anarchist revolution. The concept of the sub-society party can be considered at least in two respects. The first concerns conflicts within a sub-society party, in other words, its structure and dynamics. The second aspect concerns the phenomena that take place during the cross-party struggle for participation in state power. Before I go into the description of the party sub-society, it is necessary to stipulate that in these considerations only those societies in which there are at least two parties are taken into account. In one-party societies, the governing party does not act as a representative of the interests of civil society but identifies itself with the state. According to the etymology of the word, the so-called one-party systems are, not in fact party systems.

3.3   *Party Sub-Society Structure*

The parties are brought to life by civil society to represent its interests in the face of state power. Since the presented model of democracy is still a materialist-institutional model, therefore, only the political interest of the civic masses can be taken into consideration; Thus, the model omits phenomena related to other types of civil society interests, for instance economic interests. The political interest of the civic masses consists in suppressing the increase of the scope of the sovereign regulation of the country and increasing the sphere of civil autonomy with respect to the state power. By the very fact of its existence, the party provides its citizens with a sense of unity and thus strengthens their position towards the state apparatus. Even so, the sphere of civil autonomy over state power is growing, and the party enjoys the endorsement of some sections of civil society. However, any increase of civic autonomy with respect to state power raises the opposition of the latter. And since the state power has the means of coercion, it does not allow for far-reaching limitations of its scope of government regulation. Thus, over time, it is becoming increasingly difficult to obtain further increases in the sphere of autonomy towards the state for the benefit of the citizens. Ultimately, each party can reach at most a certain limit (threshold of influence on state power), beyond which the state prohibits the further growth of civil autonomy.

There is a hierarchy of power within the party, which, as it was mentioned, strives to maximize its own scope of regulation over party members (area of party regulation).

In the system, power of the party/party members, there is an enslavement analogous to that which occurs in the system of state power/civil society. In the relations of state power and civil society, the rising level of civil enslavement of citizen masses by the state leads to resistance. Thus, the party power that seeks to subdue the members should meet their resistance. However, the party authorities plays a dual role in relation to party members. On the one hand, it subdues them, and on the other hand it stops the increase of the scope of regulation of state power and enlarges the area of civil autonomy with respect to the state. And the latter requires the existence of a strong party power capable of opposing state power. As long as the party members register an increase in their autonomy with regard to the state, they do not rebel against the party power, even if it has managed, to some extent, to subdue the party members. Party authorities only meets the resistance of the masses when it is, on one hand, no longer able to provide them with an increase in the sphere of civil autonomy, and on the other hand, as any authority, it increases its own scope of regulation beyond the patience threshold of subordinate members of the party. Since the party authorities do not dispose the means of coercion, the form of rebellion of the members is simply to leave the party until the party is transformed into so-called "couch party."

The party's position in society depends on two components: the extent of party regulation and the degree to which the party allows the control of the state over its citizens to be reduced. The attitude of the citizens towards the party (P_{cit}) can be defined as the difference in the number of (N) increases in the sphere of civil autonomy with respect to state power (ΔAut_{cit}) and the strength in the sphere of party regulation (ΔReg_p): $N(\Delta Aut_{cit}) - N(\Delta Reg_p) = P_{cit}$. When $N(\Delta Aut_{cit}) > N(\Delta Reg_p)$, then the support for the party authorities grows up to the ceiling of the party's influence on the state. When $N(\Delta Aut_{cit}) < N(\Delta Reg_p)$, then the support for party authorities drops to the point where the party breaks down.

3.4   The Dynamics of the Party Sub-Society

Based on the above assumptions, let us try to recreate the dynamics of development of party/member state relations, i. e. the party sub-society.

At the time of its formation, the party has public support higher than zero. The party is set up by a part of civil society in order to ensure its protection against state power and must therefore, by definition, have some support from citizens. Since the party is an organisation of strong democratic civic masses, so the state power is inclined to make certain compromises at the beginning of party activity. These concessions can be obtained even by a small party, and this is because any area of state regulation consists of civil activities controlled illegally, that is to say, in violation of the applicable law recognised by the state authority. An official organization, even a small one, may, if only under threat of revealing these facts, result in a democratic state withdrawing from the outlawed regulation of citizens. Thus, at the beginning of party activity, the sphere of civil autonomy in relation to state power is growing and it is far ahead of the increase in the sphere of party regulation. There is, however, as has been said, a boundary of compromise between the state and the party. There is, therefore, a time when the party, at least as long as it remains in opposition, cannot do anything more to increase the level of civil autonomy. Ultimately, the indicator of the social party's position reaches the ceiling of influence on state power, and the sphere of civil autonomy stops growing. At the same time, because party power by nature tends to increase its influence on members, the party's sphere of party regulation is constantly growing. As a result, a party's social status indicator declines. The high level of growth of party regulation and the lack of an increase in civil autonomy towards the state cause the indicator of a party's social position to take negative values. This leads to the spread of rebellious attitudes among the member masses towards party power, and thus to a high level of outflow of party members. As a consequence, the party is at risk of collapse.

However, the concept of a ceiling on the influence of state power is a model one. In fact, the party rarely achieves it, which can be explained by the fact that party elites who are reluctant to conflict with state authority slow down the activities of the party apparatus in favour of an increase in civil autonomy in relation to the state and change the program of the party from a reformist to a conservative one.[3] Each party, in order to be distinguished from other parties operating in a given society, must possess its own identification symbols, in other words, its own political program. The elaboration of the program belongs to the party elite. When the party is formed, its main task is to gain support from the masses of citizens. Only this support will allow parties to gain a sustainable place on the country's political map. Therefore, at the beginning

---

3 The concept of the reformist and conservative party program was built by analogy with the Model VIII of the theory of power from the non-Marxian historical materialism with the concepts of conservative program of power factions and the reformist program of power factions; compare Nowak: 1991a, pp. 159–160; 1991b, pp. 207–208.

of the party's activity, the party elites proclaim a reform programme, that is to say, one that refers to the interests of civil society. Since only the political interest of civil society is taken into account in the current deliberations, the concept of the reform programme can be understood as, for example, popularising the right to vote. When a party's social position reaches the ceiling of influence on state power, the party elites, apart from suppressing the party apparatus actions to increase civil autonomy towards the state, are forced to change the party's current political reform program. Therefore, the new party programme must be of a conservative nature – the party elites, for fear of conflict with the state authority, proclaim slogans referring to the interests of the latter. This could be, for example, the following: the postulate to strengthen the executive power and to expand the state apparatus and, consequently, the increased control of citizens by the state. Thus, conservation of the party's program prevents the maximum national impact of a given party from being reached.

Just like the concept of a ceiling of influence on state power, the concept of a party's threshold for durability is of a model nature. In reality, the party elites, aware of the upcoming disintegration of the party, persuade the party apparatus to work for an increase in civil autonomy towards the state, and also change the party's conservative programme to a reformist one. As a result, reformism counteracts party breakdown. The dynamics of the party sub-society is therefore a cycle: the support of party power by citizens (area of acceptance) – the rejection of party power by citizens (the area of refutation), whose amplitude is in any case between the ceiling of influence on state power and the threshold of the party's endurance. Recognition of the above cycle by party elites causes the amplitude of fluctuations to decrease at a level dependent on the elite of a given party.

3.5   *Political Corporations and Their Role*

We have not considered the relations between parties yet. The power of a political party can be defined as the relation between its regulatory area and the scope of all the governing regulations, both state as well as all parties.

A political corporation can be called disposers of coercive powers and party authorities of all parties operating in a given society. In the theory of power of non-Marxian power of historical materialism, the class of rulers is defined as disposers of coercive powers. There, society is divided into a class of rulers and civil society, which does not have coercive means of restraint. However, this term does not allow us to describe the phenomenon of state power in societies with advanced party systems. In these societies, the political control sphere in the broadest terms consists of two elements: the scope of regulation of coercive disposers and the scope of regulation of all parties, both the ruling party and opposition parties. For the peculiarities of the phenomenon of power in democratic systems, it is therefore necessary to broaden the historical notion of the class of rulers existing in non-Marxian historical materialism of the notion of the class of rulers by its dimension, which is related to the presence of the party system. Therefore, a political corporation is a power in democratic systems.

Each party is committed to increasing its own regulatory power. The most significant increase in this energy is provided by participation in the state power. As parties do not have the means of coercion, they must resort to other types of resources in inter-party competition. It may be the party's support by civil society, i.e. the party's social position. When the indicator of social position is relatively high, it means that the increase in the sphere of civil autonomy is higher than that of party regulation. The party with the highest social standing index in relation to other parties has the highest support from civil society. This party wins the next elections and becomes the ruler, which results in it having the highest regulatory power compared to other parties. However, the party's assumption of state authority also means that it must withdraw from unrealistic promises, which were only intended to gain pre-election support. In addition, further action by the ruling party in order to increase its civil autonomy in respect of the state would soon lead it to a maximum impact on state power. Whether desired or not, the elites of the ruling party must change the party's programme from a reformist party to a conservative one, relying more on consensus with a part of political corporation, of an unassisted inter-party game, rather than on further support from civil society.

The ruling party's elites also put pressure on its apparatus to refrain from action to increase the sphere of civil autonomy with regard to the state. The increase in this autonomy decreases, which means that the indicator of the social position of the governing party falls. In the next elections, therefore, one of the opposition parties wins, which at that time managed to gain higher support than other opposition parties. A political corporation is made up of the authorities of all the parties operating in a given society and the disposers of coercive resources. The latter, like any power, seek to increase their own scope of ruling regulation, i. e. to reduce the area of social life, which is subject to party supervision.

Therefore, there is a common interest, independent of the inter-party competitive mechanism, shared between all the parties operating in a given society. The concern is to stop the increase in the scope of the power regulation of coercive disposers. Therefore, parties are reliant on civil society not only because of the inter-party competition mechanism, but also because the support of civil society is their only justification in their relations with the disposers of coercive resources. If, therefore, a stable and efficient party system has emerged in a given society, it is obvious that it plays the role of a specific cushion in the relations between administrators of coercive means and civil society.

The definition of the class of rulers in non-Marxian historical materialism as disposers of the means of resources is one of the bases for defining the notion of civil alienation. Let us remind that civil alienation is the ratio of the number of actions regulated by rulers to the total number of actions undertaken by citizens. The concept of a political corporation, which is a certain broadening of the concept of the class of rulers, also necessitates a modification of the concept of civil alienation. The range of regulation of the class of rulers and the range of regulation of all parties operating in a given society can be described as a global range of power regulation. Therefore, civil alienation can be described as the ratio between the number of civil actions regulated by rulers and political corporation and the total number of civil actions.

4 The Issue of the Autocratic Trap of a Democratic System

The multi-party political systems distinguished by Arendt are characterized by the existence of a large apparatus of state power, independent from the party game. In the two-party systems, the only positions not occupied by the winning party are those relating to institutions which guarantee state integrity. The author clearly refers to only one of them – the institution of the King in the English system; however, this position is only decorative and not related to real processes of exercising power. This leads to the conclusion that Arendt understands the problem of state unity as a community of values and beliefs of a given social group, i.e. in accordance with the principles of idealistic solidarism. The problem is seen differently by not-Marxian historical materialism. Because anarchy, i. e. the system in which there are many miniature hierarchies of power, leads to a social anomie – the aggravated masses – to protect themselves from it, that is, to survive – supported the strongest of these hierarchies. The present solidarity of power and civil society is therefore a compromise between the desire to have and broaden one's own sphere of influence of power and the threat of anomie of civil society. Institutions that guarantee the unity of the state (we can describe them as institutions of public order) are thus based on the monopoly of coercive measures that are needed to establish public order – a community of values, though real, is only a secondary matter.

In the conceptual apparatus of non-Marxian historical materialism, the ideas of Arendt concerning two- and multi-party systems can be paraphrased as follows. Two-party systems are characterized by the existence of two party pyramids. The winning party fills all the state positions, except those related to public governance institutions. In contrast, multi-party systems are characterized by the existence of many party pyramids. However, the winning party only fills a small proportion of the posts related to the administration of the state. Therefore, there is a large state apparatus, independent of the inter-party competition mechanism, of which includes public order institutions are only a small part of it.

What are the dynamics of a two-party system like, considering the above assumptions? There are two strong parties. The winning party therefore has no trouble filling all the areas of administration; the regulatory power of such a party is very large. After the electoral victory, however, the ruling party transforms itself into a classical state pyramid, constantly striving to broaden its own sphere of influence. This process also has consequences for the party sub-society. The ruling party expands its own party apparatus and enlarges the sphere of party regulation, i.e. power over its own members. However, the area of civil autonomy with regard to state power is not growing, obviously. The elites of the ruling party are forced to withdraw from unrealistic promises that were intended to gain pre-election support. For fear of being in conflict with institutions of public order that are not subject to inter-party gaming, the elites of the ruling party are also forced to change the party's programme from a reformist to a conservative one. Ultimately, the indicator of the social position of the governing party is decreasing, which results in members leaving.

The opposition party, in contrast, has little regulatory power, connected only with civil institutions independent of the state pyramid. Therefore, the position indicator of the social opposition party is low. The conscious elite of opposition party, however, makes the party's programme increasingly reformist in character. The opposition party is also being supported by members flowing from the ruling party, when it can no longer effectively represent the interests of civil society. All of this has led the opposition party to gain more and more support from civil society, and therefore a higher social position indicator. Therefore, in the next elections, the opposition party wins and the process described above starts all over again, except that the current opposition party changes into the ruling party and vice versa.[4]

---

[4] The concept of a ceiling on state power has, as was mentioned, a model character. This modeling is expressed not only by the fact that rarely, in reality, does such a party reaches this threshold, but also by the fact that in reality a lot can actually exceed this threshold for certain reasons. This may be the case if state power is too weak to counteract the increasing position of the ruling party. This party will, therefore, expand the area of civil autonomy in

The sphere of power in two-party systems consists of the sphere of regulation of two strong parties and the area of regulation of coercive power holders, which does not surpass the level of public order. The changeability of the ruling party's position and the fact that the area of regulation regulated by the inter-party competition mechanism is much greater than the area of regulation of state power, allows the conclusions that the state authority has no practical possibility of extending its scope of regulation beyond the level of public order. The two-party system with the described dynamics is therefore characterized by a high probability of escaping the transformation into autocracy. So, there are three reasons why two-party democracy is not subject to the natural sequence of state systems. The first one is a small one, it is limited to the level of public order only by the holders of coercive means of regulation. The second reason is the sufficient size of the regulatory area subject to the inter-party competition mechanism to deter the increase in the scope of government regulation beyond the minimum level of public order institutions. The third reason is that the ruling party's office is alternating, which prevents the two-party system from becoming a one-party system. For a two-party democracy, the thesis of the materialist-institutionalist model on the necessity of transforming a democratic system into an autocracy is therefore a false one.[5]

The thesis on transformation of the democratic system into autocratic one maintains its relevance for multi-party systems. These systems differ from the two-party systems in terms of the number of parties, and the number of positions subject to inter-party games. These two factors make multi-party democracies doomed to becoming an autocratic system. The regulating power of each party is by definition small. A single party also regulates only a small number of citizens acting independently of the pyramid of the state. Therefore, multi-party democracy is a system in which civil society controls at most the least important elements of a state pyramid, such as the supreme ruler. This ruler must, in any case, constantly twist between the coteries in the elite of state power and he is forced, whether he wants to do it or not, to adapt to the tendencies prevailing in this part of the pyramid of power. However,

---

relation to the state, until there is a threat of social anomie. At that time, civil society will refer to conservative parties, i.e. parties that propose strengthening state power.

[5] This argument is not simply a repetition of Arendt's argumentation, but that two-party democracies do not have to turn into autocracy. According to the latter, the existence of an opposition party is an essential factor for the sustainability of two-party democracy. As the paper states, this fact of opposition is a necessary condition, but not sufficient to prevent the growth of the scope of state regulation in two-party democracies. The size of the party and the size of the area subject to the inter-party competition mechanism are more significant than it.

the administrative apparatus is not subject to inter-party competition. The regulatory power of such a party, which receives more or less facade positions as a reward for election victory, is small and not sufficiently capable of holding back an increase in the range of state government regulation.[6] In a situation where there is a significant state pyramid independent of the inter-party game, the changeability of the ruling party and one of the opposition parties in power is also not very significant. Even a party with the highest social standing index and the most reformist programme in a given society will have to give way to the interests of the hierarchy of state power. These interests are the main reason why the multi-party system, as illustrated above, is doomed – in its model – to become an autocratic system.

In conclusion, it should be noted that the observation of modern European democracies, which are characterised by a high degree of stability – German or French – shows that there is a tendency for them to transform into the two-party systems as described above. The parties operating in stable European democracies during the elections organise themselves into two major coalitions. How many parties are in a coalition is not really significant. Classical two-party systems – the United Kingdom or the United States – also have a representation of particular interests – as the right or left wing of a party. Therefore, in overall terms, Nowak's thesis is false for the two-party systems, and these are not only the systems so defined, but also some of Europe's systems called multi – party ones.

References

Arendt, H. (1962). *The Origins of Totalitarianism.* New York: A Harvest Book.
Arendt, H. (1963). *On Revolution.* New York: The Viking Press.

---

[6] In the light of the theses presented in previous deliberations, it is easy to notice that the outflow of members' masses from one party to another is, in a way, natural, i. e. resulting from the very essence of social processes in party societies. This phenomenon may be used to explain the so-called crises of democratic systems. These crises can be defined, at least in purely institutional terms, as the inability of a given political system to represent the interests of civil society. This inability can be of a twofold nature: temporary or permanent. The temporary inability of the political system to represent the interests of civil society is a two-party system due to the excessive 'nationalisation' of the governing party. In multi-party systems, on the other hand, this inability results from a sustained weakness of the party system and its inability to resist the increase in the regulation of state power. Therefore, it can be said that multiparty democracies are in a state of permanent crisis, while in two-party democracies this crisis is of a temporary nature, linked to the renewal of the political system.

Nowak, L. (1983), *Property of Power: Towards a non-Marxian Historical Materialism*. Dordrecht: Reidel.

Nowak, L. (1991a). *Power and Civil Society. Toward a Dynamic Theory of Real Socialism*. New York: Greenwood Press.

Nowak, L. (1991b). *U podstaw teorii socjalizmu* [*The Foundations of the Theory of Socialism*]; vol. 3: *Dynamika władzy. O strukturze i konieczności zaniku socjalizmu* [The Dynamics of Power. On the Structure and Necessity of the Disappearance of Socialism]. Poznań: Nakom.

Simon, Y.R. (1951). *Philosophy of Democratic Government*. Chicago: Chicago University Press.

CHAPTER 13

On Coalitions and Party Splintering: A Contribution to the Theory of Power in Non-Marxian Historical Materialism

Marcin Połatyński

Abstract

The aim of this article is to expand the concept of political parties in non-Marxian historical materialism's theory of power. The author distinguishes various types of party organization: autocratic, democratic, oligarchic, and leader-led. Next, the author presents possible paths of development for a typical political party, which can end in a coalition (in the form of a merger, a federation, or an alliance) or a split (split-up and secession). The latter path of development results in the emergence of a new political party.

Keywords

non-Marxian historical materialism – political party – coalition – splintering – party system

1 Introduction. On the Conceptualization of a Party within the Framework of Non-Marxian Historical Materialism

Model I of the theory of power in non-Marxian historical materialism contains a rather general – for the purposes of political science – distinction between political power and the class of citizens (Nowak 1991a, pp. 55–68; 1991b, pp. 81–105). That is not changed in a significant way by the materialist-institutionalist model of the theory of power which considers the influence of state systems on the relationship between rulers and the civil society (Nowak 1991a, 69–92; 1991b, pp. 105–131). That theory was refined, to a degree, in Tomasz Banaszak's conception (1997; 2021) of a political party in which, however, a large part of the political phenomena characteristic of the activity of political parties is also omitted.

In this article, I will present a critical analysis of Banaszak's concept, and then complement it with new categories: a distinction between the party members and the party electorate, a typology of forms of party organization, and a discussion of the phenomena of a coalition and political party splintering.

1.1 Static Assumptions

Banaszak replaces assumption Z-5 of Model 1 of the theory of power, which asserts that society is not organized in the form of any political institutions (Nowak 1991a, p. 50), with the assumption that "society S is divided into organized power and a civil society organized in the form of political parties" (Banaszak 1997, p. 387; 2021). That idealizing assumption is used to analyze the internal structure of a party and the attitude of a party toward the authorities. This is how Banaszak characterizes the internal structure of a party:

> A political party, at least as we know it from history and the present political reality, is always divided into the sphere of party power and, somehow dependent on it, the grassroot members of the party; together these categories make up the given party sub-society. This fact, based on non-Marxist historical materialism, can be explained as follows. In each sufficiently large population, there are individuals maximizing their influences. This goal can be achieved through a mechanism of competition existing in a given society. Therefore, party power is the part of the sub-society party, which, thanks to the mechanism of competition, has the greatest influence in it. According to the assumed nature of power, party power seeks to broaden its own scope of power regulation.
>
> BANASZAK 2022, p. 245

Later, by way of an analogy to the concept of a state pyramid, the author introduces the concept of a party pyramid consisting of: a party leader, a party elite, a party apparatus, and party members. The first three components constitute party authorities.

Through its activity, a party realizes two interests. The first one concerns the relation between the authorities of a party and its members – the party leadership increases the sphere of party regulation, that is, the scope of the citizens' actions of the members which is controlled by party authorities. The second interest concerns the relation between the party and the state power hierarchy; its subject matter is the broadening of the sphere of citizens' autonomy.

When a party is formed, it has few members. The very existence of a party decreases the sphere of power regulation and increases the number of party members. A party sub-society operates gradually and reaches a point at which the growth of the sphere of citizens' autonomy as well as of the number of members slows down. Banaszak calls that point a threshold of the influence on state authorities (Banaszak 1997, pp. 389–390).

That process is accompanied by another one; namely a gradual increase of the sphere of party regulation within the party. In this process, resistance of the party members would be expected. It does not take place, however, because the increase of the internal regulation of a party is compensated by the increase of citizens' autonomy. It is for this reason that the party members agree to increased party control. That process ends when, in Banaszak's words:

> Party authorities only meets the resistance of the masses when it is, on one hand, no longer able to provide them with an increase in the sphere of civic autonomy, and on the other hand, as any authority, it increases its own scope of regulation beyond the patience threshold of subordinate members of the party.
> BANASZAK 2022, p. 247

A rebellion thus ensues, that is, members keep leaving the party, and it transforms into a couch party. The attitude of a party member (Pob) toward the party authorities is a result of two components: a) the scope of party regulation within the party, and b) the scope of citizens' autonomy increased (guaranteed) by the party. According to Banaszak:

> The party's position in society depends on two components: the extent of party regulation and the degree to which the party allows the control of the state over its citizens to be reduced. The attitude of the citizens towards the party (P_{cit}) can be defined as the difference in the number of (N) increases in the sphere of civil autonomy with respect to state power (ΔAut_{cit}) and the strength in the sphere of party regulation (ΔReg_p): $N(\Delta Aut_{cit}) - N(\Delta Reg_p) = P_{cit}$. When $N(\Delta Aut_{cit}) > N(\Delta Reg_p)$, then the support for the party authorities grows up to the ceiling of the party's influence on the state. When $N(\Delta Aut_{cit}) < N(\Delta Reg_p)$, then the support for party authorities drops to the point where the party breaks down.
> BANASZAK 2022, p. 247

1.2 *The Dynamic Model of a Party Sub-Society*

In the dynamic model, Banaszak discusses the changes of the relation between party authorities and party members. A party is formed by a fraction of a civil society to protect it against the increase of state power. A party acts to increase the sphere of citizens' autonomy and forces state authorities to make concessions. Initially, the activity of the party brings about an increase of citizens' autonomy which is greater than the increase of power regulation inside the party. Consequently, the number of party members grows, and so does the influence of the party on the state. At a certain moment, the party encroaches on the range of the state's influence, and the sphere of citizens' autonomy ceases to increase, while the sphere of party regulation grows. Therefore, members begin to leave the party, and the threat of disintegration looms. The party must change in order to survive. Those changes consist in renewed actions promoting citizens' autonomy. The process is reflected in the evolution of the political program: from reformist (the phase of increasing citizens' support), through conservative (the phase of the maximal influence on the state), back to reformist (which prevents the loss of citizens' support).

1.3   Critical Remarks

Banaszak only analyzes a part of the social phenomena in party activity (which is understandable considering the methodology of social modeling he adopts). I would like to draw the readers' attention to the most important phenomena omitted in his analysis. The first one is the distinction between the party electorate and the party members. The second one is the existence of channels of grassroots institutional control of the party authorities by the members, which can lead to the creation of various forms of party organization. The third one is the fact that Banaszak only assumes one path of party development: from its creation, through its influence on the state, to a couch party. There are, however, alternative paths of party development, through the stages of unification and splintering.

2   An Attempt at Extension of the Theory of Parties in Non-Marxian Historical Materialism

2.1   *Party Proponents: The Party Membership and the Party Electorate*

I define party proponents as not only the people who are formal members of a party but also those people who occasionally express support for it. Thus, we can distinguish between the party electorate and the party members and supporters:

– the party electorate occasionally supports the party in elections, which can be viewed as an institutionalized measure of citizens' support for a party.

– party members regularly support the activity of their party authorities by renewing their membership in the party and paying membership fees.

Having introduced the distinction between the party electorate and the party members, we can observe an interesting paradox. During the phase of the maximal influence of a party on the state, the support of its electorate decreases, because the election promises have not been realized, but the support of party members (and their number) grows because the party guarantees state positions and a share in power.

2.2 The Types of Forms of Party Organization

I would like to once more enumerate the elements of a party sub-society distinguished in this analysis. They are: a party leader, a party elite, a party apparatus, and party members. There can be various forms of party organization depending on the possibilities of grassroots reciprocal control by the elements of the party sub-society. That dimension of a party is omitted in Banaszak's approach to the subject. He assumes that decisions are made by the leader or the elite of a party and executed by the party apparatus and the party members. I believe such an approach to be false. The proof can be found in any existing party's statement of organization, that is, in the party law which regulates the relationships within the party authorities and between the party authorities and the party members. A statement of organization, which defines the institutional structure of almost every party, contains provisions about regular members, party clubs and their management (a counterpart of a party apparatus), branches (for example, voivodeship branches), and central authorities (a counterpart of a party elite), as well as party leaders (a counterpart of a leader).

In a more systematic approach, there are three possibilities for the relations of grassroots control of a party pyramid:
– the party members select the party authorities (J),
– the party apparatus controls the elite (JJ),
– the elite controls the leader (JJJ).

Depending on these criteria, we can distinguish four forms of party organization (see Table 13.1 on the next page).

In order to analyze the influence of forms of party organization on the evolution of a party, we need to discuss two more issues. Parties appear in democratic political systems in two phases of the development of a political society: the beginning of the phase of citizens' growing alienation, and the phase of social order. Although there is no direct relationship between the growth of citizens' support for a party and party authorities' scope of regulation (that last factor can be compensated for by the effectiveness of party activity manifested in an increase of citizens' autonomy), it seems that, from

TABLE 13.1 The typology of forms of party organization.

Forms of party organization/ criteria	The party members control the party authorities	The party apparatus controls the elite	The elite controls the leader
Democratic	Yes	Yes	Yes
Autocratic	No	Yes	Yes
Oligarchic	No	No	Yes
Leader-led	No	No	No

among the distinguished phases of the evolution of a political society, parties with democratic and autocratic forms of organization are the most likely to be supported by citizens. The existence of effective channels of control inside a party makes it possible to correct the strategies and political program of that party in advance. That is why parties with dictatorial or leader-led forms of organization are relatively unlikely to obtain mass support from citizens who do not have any reasons to subject themselves to 'despotic' party authorities (at this point, I omit cultural factors).

2.3   The Paths of Party Development

The evolution of a party in this approach (the dynamic variant) takes the following form. After a party has been created and after it has begun its activity on behalf of a civil society, the number of proponents keeps growing until the party achieves the maximal possible influence on the state authorities – at that point, the number of proponents falls. If the party elites do not correct their political strategy, support will continue to fall until the party transforms into a couch party. However, that is only one possibility for the development of that party. There are alternatives: entering a party coalition which may entail cooperation of various kinds, from a loose alliance to a merger of parties, and splintering, that is, the emergence of new groups from within the party organism.

2.4   The Varieties of a Party Coalition

A party coalition can have one of three forms: a merger (i), a federation (ii), or an alliance (iii). The chosen form depends on the possibility of increasing citizens' autonomy and the level of party regulation in a given party. Coalitions can be attractive both to party members and to the party authorities. They are created when:

(i) the increase of civil autonomy effected by the party coalition AB is greater than the increase of citizens' autonomy effected by each party, A and B, separately; which can be symbolically represented as follows[1]:

$$N_{AB}(\Delta Aut_{ob}) > N_A(\Delta Aut_{ob}) + N_B(\Delta Aut_{ob})$$

(ii) the increase of the range of party regulation effected by the inter-coalition parties AB is greater than the level of the increase of party regulation in each party, A and B, separately; which can be represented symbolically as follows:

$$N_{AB}(\Delta Reg_p) > N_A(\Delta Reg_p) + N_B(\Delta Reg_p)$$

In the first case, only the party members are interested in a coalition, in the second one – only the party authorities. For a coalition to be created, both of those conditions must be fulfilled. A coalition can have the form of a merger, a federation, or an alliance.

A merger is the creation of the one party sub-society AB from two previously separate parties, A and B. The composition of the party members changes – there can be fewer members than when the parties were separate. A merger occurs when it guarantees that the party members will have greater citizens' autonomy and that the party authorities will have greater control over the party members.

In the case of a party federation, common inter-party authorities are created for two party sub-societies which retain their structures, especially separate memberships. The federation authorities make decisions which are respected by the party authorities and the membership masses of both parties. A federation is formed when it guarantees that citizens will have greater autonomy. A federation is also beneficial for the authorities of both parties because it allows them to freely broaden the scope of their control over the party members.

An alliance is the weakest type of an inter-party coalition. Two (or more) parties form an alliance when their cooperation brings about an increase of citizens' autonomy and enables an increase of party power in both parties. However, this type of cooperation does not lead to the creation of political institutions which would be shared by the parties.

---

[1] I assume, in a simplifying manner, that only two parties form a coalition, although in reality there occur multi-party coalitions.

2.5   Splintering and its Types

Political parties can also be created by way of splintering, which consists in the creation of two party sub-societies, A and B, from the one party sub-society AB. There are two types of splintering: a split-up or a secession. Splintering takes place when:

(i) the increase of the sphere of civil autonomy effected by the united party AB is lower than the increases of civil autonomy effected by each party, A and B, separately:
$$N_{AB}(\Delta Aut_{ob}) < N_A(\Delta Aut_{ob}) + N_B(\Delta Aut_{ob})$$

(ii) the level of party regulation in the party AB is lower than the scopes of power regulation in each party, A and B, separately:
$$N_{AB}(\Delta Reg_p) < N_A(\Delta Reg_p) + N_B(\Delta Reg_p)$$

Splintering occurs when the two conditions are fulfilled at the same time. I will now characterize the two types of splintering.

In the case of a split-up, the mother party completely disappears. Two new parties, A and B, are formed, and the party sub-society AB ceases to exist. This happens when the two tendencies are combined: the maintenance of the party is not in the interest of the elites and does not guarantee that the existing level of citizens' autonomy will be preserved.

A secession happens when a new party emerges from the existing party, and the old party continues to exist, without the members who operate in new the party sub-societies A or B.

3   Conclusion. A Few Notes on the Conditions of the Stability of a Democracy

Banaszak claims that democracies with two-party systems do not undergo autocratization because the existence of two strong parties makes it possible to effectively control power. Multi-party political systems do not guarantee this and cannot prevent the transformation of a democracy into an autocracy. However, in the light of the reflections above, the role of the type of party system appears to be exaggerated because multi-party political systems can, through various kinds of coalitions, function, in practice, as two-party systems. Also, empirical examples prove the falsity of the thesis about the autocratization of democracy – *vide* Switzerland or the Netherlands. It is worth noting that two-party systems can change into multi-party systems as a result of political splintering. The model of the dynamics of a party sub-society sketched above, then, requires further development in order to determine which tendencies – unifying or splintering ones – are prevalent at which moment in the development of a party.

References

Banaszak, T. (1997). Problem autokratyzacji ustroju demokratycznego [The Problem of Autocratization of Democratic System]. In: L. Nowak and P. Przybysz (eds.) *Marksizm, liberalizm, próby wyjścia*, pp. 381–399. Poznań: Zysk i S-ka.

Banaszak, T. (2022). How does Democracy Evolve into Autocracy? In: K. Brzechczyn (ed.) *New Developments in Theory of Historical Process. Polish Contributions to Non-Marxian Historical Materialism*. Poznań Studies in the Philosophy of the Sciences and the Humanities, vol. 119, pp. 239–255. Leiden/Boston: Brill.

Nowak, L. (1991a). *Power and Civil Society: Toward a Dynamic Theory of Real Socialism*. New York: Greenwood Press.

Nowak, L. (1991b). *U podstaw teorii socjalizmu* [The Foundations of Socialism], vol. 3: *Dynamika władzy. O strukturze i konieczności zaniku socjalizmu* [The Dynamics of Power. On the Structure and the Necessity of the Disappearance of Socialism]. Poznań: Nakom.

CHAPTER 14

On Two Types of Democratization. Poland and Czechoslovakia. An Attempt at Theoretical Analysis

Lidia Godek

Abstract

The present paper seeks to conceptualize the political changes that took place in Poland and in Czechoslovakia in 1989 through the prism of the theory of power in non-Marxian historical materialism (n-Mhm). Nowak's framework for theorizing the process of political transformation continues to be influential for pertinent research. However, due to the complexity of Nowak's arguments, there is some confusion on how to classify and measure the process of democratization in the existing research. Building upon Nowak's arguments, we propose a two-dimensional framework to examine democratization, which not only adequately captures Nowak's essential arguments but also effectively describe the consequences of the two main models of the process of political transition which occurred in Poland and Czechoslovakia in 1989. A comparison of democratic processes from the perspective of that theory makes it possible to distinguish two democratization models: top-down and bottom-up democratization. Choosing between the two paths has an effect both on the shape and character of the emergent democratic political system and the speed and dynamics of the transformation process.

Keywords

non-Marxian historical materialism – democratizations – political transformation – Velvet Revolution – Round Table

1   Introduction

The notion of democratization is often used with the underlying assumption that there exists a certain normative pattern exists which may serve as a benchmark for evaluating the process of transition to a more democratic political regime. Western European democracies are commonly believed to represent such a model. Recent studies show, however, that maintaining this research assumption is both theoretically erroneous and useless in practical terms, as there is no single normative model of democratization (Pulkkinen, Rosales 2008, p. 1). Notwithstanding the above, attempts can be made to describe the constituent processes of democratization (also via comparative studies) on the basis of available social theories.

The present paper seeks to conceptualize political changes that took place in Poland and in Czechoslovakia in 1989 through the prism of the theory of power articulated in non-Marxian historical materialism (hereinafter also n-Mhm).[1] A comparison of democratic processes from the perspective of that theory makes it possible to distinguish two democratization models: *top-down* (a pre-emptive state system change in n-Mhm terms) and *bottom-up democratization* (an adaptive state system change in n-Mhm terms). A selection between the two paths has an effect both on the shape and character of the emergent democratic political system and the speed and dynamics of the transformation process. Seen from the viewpoint of the presented theory, the cases of Poland and Czechoslovakia can be regarded as paradigmatic. The model of top-down democratization involves the active role of the communist power apparatus striving to control the direction and nature of social transformations (case of Poland)[2]. The model of bottom-up democratization is characterized by the lack of response from the communist authorities to mounting social dissatisfaction and their attempts to hold on to power without any intention of sharing it with the democratic opposition (case of Czechoslovakia).

In this paper I seek to elaborate on the two distinct models of democratization. The goal is pursued within the framework of Nowak's the theory of political power in non-Marxian historical materialism. As will be shown in the forthcoming sections, the theory is useful for gaining insights into the essence of political regime transformations. A suitable starting point is an outline of the main tenets of the theory of power. The next step is a detailed classification of political system transformations. On that basis, in the final part of the study,

---

1   What I assume is a simplified model of the theory of power formulated on the basis of non-Marxian historical materialism. A full account of the theory can be found in: Nowak 1983; 1991a; 1991c. On methodological approach of Leszek Nowak and Poznań School, see: Coniglione 2010, Borbone 2016: 2021.
2   The first fully free elections in Poland did not take place until 1991, which makes Poland the last country in Eastern Europe to hold entirely democratic elections. Therefore, paradoxically, Poland was the first country to set in motion democratic processes and the last country in which democracy was fully embraced (if the institution of free elections is to be regarded as a criterion of democratic transition). See Berend (1996, p. 254), Castle (1996, p. 232), Godek (2004, pp. 117–131).

I will attempt to conceptualize the introduction and consequences of the two main models of the process of political transition which occurred in Poland and Czechoslovakia in 1989.

2 The Theory of Political Power in non-Marxian historical materialism

2.1 Model 1: Static Assumptions and the Development of the Political System

The underlying assumption in the first model of the theory of power is that a specific social minority holds a monopoly on using the means of coercion for the exercise of power[3]. The main actors of social life include, on the one hand, the class of rulers having ways and means to control social activity (disposers) and, on the other hand, the civil society which is deprived of such a possibility (Nowak 1991a, pp. 25–31; 1991c, pp. 54–56).[4] Every ruler manages a certain sphere of influence which can be defined as the set of civil activities which are subject to their control. The sum total of spheres of influence of all rulers forms the so-called scope of authoritative regulation. The main interest pursued by the class wielding control over coercive means (disposers) is to maximize the scope of authoritative regulation via competition between different rulers. Those who prove themselves to be the most efficient and effective at expanding their spheres of influence gain an advantage in the structure of power. Conversely, the rulers who enlarge their spheres of influence less successfully are either driven out of the power structure or learn to expand their scope of control of social life more adequately.

---

[3] The assumption is in accord with the view put forth by Max Weber who states explicitly that political power is to be viewed in the context of the state having the monopoly on the legitimate use of violence. See Dreijmanis 2008.

[4] Model 1 of political society in non-Marxian historical materialism is based on the following idealizing assumptions: the society S is completely isolated from all other societies (assumption 1); the society S is divided into two classes only: rulers (disposers of means of coercion) and citizens (assumption 2); coercive means in the disposition of the ruling class remain constant (i.e. technological advancement in the area of means of coercion is eliminated from the picture) (assumption 3); the disposers of means of coercion (rulers) apply the means themselves (this is to disregard the relation between rulers and special forces they may use for applying means of coercion) (assumption 4); the fact that society S is organized into certain political institutions is ignored (assumption 5), and finally the fact that the classes of society S believe in certain political and social doctrines is disregarded (to ignore the influence produced by class consciousness on the social thinking of particular citizens from a given class) (assumption 6); see Nowak (1991a, pp. 49–54; 1991b, pp. 81–84).

On the other hand, it is in the interest of civil society to maintain the largest possible sphere of autonomy free from the control exercised by disposers of coercive means. The potency of civil resistance depends on the level of civil alienation which, in the spirit of the theory presented in this paper, is defined as the ratio of the number of social actions subject to authoritative regulation to the sum total of social actions. The relationships between social alienation and social resistance can be expressed in the form of the statements given below (Nowak 1991a, pp. 33–36; 1991c, pp. 65–66):

a) If the level of civil alienation is low, social resistance is also low; this state of affairs is referred to as social peace.
b) If the level of civil alienation is medium-high, social resistance increases to the point of outbreak of a revolution of the first type.
c) If the level of civil alienation is high, social resistance is low; this state of affairs is referred to as declassation.
d) If the level of civil alienation achieves an extreme level, social resistance rises to an extreme level as well, culminating in a political revolution of the second type.

Let us assume that at the starting point of the evolution of the political system the scope of regulation is so minimal that the society operates in a state of social peace (Nowak 1991a, pp. 55–67; 1991c, pp. 87–103). However, during the phase of the growth of civil alienation rulers push to expand their spheres of influence at the expense of citizen autonomy. This is a consequence of political competition forcing rulers to strive towards expanding their powers. An increase in the scope of authoritative regulation, which is equated with increased civil alienation, intensifies civil resistance which ultimately causes an outbreak of a revolution of the first type (civil alienation rises from the threshold of class peace to the point of first-type revolution).

There are two possible outcomes of the revolution of the first type. A victorious revolution results in the revolutionaries seizing power (the civil loop variant). The mechanism of political competition begins to appear among the revolutionary authorities, gradually causing the scope of authoritative regulation to increase again. Those in power who fail to expand and secure their realm of influence or lack efficiency find themselves displaced from the class of disposers of coercive means. Consequently, there is a resurgence in civil alienation culminating in the outbreak of another revolution of the first type, this time directed against the authorities that emerged from the victorious revolution.

Let us now consider the variant of a lost revolution. The authorities break social resistance, which opens the way to maximizing the scope of authoritative regulation. In the enslavement phase, the terror imposed by the regime is directed against the entire civil class. At this stage of social development, the majority of citizens are subordinated to those in power. Thus, it is increasingly difficult to find new social areas for political conquest. A new phenomenon, termed political overcompetition, emerges within the power structures. Instead of conquering new autonomous domains of social life, rulers take over control of social life areas which are subordinate to other rulers. Since the state of mutual competition for spheres of influence would lead to the destruction of the political control system, it is in the interest of the power circles as a whole to carry out purges. In this way, the excess of challengers for power is eliminated together with potentially dangerous consequences of political overcompetition.

As soon as enslavement engulfs the lower ranks of power, the authoritative expansion turns against other parts of the civil society (the expansion of ruling). According to the statistical assumptions of the model, an increase in civil alienation then leads to a revolution of the second type. As the revolution involves only a small part of the civil class, it is doomed to fail. The rulers launch repressions against the rebels, however at the same time, in order to prevent another wave of protests, they withdraw from regulating some domains of social life. Political concessions also bring benefits to the rulers, liberating them from the state of self-enslavement, as new areas to conquer arise.

However, competitive mechanisms among those in power again induce an increase in authoritative regulation culminating in another revolution of the second type, with a broader social base. The revolution ends in defeat, pressuring the rulers into greater concessions. A certain cyclic pattern of revolutions of the second type thus becomes established. The political system evolves in the following sequence: revolution of the second type – victorious counter-revolution of rulers – political concessions – the growth of political control – another revolution of the second type, and so forth. Importantly, each successive revolution inspires even greater mass participation than the previous one. Repeated second-type revolutions cause a steady decrease in alienation.

Ultimately, the revolution becomes so widespread that the authority is no longer able to use repressive measures against the participants. As a result, the rulers are forced to make concessions which reduce the level of civil alienation below the threshold of class peace. In the secondary stage of the revolution of the first type the readiness of civil masses to put up resistance stabilizes the level of civil alienation.

2.2 *Model II: The Development of Political Society and Sequences of the State Systems*

In the Model II (materialist-institutionalist) the idealizing assumption 5 is removed what makes it possible to analyze the structure of the class of rulers

(Nowak 1991a, pp. 69–91; 1991c, pp. 105–131). The class is no longer considered as a group of people having a monopoly for over the means of coercion but as a hierarchy of positions to which the disposition of coercive means is institutionally assigned. The starting point in Model II is thus the distinction between the actual hierarchy of power and the institutional structure referred to as the pyramid of power. The hierarchy is constituted by two relations: "the relation of domination and that of a higher social power defined by the size of the spheres of domination" (Nowak 1991a, p. 70). It consists of successive levels of rule: from the most powerful rulers with the greatest realm of influence, down to the weakest rulers. The institutional structure is represented through the concept of the state pyramid. The constituent elements of the pyramid, from the top down, include the authority, elite and apparatus. It is assumed that the sphere of regulation assigned to the position of the top ruler is smaller than the total of spheres of authoritative regulation assigned to the institutional positions of the elite, though the sphere of influence of the supreme ruler is larger than the sphere of regulation held by individual elite members. Similarly, the total of spheres of regulation assigned to the positions of the power elite is smaller than the total of spheres of authoritative regulation assigned to positions in the power apparatus. Depending on how the state pyramid is organized, four main types of state systems are distinguished. They include democracy (dem), autocracy (aut), dictatorship (dic) and despotism (des). Their differentiation is based on the observable channels of upper ranks of power by the lower ranks. Accordingly, three channels of control can be identified (Nowak 1991a, pp. 75–76):

(k) control of the state power pyramid by the civil society;

(kk) control of the leadership (elite and supreme ruler) by the apparatus of power;

(kkk) control of the supreme ruler by the power elite.

Based on the criteria given above, the four basic types of state systems are distinguished (see Table 14.1 on page 271).

One of the basic theses of n-Mhm is that political relations determine the type of state system. Hence social development corresponds to a sequence of consecutive state systems. Depending on the state of political relations, the authority introduces a particular state system to secure its own interests as far as possible. Accordingly, each state system corresponds to a particular social state (1–7) identified on the basis of society development. The emergence of politico-social forms (A1, B2, C3, D4, E5, F6, G7) ensures the maximum enlargement of the sphere of authoritative regulation. The idea can be schematically represented in the following manner on Table 14.2 on the page 271.

POLAND AND CZECHOSLOVAKIA. AN ATTEMPT AT THEORETICAL ANALYSIS 271

TABLE 14.1 Types of State Systems (Nowak 1991a, p. 75)

Institutional channels of control in	The official authority by the civil society	The leadership by the apparatus of power	The supreme ruler by the elite of power
Democracy	Yes	Yes	Yes
Autocracy	No	Yes	Yes
Dictatorship	No	No	Yes
Despotism	No	No	No

TABLE 14.2 Multilinear Development and Progress in Model II (Nowak 1991a, pp. 78-79)

(A) democracy	1) state of class peace (stage of civil alienation progressing to the threshold of class peace)
(B) autocracy	2) transitional period (from the threshold of class peace to the revolution of the first type)
(C) dictatorship	3) revolution of the first type
(D) despotism	4) enslavement
(E) dictatorship	5) revolution of the second type
(F) autocracy	6) transitional period (from the revolution of the first type to the threshold of class peace)
(G) democracy	7) class peace (below the level of class peace)

Based on the consequences of the states of the society presented in Model I, it is possible to reconstruct the natural (from the rulers' point of view) sequence of political forms which would arise following the introduction of a political system with the greatest benefits for the ruling authorities at an appropriate time (Nowak 1991a, p. 81–82). For Model I, it can be illustrated in the following manner (the presented sequence of state systems occurs in the loopless variant of the development of political society):

democracy → autocracy → dictatorship → despotism → dictatorship → autocracy → democracy

It must be noted, though, that the sequence of political changes given above does not need to be materialized in this exact form. The sequence merely outlines a certain tendency towards changes which occur as a result of the competing interests of two distinct classes: the class of rulers and the civil society.

2.3 Functional and Dysfunctional Systemic Changes

The underlying assumption is that changes in the state system are functional in nature. Introduced at an appropriate point in time, they provide those in power with the highest level of authoritative regulation in a given state of social relations. A delay or acceleration in the process of political system transformation causes losses in the sphere of authoritative regulation. Consequently, two types of changes to the state system can be distinguished in the n-Mhm paradigm: functional and dysfunctional. Functional changes in the natural sequence of state systems include:

1) democracy → autocracy
2) autocracy → dictatorship
3) dictatorship → despotism
4) despotism → dictatorship
5) dictatorship → autocracy
6) autocracy → democracy

Other changes affecting the state system, which arise from skips in the sequence, are considered dysfunctional and may take the following forms (Nowak 1991a, pp. 84–85; 1991c, pp. 122–123):

1) anticipation, when a change to the state system is introduced prematurely. An example of such a change is when an autocratic political system is established is the state of class peace, for which democracy is the optimal form of the political system. Social resistance increases automatically, leading either to further citizen enslavement or to the outbreak of a revolution;

2) retardation, when a change to the state system is introduced belatedly. An example illustrating such a change is when the democratic system is not replaced by the autocratic system at an appropriate time. In this case, striving to preserve a political system which hampers the expansion of the sphere of authoritative regulation may culminate in attempts to stage a coup d'état.

To recapitulate the ideas presented above, the following classification of state systemic changes may be given (see Figure 14.1 on page 273):

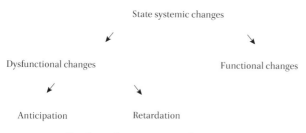

FIGURE 14.1 Typology of state systemic changes

3 On Two Types of Functional Change of the State System

So far, the theory of power in the n-Mhm framework relied on the implicit assumption that a functional change to the state system takes place concurrently with a change in political relations between the rulers and citizens. However, the situation is not always so straightforward. First, the authority must identify a given state of political relations and then design a new solution for the state system or modify the existing system in order to guarantee the maximum scope of authoritative regulation or the maintenance of political power. A certain period of time, shorter or longer, must hence pass between the transformation of the political situation and the establishment of a new political regime. Based on this line of thought, two types of functional changes to the state system can be identified:
1) pre-emptive change;
2) adaptive change.

Thus, the extended classification of state systemic changes in n-Mhm takes the following form (see Figure 14.2 on the page 274).

3.1 *Pre-emptive State Systemic Change*

A pre-emptive functional change is introduced before a shift in the balance of power between the rulers and civil society. It represents a variant of the state system transformation which involves a slightly different sequence of events. Before the state of class balance is achieved, the rulers offer to make concessions, thus pre-empting the outbreak of a revolution. In this variant, the rulers are able to prepare themselves better for a new political situation. They proactively propose state system reforms at the most convenient point in time and in the optimal sequence to serve their interests. What is more, they choose a variant of the political system that is expected to secure their position most effectively. By introducing the optimal political regime, the rulers

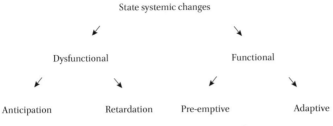

FIGURE 14.2 Extension of typology of state systemic changes

cut their losses in the sphere of authoritative regulation resulting from gradual adjustment of the political system to a new social context.

3.2 Adaptive State Systemic Change

An adaptive change of the state system involves a reform launched by the rulers in response to a new status of class relations between them and the citizens. The shorter the period between a change in class relations and the establishment of a new state system, the smaller the rulers' losses in authoritative regulation resulting from the preservation of an increasingly dysfunctional system, maladjusted to new conditions. Crucially, in this variant, a change in the state system takes place on a bottom-up basis. As a consequence, the authority is deprived of the freedom to choose the most suitable moment for the reform, and to plan and control its course.

3.3 Functional vs. Dysfunctional Changes

An extension of the classification of state system changes requires a differentiation between functional change in its pre-emptive variant and dysfunctional change manifesting as anticipation. Also, by analogy, it is necessary to make a distinction between dysfunctional change assuming the form of retardation and functional change in its adaptive variant. The main principles governing the distinction include the timing and degree of changes affecting the sphere of authoritative regulation.

Comparing anticipation with pre-emptive change in the state system, an essential factor to consider is the elapse of time between the transformation of social relations and the response of the rulers. It is assumed that a transformation of the state system by anticipation pre-dates pre-emptive change. The rulers respond well in advance to a change in social relations, which may contribute to a decrease in the level of civil alienation. In pre-emptive changes, the rulers react to signals heralding social transformations and respond to them by introducing new elements into the state system.

It must also be noted that anticipatory changes cause greater losses in the sphere of authoritative regulation than pre-emptive changes. What is more, the longer the state system anticipation prevails, the more prominent the losses become. In contrast, persistent pre-emptive functional changes in fact contribute to a reduction in losses, as the time progresses, since the social situation ripens to the point of establishing a new state system.

The differences between retardation and functional adaptive change are analogous in nature. Adaptive changes precede retardation. Consequently, the reduction of losses in functional adaptive change occurs earlier, with the political system adjusting to a new social situation. In retardation, the level of losses keeps rising, as the preservation of a non-functional system takes longer.

It is worth emphasizing that the differences between functional and dysfunctional state changes are gradable, not dichotomous.

3.4 Pre-emptive vs. Adaptive State Systemic Change: An Attempt at Comparison

A comparison of pre-emptive and adaptive changes of the state system can be shown on the example of political transition between the dictatorial regime and democracy. This kind of transformation occurs during the final stage of the phase of cyclical revolutions of the second type. Under the influence of resistance put up by citizens, the level of civil alienation decreases from the spectrum of declassation to the spectrum of class peace. Let us, therefore, briefly consider two variants of democratization of the political system. The first takes the form of pre-emptive change of the state system ("top-down democratization"), and the other – adaptive change of the state system ("bottom-up democratization").

In the mechanism of top-down democratization, introduced through pre-emptive change of the state system, the rulers make political concessions suitably in advance and, in this way, prevent the outbreak of a revolution and introduce a variant of the democratic system which is best aligned with their interests.

The sequence of events is different in bottom-up democratization initiated via adaptive change of the state system. In this case, all-encompassing civil revolution forces the authorities into making considerable concessions which push the level of civil alienation below the threshold of class peace. Under these circumstances, the most optimal political system – from the viewpoint of the authorities – is democracy, which becomes established under pressure from citizens. The rulers have only a limited room for manoeuvre in deciding how the political system will be democratized, and a minor influence on what shape it will ultimately take.

As a result, both democratization variants entail a decrease in the level of civil alienation. In top-down democratization, civil alienation is reduced through the political concessions made by the rulers in an attempt to prevent the eruption of a revolution. In contrast, in bottom-up democratization the driving force is revolution launched by citizens on a mass scale. It seems, though, that political concessions are always less effective than the revolutionary pressure in inducing a decrease in the extent of civil alienation. Moreover, democracy established in the top-down mechanism is always more favourable for the authorities than the bottom-up democratization path. This is because the former approach enables those in power to choose a more beneficial variant of the electoral system, constitution, etc.

4   Two Types of Democratization

4.1   *The Democratization of the State Systems in Poland and Czechoslovakia*

Let us now provide a concise outline of the model of state system changes developed in the n-Mhm paradigm[5]. An example of functional pre-emptive change in the political system in the form of *pre-emptive state system change* is the transition which happened in Poland in 1989. To illustrate the adaptive change of the state system manifesting as *adaptive state system change*, one can refer to the process of democratization of the political system in Czechoslovakia.[6] A comparison of democratization processes which occurred in both countries shows that they followed different paths of transitioning from the non-democratic to democratic regimes. The path, adopted by the

---

5   I will exam this aspects of political transformation which are approached from the perspective of the materialist-institutional model of power in n-Mhm. Theorists who pursue this line of reasoning for recognise nature of process of political transformation (changes of 1989 in East Central Europe) include, among others: Nowak (1991b; 1993; 2022), Brzechczyn (2011). In this analysis, I disregard the economic and international dimensions of the transformation processes in Poland and Czechoslovakia, e.g. the election of a Polish Pope, the coming to power of Mikhail S. Gorbachev or the election of Ronald W. Reagan as US president (Petrescu 2014, 45–47). On the one hand, the perspective of the materialist-institutional model of power in n-Mhm allow to avoid discussing the relationship between international aspects and final cause the collapse of the communist regimes in East-Central Europe. On the other hand, this lack of international perspective can be analyse as limitations of this theory. The literature devoted to political transformation's theory has undoubtedly been enriched by various analysis of multicausal explanations. See e.g. Edwards (2000), Petrescu (2014).

6   Petrescu (2014, pp. 18–19) adopts the term of "negotiated revolution" (Poland's case) and "non-negotiated revolution" (Czechoslovakia's case).

communist authorities in Poland, involved an active approach of the power apparatus, as it sought to retain as much control as possible in the context of inevitably changing social relations. In the other path, which was followed by the Czechoslovakian authorities, there was no reaction to the transformation of social relations. The rulers made every effort to stay in power, regardless of the cost, without any willingness to share power with the opposition. The selection between the two paths has an effect both on the shape and character of the emergent political system. Pre-emptive change allows the authorities to hold on to power even after engaging the opposition in talks (the so-called "leap forward" strategy) and shape the state system in such a manner as to retain their influence, chiefly in determining the level of democratization of the new system. No such possibility is available in the framework of adaptive change. Under mounting social pressure, the authorities are forced to make much more far-reaching concessions to introduce a fully democratic system.

4.2   Poland: A Case of Pre-Emptive State Systemic Change

A good starting point for a discussion about the political transition which occurred in Poland at the turn of the 1990s is the year 1988, when two major strike waves broke out. The first spate of strikes happened in the spring, in response to increases in the prices of food and services introduced by the communist government. The second wave broke out in the summer, in mid-August, with workers demanding wage rises in order to compensate for rising commodity prices[7]. However, as the protests escalated, the protesters also started to voice political demands. This was particularly pronounced among striking factory workers in Gdańsk and Szczecin) (Sebestyen 2007, p. 216, 219). The spate of strikes which erupted in August was larger in scope than the strike actions of April and May. Nevertheless, they also lost their impetus and gradually began to wither away (the strikes broke out in the Manifest Lipcowy mine, in the Szczecin Port and Northern Port in Gdańsk, Lenin Shipyard, and in the Huta Stalowa Wola steelworks).[8] Faced with social unrest, the authorities responded with a variety of tactics. On the one hand, negotiations were held with the striking workers, and certain concessions were made, chiefly a rise in wages (for example in Bydgoszcz). On the other hand, however, the authorities initiated repressions against the strikers, since whenever political demands were

---

7   For a detailed account of the underlying causes and the course of the strikes, see Castle (1996, pp. 222–227).
8   More on the weakening strike mobilization and the importance of protest forms can be found in: Ost (1989, p. 85).

voiced, the authorities resorted to using force. This is precisely how the protest in Nowa Huta ended, with the protesters being subdued by ZOMO (Motorized Reserves of the Citizens' Militia). These formations entered the stage when it turned out that despite meeting the wage demands being met, the strikers had no intention of stopping the protest and called for the reinstatement of fellow workers who were made redundant as early as during the Martial Law period (Marciniak 2002, pp. 29–45; Gortat, Marciniak 1991, pp. 27–37; Dudek 2007, pp. 14–16). The striking workers also suffered repressive measures. They were laid off or restricted to jobs with poorer pay and benefits. Some were also ordered to pay fines (Janowski 2003, pp. 182–195). Striking miners were forcefully drafted into the army. Furthermore, one of the first measures taken by the authorities was to convene a session of the State Defence Committee which resolved to start preparations for declaring a state of emergency (Dudek 2004, pp. 131–132).

The second wave of strikes, however, led to the first talks between the authorities and the opposition (Lech Wałęsa and Czesław Kiszczak). Inasmuch as the spring strikes failed to persuade the authorities to change their policies, the surge of strikes in August compelled them to enter into talks, since they were faced with a growing radicalization of public opinion and there were fears that tempers could reach boiling point. General Wojciech Jaruzelski and general Kiszczak decided to expand the co-optation strategy with a negotiation manoeuvre. That was the moment when the offer to hold *Round Table* talks was first extended by Kiszczak. The precondition for initiating negotiations was the termination of strikes (Sebestyen 2009, p. 248).[9] Lech Wałęsa took up the task, calling on strikers to resume work (the strikes ended, however without bringing any concessions from the communist authorities). During the meeting, Kiszczak outlined the topics to be addressed during future meetings, including proposed changes to the electoral system, establishment of the Senate and the status of the opposition in the future political regime. He stressed that even though Solidarity activists would be invited to take part in the Round Table talks, the Solidarity movement as such would not participate in negotiations with the communist authorities as an equal partner. The underlying intention was to draw oppositionists into the system, to pressure them into taking co-responsibility for the effects of social changes introduced at that time, but also to deprive the opposition of any opportunities to create a real alternative to

---

9   It is worthwhile to note that the name "round table" was not first used by Wojciech Jaruzelski in June 1988. In fact, the expression first appeared in two letters to the authorities (1982 and 1983) drawn up by the Free Democrats' Movement (one of Poland's opposition parties). See Trembicka (2003, p. 10); Łabędź (1997, p. 82).

the communist power (Mianowicz 1999, pp. 159–167; Staniszkis 2001, pp. 7–8).[10] Hence the communist authorities proposed no change in the state's functioning or (re)legalization of Solidarity. Their proposals came down to offering state positions to opposition activists[11]. The appointment of general Kiszczak as the negotiator left no doubt that the authorities had no intention of giving in to public pressures. As Roman Malinowski stated:

> The fact that Kiszczak was chosen to talk to the opposition was supposed to be an element mobilizing the opposition circles. It was a subtle reminder, a delicate suggestion showing the opposition that it was still in the sphere of interest of the authorities and that its official status had not changed that much.
> MALINOWSKI 1992, p. 52

The setting up of a large round table in the Jabłonna Palace was a government propaganda gesture. However, the talks broke off in mid-October, the main point of contention being the postulate of legalizing Solidarity. The authorities refused to recognize the trade union as an independent political force. On the other hand, the opposition rejected the concept of "one trade union in one workplace" pushed by the communist party. Another contentious issue concerned the selection of Solidarity members to represent the trade union during the negotiations (Trembicka 2003, p. 244). Initially, the communist authorities called into question twelve names. The list was finally reduced to two: Jacek Kuroń and Adam Michnik. The ultimate decision to freeze the negotiation process was motivated mainly by the government's order to liquidate the Gdańsk Shipyard. To justify the decision, the authorities cited economic reasons (unprofitability). The move was seen by the Solidarity as a provocation, for the

---

10 The views of the opposition on this matter, and their awareness of the stategy adopted by the communist authorities towards the opposition is reflected in the words of Tadeusz Mazowiecki: "[A]though we do not bear co-responsibility (we don't have conditions for it) we have a feeling of co-responsibility. I think that sometimes at the beginning of this year it became more and more clear that ... we cannot simply say 'they' answer for it. The constantly worsening state of the country is becoming our concern as well". Quoted after: Castle (1996, p. 232).

11 The intentions of the communist elite are reflected in a secret document written by Mieczysław Rakowski for the Central Committee of the Polish United Workers' Party in which he argued that "the opposition had to be drawn into the orbit of power in order to remove it from its vantage point where it did not have to do anything to accumulate political capital, as everything bad was immediately blamed on the government, with the opposition reaping benefits from this;" quoted after: Żakowski (1990, p. 18).

shipyard served as a symbol of resistance to the communist regime.[12] A poignantly symbolic end to the negotiations came in the first week of November, when the round table was dismantled and placed in storage.

Concurrently, the ruling party searched for other means to gain social support (Berend 1996, p. 265). Rakowski's government took attempts to save the regime through economic liberalization, while preserving the existing reality of economic life.[13] The programme proposed by the government was meant to realize the idea of "social market economy." The main legal act was the Act on Business Activity passed by the Sejm on 23 December 1988 which granted entrepreneurs far-reaching freedoms to set up and operate enterprises. During forthcoming weeks, the Sejm adopted a number of acts liberalizing Poland's economic life. For example, the legislators unified tax regulations, introduced unrestricted trade in foreign currencies, and established a chain of deposit-credit banks (Castle 1996, p. 229).

The intentions of the authorities are most accurately described in a party-prepared study describing the so-called Internal Political Summit. In section four of the document, which outlined the reasons for making arrangements with the opposition, the authorities indicated that

> regardless of the progress observed in the dialogue between the authorities and the opposition, given the existing social situation, one cannot rule out the eruption of a large-scale social conflict. A flexible dialogue-based policy involving all constitutive forces can either postpone such an outbreak or markedly attenuate the conflict. To recapitulate, (...) there is a constant danger of social unrest on a large scale, arising from economic causes, with a potential to evolve to a fully-fledged political conflict. A radical breakthrough could come as an "internal political summit" – a protocol-based meeting of leaders of Poland's main political powers.
>
> Quoted after DUBIŃSKI 1999, p. 158[14]

---

12   The decision to shut down the shipyard coincided with the end of preparations to declare a state of emergency. There is only indirect evidence that the apparent coincidence was actually deliberate. See Paczkowski (1999, p. 154).

13   Mieczysław Rakowski was sceptical about the idea of working for a broad compromise with the opposition. At a press conference, he stated: "Poles are less interested in a round table than one which is richly laden." "Trybuna Ludu" daily, 1988 (15–16. 10).

14   The preliminary concept with preconditions for achieving a consensus with the constructive opposition by organizing the Internal Political Summit is discussed in: Dubiński (1999, p. 158).

The stance adopted by the communist authorities can be interpreted in the following manner: in order to avoid an eruption of social discontent, the authorities proposed a set of political concessions including democratization of the state system. The strategy was adopted at the 10th Plenary Session of the Central Committee of the Polish United Workers' Party (PZPR) on 20–21 December 1988 and 16–18 January 1989, though not without reluctance.[15] By giving consent to the manoeuvre of pre-emptive change to the state system, the authorities prevented outbreaks of social unrest.

On 27 January 1988, a preliminary meeting was held in Magdalenka, a village near Warsaw, to work on the details of the future agreement and resolve divisive issues. It was the last meeting before the first plenary session of the Round Table. The participants discussed planned changes to the political system and the introduction of trade union pluralism.[16] A schedule, procedure and the names of participants were established. The basis for the agreement reached on 27 January was the Solidarity's guarantee to take part in non-confrontational elections (Sebestyen 2009, pp. 338–369; Crampton 1996, pp. 391–2). Entering into talks with the opposition determined the shape of the political system in which the Polish United Workers' Party (PZPR) retained its influence and position. This was possible thanks to the agreements reached at the Round Table negotiations and during the deliberations in Magdalenka.[17] The authorities secured their interests primarily through the decision to hold non-confrontational elections for the Sejm (Petrescu 2014, p. 46). In the new Sejm, 65 percent of members would be drawn from the communist party and

---

15 A decisive majority of the party apparatus was against dialogue with the opposition, due to the belief that it would be an act of capitulation. It was only when the communist party's elite (Jaruzelski, Kiszczak, Rakowski, Siwicki) threatened to resign that the impasse was avoided. Through blackmail, the party elite gained a vote of confidence. The attitude of the party apparatus towards the transformation process is described by Gilejko (2002, pp. 46–58).

16 During one of the Round Table sessions, Bronisław Geremek said the following: "We are not interested in sharing either in the monopoly of power, or the allocation of privileges, or the allocation of positions: we are interested in the organization of civil life." Quoted after Castle (1996, p. 233). The uniqueness of Poland's Solidarity movement in the context of the debate about civil society as a political category was first discussed by Arato (1981, pp. 23–47). See also J. Kean (1988, p. 5); Arato (1992, p. 74); Ely (1992, pp. 173–178); Baker (2002, p. 14).

17 The Polish Round Table Talks as a chapter in Poland's political history has been extensively explored. Some authors addressing the topic include Skórzyński 1995; Skórzyński, 2009; Garlicki 2003; Dudek 2004; Trembicka 2003; Codogni 2009; 2012.

its allies, and the remaining 35 percent were open to the opposition to gain in normal electoral competition.[18] The term of the Contract Sejm was to last four years (Berend 1996, p. 266). A key element of the contract democracy was the introduction of the office of president. The president was meant to serve as the guarantor of the state system, i.e. secure the continuity of institutions and the structure of the existing political system. The office of president was a guarantee that after the breaking of the monopoly held by the communist party, the communist authorities would retain its decision-making powers. Based on informal consultations, it was arranged that the office of President would be filled by a representative delegated by the government.[19]

The strategy adopted by the communist power suggests that substantial uncertainty on the part of the authorities about securing their future interests promoted the resolution of the political crisis through consensus (co-optation and negotiations). If the parties to a conflict are unable to predict how their decisions might impact their interests in the future, they become more willing to engage in talks rather than be stuck in an impasse or confronted with a crisis. The achievements of the Polish Round Table discussions suggest that the communist authorities, striving to hold on to their privileges and interests, decided to take the risk of negotiating with the opposition. The communists fought to achieve a goal which, however, after being attained lost some of its significance. After 1990, the year of the presidential elections in Poland, the institutional system of guarantees negotiated during the Round Table discussions, was dismantled (O'Donnel, Schmitter 2013, chapter 4).

4.3 Czechoslovakia: A Case of Adaptive State Systemic Change

A different scenario unfolded in Czechoslovakia. The political transition which occurred in this country was more dynamic, which narrowed down the time frame and had a significant influence on the form of the state system that emerged from the transformation. The dynamics of the political changes sweeping across Central and Eastern Europe is best described with a quote from the British historian and political commentator Timothy Garton Ash who has reported having said to Vaclav Havel that the collapse of communism "in Poland (...) took 10 years; in Hungary 10 months; in East Germany 10 weeks;

---

18 During one of the Round Table sessions, Lech Wałęsa stated: "None of us want these elections. They are the terrible, terrible price we have to pay in order to get the union back." Weschler (1989, p. 64).

19 For an analysis of the Round Table Agreement between the authorities and the opposition in the categories of negotiations, see M. Castle, (1996, pp. 234–235). For an analysis of the same aspect within a framework of n-Mhm, refer to Brzechczyn (2004, pp. 26–27; 2010).

perhaps in Czechoslovakia it will take 10 days" (Ash 1990, p. 121).[20] The collapse of the communist regime in Czechoslovakia occurred through peaceful means. Negotiations were held from 19 November until 10 December. Similarly to Poland, dialogue and talks constituted the primary instruments of change. However, unlike in Poland, where the Round Table was the culmination of a long-planned initiative, the talks held in Czechoslovakia were spontaneous and improvised, and arrangements were made on the spot. Fear of riots and public retaliation forced the communist authorities, which had refrained from entering into talks with the society for dozens of years (with the exception of the Prague Spring), to engage in negotiations (Crampton 1996, p. 398). The opposition gained influence bit by bit, and finally took over political power throughout the country in the free elections of June 1990. However, it was the dynamics of the Velvet Revolution in late 1989 that had pushed the communist regime into making greater concessions to society.

The Velvet Revolution took place from 17 November to 29 December 1989. The immediate cause was the suppression of a student demonstration in Prague by the police, which sparked a series of protests in Prague and other cities across Czechoslovakia.[21] It is important to note that the Velvet Revolution happened at a time when the dismantling of the communist regimes in Central and Eastern Europe had already begun. Poland had a (partially) non-communist government. In Hungary, the communist party had been dissolved and, on 23 October 1989, the Hungarian Republic was proclaimed. In the German Democratic Republic (GDR), Erich Honecker's government had been brought down (18 October 1989) and the Berlin Wall had collapsed (9–10 November 1989), while in Bulgaria Todor Zhivkov was ousted from power. Another point to consider is that in January 1989, when the communist authorities again arrested Vaclav Havel – the leader of the anti-communist movement in Czechoslovakia – Poland's communist government was working on details of the agreement with the democratic opposition. When Tadeusz Mazowiecki's government was formed in Poland, Havel was again convicted and sentenced to prison (Sebestyen 2009, p. 346). Neither during the period preceding these events nor after them did the Communist Party of Czechoslovakia engaged in any meaningful discussions with the democratic opposition. The Czech communist government watched with great concern the transition to

---

20 See also: Ash T. G., Václav Havel: Director of a play that changed history. 18.12.2011, "The Guardian", [http://www.guardian.co.uk/commentisfree/2011/dec/18/vaclav-havel-changed-history1, accessed May 8 2021].

21 The expression "Velvet Revolution" was first used by Rita Klímová. Quoted after: Sebestyen 2009, p. 367.

more democratic political regimes in neighbouring states, and the actions of Gorbachev's government in the Soviet Union (diplomatic relations with Poland were frozen in June 1989).[22]

The starting point for the analysis of the course and nature of the democratization process in Czechoslovakia is the year 1987, when the faction of "normalizers" (Gustav Husák, Milos Jakeš) gained dominance in the KSČ (De Candole 1991, p. 8). Initially, the group ignored the need for reforms, and saw them as a sign of political weakness. Concessions or commitments towards to the society and opposition were interpreted as a likely end to the KSČ's rule and its ultimate removal from power (Suk 1999, p. 59; Bradley 1992, p. 29; Dobbs 1998, p. 348). Nevertheless, faced with major transformations sweeping through the entire Soviet Bloc and the deteriorating economic situation, the authorities pledged to pursue key reforms. Within the communist party, however, the prevailing view was that the changes were just a façade masking a less committed reality, a manoeuvre designed to "buy some time" rather than introduce meaningful social changes. As Petr Fiala, Jan Holzer, Miroslav Mareš and Pavel Pšeja point out, the proposed changes to the state system (amendments to the election law, act on state enterprises) should not be interpreted as "a well though-out political response to rapidly unfolding events but rather as a symptom of detachment of the majority of party elites from the social reality and a spasmodic attempt to hold on to at least minimal power that was slipping away" (Fiala, Holzer, Mareš, Pšeja 1999, p. 69). Another important aspect is that the ruling communist party itself was divided over the scope of proposed changes. As a result, the scale of the reforms brought in by Czechoslovakia's prime minister Lubomír Štrougal was quite limited and stood no comparison with the changes that were introduced in Poland by Mieczysław Rakowski's government.[23] Furthermore, towards the end of 1988, the KSČ leadership decided to take a tough position on protesters. In January 1989, anti-regime demonstrations were violently suppressed by the authorities. The brutal response showed, on the one hand, how determined the communist government was to crush dissent and maintain the *status quo*, and on the other exposed its complete helplessness.[24]

---

22 When, on 16 November 1989, Mikhail Gorbachev described the 1968 Warsaw Pact intervention in Czechoslovakia as unlawful, the KSČ still regarded the operation as a justified counter-revolutionary measure. See M. Bauer (2002, p. 351).

23 Soon afterwards Štrougal was replaced as prime minister by Ladislav Adamec who was a representative of the older generation and a supporter of the 1968 intervention. See Czyż, Kubas (2012, p. 94).

24 It needs to be stressed that the majority of protests held in the same year when the communists in Poland were getting ready for relinquishing some of their power were still

The immediate trigger that set off the chain reaction of events that culminated in the collapse of the communist regime in Czechoslovakia was the student demonstration staged in Prague to commemorate the anti-fascist rally of 1939. Special police forces brutally attacked the crowd, which met with the outrage and indignation of society. Across the country emotions ran high, as the violently suppressed protest was quite neutral politically, being organized by the Socialist Youth Union (SSM)[25]. The rumour about a killed student (confirmed on 18 November by Radio Free Europe) served as a pivotal trigger that mobilized the passive majority of the society to take part in subsequent protests [http://www.totalita.cz/1989/1989_1118.php.,10.11.2017.]. A wave of demonstrations swept through the entire country. The strength of the protests surprised the authorities (Berend 1996, p. 284). The only concession of the communist government during that period, however, was the abolition of visas to Western European countries (Crampton 1996, p. 397). The main burden of resistance fell on the students who planned a general strike for 27 November. On 19 November, a political platform called the Civic Forum (*Občanské forum – OF*) was established in Prague, with Václav Havel as its leader and founder, to unify the dissident forces in Czechoslovakia (Bureš 2007; Suk 1998, p. 14). In its first proclamation (18/19 November 1989), the OF demanded the removal of the compromised members of the government (accused of collaborating with the organizers of the 1968 intervention) from power and punishment of those responsible for the violent attacks on protesters on 17 November 1989 (Bureš 2007, pp. 41–48; Saxonberg 2001, p. 330).

The weakening position of the communist authorities – and the resolve and growing impatience in society – is accurately reflected in one of the messages that appeared on banners waved by protesters gathered in the Wenceslas Square on 20 November 1989, which read "End democratization, start democracy" (http://totalita.cz/1989/1989/_1120_ul.php., 10.11.2017; accessed May 8, 2021). It was also at that time that the communist government agreed to hold a meeting with representatives of the opposition forces (without Havel). The prime minister Ladislav Adamec vowed to refrain from the use of force against the protesters and promised to launch a formal investigation into the events that occurred on 17 November[26]. The authorities chose to begin talks with the

---

violently suppressed. The stance towards the protesters was not softened until August 1989. See Crampton (1996, p. 397).

25 A reference to the anniversary of Operation Prague. In November 1939, the Nazis closed down all universities and colleges. A total of 1,900 students were arrested in Prague. Nine randomly selected students were shot. See Heineman (1979, p. 203).

26 The first commission to investigate the events of 17 November (so-called Ruml's Commission) was established on 20 November, and the second (Commission of the

opposition mainly because they feared that the movement that might well produce riots and an uncontrollable social revolution. In addition, by entering into negotiations with the opposition, the communist authorities sought to boost their public prestige as a party talking to and cooperating with the protesters. At that time, however, the communist government did not plan any major concessions to the opposition and its demands. On 23 November, the authorities launched a counteroffensive, attempting to win the support of workers at the largest factories in Prague – to no avail; they were booed down. Also, a meeting was convened for the communist party activists in the army (the minister of defence argued that the military were right to intervene against the students on 17 November), and preparations were undertaken for the action under the code name Zásah: mobilization of the military units in the Western District to attack protesters (http://totalita.cz/1989/1989_1123.php;11.10.2017). On 24 November, an extraordinary session of the KSČ was held to determine how best to approach the crisis. As a result, Miloš Jakeš, General Secretary of the Communist Party of Czechoslovakia, resigned along with seven members of the presidium (Bureš 2007, pp. 55–60). At the same time, the party's activists were informed during a confidential meeting that plans were in place to quell the protests by force. At the press conference held on 25 November, the top leaders announced the party's personnel changes to the public as a proof of their open and cooperative attitude towards the opposition. However, they also reiterated their view that the intervention of 1968 was justified, and confirmed the main tenets set out in the regime's "Lessons from the Crisis" (1970) which were meant to strengthen the ideological discipline within the party. In this way, the ruling party hinted that it was not interested in a genuine dialogue with the opposition and Czechoslovak society. On the same day, at 2 o'clock in the afternoon, the greatest demonstration in the history of Czechoslovakia, involving 800,000 people, took place near Hradčany in Prague. It was a pivotal point, following which on 28 November, the authorities began official negotiations with the political opposition and integrated oppositionists into the political process. The government's ostensibly open attitude towards the demands

---

Federal Assembly and the Czech National Council) on 29 November. Both reached different conclusions: the Commission of the Federal Assembly, headed by J. Stanek, concluded that the attack on protesters was planned and orchestrated, and intended to compromise the party's leadership (mainly Jankeš). Advocates of this version of events also claim that there was a group in Czechoslovakia's special forces (StB) that was interested in launching the proceess of changes in the country. The other commission did not identify eny evidence to corroborate this fact. See Méchýř (1999, pp. 25–30). For more details about the first talks held by the authorities with the opposition, see Bankowicz (2003, p. 91).

of the opposition was intended to be demonstrated by the federal assembly's removal of article 4 of the Czechoslovak Constitution of 1960 pertaining to the leading role of the Communist Party in the state and society, which occurred on 29 November (Saxonberg 2001, p. 349). The talks, which took place between 3 and 5 December, resulted in the appointment of a new government with five non-communist ministers (the so-called "15:5" government). "The ruling elite, nevertheless, had a strategy to hold on to their power, the only difference being that the political focus would shift from 'hard-line' communists to those representatives of the communist nomenclature who could be described as 'realists'" (Méchýř 1999, p. 337). The co-optation manoeuvre aimed at drawing the opposition into the orbit of power was, however, belated and unsuccessful. "The new authorities, more than half of which were communists, were not adequate for the new situation in the country" (Suk 1998, p. 48). The government reconstruction in the proposed shape produced mounting social discontent, further student strikes and protests of the Civic Forum (Bureš 2007, pp. 97–106).

On 8 December, the first session of "round table" talks was held in Prague, involving the authorities and the opposition (Bureš 2007, pp. 118–131). All the participants agreed that a member of the communist party would be prime minister, however his power would be balanced by the make-up of the government which would be dominated by oppositionists. The communist authorities consented to all candidates for government functions put forth by the Civic Forum. Crucially, the communist party was no longer in a position to dictate anything and had to accept what was offered. For the first time after 1948, the communists lost their majority in federal government. In December, the ratio of communists to non-communists holding government functions was 10:11, but in January 1990 it decreased to 7:14. The government stayed in power until 27 June 1990.

Faced with the lack of support from the Soviet army, and painfully aware of the social and political transformation that had been set in motion in Poland, the communists relinquished their rule under the pressure of mass demonstrations. Members of the KSČ realized that, faced with the rise of radical attitudes in the Czechoslovak society, they had to agree to the opposition's demands. Some communist representatives, however, were needed in the government based on the national consensus in order to preserve the continuity of the state which, in turn, guaranteed social peace. Dialogue proved to be a critical factor for both sides, the communist authorities and the opposition, as they feared an uncontrolled revolution. The tactics adopted by the opposition, seeking to evade conflict and striving for a non-violent transition of power (*sametová revoluce* – *velvet revolution* in Czech; *nežná revolúcia* – *gentle revolution* in Slovak) through peaceful dialogue with the progressive wing of the KSČ, proved to be the most viable solution. The most important institutional guarantee for the democratic change was the election of Vaclav Havel, a playwright turned dissident, to the post of president on 29 December 1989, and conducting of free elections. It was, without any doubt, the greatest success of the Velvet Revolution. Free elections were held in June 1990, with a sweeping victory of candidates representing the opposition circles. Another milestone on the path to democracy was the adoption of the Constitution of the Republic on 16 December 1992 (which became effective on 1 January 1993).

5 Concluding Remarks

The main aim of the paper was to distinguish two major types of functional state system changes: pre-emptive state system change and adaptive state system change. Insights gained into functional changes of the state system in the framework of non-Marxian historical materialism make it possible to more accurately interpret the political breakthroughs which took place in Poland and Czechoslovakia in 1989. In the cases of functional state system transformations achieved by the pre-emptive mechanism, the authorities, by offering concessions suitably in advance, are able to avoid the eruption of a revolution and chart out a path towards the democratization of the political system in such a manner as to protect their interests. In bottom-up democratization (adaptive state system change), the authorities have no such possibility, as a breakthrough is achieved through the protest potential and pressure of civil masses. In other words, in pre-emptive state system change the rulers – at the expense of some early compromises – are able to make much more limited concessions overall than in adaptive transformations. In the latter case, the authorities withdraw from social life regulation, but the final scope of concessions is greater.

The democratization processes which occurred in Poland and Czechoslovakia show that the manner of transition from a non-democratic to a democratic political system has an important shaping influence on the formation of the new state system. The talks held between the Polish United Workers' Party (PZPR) and the opposition determined the characteristics of the democratic system in Poland, in which non-democratic authorities retained their influence (non-confrontational elections) until 1991. The Polish Round Table Agreement of 1989 can be interpreted in the categories of pre-emptive change to the state system, because the initiation of negotiations which culminated in the agreement was not a direct consequence of the strikes of 1988. However, the strike actions were seen as a potential trigger of large-scale social unrest (Pollack, Wielgosh 2004, p. XV). The communist party's top leadership realized that if they passively watched the unfolding of the events without taking any action, the strikes could jeopardize the political status of the Polish United Workers' Party (PZPR). The risk of new social upheavals forced the authorities to extend an offer of political system liberalization. As a result, the authorities evaded the threat of social revolution and, at the same time, secured themselves an important influence on the future political reforms of the state. The interests of the communist authorities during that period were supported by two state bodies established on the basis of a political contract: the parliament elected to a four-year term and the president with a wide range of powers and a mandate for a six-year term in office.

Conversely, the Velvet Revolution in Czechoslovakia can be interpreted in the categories of adaptive change of the state system. The communist authorities belatedly decided to enter into talks with the opposition. Faced with mounting social pressure (mass-scale protests), the authorities were unable to secure themselves "political fuses" to smoothen the transition process, despite attempts (such as the "15:5" government). Fully democratic elections were held as early as in June 1990, barely seven months after the outbreak of the Velvet Revolution, with the communist winning only 16% of votes. In December 1989, Vaclav Havel, a leader of the Velvet Revolution that toppled the regime, was elected president. A key element of the contract democracy in Poland was the establishment of the office of president as the guarantor of the state system, tasked with securing the institutional and systemic continuity of the previous political system. The situation in Czechoslovakia was completely different. To conclude, it is important to stress that the two presidents, Wojciech Jaruzelski and Vaclav Havel, were elected in indirect elections, by parliaments dominated by communists. Furthermore, the period preceding the adoption of the constitution in Czechoslovakia was much shorter: the Constitution was passed on 16 December 1992. In Poland, however, a constitution was enacted and approved in a referendum as late as in 1997.

References

Arato, A.(1981). Civil Society Against the State: Poland 1980–1981. *Telos* 47, 23–47.
Arato, A. (1992). *Civil Society and Political Theory*. Cambridge, MA: MIT Press.
Ash, T.G. (1990). *We the People: The Revolution of '89 Witnessed in Warsaw, Budapest, Berlin and Prague*. Michigan: Granta Books.
Baker, G. (2002). *Civil Society and Democracy Theory*. London: Routledge.

Bankowicz, M. (2003). *Zlikwidowane państwo* [A Liquidated State]. Kraków: Wydawnictwo UJ.

Bauer, M. (2002). *Changing Cleavage Structure and the Communist Successor Parties of the Visegrád Countries.* In: A. Bozóki, J. I. Ishijama (eds.), *The Communist Successor Parties of Central and Easter Europe.* Armonk-New York.

Berend, I.T. (1996). *Central and Eastern Europe 1944–1993. Detour from the Periphery to the Periphery.* Cambridge: Cambridge University Press.

Borbone, G. (2016). *Questioni di Metodo. Leszek Nowak e la scienza come idealizzazione.* Roma: Acireale.

Borbone, G. (2021). *The Relevance of Models. Idealization and Concretization in Leszek Nowak.* Műnchen: Grin Verlag.

Bureš, J. (2007). *Občanské fórum.* Plzen: Aleš Čeněk.

Bradley, J.F. (1992). *Czechoslovakia's Velvet Revolution: A Political Analysis.* New York: Colombia University Press.

Brzechczyn, K. (2004). Porozumienie przy Okrągłym Stole w świetle koncepcji kompromisu klasowego. Próba modelu [The Round Table Agreement in the light of the Concept of Class Compromise: An attempt at Model], pp. 27–46. In: S. Drobczyński, M. Żyromski (eds.), *Rola wyborów w procesie kształtowania się społeczeństwa obywatelskiego w Polsce.* Poznań: Wydawnictwo WSNHiD.

Brzechczyn, K. (2010). The Round Table Agreement in Poland as a Case of Class Compromise: An Attempt at a Model. *Debatte: Journal of Contemporary Central and Eastern Europe*, 18 (2), 185–204.

Brzechczyn K. (2011). The Forgotten Legacy of Solidarność and Obstacles in Building a Democratic Capitalist System Following the Fall of Communism in Poland. In: N. Hayoz, L. Jesień, D. Koleva (eds.), *Twenty Years after the Collapse of Communism. Expectations, Achievements and Disillusions of 1989*, pp. 395–416. Berlin: Peter Lang.

Castle, M. (1996). The Final Crisis of the People's Republic Poland. In: J. Lefwich Curry, L. Fajfer, *Poland's Permanent Revolution People vs. Elite. 1956 to the Present.* The American University Press.

Codogni, P. (2009). *Okrągły Stół, czyli polski Rubikon* [The Round Table, or the Polish Rubicon]. Warszawa: Wydawnictwo Prószyński i Spółka.

Codogni, P. (2012). *Wybory czerwcowe 1989 roku. U progu przemiany ustrojowej* [June 1989 Elections – On the Threshold of Systemic Transformation]. Warszawa: Instytut Pamięci Narodowej.

Coniglione, F. (2010). *Realtà e astrazione. Scuola polacca ed epistemologia post-positivista.* Roma: Bonanno Editore.

Crampton, R. J. (ed.) (1996). *Easter Europe in the Twentieth Century.* London and New York: Routledge.

Czyż, A., S. Kubas (2012). *Czechy i Słowacja. Politologiczne studium wspólnej i oddzielnej państwowości* [Czech Republic and Slovakia. A Political Science Study of Joint and Separate Statehood]. Katowice: Uniwersytet Śląski.

De Candole, J. (1991). *Too Velvet Revolution?*. London: Alliance Publishers.

Dobbs, M. (1998). *Precz z wielkim bratem. Upadek imperium radzieckiego* [Down with Big Brother: The Fall of the Soviet Empire], trans. by P. Kwiatkowski, Poznań: Wydawnictwo Rebis.

Dreijmanis, J. (ed.) (2008). *Max Weber's Complete Writings on Academic and Political Vocations*, transl. G.C. Wells, New York: Algora Publishing.

Dubiński, K. (1999) (ed.). *Okrągły Stół* [The Round Table]. Warszawa: Krajowa Agencja Promocyjna.

Dudek, A. (2004). *Reglamentowana rewolucja. Rozkład dyktatury komunistycznej w Polsce 1988–1990* [A Rationed Revolution. The Distribution of Communist Dictatorship in Poland 1988–1990]. Kraków: Wydawnictwo Arcana.

Dudek, A. (2007). *Historia polityczna Polski 1989–2005* [Political History of Poland 1989–2005]. Kraków: Wydawnictwo Arcana.

Edwards, L. (ed.) (2000). *The Collapse of Communism*. Standford: Hoover Institution Press.

Ely, J. (1992). The Political Civil Society, *Telos* 93, 173–191.

Fiala, P., J. Holzer, M. Mareš, P. Pšeja, (1999). *Komunismus v České republice. Vývojové, systémové a ideové aspekty působení KSČM a dalších komunistických organizací v české politice*, Brno: MPÚ MU.

Garlicki, A. (2003). *Karuzela. Rzecz o Okrągłym Stole* [The Carousel: Observations on the Round Table]. Warszawa: Wydawnictwo Czytelnik.

Gilejko, L. (2002). Elity partyjne w czasie epilogu [Party Elites during the Epilogue]. In: P. Machcewicz, A. Paczkowski, A. Dudek, A. Friszke (eds.), *Polska 1986–1989: koniec systemu. Materiały konferencji międzynarodowej* vol.1. Warszawa.

Godek, L. (2004). Wprowadzenie „demokracji kontraktowej" w Polsce. Próba interpretacji [Introduction of 'Contract Democracy' in Poland. An Attempt at Interpretation]. In: S. Drobczyński, M. Żyromski (red.), *Rola wyborów w procesie kształtowania się społeczeństwa obywatelskiego w Polsce* Poznań: Wydawnictwo WSNHiD.

Gortat, R., P. Marciniak (1991). Społeczne siły przemian [Social Forces of Change]. *Więź*, 1, 27–37.

Heineman, J.L. (1979). *Hilter's First Foreign Minister: Constantin Freiherr von Neurath, Diplomat and Statesman*. Berkeley: University of California Press.

Janowski, K.B. (2003). *Źródła i przebieg zmiany politycznej w Polsce (1980–1989). Studium historyczno-politologiczne* [Origins and Process of Political Transformation in Poland, 1980–1989]. Toruń.

Kean, J. (1988). Despotism and Democracy. In: J. Kean (ed.), *Civil Society and the State: New European Perspective*, London: Verso.

Łabędź, K. (1997). *Spory wokół zagadnień programowych w publikacjach opozycji politycznej w Polsce w latach 1981–1989* [Disputes over Programme Issues in the publications of the Political Opposition in Poland in 1981–1989]. Kraków: Księgarnia Akademicka.

Malinowski, R. (1992). *Wielka koalicja. Kulisy* [Grand Coalition: Behind the Scenes]. Warszawa: Polska Oficyna Wydawnicza "BGW".

Marciniak, P. (2002). Spiralny ruch ku demokracji. Presja społeczna a upadek systemu komunistycznego w Polsce (1986–1989) [Spiralling Towards Democracy. Social Pressure and the Collapse of the Communist System in Poland]. In: P. Machcewicz, A. Paczkowski, A. Dudek, A. Friszke (eds), *Polska 1986–1989: koniec systemu. Materiały konferencji międzynarodowej*. Wydawnictwo Trio: Warszawa.

Méchýř, J. (1999). *Velký převrat Či snad revoluce sametová?*, Progetto: Praha.

Mianowicz, T. (1999). Rok 1989 – PZPR przekracza Rubicon [Year 1989 – the PZPR Crosses the Rubicon]. *Arcana*, nr 1, 159–167.

Nowak, L. (1991a). *Power and Civil Society. Toward a Dynamic Theory of Real Socialism*. New York: Greenwood Press.

Nowak, L. (1991b). The Collapse of Communism? An Analysis of a Myth. *Polish Western Affairs* 32(1), 77–87.

Nowak, L. (1991c). *U podstaw teorii socjalizmu* [The Foundations of the Theory of Socialism]; vol. 3: *Dynamika władzy. O strukturze i konieczności zaniku socjalizmu* [The Dynamics of Power. On the Structure and Necessity of the Disappearance of Socialism]. Poznań: Nakom.

Nowak, L. (1993). The Hidden Sense of Clericalization: The Case of Eastern Europe. *The Centennial Review* 37, Michigan State University Press, 105–114.

Nowak, L. (2022). The Problem of the So-Called Social Transformation. In: K. Brzechczyn (ed.) *New Developments in Theory of Historical Process. Polish Contributions to Non-Marxian Historical Materialism. Poznań Studies in the Philosophy of the Sciences and the Humanities*, vol. 119, pp. 77–95. Leiden/Boston: Brill.

O'Donnel, G., P.C. Schmitter (2013). *Transitions from Authoritrian Rule. Tentative Conclusions about Uncertain Democracies*, Baltimore: The John Hopkins University Press.

Ost, D. (1989). Transformation of Solidarity and the Future of Central Europe, *Telos* 79, 69–94.

Paczkowski, A. (1999). *Od sfałszowanego zwycięstwa do prawdziwej klęski. Szkice do portretu PRL* [From a Stolen Victory to a Real Defeat. Sketches for a Portrait of the Polish People's Republic]. Kraków: Wydawnictwo Literackie.

Petrescu, D. (2014). *Entangled Revolutions. The Breakdown of the Communist Regimes in East-Central Europe*. Bucharest: Editura Enciclopedică.

Pollack, D., Wielgohs J. (2004). Introduction. In: D. Pollack, J. Wielgohs (eds.), *Dissent and Opposition in Communist Eastern Europe: Origins of Civil Society and Democratic Transition*. Aldershot: Ashgate Publishing.

Pulkkinen, T., J.M. Rosales (2008). On the Politics, Concepts and Histories of European Democratization. In: K. Palonen, T. Pulkkinen, J.M. Rosales (eds.), *The Ashgate Research Companion to the Politics of Democratization in Europe. Concepts and Histories*. pp. 1–14, Aldershot: Ashgate Publishing.

Saxonberg, S. (2001). *The Fall. A Comparative Study of The End of Communism in Czechoslovakia, East Germany, Hungary and Poland*, Amsterdam: Harwood Academic Publishers.

Sebestyen, V. (2009). *Revolution 1989. The Fall of the soviet Empire*, London: Phenix.

Skórzyński, J. (1995). *Ugoda i rewolucja. Władza i opozycja 1985–1989* [Settlement and revolution. Power and Opposition 1985–1989]. Warszawa: Presspublica.

Skórzyński, J. (2009). *Rewolucja Okrągłego Stołu* [The Round Table Revolution]. Kraków: Wydawnictwo Znak.

Staniszkis, J. (2001). *Postkomunizm. Próba opisu* [Post-Communism. An Attempt at Description]. Gdańsk: Słowo/Obraz Terytoria.

Suk, J. (1998). *Občanské forum. Listopad – prosinec 1989, 1. D. údalosti, 2. D. dokumenty.* Praha – Brno: ÚSD.

Suk, J. (1999). *Chronologie zániku komunistického režimu v Československu 1985–1990*, Praha: Vydal Ústav pro soudobé dějiny AV ČR.

Trembicka, K. (2003). *Okrągły stół w Polsce. Studium o porozumieniu politycznym* [The Round Table in Poland. A Study on Political Agreement]. Lublin: UMCS.

Weschler, L. (1989). *The New Yorker*, November 13, 59–64.

Żakowski, J. (ed.) (1990). *Geremek odpowiada – Żakowski pyta. Rok 1989* [Year 1989 – Bronisław Geremek Answers, Jacek Żakowski Asks]. Warszawa: Wydawnictwo Agora.

CHAPTER 15

The Social Structure of the Ottoman Society: An Attempt at a Theoretical Analysis

Eliza Karczyńska

Abstract

Within the non-Marxian historical materialism it is possible to distinguish a special form of pre-capitalistic society – state feudalism. According to Leszek Nowak, this socio-economic formation was typical for Russia between 15th and 17th centuries. Meanwhile, similar social structures developed in the Ottoman Empire in its classical period (i.e. 1300–1600), in Latin America under the reign of the Spanish Empire and in State of the Teutonic Order in Eastern Prussia. In the state feudalism, the ruling class combines the disposition of the means of coercion and the means of production. The state which is simultaneously the owner uses political methods in the economic sphere. It also tries to degrade the status of the class of owners. All of the four societies considered conducted an aggressive foreign policy. State feudalism had a chance to develop where the ruling class, after a successful use of aggression, was strong enough to take the control over the economy. In addition, these states were located on the outskirts of European civilization, which enabled them to expand.

Keywords

feudalism – non-Marxian historical materialism – Ottoman Empire – power – property – state feudalism

1   Introduction

The purpose of my article is to analyze the structure of the society of the Ottoman Empire in the classical period of its history – from the 14th to the end of the 16th century. The interpretation of existing social relations in this society will be conducted from the perspective of non-Marxian historical materialism[1] (hereinafter also referred to as n-Mhm). This theory of historical process elaborated by Leszek Nowak (most important: 1983; 1991a) interprets the history of societies that belonged to the European line of development in the course of two and half thousand years.

The base of the conceptualization of the feudal formation developed in Western Europe is provided by the relations between the power and the property. However, Leszek Nowak noted that it is possible to distinguish, in addition to standard feudalism, another form of pre-capitalist society – which he called 'state feudalism.' This type of feudalism, which is different from Western European feudalism, appeared in Russia in the 15th century and prevailed until the mid-17th century. According to Nowak this social system should be treated as an anomaly in the historical development of Russia (Nowak 1983, pp. 239–378).

However. in this article I will argue that state feudalism was not only characteristic for Russian society. Analogical social structures emerged in the Ottoman Empire in the classical period of its history (1300–1600). Other examples may be found in Latin America under Spanish rule (Brzechczyn 2004a; 2004b; see also Žiemelis 2016) and in the society of the Teutonic Order in the Eastern Prussia (Brzechczyn 1993; 2020, pp. 184–197). Therefore, I claim that state feudalism was not unique to Russian society but was a broader historical tendency in development of some societies.

In the first part of the article I will describe state feudalism with the use of conceptual apparatus of non-Marxian historical materialism. The second part will deal with the analysis of the Ottoman society in its classical period. In the third part I will compare the social structure of this society with Latin America, the state of the Teutonic Order and Russia.

2   On the Two Types of Feudalism in non-Marxian Historical Materialism

One of the basic assumptions of non-Marxian historical materialism is the claim that three domains of social life: economy, politics and culture have a similar internal structure. Namely, it is possible to distinquish the material means of production, coercion and indoctrination. The relation to these means

---

[1]   The methodology of the Poznań School and Leszek Nowak, see: Borbone (2016; 2021) and Coniglione (2010)..

determines the division into classes of society. Disposition of the material means of production is the basis of the division of the society into owners of means of production and direct producers. Disposition of the material means of coercion divides the society into rulers and civil society. Finally, disposition of the material means of indoctrination leads to a division into priests and believers. In each case interests of two antagonistic classes are contradictory:

> The greater is the income of the owners, the lower that of direct producers; the greater is the power of rulers, the lesser the autonomy of the citizens; the deeper is the control over the spiritual life of the faithful, the less the latter have to say as far as their ability to create their own life is concerned. All this factors justify calling the divisions in question *class* ones, and members of those divisions *classes* of society.
> NOWAK 1983, p. 179.

These divisions may overlap – one social class may dispose more than one type of material means. Distinguishing the disposers of material means in society and their mutual relationships forms the basis for building a typology of societies. We can, therefore, speak about class and supraclass societies. A class society is determined by the fact that there are three separate classes: rulers, owners, and priests. Each of them disposes a different kind of material means. In class societies, one of the classes usually dominates over the other two. Therefore, we can distinguish three types of class societies: economic, political and hierocratic societies (Nowak 1983, p. 182).

In supraclass societies one social class has simultaneously disposition over more than one kind of material means. It is distinguish a double class of rulers-owners, rulers-priests or owners-priests. There may also be a society where the one triple class disposes the means of production, coercion and indoctrination (Nowak 1983, p. 183).

For the purpose of further investigations of the state feudalism, the analysis of relations between the class of rulers and the class of owners are crucial. It is possible to distinguish a society where two separate classes existed: the rulers and the owners. Additionally, the class of owners is divided into progressive (merchants) and traditional (landed aristocracy) owners. In the light of non-Marxian historical materialism this kind of social structure was characteristic for standard feudalism in Western Europe.

In the second case one double class of rulers-owners combines the disposition of means of production and means of coercion. Within n-Mmh such a society is called a totalitarian society:

> The rulers seize the disposal over the productive forces and with the aid of force change the content of the economic institutions; and all of this, together with the action of the state apparatus, influences the economic consciousness of the society.
>
> NOWAK 1983, p. 193

The intermediate type of society is state feudalism in which

> „the state organization is the greatest owner, hence it is an intermediate form between the Marxian society (where the two classes, of rulers and of owners, are in principle exclusive) and the totalitarian one (where the two classes are identical".
>
> NOWAK 1983, p. 271

This difference can be graphically presented on Figure 15.1.

In feudal society (A), the class of rulers and class of owners exist separately. In case of state feudalism (B), both classes dispose the material means of production. The authority of rulers is not limited to the means of coercion. Apart from them, we can distinguish a single class of owners. In totalitarian society (C), the class of rulers is identical with the class of owners. Therefore, there is no single class of owners as in cases (A) and (B).

The fact that in state feudalism the means of production are divided between two classes: single owners and double rulers-owners affects the actions of the state (which is at the same time the largest owner). Nowak identifies four features of this kind of feudalism:

1. In case of state feudalism the state, which is at the same time the biggest owner, uses political instead of economical methods to deal with its direct producers. It does not act like a typical owner of the means of production. In contrast to the typical owner, the state has the ability to use coercive means in the case of conflict. Direct producers in

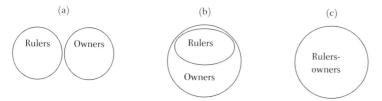

FIGURE 15.1 The structure of feudal society (A), society of state feudalism (B) and totalitarian society (C). In order to simplify, the division of the class of owners into the owners of urban and rural economic subsystems is omitted.

the public sector are also citizens and their resistance, even if caused by economic reasons, is always harmful to the interests of political power. Hence, economic conflict turns into a political conflict and thus may cause riots among all the citizens, not just among those who are the direct producers of political authority (Nowak 1983, p. 273).
2. The state authority tries to declass its direct producers and at the same time shows a tendency to broaden the influence at the expense of other citizens:

> The conclusion is evident: in state feudalism the repressiveness of the state apparatus, and, in general, the severity of the relations of power between the state and the citizens are more much advanced than in standard feudalism.
> NOWAK 1983, p. 271–272.

3. Simultaneously, the state authority applies a similar politics of the reinforcement of repressions towards the class of single owners. It treats them as citizens, with respect to whom political methods also have to be used. However, as it is not a totalitarian society, until a certain moment a class of single owners is in a better position than the rest of the citizens. Political authority is not the only owner and requires their support:

> That is why the state cannot simply suppress the private owners as it does with the remaining citizens. It still has to tolerate them and even to help in the common interest against the direct citizens. But the government already can press them a little bit. (...) And so, in state feudalism the class of disposers of coercion makes the private owners much more dependent on itself than is possible under standard feudalism.
> NOWAK 1983, pp. 272–273.

As a results, the direct producers become more and more suppressed by the single class of owners. The latter, trying to become more independent from the state, start to use methods of coercion on their own.

4. Ultimately, the productivity of direct producers declines and the entire economy, both in private and public sector, stagnates (Nowak 1983, p. 273).

It is clear that state feudalism has a tendency to change into totalitarian society. Whether such a transformation happens, depends on the relation between the owners and the rulers-owners. State feudalism will last as long as the class of rulers-owners class does not absorb the class of single owners class.

State feudalism emerged in Russia in the 15th century. According to Nowak, until that time Russia had been following the similar pattern as societies of classical European feudalism. The reason for the development state feudalism was the Mongol domination, which led to the alienation of the state apparatus from the society. However, such an explanation suggests that this system emerged by accident; if Russia had not succumbed to Tatar aggression, state feudalism simply would not have arisen.

After gaining independence, the authorities started to change the state apparatus into a double class of rulers-owners by granting them land *pomiestija*. In 1488, 8000 *boyars* were deprived of land and their places were taken by Moscovian citizens obedient to the prince. They constituted a group of *dvorianins* – "numerous personnel" of the state apparatus. The prince gave them land under regulation of *pomiestija* in return for their personal dependence. After the *dvorianin's* death the land went back into the prince's hands, or with his consent, was given to the son of the *dvorianin*:

> In this way the prince makes a *dvorianin* additionally dependent with respect to the fate of his family, and the children of a *dvorianin* in this way are somehow automatically called to be *dvorianin* again.
> NOWAK 1983, p. 259

The power of the single class of owners was limited in the interest of the thus conceived double class of rulers-owners. The politics of the *oprichnina* – introduced by Tsar Ivan IV, commonly known as 'Ivan the Terrible,' in 1565–1572 – may be interpreted as an expression of these interests. Over 30% of the territory was to be under the tsar's exclusive authority. Lands that belonged to the *boyars* came into the possession of selected *dvorianins* called *oprichniki*, whereas the former owners were resettled to new lands under the law of *pomiestija* (Nowak 1983, p. 262). These actions began to raise opposition from the single class of owners, which prompted the class of rulers-owners to use social terror and the destruction of the autonomous ownership structure of feudal society. This resulted with the collapse of the peasant economy, which affected not only the old class of owners, but also the rulers-owners (Nowak 1983, pp. 263–264).

Ivan Bolotnikov's Rebellion (1606–1607) was a reaction to this terror. At the beginning peasants took part in the riots, later also urban dwellers and other social layers together with *boyars* joined in. Apart from the abolition of the serfdom, they also demanded extensive reform of the state, which was to be governed by citizens. An important aspect of Bolotnikov's Rebellion was the fact, that it encompassed not only direct producers, but the class of owners as well. Therefore, revolutionary riots in state feudalism concern all social classes (Nowak 1983, pp. 266–268).

Although Bolotnikov's Rebellion ended with defeat, its consequences were significant. Evolutionary transformation in favour of the civil class subsequently occured. The state withdrew to political rule and changed its relation both with the class of owners and the class of direct producers (Nowak 1983, pp. 268–269).

It turns out that the division within n-Mmh into societies where the class of rulers and the class of owners exist separately, and societies where one class combines disposition of the means of production and the means of coercion, is not sufficient for analyzing certain cases. State feudalism can be treated as supplement of this classification due to the fact a special form of pre-capitalistic society is distinguished (see analyses, e.i. of Babinskas 2009; 2016; 2018).

3 Ottoman Society. An Attempt of Theoretical Analysis

According to Nowak, state feudalism was an anomaly in history of Russia. Meanwhile, a similar social structure emerged in the Ottoman Empire. In the second half of 16th century, at the peak of its power, the Ottoman Empire covered lands in Europe, Asia and Africa. It consisted of two main provinces: Anatolia and Rumelia (the Balkans), and other territories: Egypt, Iraq, Algiers, Trypolis, Georgia, Cyprus and Palestine. At the end of 16th century it was inhibited by 22 million people.[2] Istanbul, the capital of the Empire, was at that time the largest city in the world – around year 1600 it was inhabited by 800,000 people. At the same time Paris had 400,000 inhabitants, and London – 200,000 (Karaman 2009, p. 699).

In the 1550s, Mehmed the Conqueror divided all citizens into two groups: *askeri* – consisted of soldiers, officials and *ulemas* (Muslim clerks) and *reaya* which was composed of traders, artisans and peasants (Barkey 2008, p. 76). Within the conceptual apparatus of n-Mmh, *askeri* can be identified as a class of rulers, whereas *reaya* can be seen as a class of people together with a class of owners of the urban economic subsystem.

---

2 As compared to the Western countries, the population density in the Emipre was very low. In 1600, the estimated population density (the number of people per square kilometer) for particular countries equalled: Italy – 37; France – 33; Holland – 43; Great Britain – 21; European Turkey – 16; Asian Turkey – 8 (Inalcik, Quataert 2008, p. 25).

The class of rulers was at the same time the biggest owner of land in the Empire – by combining disposition of the material means of production and coercion, it represented a double class of rulers-owners. In other words, being a ruler entailed the privilege of the disposition of land. On the other hand, there was a group of individual owners, who at various times possessed different strength. Apart from these two classes, one should mention the class of priests and a folk class (consisting of the rural and urban population).

To start with, we shall analyze the structure of the class of rulers-owners class, as this structure influenced the politics in the field of land ownership. The state administration consisted of a central, strictly hierarchical authority and its representatives in the provinces. The sultan, who was at the top of the central government, was the most important person in the country and was not subject (at least theoretically) to any control. Additionally, the sultan had an authority over all the land in the Empire. Thus, he was the biggest owner. Furthermore, he claimed the right to command over material and spirituals means. In the 40s of XVIth century, Suleiman I announced that the Osman Sultan was also a caliph – a successor of the Prophet Muhammad and four caliphs. At this moment he became a priest of the highest rank (imam), although the class of priests itself managed to maintain a certain independence.

Divan (*Divan-ı Hümayun*) was an elite of the authority subordinated to the sultan. Initially it was an advisory body of the sultan. Over time, sultans stopped attending the *Divan* assemblies and the grand vizier started to play the major role in the politics.

All the representatives of the central authority operated within *kul* system – they were private slaves of the sultan. They did not possess personal freedom and were completely dependent on the sultan's will. In Ottoman society, the social status of an individual person was determined not by the fact of whether he or she was a free man or slave, but by the importance of the household. Thus, the vizier and other members of *Divan*, despite of being slaves, due to their belonging to the sultan's palace, had a higher social position than other lieges (Imber 2002, p. 148).

Central government was staffed by a majority of non-Turkish people. Until Mehmed the Conqueror's reign, the slaves captured during wars fulfilled predominantly military roles. Later they took up clerical functions in the direct surroundings of the sultan. During 150 years between the reign of Mehmed the Conqueror and of Ahmed I (in the beginning of the 17th century) out of 37 grand viziers only three were of Turkish origins (Ergil 1979, p. 186).

Officials performing duties in the palace of the sultan as well as janissaries – the personal army of the Sultan – were recruited within the *devşirme* system. It involved Christian boys of the rural non-Muslim population, with the exception of Bosnia where Mehmed the Conqueror let the children of Bosnians converted to Islam, become janissary troops (Radushev 2008, p. 451). This way Muslims were deprived of the possibility to occupy the highest offices. One of the sources from the early 17th century justifies this policy in the following way:

> If they [the Muslim Turks] were to become the sultan's slaves, they would certainly abuse the privilege. Their families in the provinces would oppress the *reayas* and would avoid taxes. They would oppose the *sanjakbeys* and caused rebellions. Meanwhile, when Christian children convert to the faith of Muhammad, they become fervent in faith and treat with hostility their relatives.
>
> INALCIK 2006, p. 91

Devşirme levies were organized every 3–7 years in accordance with the needs. Each time 1 000 boys were recruited (some of the authors claim it was 3 000 boys). Some of them were directed to palace service, while the other became soldiers of janissary units (the sultan's personal army) or were sold to rural Turkish families in Anatolia for a 7–8-year period. During that time they worked on the land (which would develop the discipline and ability to hard work) and learned the Turkish language, as well as the principles of Islam. After this period, they were used to supply *sipahis* units (cavalry) and were allowed to hold *timars*. They were a major source of the workforce in Anatolia. Through recruiting non-Turkish people into their ranks, the authority intended to weaken the influence of the Ottoman aristocracy.

Provincional representatives of the Ottoman authority joined the military and administrative functions. This was connected with the structure and development of the Empire, which was divided into provinces. Every province was ruled by a *beylerbey*. The provinces were divided into *sanjaks* managed by *sanjakbeys*. At the level of a single village the government was represented by a *bey*. The bey, who also participated in the military structure, had the task of maintaining law and order. At the lowest level were *sipahis* – soldiers who were at the same time land holders.

The primary function of the *bey* during peacetime was that of an administrator. One of his tasks was to ensure the order in the country. The *bey* in the province represented the executive power while the judicial power was exercised by a judge – *qadi* who came from *ulema* group. The sultan took care that none of these bodies had a chance to dominate the other: "A *Bey* was unable to award any punishment without a *qadi's* judgment, a *qadi* on the contrary was not allowed to enforce any judgment on his own" (Inalcik 2006, p. 117).

The above account concerned political structure of the Ottoman society. Now it is time to examine its economical arrangement. Traditional Islamic regulations strongly influenced the way Osmans managed the land in the Empire. According to Islamic law, land property consisted of three elements that were independent of each other elements: *rakaba* – ownership, *tasarruf* – possession and *istiglal* – usufruct (Inalcik, Quataert 2008, p. 91). Osmans adopted this conception of property. In the Ottoman Empire the sultan kept in his hands the right of *rakaba*, and he handed over *tasarruf* and *istiglal* to specific persons or communities.

Most of the land within the Empire was classified as *miri* and belonged to the state. On these areas the rulers class introduced the *timar*[3] system – the system of disposing of land distinctive for the Empire. However, some of the *miri* lands were not included in this system. According to sharia, *rakaba* – ultimate ownership of lands, belonged to central government – the class of rulers, while *tassaruf* and *istiglal* could be transferred to people who were not members of this class. Such lands could be divided into *tapulu* and *mukataalu*. The first kind of land was allotted to peasants under *tapu* regulation, whereas *mukataalu* lands were leased under lease-contract.

The origin of the *timar* system is not clear. Some of the researchers see a certain resemblance to the Byzantine *pronoia*, whereas others link it with the Sassanids or Seljuks states. Murat I (1326–1389) is considered to be the first ruler who distributed *timars*. In the Ottoman Empire this system of land distribution was integrated with a military function: *timar* holders constituted the basis of the Ottoman army – out of 103,500 soldiers in 1473 there were: 12,000 janissaries, 7,500 cavalry of the Porte, 40,000 *sipahis* from Rumelia, 24,000 *sipahis* from Anatolia and 20,000 *azabs* (İnalcık, Quataert 2008, p. 77).

Typical *timar* consisted of a village or a group of villages and their surroundings and was granted to cavalryman – *sipahi* called *timoriat*. In return for military service he was allowed to collect taxes from peasants within entrusted land, however, unlike feudal lord in Western Europe, he did not posses juridical authority over these people. Although *sipahi* was obliged to ensure order and security within his *timar*, he was not allowed to punish or to arbitrate a dispute on his own.

Lands that constituted *timar* can be divided according to several criteria. Within individual *timar* two kinds of land could be distinguished – *kiliç* and *hisse*. *Kiliç* (meaning "saber") was an indivisible part of *timar* given to a person in return for his military service. Therefore, *kiliç* was the minimal form of *timar* of around 3 000 *akçe* (a monetary unit in the Ottoman Empire) in the case of

---

3   The class of rulers did not introduce *timar* on all conquered territories. In Eastern Anatolia, Iraq, Egypt, Yemen, Wallachia, Moldavia and the Maghreb, the Ottomans limited themselves to the collection of taxes, leaving solutions in use unchagned. Apparently, this is how they sought to avoid social unrest. (Pamuk 2004, p. 230).

European provinces, and of around 2 000 *akçe* in case of the Anatolian provinces of the Empire. Any amount of land that exceeded the *kiliç* was counted as *hisse*, a supplement, for which a *sipahi* was additionally obliged to maintain military unit as well to provide military equipment (Moutafchieva 1988, p. 19).

Taking into consideration the persons granted *timars*, we can distinguish *eşkinci* (a holder of such land was obliged personally to serve in the army), *benövbet* (*timar*, which was granted to several persons who took it in turns to serve) and *mustahfiz*, the land distributed to non-military representatives of the state – *kadi* (a judge), *defterdar* (a scribe whose duty was to conduct registers) etc. (Moutafchieva 1988, p. 20).

The third criterion was the military rank of the *timar* holder, which determined the size and expected income. The highest officials: viziers and *beylerbeys* (who governed provinces of the Empire) received *hass* lands which generated an income of 100,000 *akçe*. Lower rank commanders possessed *ziamets* with income ranging from 20,000 to 99,000 *akçe*. *Timars* granted to *sipahs* generated income below 20,000 *akçe* (Matuz 1982, p. 286).

A *timar* holder did not own the land from which he drew his revenues. The sultan could revoke it if the cavalryman failed to perform his duties (Imber 2002, p. 194). The authorities did not want to grant one person with a big plot of land. Instead, *timar* holders had right of usage of a number of smaller plots in several villages. On the one hand, such a solution enabled the flexibility of rewarding *timar* holders in the case of promotion, without the necessity of dividing existing timars. On the other hand, it was "a deliberate politics that prevented *sipahi* from seizing complete and autonomous administration over the land and people within the area of one village, as it happened in the case of feudal lords" (Inalcik, Quataert 2008, p. 98).

After the death of *sipahi*, a *timar* could be transferred, along with all the obligations it included, to his son. However, desrcribing the *timar* lands as hereditary would be oversimplification. Indeed, in most cases, after death of a *sipahi*, the *timar* was passed into the hands of persons not related to the previous owner.[4] Another issue is the fact that the *timar* inherited by children was much smaller than the original one. Transfers of these lands were much more frequent than was in the case of inheritance. There were cases that *timar* changed ownership even every year.

---

4 For example, among 335 *timars* registered in the Sanjak of Arvanid, only 59 remained in hands of sons after the *sipahi*'s death, and afurther 6 were inherited by his grandsons. The remaining *timars* were passed to persons not related with the previous owners (Moutafchieva 1988, p. 37).

Rotation of *timars* as well as the frequent relocation of local representatives of the state authority (this mechanism included both *sipahis* and higher officials) caused lack of long-term interest among *timar* holders. Instead, they tried to exploit their temporary field for all was worth as quickly as possible. Furthermore, they were not interested in the development of the local community (Barkey 1996, p. 471).

At the same time timar-holders were restricted, in terms of additional revenue. Taxes and profits beyond the center's cap were illegal and subject to punishment. Frequent land registers entailed that all illegal gains would be easy to detect. As a result, *timar* holders withdrew from production activity. According to Karaman, it was one of the causes of stagnation of the Ottoman economy (Karaman 2009, p. 698).

At the end of the 16th century the *timar* system started to erode. Due to the introduction of firearms, the importance of cavalry forces declined and an increasing number of *timar* lands were converted into taxed farms. The system was officially abolished by Mahmud II in 1831 (Somel 2003, p. 299).

Within the historiography there are various explanation concerning *timar*. According to Moutachieva its essential function was to maintain cavalry – *sipahi* (Moutafchieva 1988, p. 8). It was at the same time a method of land management and a way of remunerating soldiers. At the same time, Karaman argues that the reason for the introduction of *timar* was the shortage of coins in the Ottoman Empire. This problem concerned other pre-capitalistic societies as well. This scarcity rentailed that most of taxes had to be collected in kind. Because of the extensiveness of the Empire and underdevelopement of transport, these goods could not be sent to the capital. Thus, instead of products, representatives of the authorities in the provinces supplied the central government with military troops (Karaman 2009, pp. 692–693).

Meanwhile, when seen from the perspective of non-Mhm, these processes may be interpreted as a sign of accumulation of power and property in the hands of one social class. *Timoriats* and other members of the hierarchy of authority who dispose a land, on account of fulfilling the office, constituted a double class of rulers-owners. The *Timar* system was reinforced after the conquest of Constantinople in 1453, when the authority, as a result of successful aggression, strengthened enough to be able to intervene in economic activities of the class of owners.

Apart from a double class of rulers-owners, we may distinguish a separate single class of owners, which consisted mainly of the clan aristocracy. They owned private properties – *mülks,* and were often founders of charitable foundations – *vakifs*. The purpose of a *vakif* was mostly religious, however, quite often they served other social functions, such as educational and nursing.

Thanks to legally guaranteed immunity, such foundations could not be subject to confiscation.

The interest of the class of rulers-owner was to weaken influence of the class of single owners. The conquest of Constantinople strengthened the power of Sultan Mehmed the Conqueror. Therefore, he was able to deal with Turkish families that had gained political influence during the interregnum period. Two days after the collapse of Constantinople grand vizier Çandarlı Halil, who came from one of the most influential clan, was dismissed and executed. All of his possessions were confiscated. His office was taken by Zaganos Paşa, a representative of the *kul* class. Other Turkish clans within the class of rulers were also replaced by non-Turkish people (Shaw 1976, p. 58).

Land registers constituted one of the methods of keeping the single class of owners under surveillance. During Mehmed the Conqueror's reign, three of such inventories were conducted; the first one in 1454–1455, the second in 1464–65 and the third one in 1476 (Özel 1999, p. 234). The last one preceded the land reform carried in the late1470s. In the course of this reform, approximately twenty thousand villages and farms, which had previously been held as freeholds *mülks* or pious foundations – *vakifs*, were converted into state ownership within the *miri* system. Some of the owners were transformed into *timar* holders (Özel 1999, p. 227). Others were conscripted into personal the sultan's personal units or regular army – *eşküncü*. The rest lost definitely their possessions. These decisions prompted discontent among the *ulemas* and aristocracy.

According to Nicoar Beldiceau, it is possible to distinguish three causes for the land reform introduced by Mehmed the Conqueror. The first one was the military and financial needs of the Ottoman government. The second one was the urge to weaken the economic power of the dervish orders, which was based on *vakif* holders. Finally, Ottoman lawyers were able to influence the sultan in order to purge Islamic law. According to certain interpretations, *vakif* and *mülk* lands stood in opposition to sharia (Özel 1999, p. 228).

The reform implemented by Mehmed the Conqueror can be interpreted differently from the perspective of n-Mmh. The class of rulers treated treated the owners as citizens whose field of autonomy was wider than that of citizens without the means of production. Thus, owners constituted greater threat to authority than direct producers. Mehmed the Conqueror's land reform can be compared to *oprichnina* introduced by Ivan IV the Terrible. In both cases the authority did not deprive the owners of the means of productions entirely, but it managed to limit their autonomy due to conditional granting of land either as *timar* or as *pomiestija*. The similarity between these two societies was emphasized by Karen Barkey.

A peasant, unlike a *timar* holder, possessed some inherited proprietary rights either as an individual or as a member of the village community. He had the right to own a house, farm buildings, a garden plot, and the fruit trees and vines he cultivated – although he did not own the land on which they grew (Sugar 1978, p. 298). According to law, a *timar* holder "had no right to interfere in the peasant's agricultural activity, except for in situations where the peasant changed the way of using the land in such a way that it hindered grain production or was contradictory to its *miri* status" (Inalcik, Quataert 2008, p. 95).

Low tax charges were characteristic for the provincial economy. This was visible both in the tax code introduced by Mehmed the Conqueror and in tax registers that survived until the present day. The two most significant taxes on the peasantry were the *öşür* tithe and the fodder for horses belonging to the *timar* holder – *salariye*, which corresponded to 1/10th and 1/40th of the grain production, respectively. When compared to the tax rate in feudal Western Europe, which sometimes amounted to 50% of production, these taxes were relatively low (Karaman 2009, p. 692).

The *reaya* group consisted of urban and rural plebs. The Ottoman urban economy differed considerably from contemporary European cities. The class of rulers controlled trade and craft by determining what should be produced, imported and exported. In consequence, economic life developed as a by-product of bureaucratic activities (Çaha, Karaman 2004, p. 56). In other words, the motives of economic actions of the class of rulers were not purely economic. They rather aimed in satisfying the needs and priorities of the government. Thus, economic policy was subordinated to the requirements of the palace and the army. This was evident in the policy of the customs – the duty on exported products was 12%, while on imported it was 3% (Mardin 1969, p. 262).

As a result of the government's policy aimed at satisfying the needs of Istanbul, the development of nearby towns was curbed. According to Suraya Faroqhi, in Anatolia the towns that were not in proximity to trade routes had a chance to developed. As an example she refers to Kayseri which in around 1580 became the second most important town (after Bursa). The provision of supplies for Istanbul from such a location would have been unprofitable. As a result, the town was left alone and had a chance to develop (Faroqhi 1990, pp. 138–139).

The above analyzes allow Ottoman society to be described as an example of the state feudalism. Although the state assumed control over economic life it failed to eliminate the class of owners. Tensions between the rulers-owners and the owners persisted throughout the classical period of the Ottoman Empire.

4 State Feudalism: An Anomaly or a Developmental Trend?

According to several scholars, the Ottoman society can be interpreted as an example of a feudal formation, since it took the in the same form as the feudalism developed in Western Europe. Josef Matuz claims, that despite some exceptions, this society was feudal in essence:

> When trying to decide whether a society is feudal or not, we consider the decisive criterion to be the existence of the land rent *as a major instrument for the acquisition of surplus product.* These features of feudalism quite conform to conditions which prevailed in the Ottoman Empire, particularly since in agriculture, the main branch of production here, slave labor was of little importance and hired labor of none at all
> MATUZ 1982, p. 283

Matuz claims that the way the surplus product was acquired in the form of land rent was typical for feudalism. However, the adoption of such a criterion does not allow us to make further divisions within feudal society. Such a division is possible when we use the level of accumulation of class divisions as a criterion. According to non-Marxian historical materialism, class divisions arise independently in the economic and political spheres. From this perspective the state feudalism developed in the Ottoman Empire because the class of rulers that had a monopoly over the means of coercion took over the disposition of the means of property. Within the conceptual apparatus of non-Mhm the hierarchy of state power was a double class of rulers-owners, combining the political and economic power. In this respect there is a similarity between the *timar* and the *pomiestija* system in the Russian society. Similarly to *dvorianins (pomeshchiks)*, *timar* holders were part of the power apparatus (civilian or military) and thus they were administrators of the land.

In the Ottoman Empire, as in Russia, the main interest of the class of rulers, even though it was the largest owner, was a political interest rather than economic:

> It is not a coincidence that the biggest exploiter was at the same time the most conservative – it was interested neither in the economic development of Russia (more precisely, only to the extent necessary for the maintenance of coercive measures at the appropriate level), nor in the elimination of stagnation, but in the expansion of control over the citizens. Over the "modern slaves" there was very little to expand and the nobility, despite of ages of fighting, did not allow themselves to be turned

into average lieges. In this situation the external expansion and maintenance of internal *status quo* remained.

NOWAK 1991b, pp. 91–92

In light of the above analysis the key issue seems to be the answer to the question of whether the state feudalism was an anomaly in the development of particular societies or a broader trend.

The accumulation of power and property can be seen in the indigenous societies of Latin America conquered by the Spaniards. According to Brzechczyn (2004a, pp. 116–117; 2004b, p. 177–182; 2007, pp. 240–243), the spread of the *Encomienda* system can be interpreted in the light of process of accumulation of class divisions.

It was introduced by the Spaniards in Latin America for the first time in Hispaniola in 1503. The Spaniards provided a group of colonists with indigenous people who were to perform for them, and to pay them tribute. On the other hand, the indigenous people, being subjects to *encomienda*, were recognized as free people, and thus did not constitute the property of their *encomenderos* (Brzechczyn 2004b, p. 177). The latter were granted at the same time land for use. However, being granted land did not mean being an owner of this land. Like the *timar* in the Ottoman Empire, *encomienda* was non-hereditary (although after some time it began to be passed to the descendants of the *encomendero*) and imposed on the recipient numerous duties, e.g. education of the indigenous people in accordance with the Catholic religion or building of a church within six months of receiving *encomienda*. Maltreatment of the indigenous population could lead to the withdrawal of privileges. Therefore, the holders of *encomienda* were a double class of owners-rulers.

Excessive exploitation of the indigenous population resulted in a decrease of its size. A further consequence was a destabilization of the economy, which facilitated state interference in this field. In 1549, the forced labour of indigenou people within the *encomienda* system was replaced by forced labour controlled by the state – *repartimiento de trabajo*. However, some remnants of *encomienda* lasted until 1718, when the system was definitely abolished. Thanks to *repartimiento de trabajo,* the class of rulers controlled distribution of indigenous labour. The class of owners could use this labour, however, it did so only through the intermediary of the state authority.

The last phase of evolution of the ownership relation was the introduction of haciendas, which was based on hiring workers coming from indigenous communities. Owners of haciendas were frequently recruited from *encomenderos*: "This form of hiring was favourable to owners as it assured them a constant access to workforce without the necessity of using the state's agency."

Such labour turned out to be more effective than *repartimiento de trabajo* (Brzechczyn 2004b, pp. 178–198).

Another example of the accumulation of class divisions can be founded in the state of the Teutonic Order between 12th and 16th centuries, where approximately a thousand monks-knights ruled over half a million subjects. The monks were organized in *convents* – basic administrative units of the state controlled by *komturs* who wielded military, administrative, juridical and financial power. The monks were in possession of 2/3 of the lands of Eastern Prussia and significantly influenced economic life of the country by limiting the rights of local knights and founding new towns as a balance to the old ones. Thus, the Teutonic knights controlling the means of coercion and means of production exemplified a double class of rulers-owners. (Brzechczyn 1993, pp. 400–402; Brzechczyn 2020, pp. 185–190). Additionally, they also controlled the means of indoctrination.

Similarities among these four societies may indicate that the accumulation of power and property was not a peculiarity of Russia but was rather a broader development tendency. It is worth considering factors favourable to the creation of such a system. Provisionally, one can point out such factors as: the imperial structure of a society and its peripheral location.

All the considered societies: the state of the Teutonic Order, Turkey, Russia and Spain – employed an aggressive foreign policy. According to the n-Mhm, a successful use of aggression strengthens the position of political power against the property both in the conquered and annexed provinces and in the metropolis of the empire, which may manifest itself in the accumulation of power and property. State feudalism had a chance to develop in these societies where the class of rulers, after successful aggression, was strong enough to be able to weaken the class of owners and take control over the economy. In addition, it is worth noting that all four states were located on the outskirts of European civilization. We may risk the hypothesis that the peripheral location of these countries facilitated political expansion. International political competition in the periphery was usually less intense than in the center of European civilization. The advantageous geopolitical location of the analyzed states made it easier to conquer new territories, which significantly changed the relationship between the government and the property giving rise to a system of state feudalism. There were many more similar factors in these societies, however, these two can be conceptualized in the light of non-Marxian historical materialism.

References

Babinskas, N. (2009). The Concept of Tributalism: A Comparative Analysis of S. Amin's, J. Haldon's and H. H. Stahl's Approaches. *The Romanian Journal for Baltic and Nordic Studies*, 1(1), 65–85.

Babinskas, N. (2016). Od feudalizmu do afrykańskiego sposobu produkcji. Problem typologii przednowoczesnych peryferyjnych społeczeństw europejskich [From Feudalism to the African Mode of Production: the Problem of Typology of the Pre-Modern Peripherial European Societies], *Człowiek i Społeczeństwo*, 42, 119–133.

Babinskas, N. (2018). Typologies of pre-modern societies beyond feudalism: exploring alternative possibilities and the problem of their applicability in cases of peripheral European societies *The Romanian Journal for Baltic and Nordic Studies*, 10(2), 9–25.

Barkey, K. (2008). *Empire of Difference. The Ottomans in Comparative Perspective.* Cambridge: Cambridge University Press.

Barkey, K. (1996). In Different Times: Scheduling and Social Control in the Ottoman Empire, 1550 to 1650. *Comparative Studies in Society and History* 38 (3), 460–483.

Borbone, G. (2016). *Questioni di Metodo. Leszek Nowak e la scienza come idealizzazione.* Roma: Acireale.

Borbone, G. (2021). *The Relevance of Models. Idealization and Concretization in Leszek Nowak.* München: Grin Verlag.

Brzechczyn, K. (1993). The State of Teutonic Order as a Socialist Society. In: L. Nowak, M. Paprzycki (eds.), *Social System, Rationality and Revolution. Poznań Studies in the Philosophy of the Sciences and the Humanities*, vol. 33, pp. 397–414. Amsterdam – Atlanta, GA: Rodopi.

Brzechczyn, K. (2004a). The Collapse of Real Socialism in Eastern Europe versus the Overthrow of the Spanish Colonial Empire in Latin America: An Attempt at Comparative Analysis. *Journal of Interdisciplinary Studies in History and Archaeology*, 1 (2), 105–133.

Brzechczyn, K. (2004b). O wielości linii rozwojowych w procesie historycznym. Próba interpretacji społeczeństwa meksykańskiego [On the Multitude of the Lines of Developments in the Historical Process. An Attempt at Interpretation of the Evolution of the Mexican Society]. Poznań: Wydawnictwo Naukowe UAM.

Brzechczyn, K. (2007). On the Application of the non-Marxian Historical Materialism to the Development of non-European Societies. In: J. Brzeziński, A. Klawiter, T.A.F. Kuipers, K. Łastowski, K. Paprzycka & P. Przybysz (eds.). *The Courage of Doing Philosophy. Essays Presented to Leszek Nowak*, pp. 235–254. Amsterdam – New York: Rodopi.

Brzechczyn, K. (2020). *The Historical Distinctiveness of Central Europe: A Study in Philosophy of History*, Berlin: Peter Lang.

Çaha, Ö., M.L. Karaman (2004). Civil Society in the Ottoman Empire, In: *Journal of Economic and Social Research* 8 (2), 53–81.

Coniglione, F. (2010). *Realtà e astrazione. Scuola polacca ed epistemologia post-positivista*. Roma: Bonanno Editore.

Ergil, D. (1979). Development of Turkish Semi-Colonialism, *Islamic Studies*, 18(3), 183–229.

Faroqhi, S. (1990). Towns, Agriculture and the State in Sixteenth-Century Ottoman Anatolia, *Journal of the Economic and Social History of the Orient*, 33 (2), 125–156.

Imber, C. (2002). *The Ottoman Empire, 1300–1650. The Structure of Power*. Basingstoke: Palgrave Macmillan.

Inalcik, H. (2006). *Imperium Osmańskie. Epoka klasyczna 1300–1600* [History of the Ottoman Empire: Classical Age, 1300–1600]. Kraków: Wydawnictwo Uniwersytetu Jagiellońskiego.

Inalcik, H., D. Quataert (2008) (eds). *Dzieje gospodarcze i społeczne Imperium Osmańskiego 1300–1914* [An Economic and Social History of the Ottoman Empire, 1300–1914]. Kraków: Wydawnictwo Uniwersytetu Jagiellońskiego.

Karaman, K. K. (2009). Decentralized Coercion and Self-Restraint in Provincial Taxation: The Ottoman Empire, 15th–16th Centuries. *Journal of Economic Behavior & Organization* 71, 690–703.

Kunt, M., Ch. Woodhead (1995), (eds.). *Süleyman the Magnificent and His Age. The Ottoman Empire in the Early Modern World*. London/New York: Longman.

Mardin, S. (1969). Power, Civil Society and Culture in the Ottoman Empire. *Comparative Studies in Society and History*, 11 (3), 258–281.

Matuz, J. (1982). The Nature and Stages of Ottoman Feudalism. *Asian and African Studies*, 16, 281–292.

Moutafchieva, V. P. (1988). *Agrarian Relations in the Ottoman Empire in the 15th and 16th Centuries*. New York: Columbia University Press.

Nowak, L. (1983). *Property and Power. Towards a non-Marxian Historical Materialism*. Dordrecht: Reidel.

Nowak, L. (1991a). *Power and Civil Society. Toward a Dynamic Theory of Real Socialism*. New York: Greenwood Press.

Nowak, L. (1991b). *U podstaw teorii socjalizmu* [The Foundations of the Theory of Socialism]; vol. 2: *Droga do socjalizmu. O konieczności socjalizmu w Rosji* [The Road to Socialism. On the Necessity of Socialism in Russia]. Poznań: Nakom.

Özel, O. (1999). Limits of the Almighty: Mehmed II's 'Land Reform' Revisited, *Journal of the Economic and Social History of the Orient*, 42 (2), 226–246.

Pamuk, Ş. (2004). Institutional Change and the Longevity of the Ottoman Empire, 1500–1800, *Journal of Interdisciplinary History*, 35 (2), 225–247.

Radushev, E. (2008). "Peasant" Janissaries? *Journal of Social History*, 42 (2), 447–467.

Shaw, S. (1976). *History of the Ottoman Empire and Modern Turkey*; vol. 1: *Empire of the Gazis: The Rise and Decline of the Ottoman Empire, 1280–1808*. Cambridge: Cambridge University Press.

Somel, S.A. (2003). *Historical Dictionary of the Ottoman Empire*. Lanham/Maryland/Oxford: The Scarecrow Press.

Sugar, P.F. (1978). Major Changes in the Life of the Slav Peasantry under Ottoman Rule, *International Journal of Middle East Studies*, 9 (3), 297–305.

Žiemelis, D. (2016). Próba analizy porównawczej litewskiej gospodarki folwarczno-pańszczyźnianej i latynoamerykańskiej gospodarki hacjendowej od II połowy XVIII do II połowy XIX wieku w kontekście kapitalistycznego systemu-świata [An Attempt at Comparative Analysis of Lithuanian Manorial-Serf Economy and Hacienda Economic System of Latin America from the Second Half of 18th to the Second Half of the 19th Century in the Context of Capitalist World System]. *Człowiek i Społeczeństwo*, 42, 135–160.

CHAPTER 16

The Dynamics of Power in Postwar China: An Attempt at a Theoretical Analysis

Dawid Rogacz

Abstract

The aim of this paper is to analyze the dynamics of the political power in the People's Republic of China, using the conceptual apparatus of Leszek Nowak's non-Marxian historical materialism. By applying his Model I of the theory of power, I am going to generalize theoretically the main political changes in post-war China, from the foundation of the People's Republic of China, through the Cultural Revolution and the Opening-Up program, to the Chinese politics after 1989. The analysis will allow me to make three wide-ranging predictions concerning further development of China in the fields of politics, economy, and ideology.

Keywords

Chinese Communism – Leszek Nowak – Mao Zedong – non-Marxian historical materialism – People's Republic of China – real socialism

1   Introduction[1]

The aim of this article is to carry out a theoretical analysis of the dynamics of political power in the Chinese society, with the use of the conceptual apparatus of non-Marxian historical materialism (hereinafter: n-Mhm), a theory created by Leszek Nowak (1983; 1991abc; 1991d), a co-creator of the Poznań School of Methodology. By applying the theory of power constructed by Nowak, or, to be more precise, Model I, I intend to interpret the political, economic, and ideological transformations in post-war China.

---

[1] The research leading to this paper was supported by National Science Centre (Poland) grant no. 2019/33/B/HS1/00244. I would like to thank Prof. Krzysztof Brzechczyn for all the remarks and suggestions to the initial version of the article.

One dominant feature of the analyses of the history and economic transformations of China is their division into two periods: before and after the opening-up reforms (*gǎigé kāifàng*). Deng Xiaoping's reforms from 1978 are treated as an abandonment of Mao Zedong's radical projects and an acceptance of Western capitalist models while preserving the appearance of a communist system. Assuming such an extreme discontinuity in the historical development of post-war China does not correspond to the standards of social science which obligate the researcher to find the most general rules possible which would describe the nature of human societies both in the synchronic and diachronic dimensions, not to mention the ultimately discarded ambitions of predicting social phenomena. In this article, I will nevertheless try to analyze theoretically the dynamics of power in post-war China and make a few political predictions based on my assumptions.

The purportedly sudden transition from Maoism to (hidden with shame) capitalism suggests an ideological key as the starting point for the analyses. However, the very instrumental nature of the Chinese politicians' use of the communist nomenklatura belies that interpretation. The consciousness of that fact, combined with the inability to reject the ideological key, resulted in the trend of presenting the transformation of 1978 as stemming from the 'spirit' of Confucianism, by analogy to Max Weber's famous analyses of the influence of Protestant ethics on the emergence of capitalism. However, that approach does not take into account that after the Cultural Revolution, the influence of Confucianism on the public sphere and politicians' motivation was negligible, and that elements of Confucian teachings only reappeared in the content of the People's Republic of China presidents' speeches at the beginning of the twenty-first century (Bell 2010, pp. 3–18). Confucianism itself has never – in the two thousand years of its existence – been the driving force of economic transition toward capitalism. Even in the nineteenth century, the most 'radical' reformists such as Gong Zizhen (1792–1841) still idealized the economic well-field system and feudalism from the times of the early Zhou dynasty (11th–8th c. BCE) (Gong 1975, pp. 78–80). In practice, the attempts at showing the contribution of Confucianism to the formation of the Chinese variety of capitalism refer not so much to Confucianism *per se* as to its contemporary, very syncretic variant forged under the influence of polemics with Marxism, Western philosophy, and Christian thought (Makeham 2003, pp. 16–17).

The theory of power in non-Marxian historical materialism offers the possibility of analyzing the political transformations in post-war China in a systematic way, with a reference, in the first place, to the dynamics of political power itself – which has at its disposal the means of coercion and is created in the clash of the interests of the rulers and the citizens – and not to social consciousness (Nowak 1983). Another task of n-Mhm is to theorize about the changes of the relationship between the authorities and the civil society, so the models in n-Mhm cannot be treated as the usual simplifications of complex processes or as rectifications of previously made assumptions (Nowak 1991d). The idealizational theory of science (Nowak 1980), which is the methodological foundation of n-Mhm, precludes such interpretations of Nowak's theory of historical process, as it provides terminological precision for the whole concept and, consistently, supplies clear criteria of its application to particular empirical cases (see: Coniglione 2010; Borbone 2016; 2021).

In the first part of my article, I will present the basic assumptions of n-Mhm, especially Model 1 of the theory of power. Next, I will carry out a historical application of Model 1, and I will present some predictions concerning further political transformations in China, on the basis of the assumed model and the whole concept.

2   The Basic Assumptions of Non-Marxian Historical Materialism

The basic assumption of n-Mhm is distinguishing three spheres: economic, political, and cultural within the framework of every society. In each of those spheres, there arise inner divisions resulting from the disposal of certain material forces. The disposal of the material forces of production determines the division of a society into the owners and the direct producers, the disposal of the material forces of coercion determines the division of a society into the rulers and the citizens, and the disposal of the material forces of indoctrination determines the division of a society into the priests and the direct followers. The interests of the groups within each of those divisions are contradictory, so they are class divisions (Nowak 1991a, pp. 176–177). Waldemar Czajkowski points to five features distinguishing n-Mhm from Marx's historical materialism in Oskar Lange's canonical interpretation:
- the basic source of historical dynamism is not, as in Marx's theory, the development of productive forces but the conflicts between social classes;
- politics and culture are not a 'superstructure' of the economy but spheres independent from it;
- instead of two main classes determined by the disposal of the means of production, we have three class divisions which can also intersect or overlap, which complicates the image of social structure;
- not only the struggle between classes but also within them – the competition between the members of the ruling class – must be taken into account; and

– Nowak's philosophy of history is rooted in a clearly defined philosophical anthropology, that is, the non-Christian model of man (Czajkowski 2013, pp. 196–197; see also Czajkowski 2022).

A given social class can, as has been mentioned, have at its disposal more than one type of material forces at a time, so we distinguish class and supra-class societies in n-Mhm. In class societies, there are three separate dominant classes: the rulers, the owners, and the priests. One of them usually dominates the remaining two. For that reason, three basic types of society are distinguished: economic, political, and hierocratic. In supraclass societies, one social class takes over control over two or three material social means. Therefore, we can combinatorially distinguish the classes of rulers-owners, rulers-priests, and owners-priests.[2] In an extreme case, the means of coercion, production, and indoctrination are aggregated in the hands of one triple class. That case is the socialist society (Nowak 1991a, pp. 178–180).

The theory of power in n-Mhm is based of a number of idealizing assumptions. They make it possible to (1) construct a general model of the structure and dynamics of power and (2) apply models of power to increasingly complex political (and historical) reality, by way of gradual concretizations, that is, cancellations of the idealizing assumptions. That procedure led Nowak to the analysis of the evolution of the theory of power within the framework of eight models, the foundations of which are particular static and dynamic assumptions. The main static assumption is the premise that every ruler maximizes the sphere of control over the citizens' actions, while it is in the interest of the civil society to increase the civil autonomy.[3] Rulers who do not follow that principle are 'eliminated' by their political competition. The sphere of individual action which is outside of the rulers' control is the area of the citizens' autonomy which stands in opposition to the area of regulation. The civil alienation is a ratio between the number of civil actions regulated by rulers and the sum of all actions undertaken by citizens. The civil resistance depends on the level of such understood civil alienation. The relationship is characterized as follows:

– for low levels of the civil alienation, civil resistance is also weak – only people from the social margins rebel (the area of class peace);

---

[2] Nowak's initial typology of societies in n-Mhm was developed many times, see Brzechczyn (2004, pp. 73–86), Ciesielski (2013; 2022), Zarębski (2003; 2022).

[3] It is in the owners' interest to maximize the surplus product, while the direct producers want to increase the variable capital. It is in the priests' interest to dominate the set of ideas professed by the followers, and it is in the followers' interest to maintain inner freedom.

- for average levels of the civil alienation, social resistance reaches its maximum (the area of the revolution of the first kind);
- when the level of the civil alienation grows even more, civil resistance decreases significantly (the area of enslavement) (Nowak 1991c, pp. 178–180).

Another static assumption of the theory of power is the thesis about the re-valorization of autonomous social ties. When the level of political control exceeds a certain threshold, people strive to replace (or go around) the etatized forms of collective life by means of direct relationships entered into within the framework of autonomous social structures, outside of the structures of power.

Moreover, a number of idealizing assumptions are made in Model 1:
- the society exists in a state of total isolation, unperturbed by any external influences;
- the society is purely political, that is, there are only two classes in it: the rulers and the citizens (that is, groups of people who have or do not have the means of coercion at their disposal), without any political institutions, political doctrines, etc.;
- the technology remains at a constant level, and there is no technical progress;
- the rulers make use of the means of coercion directly, that is, without the intermediation of special forces;
- there is no state organization, especially a hierarchy of power; and
- class consciousness does not have an influence on the social thinking of particular members of the class.

In Model 1 (in its the no-loop variant), there are the following phases of political development: the phase of the growth of civil alienation, the phase of civil revolution, the phase of enslavement with the subphase of the self-enslavement of the authorities, the phase of cyclical declassations, and the phase of cyclical revolutions.

In the phase of the growth of civil alienation, the level of power regulation is low. The mechanism of political competition forces a typical ruler to broaden his or her sphere of influence. Consequently, the level of regulation in the society as a whole systematically grows, which contributes to the constant rise of the level of the civil alienation. After a time, the society enters the phase of the civil revolution. That process can end in the stifling of the revolution or in the citizens' victory, *secundum non datur*.[4] A lost revolution is followed by the enslavement

---

4 Only of model 1. The concretization of that part of political development is discussed by Brzechczyn (1993).

phase in which post-revolutionary terror is prevalent. It destroys autonomous social relations by eliminating the most socially active citizens. The disintegration of the civil society results in the declassation of the citizens.

The second possible outcome is the citizens' victory which in practice turns out to be the revolutionists' victory. They establish a new power elite which can use the means of coercion against the revolutionary masses. The revolutionary elite is the germ of a new class of rulers. From the perspective of n-Mhm, a revolution, although it is called 'civil,' only means replacing the old class of rulers with a new one. The mechanism of political competition triggers a conflict among the revolutionists – those who oppose the transformation of the revolutionary elites into a class of political rulers are deprived of power if not of their lives. When the masses have been sufficiently enslaved, the newly formed class of rulers begins to broaden its sphere of regulation within itself – the sub-phase of the self-enslavement of the authorities (in the enslavement phase) begins. The purges are followed by further broadening of the area of regulation. Once the critical threshold is reached, the so-called civil awakening takes place. A new revolution begins (Nowak 1991c, pp. 87–92). It initiates the phase of cyclical declassations.

Contrary to the revolution of the first kind, a defeat in the revolution of the second kind does not result in terror but in concessions on the part of the authorities. The sphere of power regulation decreases, and the sphere of social autonomy grows, which causes new revolutions. The scale of each such revolution, then, is bigger. As long as those revolutions are lost (a victory would bring about a civil loop and, consequently, a return to the beginning of the phase sequence), the declassation cycle continues. Nowak explains:

> The cyclical process from revolution through a victorious revolution, concessions, and etatist pressure, to another revolution lasts until there is a revolution on such a large scale, involving so many citizens that mass repressive action becomes unfeasible and the authorities must immediately make concessions.
> NOWAK 1991C, p. 93

In the end, there is a revolution which involves so many people that the authorities must react with concessions rather than repression. In the phase of cyclical revolutions, subsequent concessions reduce the authorities to the role of an administrator of public life. However, the competition between rulers forces them to increase (regain) the area of power regulation. Consequently, the civil alienation grows, and a revolution breaks out. That revolution is on such a large scale, with revolutionary attitudes among the citizens so strong that neither the existing authorities nor the new (revolutionary) ones can pacify it. The citizens' loops do not disappear, and the citizens' revolution would not lead back to the starting point. In the phase of class peace, the level of civil alienation remains below the threshold of class conflict.

Nowak applied the presented models to the dynamics of power in the Union of Soviet Socialist Republics. The February and October revolutions were two subsequent citizens' loops, that is, a phase of the initial political revolution following a phase of the growth of civil alienation. In the second half of the twentieth century, there was declassation. Collectivization and the increase of the number of Gulag prisoners could be interpreted as the phase of enslavement, and the purges – as the subphase of the self-enslavement of the authorities. The continued enslavement resulted in a revolution of the second kind, that is, a wave of strikes and uprisings in the Gulag Archipelago, which led to the closing of the camps and necessitated a condemnation of the cult of personality. Next, the system entered the phase of cyclical declassation: in 1959–1963, the army intervened in fourteen protesting cities of the Union of Soviet Socialist Republics. After that phase, the authorities made certain concessions, and the phase of cyclical revolutions began. It was represented by Gorbachev's perestroika and the dissolution of the Communist Party of the Soviet Union and the Union of Soviet Socialist Republics (1985–1991).[5]

3   The Historical Application of the Model I of the Theory of Power. The Political Evolution of the Chinese Society

Let us apply the n-Mhm model to the political development of the Chinese society.[6] The structure of the Chinese society can be interpreted with the use of the categories of the triple-class society. It means that the rulers' class has at its disposal three types of the means of class rule: coercion, production, and indoctrination. The political rule manifests itself as the one-party system maintained since the creation of the People's Republic of China. The Communist Party of China has the leading role in the socialist state. In the peak period of enslavement, that is, in 1975 – the year the new constitution was

---

5   For a detailed discussion of dynamics of power in the Soviet Union, including an innovative application of the phase of political enslavement see Siegel (1992; 1993; 1998).
6   Non-Marxian historical materialism has already been employed to interpret the history of non-European societies, cf Brzechczyn (2004; 2007), Karczyńska (2013; 2022), and to interpret the sacred texts created in other civilizations (Bręgiel-Benedyk 2013; Bręgiel-Pant 2022), or to paraphrase other theories which describe the development of non-European societies (Zarębski 2022a).

TABLE 16.1 Power hierarchy in China (source: Bogusz, Jakóbowski (2020), p. 16–20)

Body of political power	Number of members
The Communist Party of China (CCP)	86,500,000
The Central Committee of CCP	376
The Politburo of CCP	25
The General Secretary	1

passed – the prosecutorial branch, the independence of the judiciary, the right of an accused to be defended, and equality before the law were abolished. The revolutionary committees and people's communes kept the range of the regulation of the class of rulers at the 'bottom' level of the society. Nowadays, those rights are respected but only to the degree to which they are not a threat to the monopoly of the rulers' class. Political prisoners are kept, without due process, in the forced labor camps (劳改, *láogǎi*) modeled on the Gulag camps, and they are tortured there.[7] According to the Amnesty International 2009 report, most human rights are violated in China, including the right of association. The power hierarchy in the Chinese society is both a party and a state hierarchy. It consists of the state apparatus, the power elite, and the supreme ruler (see Table 16.1).

The General Secretary is the supreme ruler, the Politburo – the power elite, and the Central Committee – the state apparatus. The state apparatus constitutes 0.0005% of the Party – the greatest political party in the world – despite the fact that about 5% of the citizens are its members (Payette 2015).

The party, having at its exclusive disposal the means of production and indoctrination, also controls the remaining areas of public life, that is, the economy and culture. Private property has been allowed by the party by way of successive amendments of the constitution, first as a 'supplement' (1988) and then as an 'important component' (1999) of the socialist market economy. In compliance with the law, the economy is subject to the control of the state (that is, the party). All Chinese natural resources and land are also the property of the state – in China, one cannot buy land, one can only obtain the rights to

---

[7] Information about the camps: Laogai Research Foundation (www.laogairesearch.org; date of access: 16.04.2021).

use it (Rowiński, Jakóbiec 2006). Clearly, the rulers' class has the disposal of the means of production.

The cultural sphere functions in a similar manner. During the Cultural Revolution, foreign books were no longer published (with the exceptions of Stalin's and Hoxha's works), an attempt was made to replace the Beijing opera with the revolutionary opera, and from 1970 to 1976 "film-making was under the control of Jiang Qing and her allies in cultural leadership" (Clark 1983, p. 309). The youth did not attend school, and it had to learn Mao's *Little Red Book* by heart. The thesis about the intensifying "class struggle" justified the enslavement. Mao called class struggle "the highest form of revolution" and "logic of the people": every thought which encourages one to stop that fight even for a moment is wrong (Mao 1967, pp. 121, 135, 139). Despite the reforms of 1978, the party did not give up its monopoly on the means of indoctrination. In the 1999 amendment of the constitution, Deng Xiaoping's theory is described as the "ideological signpost for the state." In 2002, the principle of three representations (三个代表 *Sāngè Dàibiǎo*) was introduced. The groups which did not want to acknowledge the ideological monopoly of the party went underground or were persecuted. It is estimated that there are 6,000,000 Chinese Catholics in the official church, while there are at least 4,000,000 outside of it (Wenzel-Teuber 2020). Newly built church buildings were destroyed, and the government continues to imprison Catholic priests (CNA 2020). Nevertheless, the number of Christians continues to rise – each year, half a million Chinese are baptized in one of the protestant churches (Wang 2014). Last but not least, the party carefully supervises the Internet and blocks particular portals and websites (for example, Google and Facebook).

There is no doubt, then, that the Chinese society is ruled by the class of the triple lords. The system of government is the political version of the triple rule because the class of triple lords controls the means of production and indoctrination, while its economic and cultural power is used to maximize the area of power regulation. The changes in the structure of the classes of owners and priests after Deng's reforms did not entail any loss of power of the class of rulers which is superior to the other two classes. Since 1949, "the party is the state." During the Cultural Revolution, it was more apparent, but the Communist Party of China has never – not for a single moment – resigned its monopoly of the means of coercion, production, and indoctrination. The economic reforms in recent years could be treated as the emergence of the owners' classs from the triple class, but that process is slow and fully controlled by the authorities.

It is time to apply the conceptual apparatus of Model I of the theory of power of non-Marxian historical materialism to the analysis of the dynamics of power in post-war China. The directly analyzed period encompasses half a century (1949–1989). In this part, I shall distinguish the following phases of the history of China at that time: the growth of civil alienation, initial political revolution, enslavement with the subphase of the self-enslavement of the authorities, cyclical declassations, and cyclical revolutions.

The Communist Revolution, usually packed into the "Chinese civil war" in history course books, seems to be a political conflict between two parties rather than a citizens' revolution with a broad social base. Indeed, the Kuomintang acted as the ruling party in that war, after decades of the rule of the military junta and after the war with Japan, with its disastrous results. However, the misery caused by the events of the 1930s and 1940s significantly raised the level of the civil alienation, and the citizens' support became the decisive factor in the victory of Mao and the communist party over the Kuomintang. Lung Ying-tai states that during the Battle of Xuzhou alone, the communists mobilized 5.34 million peasants (Lung 2009, p. 184). The promise of an agrarian reform attracted masses of landless peasants who had nothing to lose to the Communist Party of China. It was mainly for them that the 1945–1949 was revolutionary. The Kuomintang, instead of making concessions to the urban population which were not allied with the communists, began taking over banks and factories (a few years after the Japanese had done the same), as well as civilians' supplies, to use them in the fight with the communists, which led to student and intelligentsia strikes and to mass desertions from the Kuomintang army (Leung 1996, p. 96). That corresponded to the phase of progressive civil alienation. The increase of power regulation did not trigger an outbreak of the initial citizens' revolution because, in return for the carrying out of the agrarian reform, the authorities gained the support of the peasantry which was the most numerous social group in the Chinese society.[8] Thus, the communist party became the core of the new state authorities. As early as 1949, that is, after the proclamation of the People's Republic of China, the Chinese People's Political Consultative Conference was formed. It was headed by Zhou Enlai.

The tightening of political control took the form of the first five-year plan and the agrarian reform (1950–1953), the scope of which far exceeded the subdivision of land and was a pretext for the use of repression and terror:

> A small cadre would find out who in a given village were the worst "enemies of the people" (…) They would gather all the persons in the village

---

[8] Perhaps, if the economic dimension of social life were introduced to the model, it could be explained with the so-called NEP effect: the satisfaction of the economic aspirations of the peasantry contributed to the growth of support for the authorities; surely, it stabilized their rule. See Nowak (1991c, pp. 227–229).

and encourage them in "struggle meetings" to denounce those who had exploited them. When hatred had erupted or been worked up, certain of the most grasping landlords and richest farmers would be paraded before a People's Court, accused, and condemned, some to execution, which the people would be compelled to witness, and some to reeducation and rehabilitation by labor.

MORTON, LEWIS 2004, p. 206

A few million people (the exact number is difficult to evaluate) lost their lives in such executions and show trials combined with dispossession (Fairbank, Goldman 2006, p. 350). As the communes were created (about seventy thousand of them), villagers were recruited to the triple class which had (sometimes unlimited) power over the peasants working in the communes. In consequence, Chinese peasants' freedom was restricted even more than during feudalism. New duties were imposed of them in relation to the membership in production teams and communes (Oi 1989, p. 5). The multi-level tax system only left a tiny part of the grain for a peasant's consumption – the amount was much lower than the daily portion of 7,000 calories considered to be sufficient for one person (Fairbank, Goldman 2006, p. 356). The declassation was the more hurtful as it was the smallholders that had supported the communist party and helped it win.

The party control reached new social groups. The aim of the so-called Hundred Flowers Campaign run with the slogan of "letting a hundred schools of thought contend" was to appease the intelligentsia by encouraging it to put forth critical opinions (提意见 *tíyìjiàn*), but the movement led to mass critique of the Communist Party of China and of the postulates of the democratization of politics. As the rulers' class noticed the excessive loosening of the area of regulation, it began a campaign against the rightists, which cost about half a million Chinese people their lives (Prybyla 1981, pp. 254–259). About seven hundred thousand educated Chinese were dismissed from their positions, and most of them were sent to re-education camps in villages. After ten years of the communist rule, there were only two hundred thousand graduates of higher (mainly technical) education institutions in China, a country with a population of half a billion people (Fairbank, Goldman 2006, pp. 363–365).

Although it was officially presented as an attempt at a sudden invigoration of the Chinese economy, the policy of the Great Leap Forward, initiated in 1957–1958 made it possible to extend the authorities' area of regulation to new spheres of social life. As the campaign began, units of people's militia were formed. Their task was to militarize the everyday life of the Chinese. In one year, the movement encompassed three hundred million citizens, that is more than half the population (Lüthi 2008, p. 105). All citizens (650 million) were mobilized to build the Chinese industry – one hundred million for steel production alone (Fairbank, Goldman 2006, p. 371). Scrap melting and steel production in primitive bloomeries ruined the industry, and progressive collectivization combined with natural disasters led to a great famine. At least thirty million human lives were lost during the famine. Cases of cannibalism were reported (Vardy, Vardy 2007). The survivors' life was subjected to radical control, with a complete prohibition of any private property and extreme organization of the life of the rural population in communes: women and men lived in separate dormitories and could only meet at certain times (Morton, Lewis 2004, p. 213). According to Model 1 of the theory of power of non-Marxian historical materialism, the period of time called the "twenty lost years" in Chinese historiography (1955–1975) represented the phase of political enslavement.

It is worth noting that in the model of power in n-Mhm, the 'aggressiveness' of the rulers' class grows during the enslavement phase – they strive to expand their area of regulation to the citizens of other states. Indeed, we could make a general observation about the trend toward greater outward aggressiveness. For example, in 1949, the People's Republic of China joined the war in Korea. Propagandists presented it as a glorious victory of China over the bourgeoisie United States of America (in reality, an armistice agreement was signed). Also in that year, the People's Republic of China 'freed' Tibet. In 1958, the Union of Soviet Socialist Republics attacked Taiwan. That conflict ended with a quick reaction of the United States of America and with the withdrawal of support by the Soviet Union. In 1962, the Aksai Chin territory was annexed in the course of the Sino-Indian War. Thus, in the 1960s and 1970s, the enslavement intensified. The Great Proletarian Cultural Revolution of 1966–1976 could be interpreted as the phase of enslavement with the subphase of the self-enslavement of the authorities. The direct impulse for the announcement of the Cultural Revolution was the desire of the rulers' class, especially Mao, to prevent events similar to those which took place in the Union of Soviet Socialist Republics, that is, to post-Stalinist 'revisionism,' as it would mean a significant restriction of the area of power regulation of the party. About thirty million Chinese people were imprisoned or killed in the course of the elimination of the 'bourgeoisie element' (Walder, Su 2003). The Red Guards (红卫兵 *Hóngwèibīng*) a paramilitary student organization which consisted of seven hundred thousand people, struck terror in the country. The Red Guards themselves were enslaved to enslave others. In their own words, president Mao defined their future, and nothing would stop them on the way (Chong 2002, p. 105). During their campaign of destroying the "old four" (四旧 *sìjiù*), the Red Guards attacked everything related to the old customs, ideas, traditions, and culture. An immense number of Confucian, Buddhist, and Taoist historical objects. Buildings, cemeteries, sculptures, and bronzes were destroyed. Even the corpses of the emperor couple from the Ming dynasty were dragged out of their grave. Traditional books were burned. Also, all schools were closed, so the Chinese literature calls the youth of that time the "lost generation." Factory production fell by 10% (as much as 40% in southern and eastern China). Great factories built in Henan, Hebei, and Hunan lost twenty-five million dollars because they became unprofitable, and then they were closed (Bai 2014, p. 12).

As noted by John King Fairbank, the pervasive terror was possible because of the complete erosion of the civil society; the Chinese were passive and obedient with respect to the authoritarian rule. Importantly, they were also told for many years that the concept of human rights is essentially egoistic and anti-socialist (Fairbank, Goldman 2006, p. 383). Let us note that in n-Mhm, enslavement is defined in terms of a reduction of the civil society and the popularization of the attitude of enslavement and of lack of resistance. The counterpart of the subphase of the self-enslavement of the authorities would be the period of Cultural Revolution when members of the rulers' class were repressed. In 1966, Mao issued a circular which informed about the "representative of the bourgeoisie who broke into the party." Liu Shaoqi, the head of the state, died in 1968, in prison. His successor, Lin Biao, died in a mysterious air plane accident in Mongolia. Generals Peng Duha and Zhu De, leaders of the Great March, were removed. Deng Xiaoping, the General Secretary at the time, was also repressed. During the Cultural Revolution, the purges included about 60% of the members of the party. Four hundred thousand party members were killed, and seven hundred thousand were imprisoned after illegal show trials (Fairbank, Goldman 2006, p. 387).

In the second half of 1968, the Red Guards themselves fell victim to the purges which had been initiated by its functionaries. The army sent from twelve to twenty million Red Guard soldiers to the country. Three million of them were arrested, and a few million were executed (Margolin 1999, p. 534). The failure of the Red Guards meant the end of Mao's career as the Great Helmsman:

> People still pretended to be faithful to their leader. But underneath, civil society was emerging from its torpor, prior to its explosion in the years 1976–1979 (...) When Mao finally died in September 1976, he had been a spent force politically for some time. The muted nature of popular response to his death was sufficient proof of that, as was his obvious incapacity to assure his own succession.
>
> MARGOLIN 1999, p. 538

It was not the death of an individual but the internal dynamics of power that brought about the political transformation of 1976. Deng Xiaoping's reforms included the creation of economic zones for the Western capital, liberalization of the activity of the private sector, and dissolution of the system of people's communes in the country. All of them could be interpreted as concessions on the part of the Chinese triple lords. In the case of China, the transition to the phase of cyclical declassations is not typical in that concessions were not preceded by revolutionary unrest. In the light of the theory of power in non-Marxian historical materialism, a low level of social resistance is explained with either extremely low or extremely high – destructive for human relationships – level of enslavement.

It seems that it is the latter situation in China. It is worth noting that in the Chinese society, the nature of concessions was economic, not political. As there were no revolutionary outbreaks, the party monopoly of power was not violated, but the concessions did help initiate a process of the gradual emergence of a separate owners' class. A decade later, an amendment of the constitution of the People's Republic of China of April 2, 1988 sanctioned that state of things as it declared the private sector to be a "supplement" for the socialist economy and made it possible to trade the rights to use land.

We should not, however, be misled by the direction of those changes. Let us remember that the phase of cyclical declassations is characterized by the following pattern of development: "revolution – concessions – etatization – revolution, etc." In the Chinese society, the first demands for a liberalization and democratization appeared quite early: already in 1978, Wei Jingsheng presented an essay titled "The Fifth Modernization" in which he wrote that the Chinese needed democracy and freedom and not being a dictators' tool of modernization (Wei 1997). In consequence, Wei Jingsheng was imprisoned from 1979 to 1997. The governing style of the Chinese authorities did not change significantly, as proven by, among other things, the radical implementation (at the beginning of the 1980s) of the policy of one child – the area of the rulers' control (and punishment) extended to one of the most basic aspects of personal life. Social inequalities grew, and the citizens, deprived of legal protection and social benefits, were more helpless in the face of the expanding system of the corrupted *guanxi* ties. That facilitated even greater etatization of political life.

In 1989, during the strikes on the Tiananmen Square in Beijing, a group of one hundred thousand citizens, most of them young, demanded the same as dissident Wei: a liberalization and democratization of the public life in China (Nathan 2001). The demonstrations could be interpreted as a beginning of the citizens' revolution which was to lead to a restriction of the area of regulation by demanding that the authorities withdraw their control of politics, the economy, and culture. The rebellion was brutally suppressed, and the revolution ended in defeat before it even began. Like every lost revolution, the one from 1989 brought about concessions on the part of the authorities, which initiated the second cycle of the phase of cyclical declassation. However, those concessions are gradual, as exemplified by the slow liberalization of private property law or by the progressive weakening of the policy of one child, which was finally abolished in 2015.

Communist officials have also successfully avoided that policy: in 2000–2005, in Hunan alone, about two thousand officials had more than one child (Xinhua 2007). The promises of the introduction of a social security system within the framework of the new five-year-old plan is another example of concessions made to delay, as much as possible, another rebellion and to maintain the authoritarian rule of the Communist Party of China. The Chinese civil society is too weak, and the rulers' class is too strong for the occurrence of the phase of cyclical revolutions. There are no signs of that happening in the near future, either. Thus, the Chinese society is stuck in the second cycle of the phase of declassation. The dependencies are presented in the Figure 16.1.

To sum up, in the history of the Chinese society, we can distinguish counterparts of the phase of the growth of civil alienation (1945–1949), the phase of enslavement (1956–1976), the subphase of the self-enslavement of the authorities (1966–1976), and the phase of cyclical declassations (the first cycle in 1976–89 and the second cycle since 1989). The society is unique in that there is no clear and separate phase of the initial citizens' revolution and of the citizens' revolution initiating the first cycle of the phase of cyclical declassations. There was such an initiating revolution, though, before the second cycle of

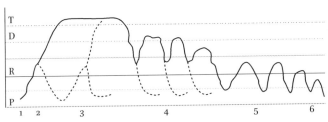

FIGURE 16.1 The dynamics of relation between the class of rulers and the class of citizens in the People's Republic of China. Explanations: P – the threshold of class peace, R – the area of revolutions, D – the threshold of declassation, T – the threshold of totalitarianism; development phases: 1– the phase of the growth of civil alienation, 2 – the phase of the civil revolution, 3 – the phase of enslavement, 4 – the phase of cyclical declassations, 5 – the phase of cyclical revolutions; 6 – the phase of class peace.

that phase, in 1989. Still, considering the strong idealizing assumptions, the model of power is a satisfactory approximation of the post-war development of the Chinese society.

4 Predictions and Perspectives

In the last part, I would like to present few general predictions or trends inspired by the n-Mhm conceptualization of the social world.

As regards internal politics, we can predict a gradual decrease of power regulation, which will continue until the threshold of a political revolution (Stepan 2015). As long as a strong civil society does not emerge in the Chinese society, the political concessions of the triple rule will not step out of the phase of cyclical declassations.

That decrease of power regulation in the internal politics will be compensated by an increase of power regulation in foreign policy. That will happen through cultural centers (such as Confucius Institutes) and general pressure upon censoring hostile comments on China's policy. Most importantly, however, the compensation will be made through new economic initiatives such as One Belt, One Road, or lately – the Polar Silk Road. The economic subjugation of African states will also follow the gradual decrease of internal control. In all cases, the economic expansion of China will be instrumental to the broadening of its external sphere of influence.

On the one hand, the concessions of the triple rule in the economic realm – that is, the consent to the activity of foreign capital and domestic companies and to individual use of land by the peasants – will ensure the internal stabilization of the triple rule; on the other hand, the growing effectiveness of the Chinese economy will help the country expand its influence abroad. That kind of economic domination in inter-social relationships will manifest itself in the construction of economic hegemony (see Brzechczyn 2007a, p. 247). Economic concessions will enrich the citizens and lead to the emergence of a separate owners' class.

In the cultural sphere, we will observe further distancing from the remnants of Marxism-Leninism which started in 1978. In order to ideologically justify the Chinese position on the international arena, the official discourse will increasingly contain references to the Confucian and imperial past. The image of Mao as the founding figure of Chinese communism, along with his theory of permanent revolution will be gradually superseded by model works created by Xi Jinping and his successors, with a clear preference for the language of interstate harmony and mutual co-operation (cf. Xi 2014).

However, the triple rule will not give up its spiritual monopoly, that is, it will not allow the formation of a separate priests' class because, given the appearance of the owners' class we have predicted above, it would cause a total erosion of the party triple rule. The state censorship will continue to control the citizens' cultural activity and preclude any pluralism of world views which – in connection with calls for democratization – would threaten the rulers' class and the maintenance of the area of power regulation.[9]

The particular predictions made on the basis of the application of n-Mhm prove the methodological efficacy of that concept. N-Mhm allows us to capture and describe the dynamics of power in post-war China in a consistent and precise manner.

As I have mentioned before, from the perspective of n-Mhm, the Chinese history is unique in that there was no revolution which would initiate the phase of cyclical declassations. For that reason, the theory faces the challenge of constructing a vision of the Chinese expansion which would include the economic factors alongside the political ones. That, however, would require further concretization of the assumed models. Another research obstacle to overcome would be the necessity to adapt the subsequent models and broaden of the scope of the adaptation of Models I and II (for example, for the years 1912–1949). The prospect of developing that concept – with its confirmed explanatory and prognostic power – should be encouraging for researchers and arouse interest in its expansion and even broader application.

Acknowledgement

The research leading to this paper was supported by National Science Centre (Poland) grant no. 2019/33/B/HS1/00244. I would like to thank Prof. Krzysztof Brzechczyn for all the remarks and suggestions to the initial version of the article.

References

Bell, D. (2010). *China's New Confucianism: Politics and Everyday Life in Changing Society*. Princeton: Princeton University Press.

---

[9] In 2013, in response to Xi Jinping's speech about the "Chinese dream," many articles were written with appeals for democratic and constitutional China. However, the censors did not allow their publication, which caused protests, see Stępień (2015, pp. 143–147).

Bogusz, M, J. Jakóbowski (2020). *The Chinese Communist Party and Its State. Xi Jinping's Conservative Turn*. Warsaw: Centre for Eastern Studies.

Borbone, G. (2016). *Questioni di Metodo. Leszek Nowak e la scienza come idealizzazione*. Roma: Acireale.

Borbone, G. (2021). *The Relevance of Models. Idealization and Concretization in Leszek Nowak*. Műnchen: Grin Verlag.

Bręgiel-Benedyk, M. (2013). Obraz struktury społecznej w Manusmryti. Próba analizy teoretycznej [The Image of the Social Structure in Manusmriti. An Attempt at a Theoretical Analysis]. In: K. Brzechczyn, M. Ciesielski, and E. Karczyńska (eds.), *Jednostka w układzie społecznym. Próba teoretycznej konceptualizacji*, pp. 291–319. Poznań: Wydawnictwo Naukowe WNS UAM.

Bręgiel-Pant, M. (2022). The Image of a Social Structure in Manusmṛti: An Attempt at a Theoretical Analysis. In: K. Brzechczyn (ed.) *Non-Marxian Historical Materialism: Reconstructions and Comparisons*. Poznań Studies in the Philosophy of the Sciences and the Humanities, vol. 120, pp. 127–160. Leiden/Boston: Brill.

Brzechczyn, K. (1993). Civil Loop and the Absorption of Elites. In: L. Nowak, M. Paprzycki, (eds.), *Social System, Rationality and Revolution. Poznań Studies in the Philosophy of the Sciences and the Humanities*, vol. 33, pp. 277–283. Amsterdam/Atlanta, GA: Rodopi.

Brzechczyn, K. (2004). *O wielości linii rozwojowych w procesie historycznym. Próba interpretacji ewolucji społeczeństwa meksykańskiego* [On the Multitude of the Lines of Developments in the Historical Process. An Attempt at Interpretation of the Evolution of the Mexican Society]. Poznań: Wydawnictwo Naukowe UAM.

Brzechczyn, K. (2007a). On the Application of non-Marxian Historical Materialism to Development of non-European Societies. In: J. Brzeziński, A. Klawiter, T.A.F. Kuipers, K. Łastowski, K. Paprzycka, P. Przybysz (eds.), *The Courage of Doing Philosophy: Essays Dedicated to Leszek Nowak*, pp. 235–254. Amsterdam/New York: Rodopi.

Brzechczyn, K. (2007b) Paths to Democracy of the Post-Soviet Republics: an Attempt At Conceptualization. In: E. Czerwińska-Schupp (ed.), *Values and Norms in the Age of Globalization*, pp. 529–571. Berlin: Peter Lang.

Chong, W.-L. (2002). *China's great proletarian Cultural Revolution: master narratives and post-Mao counternarratives*. Lanham: Rowman & Littlefield.

Ciesielski, M. (2013). Problem kumulacji podziałów klasowych we współczesnym kapitalizmie [The Problem of the Accumulation of Class Divisions in Contemporary Capitalism]. In: K. Brzechczyn, M. Ciesielski, and E. Karczyńska (eds.), *Jednostka w układzie społecznym. Próba teoretycznej konceptualizacji*, pp. 131–152. Poznań: Wydawnictwo Naukowe WNS UAM.

Ciesielski, M. (2022). The Problem of the Accumulation of Class Divisions in Contemporary Capitalism: An Attempt at a Theoretical Analysis. In: K. Brzechczyn (ed.) *New Developments in Theory of Historical Process. Polish Contributions to*

Non-Marxian Historical Materialism. Poznań Studies in the Philosophy of the Sciences and the Humanities, vol. 119, pp. 217–238. Leiden/Boston: Brill.

Clark, P. (1983). Film-Making in China: From the Cultural Revolution to 1981. *The China Quarterly* 94 (June), 304–322.

Coniglione, F. (2010). *Realtà e astrazione. Scuola polacca ed epistemologia post-positivista*. Roma: Bonanno Editore.

Czajkowski, W. (2013). Kilka uwag o Leszka Nowaka nie-Marksowskim materializmie historycznym oraz Immanuela Wallersteina i Andre G. Franka teoriach systemu światowego [A Few Remarks about Leszek Nowak's non-Marxian Historical Materialism and on Immanuel Wallerstein's and Andre G. Frank's Theories of the World System]. In: K. Brzechczyn, M. Ciesielski, and E. Karczyńska (eds.), *Jednostka w układzie społecznym. Próba teoretycznej konceptualizacji*, pp. 187–205. Poznań: Wydawnictwo Naukowe WNS UAM.

Czajkowski, W. (2022). Leszek Nowak's Historiosophy from Historical and Systematical Perspectives. In: K. Brzechczyn (ed.) *Non-Marxian Historical Materialism: Reconstructions and Comparisons. Poznań Studies in the Philosophy of the Sciences and the Humanities*, vol. 120, pp. 16-39. Leiden/Boston: Brill.

Fairbank, J.K., M. Goldman. (2006). *China. A New History*. Cambridge–London: The Belknap Press of Harvard University Press.

Gong, Z. (1975). *Gong Zizhen quanji*. Shanghai: Shanghai Renmin Chubanshe.

Karczyńska, E. (2013). Struktura społeczna Imperium Osmańskiego. Próba analizy teoretycznej [The Social Structure of the Ottoman Empire. An Attempt at a Theoretical Analysis]. In: K. Brzechczyn, M. Ciesielski, and E. Karczyńska (eds.), *Jednostka w układzie społecznym. Próba teoretycznej konceptualizacji*, pp. 273–290. Poznań: Wydawnictwo Naukowe WNS UAM.

Karczyńska, E. (2022). The Social Structure of the Ottoman Society: an Attempt at a Theoretical Analysis. In: K. Brzechczyn (ed.) *New Developments in Theory of Historical Process. Polish Contributions to Non-Marxian Historical Materialism. Poznań Studies in the Philosophy of the Sciences and the Humanities*, vol. 119, pp. 294–313. Leiden/Boston: Brill.

Leung, E.P. (ed). (1996). *Historical Dictionary of Revolutionary China, 1839–1976*, Westport: Greenwood Publishing Group.

Liang, B. (2014). Economic Legacies of the Cultural Revolution. *Job Market Paper*. January 14.

Lung, Ying-tai. (2009). *Dajiang Dahai 1949*. Taipei: Commonwealth Publishing Press.

Lüthi, L.M. (2008). *The Sino-Soviet Split: Cold War in the Communist World*. Princeton: Princeton University Press.

Makeham, J. (2003). *New Confucianism. A Critical Examination*. New York: Palgrave MacMillan.

Mao, Z. (1967). *Mao Zhuxi yanlu*. Huhehaote: Xinhua Shudian.

Margolin, J.-L. (1999). China: A Long March into Night. 463–546. In: S. Courtois (ed.), *The Black Book of Communism: Crimes, Terror, Repression*, pp. 463–546. Cambridge, MA: Harvard University Press.

Morton, W.S., C.M. Lewis. (2004). *China: Its History and Culture*. New York: McGraw-Hill Education.

Nathan, A. (2001). The Tiananmen Papers. *Foreign Affairs* Jan.-Feb. 2001.

Nowak, L. (1980). *The Structure of Idealization. Towards a Systematic Interpretation of the Marxian Idea of Science*. Dordrecht: Reidel.

Nowak L. (1983). *Property and Power. Towards a non-Marxian Historical Materialism. Theory and Decision Library*, vol. 27 . Dordrecht/Boston/Lancaster: Reidel.

Nowak, L. (1991abc). *U podstaw teorii socjalizmu* [The Foundations of the Theory of Socialism]; vol. 1: *Własność i władza. O konieczności socjalizmu* [Property and Power. On the Necessity of Socialism]; vol. 2: *Droga do socjalizmu. O konieczności socjalizmu w Rosji* [The Road to Socialism. On the Necessity of Socialism in Russia]; vol. 3: *Dynamika władzy. O strukturze i konieczności zaniku socjalizmu* [The Dynamics of Power. On the Structure and Necessity of the Disappearance of Socialism]. Poznań: Nakom.

Nowak L. (1991d). *Power and Civil Society. Toward a Dynamic Theory of Real Socialism*. New York: Greenwood Press.

Oi, J.C. (1989). *State and the Peasant in Contemporary China*. Berkeley: University of California Press.

Payette A. (2015). Institutionalisation of the Party's Leadership Nomination System: The „Path" to the Top in Communist China. *International Journal of China Studies* 6 (3), 231–272.

Prybyla, J.S. (1981). The Hundred Flowers of Discontent. *Current History* 80 (476), 254.

Rowiński J., W. Jakóbiec. (2006). *System konstytucyjny Chińskiej Republiki Ludowej* [The Constitutional System of the People's Republic of China]. Warsaw: Wydawnictwo Sejmowe.

Siegel, A. (1992). *Der Dynamik des Terrors im Stalinismum: Ein strukturtheoretischer Erklärungsversuch*. Pfaffenweiler: Centaurus.

Siegel, A. (1993). The Overrepression Cycle in the Soviet Union. An Operationalization of a Theoretical Model. In: L. Nowak, M. Paprzycki (eds.), *Social System, Rationality and Revolution*, pp. 371–396. Amsterdam-Atlanta: Rodopi.

Siegel A. (1998). Ideological Learning Under Conditions of Social Enslavement: The Case of the Soviet Union in the 1930s and 1940s. *Studies in East European Thought* 50 (1), 19–58.

Xinhua. (2007). Over 1,900 officials breach birth policy in C. China. *Xinhua*, July 8, 2007.

Stepan M. (2015). Two Years of Refurbishing the Command and Control Apparatus: the Chinese Communist Party strengthens its hold on the judicial system and societal forces. *China Monitor* 28, 3–8.

Stępień M. (2015). *Chińskie marzenie o konstytucjonalizmie* [Chinese Constitutional Dream]. Kraków: Wydawnictwo Uniwersytetu Jagiellońskiego.

Vardy S., Vardy A. (2007). Cannibalism in Stalin's Russia and Mao's China. *East European Quarterly* 41 (2), 223–238.

Walder A., Yang S. (2003) The Cultural Revolution in the Countryside: Scope, Timing and Human Impact. *The China Quarterly* 173 (March).

Wang H. (1997). China plans establishment of Christian theology. *China Daily* 07.08.2014.

Wei, J. (1997). *The Courage to Stand Alone: Letters from Prison and Other Writings.* New York: Penguin Books.

Wenzel-Teuber K. (2020). Statistics on Religions and Churches in the People's Republic of China – Update for the Year 2019. *Religions & Christianity in Today's China* 10 (2), 21–41.

Xi, J. (2014). *The Governance of China*, vol. 1. Beijing: Foreign Languages Press.

Zarębski T. (2003). Problem totalitaryzacji kapitalizmu [The Problem of Totalitarization of the Capitalist Society]. In: K. Brzechczyn (ed.), *Ścieżki transformacji. Ujęcia teoretyczne i opisy empiryczne*, pp. 229–260. Poznań: Zysk i S-ka.

Zarębski T. (2013). Struktura klasowa społeczeństw hydraulicznych. Próba parafrazy teorii Karla Augusta Wittfogla w aparaturze pojęciowej nie-Marksowskiego materializmu historycznego [Class Structure of Hydraulic Societies. An Attempt at the Paraphrase of Karl August Wittfogel's Theory in the Conceptual Apparatus of non-Marxian Historical Materialism]. In: K. Brzechczyn, M. Ciesielski, and E. Karczyńska (eds.), *Jednostka w układzie społecznym. Próba teoretycznej konceptualizacji*, pp. 207–221. Poznań: Wydawnictwo Naukowe WNS UAM.

Zarębski T. (2022). The Problem of Totalitarization of the Capitalist Society. In: K. Brzechczyn (ed.) *New Developments in Theory of Historical Process. Polish Contributions to Non-Marxian Historical Materialism. Poznań Studies in the Philosophy of the Sciences and the Humanities*, vol. 119, pp. 189–216. Leiden/Boston: Brill.

Internet Sources:

Catholic News Agency (2020). *Report: Chinese government imprisoning more priests, bishops* (https://www.catholicnewsagency.com/news/45889/report-chinese-government-imprisoning-more-priests-bishops%C2%A0; date of access: 16.04.2021).

Laogai Research Foundation www.laogairesearch.org; date of access: 16.04.2021).

Name Index

Abramowski, Edward   83
Adamec, Ladislav   284, 285
Ahmed I, sultan   301
Amoretti, Francesco   233, 236
Arato, Andrew   281, 289
Arendt, Hannah   239, 243–245, 251, 253, 254
Aron, Raymond   136, 139
Arrow, Kenneth J.   190, 213
Ash, Timothy Garton   282, 283, 289

Babinskas, Nerijus   300, 311
Bäcker, Roman   200, 213
Baker, Gideon   281, 289
Bakunin, Mikhail Alexandrovich   29, 29
Balicki, Władysław   ix, xxii
Banaszak, Tomasz   xxii, xxxi, 160, 167, 182, 203, 213, 219, 236, 256–259, 263, 264
Bankowicz, Marek   286, 290
Barber, Benjamin   217, 229–232, 235, 236
Barkey, Karen   300, 305, 306, 311
Bartkowiak, Jacek   xi, xii, xxii
Bauer, Michael   284, 290
Bauman, Zygmunt   230, 236
Becker, Garry Stanley   190, 213
Będkowski, Marcin   xxiii
Bell, Daniel   12, 49, 315, 330
Berdyaev, Nikolai Alexandrovich   26, 49, 92, 93
Berend, T. Iván   266, 280, 282, 285, 290
Berlin, Isaiah   82, 93, 166
Berlusconi, Silvio   233
Berthold, Ludwig   xv, xxii
Bhaskar, Roy   108, 117
Blakekey, Thomas   xxvii
Bogusz Michał   321, 331
Bolotnikov, Ivan   299, 300
Borbone, Giacomo   xvi, xxiii, 192, 213, 218, 236, 266, 290, 295, 311, 316, 331
Bozóki, András   290
Bradley, John F.   284, 290
Bręgiel-Benedyk, Marta   320, 331
Brożek, Anna   xxiii
Brzechczyn, Krzysztof   vii, xiii, xv, xviii, xx, xxii, xxiii, xxiv, xxvi, xxxi, 76, 95, 99, 103, 104, 118, 149, 150, 151, 153, 160, 171, 179, 182, 185, 213, 215, 219–222, 236, 238, 264, 276, 282, 290, 292, 295, 309–311, 314, 317, 320, 329–332, 334
Brzeziński, Jerzy   xxiii, xxiv, xxvii, 33, 50, 94, 95, 182, 236, 237, 311, 331
Buchanan, James   191, 213
Buczkowski, Piotr   x, xxi, 4, 8, 50, 51, 82, 93, 97, 103, 125, 132, 150, 159, 182, 185, 229, 237
Burbelka, Jolanta   97, 103, 150
Bureš, Jan   285–287, 290

Çaha, Ömer   307, 312
Çandarlı, Halil   306
Castle, Marjorie   266, 277, 279–282, 290
Chavance, Bernard   132
Chong, Woei Lien   325, 331
Chybińska, Alicja   xxiii
Ciesielski, Mieszko   xx, xxiii, xxiv, xxxi, 217, 219, 237, 317, 331, 332, 334
Clark, Paul   322, 331
Codogni, Paulina   281, 290
Cohen, Gerald Allan   108, 138, 148, 190, 213
Cohen, Marshall   108, 138
Coniglione, Francesco   xiv, xvi, xxiv, xxv, 117, 192, 214, 218, 237, 266, 290, 295, 312, 316, 331
Constant, Benjamin   70, 75
Crampton, Richard   281, 283, 285, 290
Curry, Jane Leftwich   290
Czajkowski, Waldemar   316, 317, 332
Czerwińska-Schupp, Ewa   182, 331
Czyż, Anna   284, 291

Da Costa, Newton C. A.   108, 117
De Candole, James   284, 291
Deng Xiaoping   315, 322, 326, 327
Deutscher, Isaac   160, 182
Djilas, Milovan   xviii, xxiv
Dobbs, Michael   284, 291
Dobek-Ostrowska, Bogusława   234, 236, 237
Dreijmanis, John   267, 291
Drobczyński, Sebastian   290, 291
Dubiński, Krzysztof   280, 291
Dudek, Antoni   278, 281, 291, 292
Dźwiniel, Marian   xxvi

Egiert, Robert   xx, xxiv
Eliade, Mircea   12, 13, 50
Elster, Jon   108, 117, 138, 148, 190, 191, 214
Ely, John   281, 291
Engels, Friedrich   vii, 5, 50, 97, 114, 204, 206
Ergil, Dogu   301, 312

Fairbank, John King   324, 325, 326, 332
Fajfer, Luba   290
Falkiewicz, Andrzej   30, 50
Faroqhi, Suraiya   307, 312
Fest, Joachim   24, 50
Fiala, Petr   284, 291
Fisk, Milton   108, 117
Friszke, Andrzej   291, 292
Fukuyama, Francis   83, 136, 159, 217, 218, 237

Garcia de la Sienra, Adolfo   xx, xxiv, 108, 117
Garlicki, Andrzej   281, 291
Geremek, Bronisław   281, 293
Giddens, Anthony   108, 117
Gilejko, Leszek   281, 291
Gilowski, Paweł   21
Godek, Lidia   xxii, xxxi, 266, 291
Godelier, Maurice   80, 94, 97, 103, 112, 117, 138
Goldman, Merle   324, 325, 326, 332
Gombrowicz, Witold   153, 154
Gong, Zizhen   315, 332
Gorbachev, Mikhail Sergeyevich   276, 284, 320
Gortat, Radzisława   278, 291
Grad, Jan   xxvi
Gratian, an emperor   30

Habermas, Jurgen   92, 94
Hamminga, Bert   114, 117, 191, 214
Havel, Vaclav   282, 283, 285, 288, 289
Hayek, Friedrich   136, 166
Hegel, Georg Wilhelm Friedrich   57, 59–63, 65, 67–70, 72, 74, 75, 109, 134, 135, 154
Heineman, John L.   285, 291
Heller, Włodzimierz   96, 184, 214
Hobhouse, Leonard   68, 75
Holzer, Jan   284, 291
Honecker, Erich   283
Hübner, A.   183
Husák, Gustav   284

Imber, Colin   301, 304, 312
Inalcik, Halil   300, 302–304, 307, 312

Ishijama, John   290
Ivan IV, Tsar of Russia   299, 306
Ivanyk, Stepan   xxiii

Jakeš, Milos   284, 286
Jakóbowski, Jakub   321, 331
Jakubiec, Wojciech   322, 333
Janowski, Karol Boromeusz   278, 291
Jaruzelski, Wojciech   278, 281, 289
Jaśkowski, Stanisław   109, 117
Jedlicki, Jerzy   69, 75
Jermakowicz, Władysław   92, 94
Jiang, Qing   322
Johnson, H.J.   216

Kaczyński, Lech   xii, xiii, xxiv
Karaman, Kamil Kıvanç   300, 307, 312
Kean, John   281, 291
Keynes, John Maynard   54
Kiszczak, Czesław   278, 279, 281
Klawiter, Andrzej   vii, x, xi, xxi, xxiii, xxiv, xxvii, 4, 8, 50, 51, 82, 93, 103, 125, 132, 150, 159, 182, 185, 192, 214, 229, 236, 237, 311, 331
Klímová, Rita   283
Kmita, Jerzy   50
Kołakowski, Leszek   82, 94, 135, 136, 138, 139, 146, 148, 166, 204, 214
Kornai, Janos   92, 94
Kotarbińska, Janina   viii
Kowalik, Tadeusz   140, 148
Kowalewski Jahromi, Piotr   xvi, xxiv
Kozielecki, Jerzy   xxv
Krause, Ulrich   108, 117
Kubas, Sebastian   284, 291
Kubik, Jan   xv, xxiv
Kuipers, Theo A. F.   xxiii, xxiv, xxvii, 117, 182, 236, 311, 331
Kuokkanen, Martti   85, 94
Kuroń, Jacek   83, 279

Lange, Oskar   109, 117, 139, 316
Leach, J.   216
Leinfellner, Elisabeth   183
Leinfellner, Werner   183
lem   151, 182
Leung, Pak-Wah   323, 332
Lewis, Charlton M.   324, 325, 332
Liedman, Sven-Eric   184

NAME INDEX

Lin, Biao 326
Lissewski, Piotr xii, xxiv
Liu, Shaoqi 326
Luce, Robert Duncan 211, 215
Lukács, György 18, 162
Lukes, Steven 108, 117, 118
Lung, Ying-tai 323, 332
Lüthi, Lorenz M. 325, 332
Luxemburg, Rosa 156, 158
Łabędź, Krzysztof 278, 292
Łastowski, Krzysztof vii, xxiii, xxiv, xxvii, 82, 94, 95, 97, 103, 125, 132, 150, 182, 192, 214, 236, 311, 331

Machcewicz, Piotr 291, 292
Majchrzak, Grzegorz xxiv
Makeham, John 315, 332
Małachowski, Andrzej xii
Malawski, Marcin 190, 214
Malinowski, Roman 279, 292
Mao Zedong 181, 314, 315, 322, 323, 325, 326, 329, 332
Marciniak, Piotr 278, 291, 292
Mardin, Şerif 307, 312
Mareš, Miroslav 284, 291
Margolin, Jean-Louis 326, 332
Margul, Tadeusz 20, 21, 22, 50
Maruszewski, Tomasz 95
Marx, Karl vii, viii, ix, x, xv, xix, 5, 6, 10, 11, 25, 28, 46, 50, 54, 55, 57, 72–76, 80, 97, 108, 109, 112, 114, 116, 135–138, 142, 145–148, 154–160, 169, 170–172, 181, 192, 204–207, 212, 214, 316
Matuz, Josef 304, 308, 312
Mazowiecki, Tadeusz 84, 279, 283
Méchýř, Jan 286, 287, 292
Mehmed, the Conqueror 300, 301, 306, 307
Meissner, Boris 92, 94
Meyer, Robert K. 108, 118
Mianowicz, Tomasz 279, 292
Michalski, Kazimierz 133
Michnik, Adam 279
Mill, John Stuart 101, 114, 116, 118, 136, 163
Miśkiewicz, Benon xiv
Moczulski, Leszek 91
Mohl, Alexa 120, 132
Morishima, Michio 107, 118, 138, 148
Morton, W. Scott 324, 325, 332
Moseley, Fred 108, 118

Moutafchieva, Vera P. 304, 305, 312
Muehlman, R. 216
Muhammad, Prophet 301, 302
Murat I, sultan 303
Murray, Patrick 108, 118

Nagel, Thomas 117
Nathan, Andrew J. 328, 332
Niedźwiadek, Krzysztof 150, 229, 237
Niewiadomski, Marek 100, 104, 160, 183
Nowak, Leszek vii–xxii, xxiv–xxvii, xxxi, 3, 4, 6–10, 12, 14, 27, 31, 32, 46–52, 55–57, 64, 75–77, 80, 82, 83, 85, 88, 89, 90, 92–100, 102–106, 110, 112, 117, 118, 119, 121, 123–125, 130–134, 136, 137, 139, 141, 148–156, 158–160, 162, 167, 168, 173, 180–185, 189, 192, 193, 197–200, 203, 206, 213, 214, 215, 217–222, 229, 236–239, 241, 248, 254–257, 264–268, 270, 271, 276, 292, 294–300, 309, 311, 312, 314, 316–320, 323, 331–333
Nowakowa, Izabella. xv, xxvi, xxxi, 9, 51, 152, 185, 192, 215, 218, 238
Nozick, Robert 191, 205, 215

O'Donnel, Guillermo 282, 292
Ociepka, Beata 233, 238
Oi, Jean C. 324, 333
Osman Sultan 301
Ost, David 277, 292
Owsiński, Jan xxiv
Özel, Oktay 306, 312
O'Rourke, James J. xxvii

Paczkowski, Andrzej 280, 291, 292
Palonen, Kari 293
Pamuk, Şevket 303, 312
Panasiuk, Ryszard 184, 215
Paprzycka, Katarzyna xx, xxiii, xxiv, xxvi, xxvii, 85, 95, 100, 104, 130, 133, 160, 182, 185, 236, 311, 331
Paprzycki, Marcin xx, xxiv, xxvi, xxvii, 85, 95, 130, 133, 182, 311, 331, 333
Paśniczek, Jacek 95
Payette, Alex 321, 333
Peng, Duha 326
Petrażycki, Leon 49, 51
Piłsudski, Józef 92
Połatyński, Marcin xxii, xxxii, 256

Popper, Karl Raimund   67, 72, 74, 76, 81, 82, 95, 99, 116, 118, 136, 161, 166, 168, 178, 185
Priest, Graham   108, 118
Prybyla, Jan S.   324, 333
Przeworski, Adam   167, 189, 190, 203–213, 215
Przybysz, Piotr   xxiii, xxiv, xxv, xxvii, 106, 119, 149, 182, 184, 205, 213, 215, 236, 264, 311, 331
Pšeja, Pavel   284, 291
Pulkkinen, Tuija   266, 293

Radushev, Evgeni   301, 312
Raiffa, Howard   211, 215
Rainko, Stanisław   6, 51
Rakowski, Mieczysław   279–281
Rapp, Friedrich, J.   xxvii
Ratajczak, Magdalena   233, 238
Rawls, John   79, 95, 114, 118, 191, 205, 215
Reagan, Ronald   150, 170, 276
Ritzer, George   230, 238
Roemer, John   108, 118, 190, 191, 215, 216
Rogacz, Dawid   xxii, xxxii, 314
Rogowski, Leonard Sławomir   109, 118, 139
Rosales, José María   266, 293
Rosdolsky, Roman   108, 118
Routley, Richard   108, 118
Rowiński, Jan   322, 333
Rummel, Rudolph   101, 105, 163

Saxonberg, Steven   285, 287, 293
Scanlon, Thomas   117
Schmitter, Philippe C.   282, 292
Schneck, Stephen Frederick   xv, xvii
Sebestyen, Victor   277, 278, 281, 283, 293
Sen, Amartya Kumar   190, 216
Shaw, Stanford   306, 313
Siegel, Achim   xvii, xxvii, 320, 333
Simon, Herbert A.   190, 216
Simon, Yves R.   243, 255
Siwicki, Florian   281
Skórzyński, Jacek   281, 293
Sobolewska, Barbara   75
Sobolewski, Marek   75
Sójka, Jacek   xxvi
Sołtan, Karol   xv, xxvii
Solzhenitsyn, Aleksandr Isayevich   ix, x
Somel, Selcuk Aksin   305, 313
Sosnowska, Honorata   190, 214

Stalin, Joseph Vissarionovich   53, 54, 322
Stanek, J.   286
Staniszkis, Jadwiga   279, 293
Stepan, Matthias   329, 333
Stępień, Mateusz   330, 333
Štrougal, Lubomir   284
Swiderski, Edward M.   xvi, xxvii
Sugar, Peter F.   307, 313
Suk, Jiří   284, 285, 287, 293
Suleiman I, sultan   301
Suszko, Roman   109, 118, 139
Szabała, Henryk   98, 105, 200, 216, 219, 238

Taylor, Michael   206, 215, 216
Thatcher, Margaret   131, 150, 170
Tischner, Józef   73, 76
Toeplitz, Krzysztof Teodor   134, 136, 149
Tomczak, Grzegorz   92, 95, 99, 105, 157, 185
Topolski, Jerzy   89, 95
Traczykowski, Dominik   xxiii
Trembicka, Krystyna   278, 279, 281, 293
Tullock, Gordon   191, 209, 213, 216
Tuomivaara, Timo   85, 94

Vardy, Agnes Huszar   325, 333
Vardy, Steven Bela   325, 333

Walder, Andrew G.   325, 333
Wałęsa, Lech   278, 282
Walicki, Andrzej   136
Wallerstein, Michael   204, 215
Wallerstein, Immanuel   217, 218, 238, 332
Wang, Hongyi   322, 333
Weber, Max   53, 267, 315
Wei, Jingsheng   327, 333
Weizsaecker, Carl Friedrich   128, 133
Wenzel-Teuber, Katharina   322, 334
Weschler, Lawrence   282, 293
Wieczorek, Andrzej   190, 214
Wierusz-Kowalski, Janusz   30, 51
Wigorska, Nina   151, 185
Wittfogel, Karl August   xviii, xxvii, 80, 95, 97, 105, 112, 118, 138
Wolf, Robert G.   108, 117
Wolters, Gereon   xvi, xxvii
Wołyński, Wojciech   xiii, xxvii
Wood, Allen   108, 118
Wright, Erik Olin   190, 216

NAME INDEX

Xi, Jinping   329, 334

Zaganos, Paşa   306
Zamiara, Krystyna   77, 104, 118, 214
Zaporowski, Andrzej   xvi
Zarębski, Tomasz   xxii, xxxii, 167, 185, 189, 220, 238, 317, 320, 334
Zhivkov, Todor Hristov   283
Zhou, Enlai   323

Zhu, De   326
Zielińska, Renata   14, 51
Ziembiński, Zygmunt   viii
Zinoviev, Alexander Alexandrovich   54
Zychowicz, J.   144
Żakowski, Jacek   279, 293
Žiemelis, Darius   295, 313
Żuk, Piotr   232, 238
Żyromski, Marek   290, 291

Subject Index

antagonicist-sociological paradigm 3, 5, 6, 8, 12, 22, 27, 28, 44, 48, 49
authority
   spiritual xix, 9, 22–24, 36, 40, 229, 232
   state (political) 195, 196, 198, 242, 243, 247–250, 253, 258, 269–274, 297–299, 301–303, 305, 306, 309
autocracy 198, 199, 239–255, 263, 270, 271

capitalism viii, 6, 54, 55, 78–80, 82, 84, 96–102, 107, 111, 112, 119, 121, 126, 130, 131, 134, 137–143, 145–147, 150–181, 189–213, 217–235, 315
categorial ontology xvi, 85–88
Catholic Church
   in general 84, 143
   in Poland xv, 47, 143
Christianity 20, 44, 45, 47, 48, 155
civilizational development 122, 125, 128, 130, 131, 154
class of owners 73, 90, 154, 155, 157, 189, 193, 199, 220, 221, 223, 225, 227, 295–300, 307, 309, 310
class of owners-rulers 173, 224–226, 309
class of owners-priests 224, 225, 227, 232, 235, 296, 317
class of priests 3, 30–32, 34, 36, 221–227, 301
class of priests-owners 225, 227
class of rulers 31, 189, 193, 195–197, 202, 203, 221–224, 234, 240, 241, 249, 250, 251, 267, 269, 272, 296, 297, 300, 303, 306, 307, 309, 310, 319, 321, 322, 328
class of rulers-owners 98, 121, 159, 173, 178, 199, 201, 221, 225, 226, 234, 235, 296, 297, 298, 299, 301, 305, 307, 317
class of rulers-priests 121, 235, 296, 317
class of rulers-owners-priests 121, 226, 227
class compromise 189, 204, 210, 211
communism 24, 25, 52, 72, 82, 92, 134, 141, 153, 173, 282, 314, 329
confessional society xxi, 3, 26–28, 32, 36, 43

democracy 25, 78, 80, 84, 96, 97, 100, 102, 111–113, 136–138, 142, 150, 152, 162, 165–167, 177, 198, 199, 203, 218, 219, 239–254, 263, 266, 270, 271, 275, 276, 282, 285, 288, 289, 327
democratization 69, 265, 266, 275–277, 281, 284, 285, 288, 324, 327, 330
dogmatization 3, 30–33, 37, 39, 44

ecological movement 119–121, 124, 129, 131
enslavement xvii–xx, 52, 241, 247, 268, 269, 271, 272, 318–320, 322, 323, 325–328

faith 3, 13–49, 134, 136, 143, 144, 230, 302
feminist movement 119, 121, 129
feudalism 46, 80, 107, 112, 138, 155, 158, 294–299, 300, 307–309, 310, 315, 324
formal-axiological paradigm 3, 7–9
free market 25, 54, 78, 111, 137
functionalist-sociological paradigm 3, 7–9

Hegelianism xxi, 69, 74, 136
historiosophy
   in general xi, xix, 57–59, 68, 69, 73, 74, 77, 83, 84, 96, 98, 129, 130, 134, 136, 146
   Hegelian 59–65, 67, 74, 96, 98
   liberal 6, 7, 68, 69, 74, 78–82, 93, 96, 97, 99, 102, 111, 112, 136, 137, 138, 141, 161, 166, 167, 203
   Marxist (Marxian) 72–75, 79, 80, 81, 82, 96, 97, 111, 112, 116, 122, 137, 138, 142

Idealizational theory of science vii, xv, 9, 27, 45, 152, 179, 192, 197, 218, 316

laws of history 82, 88–90
liberalism xv, xviii, xxi, 57, 59, 68, 69, 74, 75, 77, 79–84, 97, 100, 106, 107, 109, 110, 112, 113–117, 126, 134, 136–140, 142, 144, 147, 154, 157–159, 166, 167, 205, 209, 218
neoliberalism 82, 100, 101, 163, 170

Maoism 315
Marxism
   Analytical 106–110, 138, 139, 189–192, 213
   In general x, xviii, xxi, 4, 6, 55, 56, 73, 80, 82, 97, 106–110, 112–117, 134, 136–139,

SUBJECT INDEX

142–144, 154, 157–159, 169, 171, 172, 189–191, 206, 207, 213, 315, 329
mythologization   3, 13–18, 19, 44, 57, 63–67, 69–72, 74

party system   xix, 239, 243, 244, 246, 249–254, 256, 263
peace movement   119, 120
philosophy of history   vii, xxi, 57, 77, 96, 106, 317
political competition   xvii, 52, 219, 268, 317, 318, 319
political party   91, 239, 245, 246, 249, 256, 257
political (social) transformation   77, 78, 90, 91, 265, 266, 274, 276, 287, 315, 316, 327

real socialism   ix, x, xvii, xviii, 52, 58, 98, 107, 110, 135, 141, 142, 153, 154, 160, 164, 173, 193, 314

satanization   xx, 52
schism   36, 37–45, 48
solidarism   116, 119, 122, 129, 203, 251

spiritual alienation   xxi, 3
spiritual dependence   3, 26
spiritual regulation   30, 31
Stalinism   xvii, xxi, 52–56, 75
state feudalism   294, 296–300, 307–310
sublimation   3, 15–21, 36, 38, 39, 41, 42, 44, 65, 71, 73

theory of power   xvii, xix, xx, 89, 239, 240, 241, 244, 248, 249, 256, 257, 265–267, 273, 314–318, 320, 325, 327
totalitarianism   68, 98, 121, 130, 153, 158, 159, 161, 165, 173, 179, 189, 194, 196, 197, 199, 200, 202, 218, 328
triple-rule system   7, 109
truth   xii, xx, 7, 26, 29, 34, 38, 44, 52, 62, 66, 80, 93, 97, 106, 107, 109, 110, 112, 115, 116, 121, 138, 139, 155, 168, 171, 179–181
truthfulness   115, 146, 151, 209, 218
typology of societies   221–229

worldview   xxi, 3, 18–37, 46, 48, 49, 135